A Text Book Of

AF897605

CLOUD COMPUTING

(22624)

Semester - VI

THIRD YEAR DIPLOMA IN INFORMATION TECHNOLOGY GROUP

As Per MSBTE's 'I' Scheme Syllabus

Dr. Kishor S. Wagh
Ph.D (CSE)
Associate Professor, Dept. of Computer Engineering
AISSMS Institute of Information Technology
Pune

Dr. Sharmila. K. Wagh
Ph.D (Computer Engineering)
Associate Professor, Dept. of Computer Engineering
Modern Education Society's College of Engineering
Pune

NIRALI PRAKASHAN
ADVANCEMENT OF KNOWLEDGE

N4402

Cloud Computing **ISBN: 978-93-89825-27-5**

First Edition : **December 2019**

Published By :

NIRALI PRAKASHAN

Abhyudaya Pragati, 1312, Shivaji Nagar

Off J.M. Road, PUNE – 411005

Tel - (020) 25512336/37/39, Fax - (020) 25511379

Email : niralipune@pragationline.com

DISTRIBUTION CENTRES

PUNE

Nirali Prakashan (For orders within Pune) : 119, Budhwar Peth, Jogeshwari Mandir Lane, Pune 411002, Maharashtra
Tel : (020) 2445 2044, 66022708, Fax : (020) 2445 1538; Mobile : 9657703145
Email : niralilocal@pragationline.com

Nirali Prakashan (For orders outside Pune) : S. No. 28/27, Dhayari, Near Asian College Pune 411041
Tel : (020) 24690204 Fax : (020) 24690316; Mobile : 9657703143
Email : bookorder@pragationline.com

MUMBAI

Nirali Prakashan : 385, S.V.P. Road, Rasdhara Co-op. Hsg. Society Ltd.,
Girgaum, Mumbai 400004, Maharashtra; Mobile : 9320129587
Tel : (022) 2385 6339 / 2386 9976, Fax : (022) 2386 9976
Email : niralimumbai@pragationline.com

DISTRIBUTION BRANCHES

JALGAON

Nirali Prakashan : 34, V. V. Golani Market, Navi Peth, Jalgaon 425001, Maharashtra,
Tel : (0257) 222 0395, Mob : 94234 91860; Email : niralijalgaon@pragationline.com

KOLHAPUR

Nirali Prakashan : New Mahadvar Road, Kedar Plaza, 1st Floor Opp. IDBI Bank, Kolhapur 416 012
Maharashtra. Mob : 9850046155; Email : niralikolhapur@pragationline.com

NAGPUR

Nirali Prakashan : Above Maratha Mandir, Shop No. 3, First Floor,
Rani Jhanshi Square, Sitabuldi, Nagpur 440012, Maharashtra
Tel : (0712) 254 7129; Email : niralinagpur@pragationline.com

DELHI

Nirali Prakashan : 4593/15, Basement, Agarwal Lane, Ansari Road, Daryaganj
Near Times of India Building, New Delhi 110002 Mob : 08505972553
Email : niralidelhi@pragationline.com

BENGALURU

Nirali Prakashan : Maitri Ground Floor, Jaya Apartments, No. 99, 6th Cross, 6th Main,
Malleswaram, Bengaluru 560003, Karnataka; Mob : 9449043034
Email: niralibangalore@pragationline.com

Other Branches : Hyderabad, Chennai

niralipune@pragationline.com | www.pragationline.com

Also find us on www.facebook.com/niralibooks

Preface ...

We take an opportunity to present this book entitled as "**Cloud Computing**" to the students of Sixth Semester (Third Year Diploma in Information Technology Group). The objective of this book is to present the subject matter in a most concise and simple manner. The book is written strictly according to the Revised Syllabus (I-Scheme) prepared by Maharashtra State Board of Technical Education (MSBTE).

This book contains Six constructive chapters.

- First chapter gives fundamentals of cloud computing.
- Second chapter focuses on virtualization.
- Third chapter covers storage in clouds.
- Fourth chapter introduces cloud monitoring and management.
- Fifth chapter deals with security concepts in cloud computing.
- Trends and future in cloud computing is covered in Sixth chapter.

A special words of thank to Shri. Dineshbhai Furia, Mr. Jignesh Furia for showing full faith in us to write this text book. We also thank to entire staff of M/s Nirali Prakashan for their excellent co-operation.

We welcome constructive suggestions from our colleagues and students.

Authors

Syllabus ...

1. Fundamentals of Cloud Computing

1.1 Cloud Computing, Essential Characteristics of Cloud Computing.

1.2 Cloud Deployment Model: Public Cloud, Private Cloud, Community Cloud, Hybrid Cloud.

1.3 Cloud Service Models: IaaS, PaaS, SaaS.

1.4 Cloud Economics and Benefits.

1.5 Architecture of Cloud Computing.

1.6 Cloud Computing Infrastructure.

1.7 Cloud-Based Integrated Development Environment (IDE) to Write, Run, and Debug Code with a Browser.

2. Virtualization

2.1 Introduction, Virtualization Reference Model, Characteristics of Virtualized Environment.

2.2 Virtualization Types.

2.3 Technology Example: VMware, Microsoft Hyper-V, KVM Xen.

2.4 Advantages: Virtual Machine (VM), VM Migration, VM Consolidation, VIVI Management.

2.5 Disadvantages of Virtualization.

3. Storage in Clouds

3.1 Storage System Architecture.

3.2 Virtualize Data Centre (VDC) Architecture, VDC Environment, Server, Storage, Networking, Desktop and Application Virtualization Techniques and Benefits.

3.3 Block and File Level Storage Virtualization, Virtual Provisioning, and Automated Storage Tiering, Virtual Storage area Network (SAN) and Benefits.

3.4 Cloud File Systems: Google File System GFS and Hadoop Distributed File System HDFS.

4. Cloud Monitoring and Management

4.1 Service Provider and Users.

4.2 An architecture of Federated Cloud Computing.

4.3 Service Level Agreement (SLA) Management: Types of SLA, Life Cycle of SLA.

4.4 Service Catalog, Management and Functional Interfaces of Services.

4.5 Cloud Portal and its Functions.

4.6 Cloud Service Life Cycle Phases: Service Planning, Service Creation, Service Operation and Service Termination.

4.7 Cloud Resource Management:

- Ab-initio Resource Assignment.
- Periodic Resource Optimization.

5. Security in Cloud Computing

5.1 Cloud Security Fundamentals.

5.2 Cloud Risk, Cloud Risk Division

- Polity and Organizational Risks
- Technical Risks
- Legal Risks.

5.3 Technologies for Data Security, Data Security Risk.

5.4 Digital Identity and Access Management.

5.5 Content Level Security.

5.6 Security-As-A-Cloud Service.

6. Trends and Future in Cloud Computing

6.1 Cloud Trends in Supporting Ubiquitous Computing.

6.2 Enabling Technologies with the Internet of Things (RFID, Sensor Networks and ZigBee Technologies, GPS).

6.3 Innovative Applications with the Internet of Things (Ex: Smart Buildings and Smart Power Grid).

6.4 Future of Cloud-Based Smart Devices, Home Based Cloud Computing, Energy Aware Cloud Computing.

6.5 Cloud Platforms: Amazon EC2 and S3, Microsoft Azure, Cloudstack, Intercloud, Google App Engine, Open Source Cloud Eucalyptus, Open Stack, Open Nebulla, etc.

Contents ...

1...

Fundamentals of Cloud Computing

Chapter Outcomes...

- Explain the specified characteristics of cloud computing.
- Compare the given cloud deployment models on the given criteria.
- Explain the given service offered by identified cloud service model.
- Explain the given component of cloud computing architecture.
- Write steps to use cloud based integrated development environment to develop the given application.

Learning Objectives...

- To understand Basic Concepts in Cloud Computing
- To learn Cloud Development Models
- To study Architecture of Cloud Computing
- To learn Cloud Based Integrated Environment (IDE) to Writing, Running and Debugging Code with a Browser

1.0 INTRODUCTION

- Nowadays cloud computing is one of the most popular technologies that has become an integral part of the computing world. The usage and popularity of cloud computing is increasing every day and is expected to increase further.
- Cloud computing has emerged as a technology to realize the utility model of computing while using Internet for accessing applications. Cloud computing is the use of computing assets (hardware and software) that are consigned as a service over a the Internet.
- Cloud computing is the latest evolution of computing, where IT resources are offered as services. The hardware and software systems that manage these services are referred to as Infrastructure as a Service (IaaS) and Platform as a Service (PaaS), while actual applications managed and delivered by IaaS and PaaS are referred to as Software as a Service (SaaS).
- The combination of virtualization, IaaS, and PaaS hold the potential to revolutionize software application (SaaS) life-cycle management.
- Cloud computing enables simplified functionality of infrastructure and platforms used in IT and IT-enabled industries, so that the end-users can avail what they want and pay only for the service they use.
- Cloud computing can be characterized as Internet-based computing in which many remote servers are networked to enable shared data-processing ventures, centralized knowledge storage, and access to services or resources online.

- The term 'Cloud Computing' is relatively new but unknowingly, we have been engaging the cloud since 1996, when Hotmail and other Web-based emails gained popularity.
- Cloud computing allows the users to share the storage and computing resources. It also provides the infrastructure for the sharing of these resources. This helps to reduce the cost of the various applications.

What is the Cloud?

- There has been a lot of debate about what the cloud is. Many people think of the cloud as a collection of technologies. It's true that there is a set of common technologies that typically make up a cloud environment, but these technologies are not the essence of the cloud. The cloud is actually a service or group of services. This is partially the reason that the cloud has been so hard to define.
- Originally, the cloud was thought of as a bunch of combined services, technologies, and activities. What happened inside the cloud was not known to the users of the services. This is partially how the cloud got its name.
- Cloud Computing is defined as "a model for enabling convenient, on-demand network access to a shared pool of configurable computing resources (e.g., networks, servers, storage, applications, and services) that can be rapidly provisioned and released with minimal management effort or service provider interaction" .
- Cloud computing represents a new way to deploy computing technology to give users the ability to access, work on, share, and store information using the Internet.
- The cloud itself is a network of data centers, each composed of many thousands of computers working together that can perform the functions of software on a personal or business computer by providing users access to powerful applications, platforms, and services delivered over the Internet.
- It is in essence a set of network enabled services that is capable of providing scalable, customized and inexpensive computing infrastructures on demand, which could be accessed in a simple and pervasive way by a wide range of geographically dispersed users.

Features of Cloud Computing:

1. **Reliability :** Dependable accessibility of resources and computation.
2. **Agility :** Helps in rapid and inexpensive re-provisioning of resources.
3. **Maintenance :** Users (companies/organizations) have less work in terms of resource upgrades and management, which in the new paradigm will be handled by service providers of Cloud Computing.
4. **Location Independence :** Resources can be accessed from anywhere and everywhere.
5. **Multi-Tenancy :** Resources are shared amongst a large pool of users.
6. **Scalability :** Dynamic provisioning of data helps in avoiding various bottleneck scenarios.

1.1 CLOUD COMPUTING

- The term cloud has historically been used in the telecommunications industry as an abstraction of the network in system diagrams. It then became the symbol of the most popular computer network: Internet.
- The Internet plays a fundamental role in cloud computing, since it represents either the medium or the platform through which many cloud computing services are delivered and made accessible.
- Cloud is a parallel and distributed computing system consisting of a collection of inter-connected and virtualized computers that are dynamically provisioned and presented as one or more unified computing resources based on Service Level Agreements (SLA) established through negotiation between the service provider and consumers.
- Clouds are a large pool of easily usable and accessible virtualized resources (such as hardware, development platforms and/or services). These resources can be dynamically reconfigured to adjust to a variable load (scale), allowing also for an optimum resource utilization.
- This pool of resources is typically exploited by a pay-per-use model in which guarantees are offered by the Infrastructure provider by means of customized Service Level Agreements/(SLA).
- Cloud computing is a shared pool of configurable computing resource (eg. networks, servers, storage, applications, and services) network on demand over the internet.
- Cloud computing literally, is the use of remote servers (usually accessible via the Internet) to process or store information. Access is usually using a Web browser. Save files on a server via the Internet is one example.

- Cloud computing is a technological advancement it is based on the concept of dynamic provisioning, which is applied not only to services but also to compute capability, storage, networking, and Information Technology (IT) infrastructure in general. Resources are made available through the Internet and offered on a pay-per-use basis from cloud computing vendors.
- Cloud computing allows renting infrastructure, runtime environments, and services on a pay-per-use basis. End users leveraging cloud computing services can access their documents and data anytime, anywhere, and from any device connected to the Internet.
- Cloud computing is the best solution to manage our applications. It is a shared multi-tenant platform that is supported. When using an application running in the cloud, we simply connect to it, customize it and use it.
- Cloud Computing can be defined as delivering computing power (CPU, RAM, Network Speeds, Storage OS software) a service over a network (usually on the internet) rather than physically having the computing resources at the customer location.
- This principle finds several practical applications and then gives different images of cloud computing to different people.
- Chief information and technology officers of large enterprises see opportunities for scaling their infrastructure on demand and sizing it according to their business needs.
- **Examples:** AWS, Azure, Google Cloud
- The cloud makes it possible for us to access our information from anywhere at any time. While a traditional computer setup requires to be in the same location as the data storage device, the cloud takes away that step.
- The cloud removes the need for us to be in the same physical location as the hardware that stores our data. The cloud provider can both own and house the hardware and software necessary to run our home or business applications.
- This is especially helpful for businesses that cannot afford the same amount of hardware and storage space as a bigger company. Small companies can store their information in the cloud, removing the cost of purchasing and storing memory devices.
- Additionally, because we need to buy the amount of storage space we will use, a business can purchase more space or reduce their subscription as their business grows or as they find they need less storage space.
- Cloud is essentially provided by large distributed data centers. These data centers are often organized as grid and the cloud is built on top of the grid services. Cloud users are provided with virtual images of the physical machines in the data centers. This virtualization is one of the key concept of cloud computing as it essentially builds the abstraction over the physical system.
- Many cloud applications are gaining popularity day by day for their availability, reliability, scalability and utility model. These applications made distributed computing easy as the critical aspects are handled by the cloud provider itself.

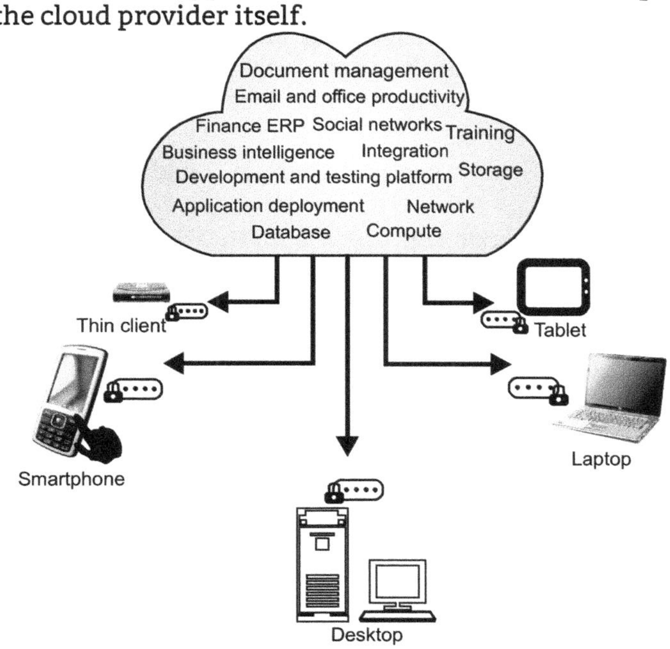

Fig. 1.1 : Cloud Computing

- Now-a-days cloud computing is growing in the interest of technical and business organizations but this can also be beneficial for solving social issues.
- In the recent time E-Governance is being implemented in developing countries to improve efficiency and effectiveness of governance. This approach can be improved much by using cloud computing instead of traditional ICT (Information and Communication Technology).
- In India, economy is agriculture based and most of the citizens live in rural areas. The standard of living, agricultural productivity etc can be enhanced by utilizing cloud computing in a proper way.
- Both of these applications of cloud computing have technological as well as social challenges to overcome.

Advantages of Cloud Computing:

1. **Scalability:** Cloud computing services sanction enterprises to only compensate for what they use like electrical power and water. As the business grows, user can put up by adding more server space.
2. **Automatic Software Integration:** Cloud ensures real-time and seamless integration of its applications to the user's environment and system.
3. **Efficiency:** Cloud computing renders the gain of divided hardware, automated and recognizable technologies. The employees have the right to use the database from everywhere by using any PC, mobile device or browser. It also reduces overall energy usage and physical presence.
4. **Easy Access to Information:** The user has unprecedented and unrivalled access to data from anywhere and at any time.
5. **Cost Reduction:** Cloud computing lessens paperwork, enterprise deal charges and minimizes the financial endeavour in hardware. Moving our enterprise to 'the cloud' in addition lessens the want for an employee.
6. **Affordable:** With cloud computing, it is possible to reduce operational costs and investment expenditures on hardware, software licenses and implementation services.
7. **Levels the Playing Field:** Sharing IT resources with other companies reduces the cost of licensing software and retail servers.
8. **Flexible:** Cloud computing can sanction to maximize supplies for better competence and lessen unused capacity. It can also scale up or downward to meet the varying demands of the business.
9. **Quick Deployment:** The cloud is ready for use once the relevant cloud functionalities and parameter settings are completed.
10. **Almost Unlimited Storage:** Cloud provides access to very large storage space based on user's requirements.
11. **Easier Collaboration:** Cloud computing services allows to access any time from any computer, it is easy to work together with employees in remote locations.
12. **Backup and Recovery:** Cloud offers backup and recovery services for the most traditional physical computing infrastructures. It is relatively much easier and safer to backup and restore important data than to store data on tertiary devices.

Disadvantages of Cloud Computing:

1. **Technical Issues:** Technical issues occur if there is a bad Internet connection or dysfunctional systems.
2. **Risk of Losing Internet Connection:** If there is no Internet connection, the database accessing is very difficult.
3. **Security and Privacy:** Cloud computing still suffers from some security and privacy challenges. The major concerns are data protection and confidentiality, disaster and data breach as well as user authentication.
4. **Limited Resources for Customizations:** One can require in-depth customizations and integration with his current systems for his daily business functions. Cloud computing may not be accommodating to his needs.
5. **Prone to Attack:** Cloud is more potentially prone to security threats and external hack attacks as there is a large amount of sensitive information on the cloud. The fact that it is in the cloud does not mean it is safe from external interference and attacks.
6. **Availability:** If it happens, the cloud service goes down unexpectedly, leaving us without important information for hours or more? Then how is it possible to get reliability in retrieval of data is yet another challenge.

1.1.1 Essential Characteristics of Cloud Computing

- Certain features of a cloud are essential to enable services that truly represent the cloud computing model and satisfy expectations of consumers, and cloud offerings must be as follows:

1. **Self-Service:**

- Consumers of cloud computing services expect on-demand, nearly instant access to resources. To support this expectation, clouds must allows self-service access so that customers can request, customize, pay, and use services without intervention of human operators.
- A consumer can unilaterally provision computing capabilities, such as server time and network storage, as needed automatically without requiring human interaction with each service provider.

2. **Per-Usage Metering and Billing :**

- Cloud computing eliminates up-front commitment by users, allowing them to request and use only the necessary amount.
- Services must be priced on a shortterm basis (e.g., by the hour), allowing users to release (and not pay for) resources as soon as they are not needed.

3. **Elasticity :**

- Cloud computing gives the illusion of infinite computing resources available on demand . Therefore users expect clouds to rapidly provides resources in any quantity at any time.
- In particular, it is expected that the additional resources can be (a) provisioned, possibly automatically, when an application load increases and (b) released when load decreases (scale up and down).

4. **Customization :**

- In a multi-tenant cloud a great disparity between user needs is often the case. Thus, resources rented from the cloud must be highly customizable.
- In the case of infrastructure services, customization means allowing users to deploy specialized virtual appliances and to be given privileged (root) access to the virtual servers.
- Other service classes (PaaS and SaaS) offer less flexibility and are not suitable for general-purpose computing, but still are expected to provide a certain level of customization.

5. **Broad Network Access:**

- Capabilities are available over the network and accessed through standard mechanisms that promote use by heterogeneous thin or thick client platforms (e.g., mobile phones, tablets, laptops and workstations).
- Cloud computing resources are available over the network and can be accessed by diverse customer platforms. In other words, cloud services are available over a network-ideally high broadband communication link-such as the Internet, or in the case of a private clouds it could be a Local Area Network (LAN).
- Network bandwidth and latency are very important aspects of cloud computing and broad network access, because they relate to the Quality of Service (QoS) on the network.

Multi-tenancy and Resource pooling:

- The provider's computing resources are pooled to serve multiple consumers using a multi-tenant model, with different physical and virtual resources dynamically assigned and reassigned according to consumer demand.
- There is a sense of location independence in that the customer generally has no control or knowledge over the exact location of the provided resources but may be able to specify location at a higher level of abstraction (e.g., country, state or datacenter).
- Examples of resources include storage, processing, memory and network bandwidth.
- Multi-tenancy allows multiple customers to share the same applications or the same physical infrastructure while retaining privacy and security over their information. It's similar to people living in an apartment building, sharing the same building infrastructure but they still have their own apartments and privacy within that infrastructure. That is how cloud multi-tenancy works.
- Resource pooling means that multiple customers are serviced from the same physical resources. Provider's resource pool should be very large and flexible enough to service multiple client requirements and to provide for economy of scale. When it comes to resource pooling, resource allocation must not impact performances of critical manufacturing applications.

6. **Rapid Elasticity and Scalability:**

- Capabilities can be elastically provisioned and released, in some cases automatically, to scale rapidly outward and inward commensurate with demand. To the consumer, the capabilities available for provisioning often appear to be unlimited and can be appropriated in any quantity at any time.
- Rapid elasticity and scalability in the cloud is related to testing of manufacturing applications. If a manufacturing organization needs, for example, a few virtual machines to test a Supervisory Control And Data Acquisition (SCADA) system before they roll it out in production, they can have it up and running in minutes instead of physically ordering and waiting for hardware to be shipped.

7. **Measured Service:**

- Cloud systems automatically control and optimize resource use by leveraging a metering capability at some level of abstraction appropriate to the type of service (e.g., storage, processing, bandwidth and active user accounts). Resource usage can be monitored, controlled and reported, providing transparency for the provider and consumer.
- Cloud computing resources usage is metered and manufacturing organizations pay accordingly for what they have used. Resource utilization can be optimized by leveraging charge-per-use capabilities. This means that cloud resource usage-whether virtual server instances that are running or storage in the cloud-gets monitored, measured and reported by the cloud service provider.
- The cost model is based on "pay for what us to use"-the payment is variable based on the actual consumption by the manufacturing organization.

1.2 CLOUD DEVELOPMENT MODEL

- Cloud development models refer to how a cloud solution is used by an organization, where the data is located, and who operates the cloud solution.
- Cloud computing supports multiple development models that can deliver the capabilities needed in a cloud solution.
- Deployment models describe the ways with which the cloud services can be deployed or made available to its customers, depending on the organizational structure and the provisioning location.
- According to deployment model, cloud computing can be categorized into four categories namely, Public cloud, Private cloud, Hybrid cloud and Community cloud.
- Although cloud computing has emerged mainly from the appearance of public computing utilities. In this sense, regardless of its service class, a cloud can be classified as public, private, community, or hybrid based on model of deployment as shown in Fig. 1.2 and 1.3.

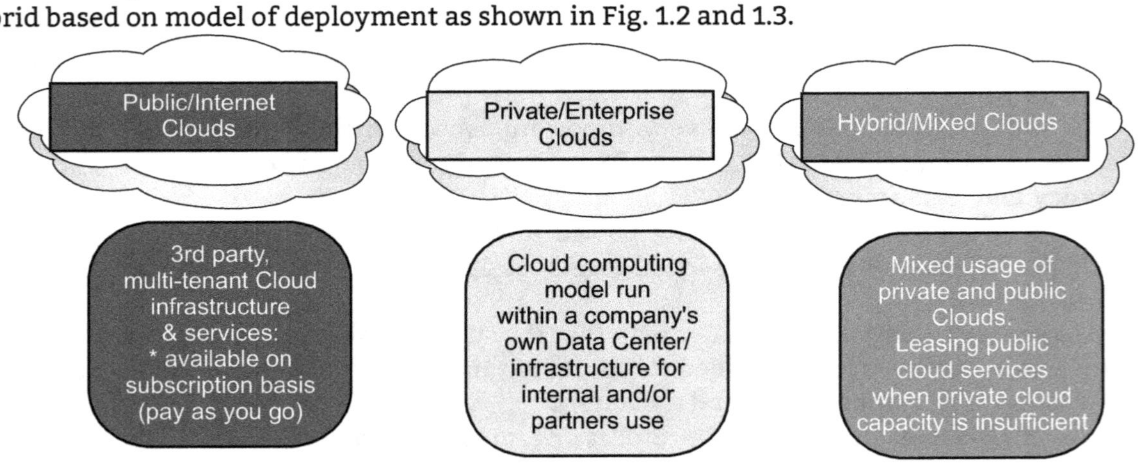

Fig. 1.2: Deployment Models of Cloud

Fig. 1.3: Cloud development models features

Host	Provider	Enterprise, 3rd Party	Enterprise, 3rd Party	Community, 3rd Party
Owner	Provider	Enterprise	Enterprise	Community
Access	Internet	Internet, VPN	Internet, VPN	Intranet, VPN
Users	Public Individuals Organizations	Business Units	Business Units	Community Members

1.2.1 Public Cloud

- A public cloud is one in which the cloud infrastructure is made available to the general public or a large industry group over the Internet.
- The infrastructure is not owned by the user, but by an organization that provides cloud services. Services can be provided either at no cost, as a subscription, or as a pay-as-you-go model.
- A public cloud or external cloud is one base on the usual mainstream model, in which service provider makes resources, such as storage and application, obtainable to the general public over the Internet or via web applications/web services.
- In public cloud hardware, application and bandwidth costs are covered by the service provider so it is easy and inexpensive set-up to the user. Using "pay-as-you-go" model it may save resource from wasting.
- Examples of public clouds include IBM's Blue Cloud, Sun Cloud, Google AppEngine, Windows Azure Services Platform, Amazon Elastic Compute Cloud (EC2).
- Applications of Public Cloud:
  1. Public facing Web pages.
  2. Public Wiki's, blogs, etc.
  3. Batch processing jobs with limited security requirements.
  4. Data intensive workloads.
  5. Software as a Service applications.
  6. Online storage solutions.
  7. Online backups/restore solutions.
  8. Isolated workloads where latency between application components is not an issue.

Advantage of Public Cloud:

1. **Simple and Easy:** Public clouds are available as a service in the Internet, they are easy to deploy.
2. **Cost:** Initial investment is very low or nil.
3. **Less Time:** The IT resources and services are available immediately saving time for the company.
4. **No Maintenance:** The hardware and networks are maintained by the cloud services provider. Internal IT staffs have no responsibility in maintaining the infrastructure.
5. **No Contracts:** No long term commitment with service provider because public clouds are usually pay-as-you-go models.
6. **Scalability:** It offers greater scalability
7. **Reliability:** It offers reliability which means no single point of failure will interrupt our service.
8. **Availability:** Services like SaaS, (Paas), (Iaas) are easily available on Public Cloud platform as it can be accessed from anywhere through any Internet enabled devices.
9. **Location Independent:** It is location independent the services are available wherever the client is located.

Disadvantage of Public Cloud:

1. **Lacks Proper Controls:** The client has no control of data or infrastructure. There are issues of data privacy and integrity. The service level policies and compliances are completely enforced by the service provider.
2. **Performance:** The performance of the network depends on the speed of the internet connectivity.
3. **Weak on Security:** Since the hardware resource is shared between multiple users, IT security issues are more profound and data is vulnerable to thefts.
4. **Customization:** Customization of resources or services is not possible.

5. **Privacy Problems:** No control over privacy or security
6. **Not used for Application:** Cannot be used for use of sensitive applications
7. **Problem of Flexibility:** Lacks complete flexibility as the platform depends on the platform provider
8. **Problems of Protocols:** No stringent protocols regarding data management
9. **Extra Expenses/Cost:** While public cloud computing allows the enterprise to avoid many infrastructure expenses, it's important to plan for other associated cost areas tied to a deployment, such as vendor management processes, capacity planning, Service Oriented Architecture (SOA), chargeback systems, incident management and Service Level Agreements (SLAs).

1.2.2 Private Cloud

- The term Private Cloud is also referred to as internal cloud or corporate cloud. Here, the provider provides services to a limited number of users behind a firewall or users access is limited to mitigate the security risk.
- For proprietary computing architecture it could be a marketing term where marketing media uses the words private cloud to offer organization that needs more control over their data than using a third-party hosted service.
- Private cloud is good for companies own privacy policies however, from up-front capital cost, it is not that much beneficial "still it cost money to buy, build and manage".
- A private cloud refers to a cloud solution, where the infrastructure is provisioned for the exclusive use of a single organization. The organization often acts as a cloud service provider to internal business units, that obtain all the benefits of a cloud without having to provision their own infrastructure.
- By consolidating and centralizing services into a cloud, the organization benefits from centralized service management and economies of scale.
- A private cloud provides an organization with some advantages over a public cloud. The organization gains greater control over the resources that make up the cloud. In addition, private clouds are ideal when the type of work being done is not practical for a public cloud because of network latency, security, or regulatory concerns.
- A private cloud can be owned, managed, and operated by the organization, a third party, or a combination. The private cloud infrastructure is usually provisioned on the organization's premises, but it can also be hosted in a data center that is owned by a third party.
- IBM uses the term Local when referring to on-premises private clouds that are owned, managed, and operated by the organization, and the term Dedicated when referring to off-premise third-party managed private clouds.
- Services of private cloud includes virtualization, multi-tenancy, consistent deployment, chargeback and pricing.
- Some examples of a private cloud include Simple Storage Service (S3), Red Hat, SaM CloudBOX and Amazon EC2.

Advantages of Private Cloud:

1. **Controls:** Better controls for data, users and information assets.
2. **Cost:** Initial investment for hardware is very high in case of an on-premise infrastructure.
3. **Security:** The cloud belongs to a single client. Hence, the infrastructure and systems can be configured to provide high levels of security.
4. **Superior Performance:** Normally private clouds are deployed inside the firewall of the organization's intranet which ensures efficiency and good network performance.
5. **Easy Customization:** The hardware and other resources can be customized easily by the company.
6. **Compliance:** Compliance is achieved easily in private clouds.
7. **Security:** Offers greater security, privacy and more control over system configuration as per the company's need.
8. **Flexibility:** Greater reliability when it comes to performance.
9. **Quality:** Enhances the quality of service offered by the clients.

Disadvantages of Private Cloud:

1. **Cost:** Costs are substantial in the case of building an on-premise private cloud. The running cost would include personnel cost and periodic hardware upgrade costs. In the case of outsourced private cloud, operating cost will include per resource usage and subject to change at the discretion of the service provider.
2. **Under-Utilization:** In some instances the resources subscribed can be under-utilized. Hence, optimizing the utilization of all resources is a challenge.
3. **Capacity Ceiling:** Due to physical hardware limitations with the service provider, there could be a capacity ceiling to handle only certain amount of servers or storage.
4. **Vendor Lock-In:** This can be a major impediment in private cloud adoption especially when the hardware and infrastructure is outsourced. This is a service delivery technique where the client company is forced to continue with the same service provider, thus preventing the client to migrate to another vendor.
5. **Expensive:** Expensive when compared to public cloud and Requires IT expertise.
6. **No optimum Promise:** It does not provide the optimum promise of cloud computing such as the lowest price and unlimited elasticity to ramp resources.

1.2.3 Community Clouds

- Community cloud is controlled by a group of organizations that have shared interests such as specific security requirements or a common mission. It implies an infrastructure that is shared between organizations, usually with the shared data and data management concerns.
- For example, a community cloud can belong to a government of a single country. Community clouds can be located both on and off the premises.
- A community cloud shares the cloud infrastructure across several organizations in support of a specific community that has common concerns (for example, mission, security requirements, policy, and compliance considerations).
- The primary goal of a community cloud is to have participating organizations realize the benefits of a public cloud, such as shared infrastructure costs and a pay-as-you-go billing structure, with the added level of privacy, security, and policy compliance that is usually associated with a private cloud.
- The community cloud infrastructure can be provided on-premises or at a third party's data center, and can be managed by the participating organizations or a third party.
- The cloud service shares among various organizations and companies which belong to the same community with the common concerns. This can manage either by the third party or internally.
- Organizations having similar computing concern and have shared interest can share it. This type of cloud computing is best compatible with ventures, business organizations, research organizations, and tenders.
- This benefits the user of community cloud to know and analyze the business demand first. The presence of the community cloud can be either onsite or offsite.
- Community cloud diminishes the cost pressure, security concerns, technical complexities, and lack of specific services.
- Examples of community clouds include Google Government Cloud, IGT Cloud, Optum Health Care Cloud, and so on.

Advantages of Community Cloud:

1. **Cheaper in Cost:** Cost of setting up a communal cloud versus individual private cloud can be cheaper due to the division of costs among all participants.
2. **No Performance of Clients:** Management of the community cloud can be outsourced to a cloud provider. The advantage here is that the provider would be an impartial third party that is bound by contract and that has no preference to any of the clients involved other than what is contractually mandated.
3. **Usages of Tools:** Tools residing in the community cloud can be used to leverage the information stored to serve consumers and the supply chain, such as return tracking and just-in-time production and distribution.

4. **Flexibility and Scalability:** The community cloud is very scalable and flexible as it is mostly compatible with every user and they can modify as per their use. The cloud will support ways like acquisitions, reductions in branches or employees, or rapid climb. It also permits credit unions to support remote users, permitting employees to figure regardless of where they are. The cloud additionally supports smartphones, tablets, and different devices. The cloud permits credit unions to secure these devices and the data on them.
5. **Available and Reliable:** The replication of data is done in the cloud to protect it against the disaster. It is replicated to various places which are safe and secure. The cloud replicates the system, applications, and data to an alternate facility, and might build it offered to we at our primary location just in case of uncertainty. As a result of the servers, applications, and data are no longer physically at the base, a disaster at a branch or in the region won't stop we from serving members. The cloud includes redundant property, networking, storage, hardware, uninterruptible power provide, generators, replicated knowledge stores, onsite fuel and more. Moreover, the data replicates to an alternate web site to make sure our systems offer once we want them.
6. **Secure and Compliance:** The data of the clients should be secure and manage properly. When applications and knowledge offer anytime and anyplace from any device, the info ought not to move. In fact, with the cloud, we will be able to block users from downloading. Sensitive data should be kept securely and on the servers. These data should not be kept elsewhere an intensive security audit revealed that the sensitive data is present on desktops, laptops, backup units, USB drives, smartphones, tablets, and even employees personal computers. Data gets unfold all over as a result of staff copy files to form them offered once and wherever they have them.
7. **Improved Services:** Community cloud includes all systems, applications, and data within the cloud which removes the requirement to own valuable IT employees to take care of and support those systems. Plus, the community cloud supplier handles computer code updates for us. This will raise a fact that the customers will target the rising companies and services.

Disadvantages of Community Cloud:

1. Costs higher than public cloud.
2. Fixed amount of bandwidth and data storage is shared among all community members.
3. Not the right choice for every organization.
4. Slow adoption to date.

Comparison between Public, Private and Hybrid Clouds:

Sr. No.	Terms	Private	Public	Hybrid
1.	Tenancy	Single tenancy (there is only the data of a single organization stored in the cloud).	Multi-tenancy (the data of multiple organizations in stored in a shared environment).	The data stored in the public cloud is usually multi-tenant, which means the data from multiple organizations is stored in a shared environment. The data stored in private cloud is kept private by the organization.
2.	Exposed to the Public	No (only the organization itself can use the private cloud services).	Yes (anyone can use the public cloud services).	The services running on a private cloud can be accessed only the organization's users, while the services running on public cloud can be accessed by anyone.
3.	Data Center Location	Inside the organization's network.	Anywhere on the Internet where the cloud service provider's services are located.	Inside the organization's network for private cloud services as well as anywhere on the Internet for public cloud services.

Contd. ...

4.	Cloud Service Management	The organization must have their own administrators managing their private cloud services.	The cloud service provider manages the services, where the organization merely uses them.	The organization itself must manage the private cloud, while the public cloud is managed by the CSP.
5.	Hardware Components	Must be provided by the organization itself, which has to buy physical servers to build the private cloud on.	The CSP provides all the hardware and ensures it's working at all times.	The organization must provide hardware for the private cloud, while the hardware of CSP is used for public cloud services.
6.	Expenses	Can be quite expensive, since the hardware, applications and network have to be provided and managed by the organization itself.	The CSP has to provide the hardware, set-up the application and provide the network accessibility according to the SLA.	The private cloud services must be provided by the organization, including the hardware, applications and network, while the CSP manages the public cloud services.

1.2.4 Hybrid Cloud

- A Hybrid Cloud, as the name implies, is a combination of various cloud types (public, private, and community). Each cloud in the hybrid mix remains a unique entity, but is bound to the mix by technology that enables data and application portability.
- The hybrid approach allows a business to take advantage of the scalability and cost-effectiveness of off-premise third-party resources without exposing applications and data beyond the corporate intranet.
- A well-constructed hybrid cloud can service secure, mission-critical processes, such as receiving customer payments (a private cloud service), and secondary processes, such as employee payroll processing (a public cloud service). The challenge for a hybrid cloud is the difficulty in effectively creating and governing such a solution.
- Services from various sources must be obtained and provisioned as though they originated from a single location, and interactions between on-premises and off-premise components make the implementation even more complicated.
- Eucalyptus and GoGrid are examples of hybrid cloud service providers.

Advantage of Hybrid Cloud:

1. It is scalable and cost efficient.
2. Offers better security and greater flexibility.
3. Flexibility and scalability depending on individual application needs within the company. For example, interacting with clients on the public cloud, but keeping their data secure on a private network.
4. More secure than strictly public cloud, and the ability to choose which portions of IT will be placed in private cloud vs. public cloud.
5. Good option for companies in transition from public cloud to private cloud.
6. Many vendors offer managed hybrid cloud options.

Disadvantage of Hybrid Cloud:

1. Infrastructure dependency.
2. Possibility of security breach through public cloud.
3. Keeping track of multiple different platforms and vendors.
4. Using both public and private clouds may require more complex IT management that could equate to higher overall costs.
5. It shares some of the risks associated with public clouds.
6. The complexity of monitoring and managing all portions of the hybrid cloud from a common portal or service desk.

1.3 CLOUD SERVICE MODELS (IaaS, PaaS AND SaaS)

- Cloud computing services are divided into three classes, according to the abstraction level of the capability provided and the service model of providers, namely, Infrastructure as a Service (Iaas), Platform as a Service (Paas) and Software as a Service (SaaS).
- Fig. 1.4 depicts the layered organization of the cloud stack from physical infrastructure to applications.

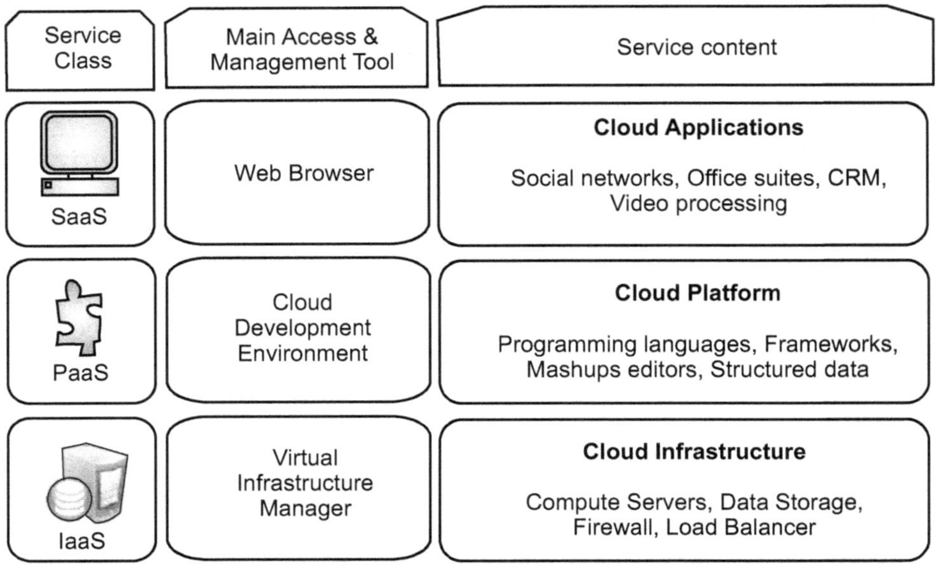

Fig. 1.4: The Cloud Computing Stack

- These abstraction levels can also be viewed as a layered architecture where services of a higher layer can be composed from services of the underlying layer. The reference model explains the role of each layer in an integrated architecture.
- A core middleware manages physical resources and the VMs deployed on top of them; in addition, it provides the required features (e.g., accounting and billing) to offer multi-tenant pay-as-you-go services.
- Cloud development environments are built on top of infrastructure services to offer application development and deployment capabilities; in this level, various programming models, libraries, APIs, and mashup editors enable the creation of a range of business, web, and scientific applications. Once deployed in the cloud, these applications can be consumed by end users.

1.3.1 Infrastructure as a Service (IaaS)

- Offering virtualized resources (computation, storage, and communication) on demand is known as Infrastructure as a Service (IaaS).
- A cloud infrastructure enables on-demand provisioning of servers running several choices of operating systems and a customized software stack. Infrastructure services are considered to be the bottom layer of cloud computing systems.
- Amazon Web Services mainly offers IaaS, which in the case of its EC2 service means offering VMs with a software stack that can be customized similar to how an ordinary physical server would be customized.
- Users are given privileges to perform numerous activities to the server, such as: starting and stopping it, customizing it by installing software packages, attaching virtual disks to it, and configuring access permissions and firewalls rules.
- At the base of the stack, Infrastructure-as-a-Service solutions deliver infrastructure on demand in the form of virtual hardware, storage, and networking.
- It involves offering hardware related services using the principles of cloud computing. These could include some kind of storage services (database or disk storage) or virtual servers. Leading vendors that provide Infrastructure as a service are Amazon EC2, Amazon S3,Rackspace Cloud Servers and Flexiscale.

- The IaaS customer rents computing resources instead of buying and installing them in their own data center. The service is typically paid for on a usage basis.
- The service may include dynamic scaling so that if the customer winds up needing more resources than expected, he can get them immediately (probably up to a given limit).
- Dynamic scaling as applied to infrastructure means that the infrastructure can be automatically scaled up or down, based on the requirements of the application.
- Additionally, the arrangement involves an agreed-upon service level. The service level states what the provider has agreed to deliver in terms of availability and response to demand.
- It might, for example, specify that the resources will be available 99.999 percent of the time and that more resources will be provided dynamically if greater than 80 percent of any given resource is being used.
- Currently, the most high-profile IaaS operation is Amazon's Elastic Compute Cloud (Amazon EC2). It provides a web interface that allows customers to access virtual machines. EC2 offers scalability under the user's control with the user paying for resources by the hour.
- The use of the term elastic in the naming of Amazon's EC2 is significant. The elasticity refers to the ability that EC2 users have to easily increase or decrease the infrastructure resources assigned to meet their needs. The user needs to initiate a request, so this service provided isn't dynamically scalable.
- Users of EC2 can request the use of any operating system as long as the developer does all the work. Amazon itself supports a more limited number of operating systems (Linux, Solaris, and Windows)
- Companies with research-intensive projects are a natural fit for IaaS. Cloud based computing services allow scientific and medical researchers to perform testing and analysis at levels that aren't possible without additional access to computing infrastructure.
- Other organizations with similar needs for additional computing resources may boost their own data centers by renting the computer hardware-appropriate allocations of servers, networking technology, storage, and data center space- as a service.
- Instead of laying out the capital expenditure for the maximum amount of resources to cover their highest level of demand, they purchase computing power when they need it.

1.3.2 Platform as a Service (PaaS)

- In addition to infrastructure-oriented clouds that provide raw computing and storage services, another approach is to offer a higher level of abstraction to make a cloud easily programmable, known as Platform as a Service (PaaS).
- A cloud platform offers an environment on which developers create and deploy applications and do not necessarily need to know how many processors or how much memory that applications will be using. In addition, multiple programming models and specialized services (e.g., data access, authentication, and payments) are offered as building blocks to new applications.
- Google App Engine, an example of Platform as a Service, offers a scalable environment for developing and hosting web applications, which should be written in specific programming languages such as Python or Java, and use the services own proprietary structured object data store.
- Building blocks include an in-memory object cache (memcache), mail service, instant messaging service (XMPP), an image manipulation service, and integration with Google Accounts authentication service.
- Platform as a Service (PaaS) involves offering a development platform on the cloud. Platforms provided by different vendors are typically not compatible. Typical players in PaaS are Google Application Engine, Microsofts Azure, Salesforce.com, force.com.
- They deliver scalable and elastic runtime environments on demand and host the execution of applications. These services are backed by a core middleware platform that is responsible for creating the abstract environment where applications are deployed and executed.
- With Platform as a Service (PaaS), the provider delivers more than infrastructure. It delivers a solution stack- an integrated set of software that provides everything a developer needs to build an application -for both software development and runtime. PaaS can be viewed as an evolution of Web hosting.
- In recent years, webhosting companies have provided fairly complete software stacks for developing Web sites. PaaS takes this idea a step farther by providing lifecycle management- capabilities to

manage all software development stages from planning and design, to building and deployment, to testing and maintenance.

- The primary benefit of PaaS is having software development and deployment capability based entirely in the cloud-hence, no management or maintenance efforts are required for the infrastructure. Every aspect of software development, from the design stage onward (including source-code management, testing, and deployment) lives in the cloud.
- PaaS is inherently multi-tenant and naturally supports the whole set of Web services standards and is usually delivered with dynamic scaling. In reference to Platform as a service, dynamic scaling means that the software can be automatically scaled up or down.
- Platform as a service typically addresses the need to scale as well as the need to separate concerns of access and data security for its customers.
- The major drawback of Platform as a Service is that it may lock one in to the use of a particular development environment and stack of software components. Platform as a Service offerings usually have some proprietary elements (perhaps the development tools or even component libraries).
- Consequently, one may be wedded to the vendor's platform and unable to move the applications elsewhere without rewriting them to some degree. If one suddenly becomes dissatisfied with the Platform as a Service provider, one may face very high expenses when one suddenly needs to rewrite the applications to satisfy the requirements of another PaaS vendor.
- The fear of vendor lock-in has led to a new variety of Platform as a Service emerging: Open Platform as a Service. This would offer the same approach as Platform as a Service, except that there is no constraint on choice of development software. It avoids the possibility of lock-in.
- Some examples of Platform as a Service include the Google App Engine, AppJet, Etelos, Qrimp, and Force.com, which is the official development environment for Salesforce.com.

1.3.3 Software as a Service (SaaS)

- Applications reside on the top of the cloud stack. Services provided by this layer can be accessed by end users through Web portals. Therefore, consumers are increasingly shifting from locally installed computer programs to on-line software services that offer the same functionally.
- Traditional desktop applications such as word processing and spreadsheet can now be accessed as a service in the web. This model of delivering applications, known as Software as a Service (SaaS), alleviates the burden of software maintenance for customers and simplifies development and testing for providers.
- Salesforce.com, which relies on the SaaS model, offers business productivity applications (CRM) that reside completely on their servers, allowing costumers to customize and access applications on demand.
- Software-as-a-Service solutions provide applications and services on demand. Most of the common applications are Office automation, photo editing, CRM, and social networking
- Examples includes Google Documents, Facebook, Flickr, Salesforce Web 2.0.
- Software as a Service Interfaces are replicated on the provider's infrastructure and made more scalable and accessible through a browser on demand.
- These applications are shared across multiple users whose interaction is isolated from the other users. The SaaS layer is also the area of social networking websites, which leverage cloud-based infrastructures to sustain the load generated by their popularity. It includes a complete software offering on the cloud.
- Users can access a software application hosted by the cloud vendor on pay-per-use basis. This is a well-established sector. The pioneer in this field has been Salesforce.coms offering in the online Customer Relationship Management (CRM) space.
- Other examples are online email providers like Googles gmail and Microsofts hotmail, Google docs and Microsofts online version of office called BPOS (Business Productivity Online Standard Suite).
- One of the first implementations of cloud services was Software as a Service (SaaS) — business applications that are hosted by the provider and delivered as a service. SaaS has its roots in an early kind of hosting operation carried out by Application Service Providers (ASPs).
- CRM is one of the most common categories of Software as a Service.

- The price of the software is on a per-use basis and involves no upfront costs from the service provider. Of course, the reality is that the company may have some upfront work to do to get the data loaded into the Software as a Service application database and one may have to deal with ongoing data integration between the internal and cloud data stores.
- Businesses get the immediate benefit of reducing capital expenditures. In addition, a business gains the flexibility to test new software on a rental basis and then can continue to use and adopt the software, if it proves suitable.

Differences between SaaS, PaaS, and IaaS

Sr. No.	Software as a Service (SaaS)	Platform as a Service (PaaS)	Infrastructure as a Service (IaaS)
1.	Software as a service is a model in which a third-party provider hosts multiple applications and lets customers use them over the internet.	This is a model in which a third-party provider application development platform and services built on its own infrastructure. Again these tools are made available to customers over the internet.	In IaaS, a third-party application provides servers, storage, compute resources, and so on. And then makes it available for customers for their utilization. Customers can use IaaS to build their own PaaS and SaaS service for their customers.
2.	SaaS is a very useful pay-as-you-use model.		
3.	**Examples:** Salesforce, NetSuite.	**Examples:** Google App Engine, AWS Lambda.	**Examples:** Google Cloud Compute, Amazon S3.

1.4 CLOUD ECONOMICS AND BENEFITS

- In the simplest term, economics of cloud computing deal with the knowledge concerning the principles, costs, and benefits of cloud computing.

1.4.1 Cloud Economics

- The main drivers of cloud computing are economy of scale and simplicity of software delivery and its operation.
- The biggest benefit of cloud economy is financial: the pay-as-you-go model offered by cloud providers.
- In particular, cloud computing allows:
  1. Reducing the capital costs associated to the IT infrastructure.
  2. Eliminating the depreciation or lifetime costs associated with IT capital assets.
  3. Replacing software licensing with subscriptions.
  4. Cutting the maintenance and administrative costs of IT resources.
- A capital cost is the cost occurred in purchasing an asset that is useful in the production of goods or the rendering of services. Capital costs are one-time expenses that are generally paid up front and that will contribute over the long term to generate profit. The IT infrastructure and the software are capital assets because enterprises require them to conduct their business.
- At present it does not matter whether the principal business of an enterprise is related to IT, because the business will definitely have an IT department that is used to automate many of the activities that are performed within the enterprise: payroll, customer relationship management, enterprise resource planning, tracking and inventory of products, and others. Hence, IT resources constitute a capital cost for any kind of enterprise.
- It is good practice to try to keep capital costs low because they introduce expenses that will generate profit over time; more than that, since they are associated with material things they are subject to depreciation over time, which in the end reduces the profit of the enterprise because such costs are directly subtracted from the enterprise revenues. In the case of IT capital costs, the depreciation

costs are represented by the loss of value of the hardware over time and the aging of software products that need to be replaced because new features are required.

- Before cloud computing diffused within the enterprise, the budget spent on IT infrastructure and software constituted a significant expense for medium-sized and large enterprises.
- Many enterprises own a small or medium-sized data center that introduces several operational costs in terms of maintenance, electricity, and cooling.
- Additional operational costs are occurred in maintaining an IT department and an IT support center. Moreover, other costs are triggered by the purchase of potentially expensive software. With cloud computing these costs are significantly reduced or simply disappear according to its penetration.
- One of the advantages introduced by the cloud computing model is that it shifts the capital costs previously allocated to the purchase of hardware and software into operational costs inducted by renting the infrastructure and paying subscriptions for the use of software.
- These costs can be better controlled according to the business needs and prosperity of the enterprise. Cloud computing also introduces reductions in administrative and maintenance costs. That is, there is no or limited need for having administrative staff take care of the management of the cloud infrastructure.
- At the same time, the cost of IT support staff is also reduced. When it comes to depreciation costs, they simply disappear for the enterprise, since in a scenario where all the IT needs are served by the cloud there are no IT capital assets that depreciate over time.
- The amount of cost savings that cloud computing can introduce within an enterprise is related to the specific scenario in which cloud services are used and how they contribute to generate a profit for the enterprise.
- In the case of a small startup, it is possible to completely leverage the cloud for many aspects, such as:
  1. IT infrastructure
  2. Software development
  3. CRM and ERP
- In this case it is possible to completely eliminate capital costs because there are no initial IT assets. The situation is completely different in the case of enterprises that already have a considerable amount of IT assets.
- In this case, cloud computing, especially IaaS-based solutions, can help manage unplanned capital costs that are generated by the needs of the enterprise in the short term. In this case, by leveraging cloud computing, these costs can be turned into operational costs that
- Last as long as there is a need for them. For example, IT infrastructure leasing helps more efficiently manage peak loads without inducing capital expenses. As soon as the increased load does not justify the use of additional resources, these can be released and the costs associated with them disappear.
- This is the most adopted model of cloud computing because many enterprises already have IT facilities. Another option is to make a slow transition toward cloud-based solutions while the capital IT assets get depreciated and need to be replaced. Between these two cases there is a wide variety of scenarios in which cloud computing could be of help in generating profits for enterprises.
- Economics of cloud computing deal with the knowledge concerning the principles, costs, and benefits of cloud computing.
- Economics refer to feasibility of the product or service. In business, profitability occurs when revenue exceeds expenses.
- Using the total cost of a product to calculate expenses gives us a more accurate picture of profitability. The total cost of a product takes into account a wide range of expenses, including all fixed and variable costs associated with producing the product.
- For any organization to derive the greatest value for the business, it must specifically determine how cloud services can affect IT budget, security and IT infrastructure.
- Cloud computing brings the benefit of unprecedented economies of scale to IT operations. Cloud technology allows large data centers to standardize and pool computing resources, resulting in highly efficient operations. At the same time, cloud automates and streamlines many maintenance tasks, offering exceptional agility to end-users.

- Many of these benefits are amplified as the size of the cloud increases due to the presence of three sources of economies of scale.
- Supply-side economies of scale result from consolidation of overhead costs, purchasing power, and power efficiency, making large data centers up to 50% more cost effective than smaller data centers. In addition to the cost of capacity, the overall cost of IT is also determined by the degree to which the capacity is efficiently utilized.
- Currently, infrastructure is built to meet peak demand. Assessment of demand-side economies of scale shows that pooling computing improves the utilization of IT resources and reduces costs by another 50%.
- Finally, multi-tenancy, which refers to multiple customers sharing the same application, allows those customers to divide the costs of operating the application and can reduce costs by an additional 20%.
- The combined impact of these economies of scale can result in long-term savings of up to 80% when comparing large and small clouds.
- While private clouds can achieve some degree of cost savings from the scale economies while addressing some concerns about cloud, analysis reveals there is a price premium associated with private clouds, as the benefits of scale do not apply equally to public clouds and private clouds.
- Through our analysis, we show that over time the cost of private clouds will increase to be 10x higher than public clouds, while barriers to public cloud adoption will be addressed to a greater degree.
- Managers must therefore weigh the implications of both choosing a private cloud for their own IT and of enacting regulation that might inhibit the use of public clouds.

Reasons Customers Save Money with Cloud:

1. Cloud helps customers replace up-front capital expense with low variable cost.
2. Massive economies of scale and efficiency improvements allow to continually lower prices.
3. Multiple pricing models allows us to optimize costs for both variable and stable workloads.
4. Cloud computing drives down IT labor costs both up-front and on an on-going basis.
5. Cloud delivers a premium security spec at non-premium prices.
6. Cloud allows customer workloads to be available for a fraction of the cost of self-hosting.

- The basis for the economic advantage is the economy of scale available to cloud computing data centers. The three areas of scale advantage:
  1. **Supply-side savings:** Cloud data centers have lower costs per server, based upon purchasing power.
  2. **Demand-side aggregation:** By supporting a mix of tenants, cloud providers are able to achieve higher server utilization rates than is possible for single-tenant data centers (even those for large companies with different departments, business units, or subsidiaries sharing the data center).
  3. **Multi-tenancy efficiency:** Hosting multiple tenants spreads administrative costs and reduces cost per data center user.

1.4.2 Cloud Benefits

- Various benefits of cloud computing are listed below:
  1. **Optimized Server Utilization :** As most enterprises typically underutilize their server computing resources, cloud computing will manage the server utilization to the optimum level. Cloud computing can lower IT barriers to innovation, as can be witnessed from the many promising startups, from the ubiquitous online applications such as Facebook and Youtube to the more focused applications like Trip It (for managing one's travel) or Mint (for managing one's personal finances).
  2. **Cost Saving :** IT infrastructure costs are almost always substantial and are treated as a capital expense (CAPEX). However if the IT infrastructure usually becomes an operating expense (OPEX). In some countries, this results in a tax advantage regarding income taxes. Also, cloud computing cost saving can be realized via resource pooling. It dramatically lowers the cost of entry for smaller firms trying to benefit from compute-intensive business analytics that were hither to available only to the largest of corporations. These computational exercises typically involve large amounts of computing power for relatively short amounts of time, and cloud computing makes such dynamic provisioning of resources possible. Cloud computing also represents a huge opportunity to many third-world countries that have been so far left behind in the IT revolution - some cloud computing providers are using the advantages of a cloud platform to enable IT

services in countries that would have traditionally lacked the resources for widespread deployment of IT services.

3. **Improved Compatibility between Operating Systems :** In the cloud, operating systems simply don't matter. One can connect the Windows computer to the cloud and share documents with computers running Apple's Mac OS, Linux, or UNIX. In the cloud, the data matters, not the operating system.
4. **Dynamic Scalability :** many enterprises include a reasonably large buffer from their average computing requirement, just to ensure that capacity is in place to satisfy peak demand. Cloud computing provides an extra processing buffer as needed at a low cost and without the capital investment or contingency fees to users.
5. **Cloud Computing Makes it Easier for Enterprises to Scale their Services :** Which are increasingly reliant on accurate information - according to client demand. Since the computing resources are managed through software, they can be deployed very fast as new requirements arise. In fact, the goal of cloud computing is to scale resources up or down dynamically through software APIs depending on client load with minimal service provider interaction.
6. **Unlimited Storage Capacity:** The cloud offers virtually limitless storage capacity. Consider that when our desktop or laptop PC is running out of storage space. The computer's 200GB hard drive is peanuts compared to the hundreds of petabytes (a million gigabytes) available in the cloud.
7. **Universal Access to Documents:** Universal access to documents with cloud computing, one doesn't have to take the documents. Instead, they stay in the cloud, where one can access them from anywhere one has a computer and an Internet connection. All the documents are instantly available from wherever one accesses them. There's simply no need to take the documents with us-as long as we have an Internet connection, that is.
8. **Latest Version Availability:** It is another document-related advantage of cloud computing. When one edits a document at home, that edited version is what he'll see when he will access the document at work. The cloud always hosts the latest version of the documents; one is never in danger of having an outdated version on the computer when working on.
9. **Shortened Development Life Cycle:** Cloud computing adopts the Service Orientates Architecture (SOA) development approach, which has significantly shorter development life cycle that that required by the traditional development approach. Any new business application can be developed online, connecting proven functional application building blocks together.
10. **Reduced Time for Implementation:** Cloud computing provides the processing power and data storage as needed at the capacity required. This can be obtained in near-real time instead of weeks or months that occur when a new business initiative is brought online in a traditional way.

1.5 ARCHITECTURE OF CLOUD COMPUTING

- Cloud Computing architecture comprises of many cloud components, which are loosely coupled. We can broadly divide the cloud architecture into two parts namely, Front End and Back End.
- Each of the ends is connected through a network, usually Internet. The following diagram shows the graphical view of cloud computing architecture:

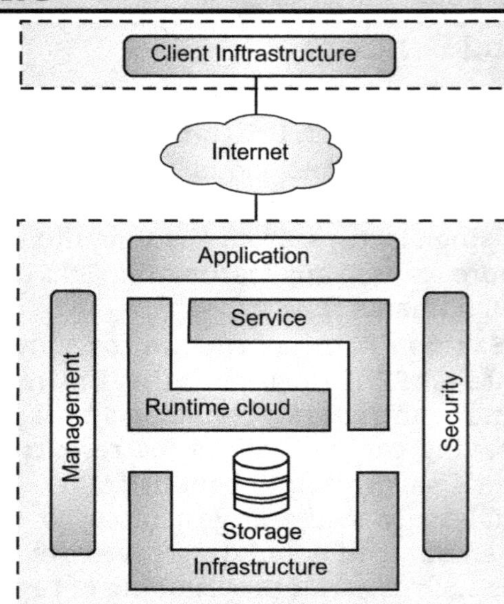

Fig. 1.5 : Architecture of Cloud Computing

1. **Front End:**

- The front end is the side of computer user or client.
- It involves the interfaces and the applications that are necessary to access the cloud computing system.
- Example, Web Browser.

2. Back End:

- The back end is the cloud section of the system.
- It involves all the resources which are necessary to give cloud computing services.
- It includes huge data storage, virtual machines, security mechanism, services, deployment models, servers etc.
- To give built-in security mechanism, traffic control and protocols is the responsibility of the back end

1.6 CLOUD COMPUTING INFRASTRUCTURE

- Cloud infrastructure means the hardware and software components. These components are server, storage, networking and virtualization software.
- These components are required to support the computing requirements of a cloud computing model.

1.6.1 Components of Cloud Infrastructure

- Fig. 1.6 shows components of cloud infrastructure.

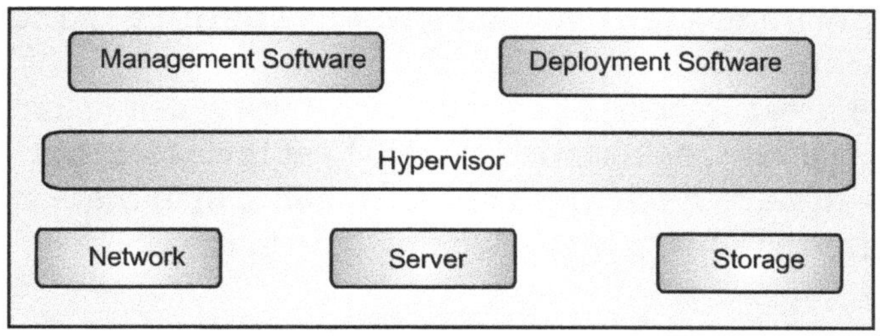

Fig.1.6 : Cloud Infrastructure Components

1. Hypervisor:

- Hypervisor is a firmware or low-level program. It acts as a Virtual Machine Manager.
- It enables to share a physical instance of cloud resources between several customers.

2. Management Software:

- Management software assists to maintain and configure the infrastructure.

3. Deployment Software:

- Deployment software assists to deploy and integrate the application on the cloud.

4. Network:

- Network is the key component of the cloud infrastructure.
- It enables to connect cloud services over the Internet.
- The customer can customize the network route and protocol i.e possible to deliver network as a utility over the Internet.

5. Server:

- The server assists to compute the resource sharing and offers other services like resource allocation and deallocation, monitoring the resources, provide the security etc.

6. Storage:

- Cloud keeps many copies of storage. Using these copies of resources, it extracts another resource if any one of the resources fails.

1.6.2 Infrastructural Constraints

- The basic constraints of cloud computing includes Transparency, Scalability, Intelligent Monitoring and Security.

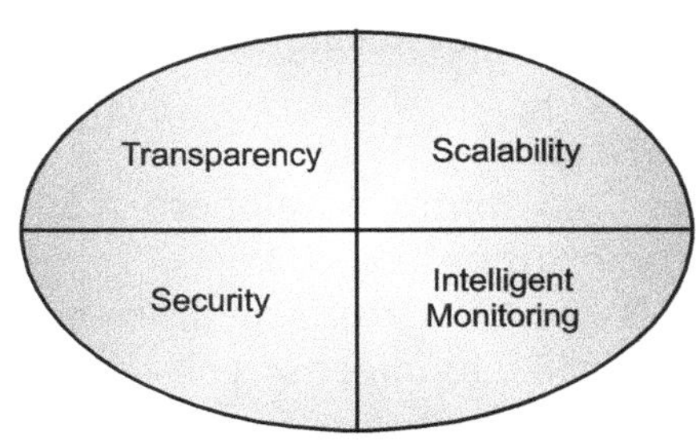

Fig. 1.7 : Infrastructure Constraints

1. Transparency:

- In a Cloud environment, virtualization is the key to share the resources.
- It is impossible to satisfy the demand with single resource or server. Hence, there should be transparency in resources, load balancing and application, so that we can scale the resources on demand.

2. Scalability:

- Scaling up an application is easy but scaling up an application delivery solution is not easy, because it includes configuration overhead or even rearchitecting the network.
- Hence, application delivery is required to be scalable that need the virtual infrastructure so that, resources are provisioned and de-provisioned easily.

3. Intelligent Monitoring:

- Application solution delivery is required to be capable of intelligent monitoring to achieve transparency and scalability.

4. Security:

- In security, the mega data center in the cloud must be securely architected.
- The control node, an entry point in mega data center also requires to be secure.

1.7 CLOUD BASED INTEGRATED DEVELOPMENT ENVIRONMENT (IDE) TO WRITE, RUN AND DEBUG CODE WITH A BROWSER

- Classic desktop coding programs aren't going anywhere. But there is a surge of cloud-based coding with many free IDEs we can run in our browser.
- These little webapps are great for practice projects or testing demos online. We can edit the code from any computer and even share links with others to get their feedback.
- If we are not sure where to start in the world of cloud coding then these apps should get you started. We have list of the best free options to get we writing code in the cloud:

1. CodePen:

- First and foremost is the wildly popular CodePen. This has been around for years and it's quickly become the go to source for online cloud coding.
- With CodePen we can write HTML/CSS/JS code and it will render live right on the page. Everything auto updates so we can see the results in real time as we type. Not to mention we can also run on top of Sass/Less or the many HTML templating languages like Pug or Haml.
- Plus if we can find CDN links for our favorite CSS or JS libraries we can include those into our pen using the include settings.
- Really CodePen is the premiere choice for browser-based coding. It's got everything we could ever need with tons of new features being released all the time.

2. JSFiddle:

- A close follow up to CodePen is JSFiddle. This site has been online for years and it's one of the most well known cloud platforms.
- With JSFiddle we build pretty much anything using HTML/CSS/JS. It works much like CodePen where we can include libraries right into the platform.
- The cool thing about JSFiddle is how they have a list of scripts & frameworks we can include with the click of a button.
- Options range from D3.js to Vue.js and dozens of others in between.

3. Codesandbox:

- CodeSandbox is totally free and open sourced with a full GitHub repo to browse.
- This site differentiates itself because it lets run code from many other frameworks natively. This includes React, Ember, Angular, and many others.
- We can even pick from a series of templates to create new projects from scratch. Our new cloud based project has its own virtual file structure that we can switch between and even add more as we go along.

4. CSSDeck:

- Not too many developers mention CSSDeck but it's still one of the cleanest frontend coding platforms online.
- This has been running since before CodePen so it's definitely a stable site. And it supports all the major JS languages so you can build demos with HTML, CSS, and JS.
- One of the coolest features here is the featured code snippets on the front page. We can browse through recent codes that others have built and dig into the source to copy, clone, or restyle if we wish.

5. Plunker:

- For real time collaboration and code sharing we can not do much better than Plunker.
- This was created specifically for developers who work in the cloud and want to share ideas with others remotely.
- All projects are public so we can browse plunks to see what others are creating.
- If we take a look at the editor page we will notice this tool has a lot more social features than others.
- We can chat with the community and even browse user created templates to help we get started.
- Plunker comes with a built-in code minifier, collaboration features, live chat, code linting, and a download button to download all our code in a .zip file. It's probably the best way to write code with other people and keep things organized.

6. JS Bin:

- Here is a really cool editor that focuses primarily on JavaScript. With JS Bin we get a coding experience much like JSFiddle but with a greater emphasis on JavaScript coding standards.
- Each snippet we create has its own console to log JS scripts, plus room for debugging right in the main editor screen. Their help guide is massive with lots of resources for beginners trying to learn the tool.
- It may not be the most popular cloud IDE but it's certainly worth saving if we do a lot of JavaScript work.

7. IDEone:

- With Ideone we'll find a whole lot more than basic frontend coding. This webapp lets we compile almost any language and test our codes right in the browser.
- From the main page we'll find a code snippet box with a small dropdown in the lower-left corner. That menu lists all the available coding languages and there's easily 50+ options to pick from.
- We probably won't use them all but it does support a lot of web friendly languages: PHP, Perl, Ruby, Python, VB .NET.
- There are plenty of limitations in this app since we can't build fully-fledged programs that run on a powerful server. But we can at least test our ideas without setting up a local dev environment.

8. MJML Editor:

- MJML is a great framework. But one of the best reasons to try this framework is the live code editor they host online.
- This works in the cloud so we never need to download anything. It does take some adjusting to figure out how the MJML syntax works.
- In fact we can build a full newsletter design right inside this webapp and download the finished code when we are done. It's basically a full program for coding our own newsletter start to finish.

9. StackBlitz :

- If we do lots of webapp development on Angular or React then we will love StackBlitz.
- This is a free cloud editor made specifically for framework development using these popular open source scripts. We can pull packages from npm and even get a custom URL to see our webapp online (hosted for free).
- It is a huge undertaking and the project is still in active development. But we can sign up with our GitHub account and start building some really cool webapps totally free of charge.

10.Eucalyptus:

- Eucalyptus is acronym standing for Elastic Utility Computing Architecture for Linking Our Programs To Useful Systems. Eucalyptus is a system for implementing on-premise private and hybrid clouds, using the hardware and software infrastructure that's in place, without modification. In effect, it's an add-on capability for data center virtualization to create genuine cloud capability such as self-service provisioning, security, performance management, and end-user customization.
- Eucalyptus is open source, so the software can be downloaded free and it is also shipped with the Ubuntu 9.04 (and later) distribution of Linux. It is thus becoming the default opensource cloud capability. It is implemented by using commonly available Linux tools and basic Web service technologies. The current interface to Eucalyptus is compatible with Amazon's EC2, S3, and Elastic

Block Store (EBS) — a storage area network (SAN) in the cloud-interfaces, so it is possible to create a private cloud by using Eucalyptus with the intention of moving some or all of it onto EC2.

11. Nimbus:

- Nimbus is a toolkit that, once installed on a cluster, provides an infrastructure as a service cloud to its client via WSRF-based or Amazon EC2 WSDL web service APIs. Nimbus is free and open-source software, subject to the requirements of the Apache License, version 2.
- Nimbus supports both hypervisors like Xen and KVM and virtual machine schedulers Portable Batch System and Oracle Grid Engine. It allows deployment of selfconfigured virtual clusters via contextualization. It is configurable with respect to scheduling, networking leases, and usage accounting.
- Nimbus overcomes these challenges like users need to find ways to allow the on-demand resources to share security and configuration context manage the deployment of potentially diverse platform Ensure reliability and scalability in the environment, etc.
- Its aim is to enable users to move to the cloud quickly and effortlessly, automating and facilitating much of the process.
- It also aims to provide a bridge allowing a user to overlay familiar concepts, such as virtual clusters, onto the resources provisioned in the cloud.

Nimbus toolkits:

- cloudinit.d is a tool for launching, controlling, and monitoring cloud applications. If the application is simple or complex, single cloud or multi-cloud, VM based or bare metal, or any combination of the above, cloudinit.d is designed to make the management and coordination of that application easy.
- Phantom is a service that provides auto-scaling and high availability for collections of resources deployed over multiple IaaS cloud providers allowing users to develop scalable and reliable applications. The Context Broker is a service that allows clients to coordinate large virtual cluster launches automatically and repeatable

12. OpenNebula:

- OpenNebula provides the most simple but feature-rich and flexible solution for the comprehensive management of virtualized data centers to enable private, public and hybrid IaaS clouds.
- OpenNebula interoperability makes cloud an evolution by leveraging existing IT assets, protecting our investments, and avoiding vendor lock-in.
- Features include:
  - (i) Openness of the architecture, interfaces, and code.
  - (ii) Flexibility to fit into any datacenter.
  - (iii) Interoperability and portability to prevent vendor lock-in.
  - (iv) Stability for use in production enterprise-class environments.
  - (v) Scalability for large scale infrastructures.
  - (vi) SysAdmin-centrism with complete control over the cloud.
  - (vii) Simplicity, easy to deploy, operate and use.
  - (Viii) Lightness for high efficiency.

13. CloudSim:

- It supports for modeling and simulation of large scale cloud computing data centers & federated clouds. It support for modeling and simulation of virtualized server hosts, with customizable policies for provisioning host resources to virtual machines.
- It support for modeling and simulation of energy-aware computational resources. It has support for modeling and simulation of data center network topologies and message-passing applications.
- It has support for dynamic insertion of simulation elements, stop and resume of simulation. It also supports user-defined policies for allocation of hosts to virtual machines and policies for allocation of host resources to virtual machines.

Individual Student Setup Account for AWS Cloud9:

- This topic explains how to set up to use AWS Cloud9 as a student, with us as the only individual using our account with AWS. To set up to use AWS Cloud9 for any other usage pattern, see Setting Up AWS Cloud9 for the correct instructions. To learn about who qualifies as a student, see Who can join AWS Educate on the *AWS*.

Step 1: Create an Account with AWS

Step 2: Sign In to the AWS Cloud9 Console

Step 1: Create an Account with AWS

- In this step, we create either an AWS Educate Starter Account or a regular AWS account, which we can then use to access AWS Cloud9.
- For an AWS Educate Starter account, note the following:
  1. We must be an eligible student.
  2. We don't need a credit card.
  3. There are some restrictions on AWS usage in the account.
  4. The account isn't eligible for the AWS Free Tier.
  5. After we graduate, we can no longer keep using the account.
  6. We can't link the account to any other account.
  7. We can't apply any additional AWS promotional credit to the account.
  8. AWS resources that we create in the account will stop working after all AWS promotional credit is used.
  9. If the account runs out of AWS promotional credit, the account is deactivated.
  10. We can't turn the account into a regular AWS account.
- For more information, see What is the difference between the AWS Account and AWS Educate Starter Account on the AWS Educate Frequently Asked Questions website.
- Create an AWS Educate Starter Account
- Create a Regular AWS Account and Apply for AWS Educate

Create an AWS Educate Starter Account

- If we already have an AWS Educate Starter Account, skip ahead to Step 2: Sign In to the AWS Cloud9 Console.
  1. Go to the Apply for AWS Educate website, at https://aws.amazon.com/education/awseducate/apply/.
  2. Choose Apply for AWS Educate for Students.
  3. On the Tell us about ourself page, follow the on-screen instructions. This includes giving AWS Educate information such as the educational institution that we attend and our student email address there. Leave Promo Code blank.
  4. Complete the security challenge, and then choose Next.
  5. On the Choose one of the following page, select Click here to select an AWS Educate Starter Account, and then choose Next.
  6. AWS will send us an email with the title Email Verification - AWS Educate Application. Choose the link in that email to confirm our email address, review the AWS Educate program terms and conditions, and complete the application process.
  7. After we complete the application process, AWS will send us an email with the title Thank You for Applying for AWS Educate. This email includes details such as how to check the status of our application and how to contact AWS Educate support with any questions.
  8. After AWS Educate approves our application, AWS will send us an email with the title AWS Educate Application Approved. Note that the approval process might take a day or longer. Do not go past this step in this procedure until we get this approval.
  9. After we get the approval email, follow the instructions in the email to set our AWS Educate Student Portal password, and then sign in to our AWS Educate Student Portal. After we set our AWS Educate Student Portal password, store that password in a secure location.
  10. Skip ahead to Step 2: Sign In to the AWS Cloud9 Console.

Create a Regular AWS Account and Apply for AWS Educate

- If we already have a regular AWS account, skip ahead to step 6 in this procedure to apply for AWS Educate.
  1. Go to https://aws.amazon.com.
  2. Choose Sign In to the Console.
  3. Choose Create a new AWS account.

4. Complete the process by following the on-screen directions. This includes giving AWS our email address and credit card information. We must also use our phone to enter a code that AWS gives us.
5. After we finish creating the account, AWS will send us a confirmation email. Do not go past this step in this procedure until we get this confirmation.
6. Go to the Apply for AWS Educate website, at https://aws.amazon.com/education/awseducate/apply/.
7. Choose Apply for AWS Educate for Students.
8. On the Tell us about ourself page, follow the on-screen instructions. This includes giving AWS Educate information such as the educational institution that we attend and our student email address there. Leave Promo Code blank.
9. Complete the security challenge, and then choose Next.
10. On the Choose one of the following page, select Click here to enter an AWS Account ID.
11. In the box next to Click here to enter an AWS Account ID, enter our AWS account ID, and then choose Next. (To get our AWS account ID, see Finding Our AWS Account ID in the *Amazon Web Services General Reference*.)
12. AWS will send us an email with the title Email Verification - AWS Educate Application. Choose the link in that email to confirm our email address, review the AWS Educate program terms and conditions, and complete the application process.
13. After we complete the application process, AWS will send us an email with the title Thank You for Applying for AWS Educate. This email includes details such as how to check the status of our application and how to contact AWS Educate support with any questions.
    After AWS Educate approves our application, AWS will send us an email with the title AWS Educate Application Approved. Note that the approval process might take a day or longer. We can start using AWS Cloud9 without waiting for this approval. To do this, skip ahead to Step 2: Sign in to the AWS Cloud9 Console.
14. After we get the approval email, follow the instructions in the email to set our AWS Educate Student Portal password, and then sign in to our AWS Educate Student Portal. After we set the AWS Educate Student Portal password, store that password in a secure location.
15. The approval email contains information about AWS promotional credit that we can apply to our AWS account. AWS promotional credit can help offset the cost of using qualifying AWS services, some of which can be used by or with AWS Cloud9. To apply AWS promotional credit to our AWS account, do the following:
    (a) With our AWS Educate Student Portal already open, choose Sign In to the Console.
    (b) To return to our AWS Educate Student Portal, go to the AWS Educate Site Login website, at https://www.awseducate.com/signin/. Enter the email address and password that we used when you initially signed in to our AWS Educate Student Portal, and then choose Sign In.
    (c) Enter the email address for our AWS account, and then choose Next.
    (d) If an email address is already displayed and it's the wrong one, choose Sign in to a different account. Enter the correct email address, and then choose Next.
    (e) Enter the password for our AWS account, and then choose Sign in.
    (f) Type the password for our AWS account, not our AWS Educate Student Portal password.
    (g) In the AWS navigation bar, choose our email address or display name, and then choose My Account.
    (h) Choose Credits.
    (i) For Promo Code, enter the Credit Code from the approval email.
    (j) Complete the Security Check, and then choose Redeem.
    (k) To see the list of AWS services that qualify for this credit, choose See complete list.

Note

- AWS Cloud9 is not in this list of qualifying AWS services, because there is no additional charge for AWS Cloud9. Instead, AWS automatically applies this credit toward qualifying AWS service usage, some of which can be used by or with AWS Cloud9. For more information, see AWS Cloud9 Pricing.

Step 2: Sign In to the AWS Cloud9 Console

- We are now ready to use either an AWS Educate Starter Account or a regular AWS account to sign in to the AWS Cloud9 console and start using AWS Cloud9.
- Use an AWS Educate Starter Account to Sign In to the AWS Cloud9 Console
- Use a Regular AWS Account to Sign In to the AWS Cloud9 Console

Use an AWS Educate Starter Account to Sign In to the AWS Cloud9 Console

1. Go to the AWS Educate Site Login website, at https://www.awseducate.com/signin/.
2. Enter the email address and password we you use to sign in to our AWS Educate Student Portal, and then choose Sign In.
3. Choose AWS Account.
4. Choose Go to our AWS Educate Starter Account.
5. Choose AWS Console.
6. Do one of the following:
   - Choose Cloud9, if it's already displayed.
   - Expand All services, and then choose Cloud9.
   - In the Find services box, type Cloud9, and then press Enter.
   - In the AWS navigation bar, choose Services, and then choose Cloud9.

We can now start using AWS Cloud9. Skip ahead to Next Steps.

Use a Regular AWS Account to Sign In to the AWS Cloud9 Console

Do one of the following:

- Open the AWS Cloud9 console, at https://console.aws.amazon.com/cloud9/.
- Go to the AWS Educate Member Login website, at https://aws.amazon.com/education/awseducate/members/, and then choose Sign In to the Console. (Do not choose Students Login Here.)
  1. Enter the email address for our AWS account, and then choose Next.
  2. If an email address is already displayed and it's the wrong one, choose Sign in to a different account. Enter the correct email address, and then choose Next.
  3. Enter the password for our AWS account, and then choose Sign in.
  4. Enter the password for our AWS account, not our AWS Educate Student Portal password.
  5. If the AWS Management Console is displayed instead of the AWS Cloud9 console, do one of the following:
     - Choose Cloud9, if it's already displayed.
     - Expand All services, and then choose Cloud9.
     - In the Find services box, type Cloud9, and then press Enter.
     - In the AWS navigation bar, choose Services, and then choose Cloud9.
     - You can now start using AWS Cloud9.

Example: A cloud program that displays Hello Cloud9.

- Steps to set up an AWS Cloud9 development environment and then use the AWS Cloud9 IDE to code, run, and debug our first application.
- It uses the AWS Cloud9 console, which enables us to perform the steps of the tutorial in a graphical user interface instead of a command line tool.

Steps

- Step 1: Create an Environment
- Step 2: Basic Tour of the IDE
- Step 3: Clean Up

Step 1: Create an Environment

- In this step, we use the AWS Cloud9 console to create and then open an AWS Cloud9 development environment.

Note

- If we have already created the environment that we want to use for this tutorial, open that environment and skip ahead to Step 2: Basic Tour of the IDE.

- In AWS Cloud9, a development environment (or just environment) is a place where we store our development project's files and where we run the tools to develop our applications. In this tutorial, we create a special kind of environment called an EC2 environment, and then work with the files and tools in that environment.

Create an EC2 Environment with the Console

1. Sign in to the AWS Cloud9 console as follows:
   - If we're the only individual using our AWS account or we are an IAM user in a single AWS account, go to https://console.aws.amazon.com/cloud9/.
   - If our organization uses AWS Single Sign-On (AWS SSO), see our AWS account administrator for sign-in instructions.
   - If we're using an AWS Educate Starter Account, see Step 2: Sign In to the AWS Cloud9 Console in Individual Student Signup.
   - If we're a student in a classroom, see our instructor for sign-in instructions.
2. After we sign in to the AWS Cloud9 console, in the top navigation bar, choose an AWS Region to create the environment in. For a list of available AWS Regions, see AWS Cloud9 in the AWS General Reference.

3. Choose the large Create environment button in one of the locations shown below.
   - If we have no AWS Cloud9 environments yet, the button is shown on a welcome page.

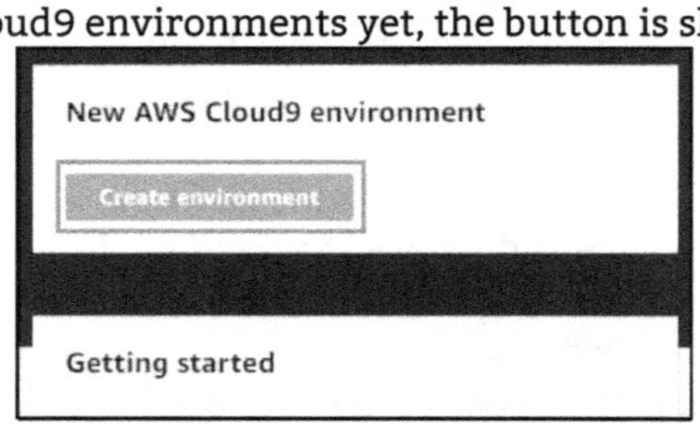

   - If we already have AWS Cloud9 environments, the button is shown as follows.

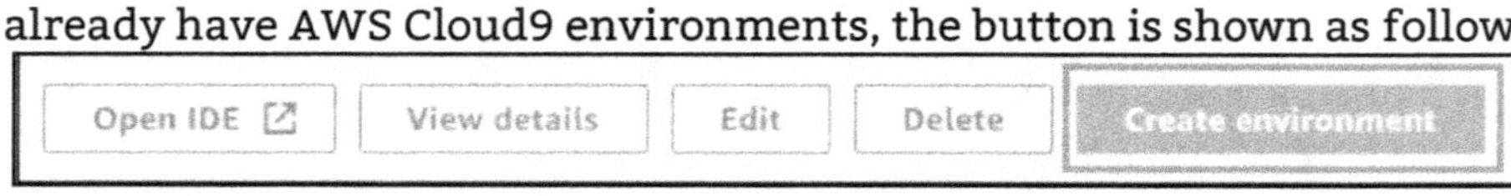

4. On the Name environment page, for Name, enter a name for our environment. For this tutorial, use my-demo-environment.
5. For Description, enter something about our environment. For this tutorial, use This environment is for the AWS Cloud9 tutorial.
6. Choose Next step.
7. On the Configure settings page, for Environment type, choose Create a new instance for environment (EC2).

   Warning
   - Choosing Create a new instance for environment (EC2) might result in possible charges to our AWS account for Amazon EC2.
8. For Instance type, leave the default choice. This choice has relatively low RAM and vCPUs, which is sufficient for this tutorial.

   Warning
   - Choosing instance types with more RAM and vCPUs might result in additional charges to our AWS account for Amazon EC2.

9. For Platform, choose the type of Amazon EC2 instance that we want: Amazon Linux or Ubuntu. AWS Cloud9 creates the instance and then connects the environment to it.
10. Choose a value for Cost-saving setting. When all web browser instances that are connected to the IDE for the environment are closed, AWS Cloud9 waits this amount of time and then shuts down the Amazon EC2 instance for the environment.

    Warning

    - Choosing a longer time period might result in more charges to our AWS account.
11. Expand Network settings (advanced).
    - AWS Cloud9 uses Amazon Virtual Private Cloud (Amazon VPC) to communicate with the newly created Amazon EC2 instance. For this tutorial, we recommend that we don't change the preselected default settings. With the default settings, AWS Cloud9 attempts to automatically use the default VPC with its single subnet in the same AWS account and AWS Region as the new environment.
    - Find more information about Amazon VPC choices in Create an EC2 Environment with the Console, and in VPC Settings for AWS Cloud9 Development Environments.
12. Choose Next step.
13. On the Review page, choose Create environment. Wait while AWS Cloud9 creates our environment. This can take several minutes.
    - After AWS Cloud9 creates our environment, it displays the AWS Cloud9 IDE for the environment.
    - If AWS Cloud9 doesn't display the IDE after at least five minutes, there might be a problem with our web browser, our AWS access permissions, the instance, or the associated virtual private cloud (VPC). For possible fixes, see Cannot Open an Environment in Troubleshooting.

Step 2: Basic Tour of the IDE

- This part of the tutorial introduces some of the ways in which we can use the AWS Cloud9 IDE to create and test applications.
  1. We can use an editor window to create and edit code.
  2. We can use a terminal window or a Run Configuration window to run our code without debugging it.
  3. We can use the Debugger window to debug our code.
- We will perform these three tasks using JavaScript and the Node.js engine.

Get Our Environment Ready

- Most of the tools we need to run and debug JavaScript code are already installed for us. However, we need one additional Node.js package for this tutorial. Install it as given.
  1. On the menu bar (at the top of the AWS Cloud9 IDE), choose Window, New Terminal (or use an existing terminal window).
  2. In the terminal window (one of the tabs in the bottom portion of the IDE), enter the following.

```
npm install readline-sync
```

- Verify that the result is similar to the following.

```
+ readline-sync@1.4.10
added 1 package from 1 contributor and audited 5 packages in 0.565s
found 0 vulnerabilities
```

Write Code:

- Begin by writing some code.

  On the menu bar, choose File, New File.

  Add the following JavaScript to the new file.

```
varreadline = require('readline-sync');
var i = 10;
var input;

console.log("Hello Cloud9!");
console.log("i is " + i);
do {
    input = readline.question("Enter a number (or 'q' to quit): ");
if (input === 'q') {
console.log('OK, exiting.')
    }
else{
```

```
            i += Number(input);
    console.log("i is now " + i);
        }
    } while (input != 'q');

    console.log("Goodbye!");
```

Choose File, Save, and then save the file as hello-cloud9.js.

Run Our Code

- Next, we can run our code.
- Depending on the programming language we are using, there might be multiple ways in which we can run code. For this tutorial, we are using JavaScript, which we can run using a terminal window or a Run Configuration window.

To Run the Code Using a Run Configuration Window

1. On the menu bar, choose Run, Run Configurations, New Run Configuration.
2. In the new Run Configuration window (one of the tabs in the bottom portion of the IDE), enter hello-cloud9.js in the Command field, and then choose Run.
3. Be sure that the Run Configuration prompt is active, and then interact with the application by entering a number at the prompt.
4. View the output from our code in the Run Configuration window.

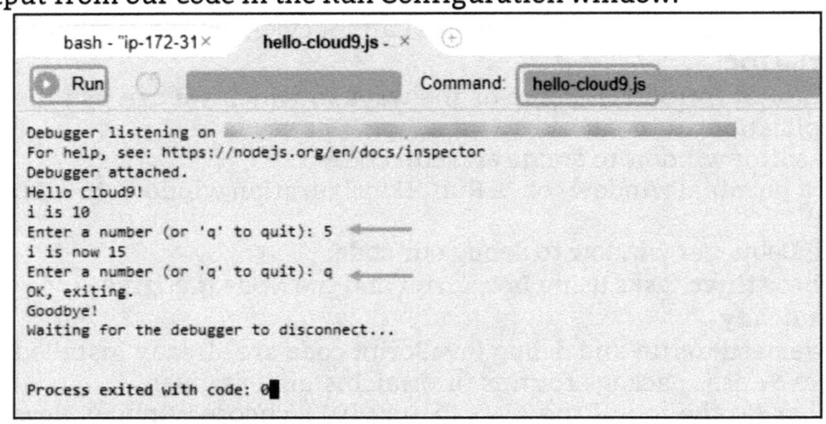

To Run the Code Using a Terminal Window

1. Go to the terminal window that we used earlier (or open a new one).
2. In the terminal window, enter ls at the terminal prompt, and verify that our code file is in the list of files.
3. Enter node hello-cloud9.js at the prompt to start the application.
4. Interact with the application by entering a number at the prompt.
5. View the output from our code in the terminal window. It should be similar to the following.

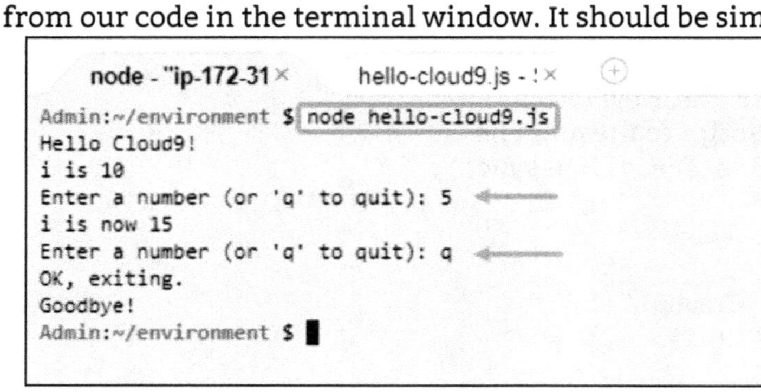

Debug Our Code

- Finally, we can debug our code by using the Debugger window.

1. Add a breakpoint to our code at line 10 (if (input === 'q')) by choosing the margin next to line 10. A red circle is displayed next to that line number, as follows.

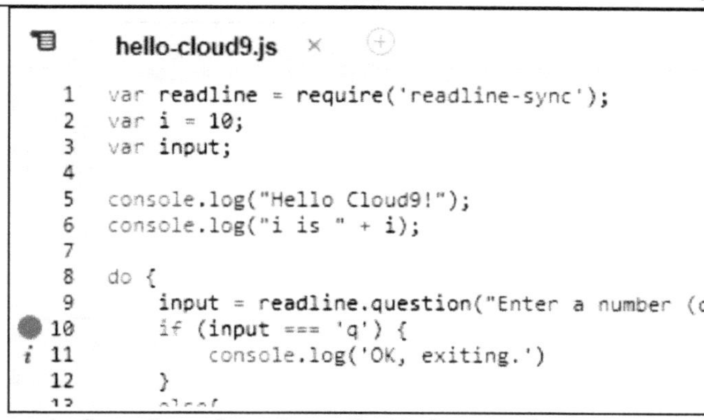

2. Open the Debugger window by choosing the Debugger button on the right side of the IDE. Alternatively, choose Window, Debugger on the menu bar.
   Then, put a watch on the input variable by choosing Type an expression here in the Watch Expressions section of the Debugger window.

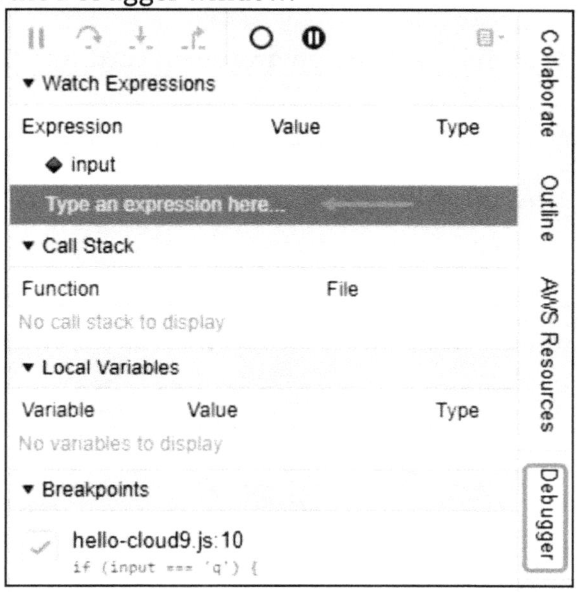

3. Go to the Run Configuration window that we used earlier to run the code. Choose Run.
   Alternately, we can open a new Run Configuration window and start running the code by choosing Run, Run With, Node.js, from the menu bar.
4. Enter a number at the Run Configuration prompt and see that the code pauses at line 10. The Debugger window shows the value we entered in Watch Expressions.

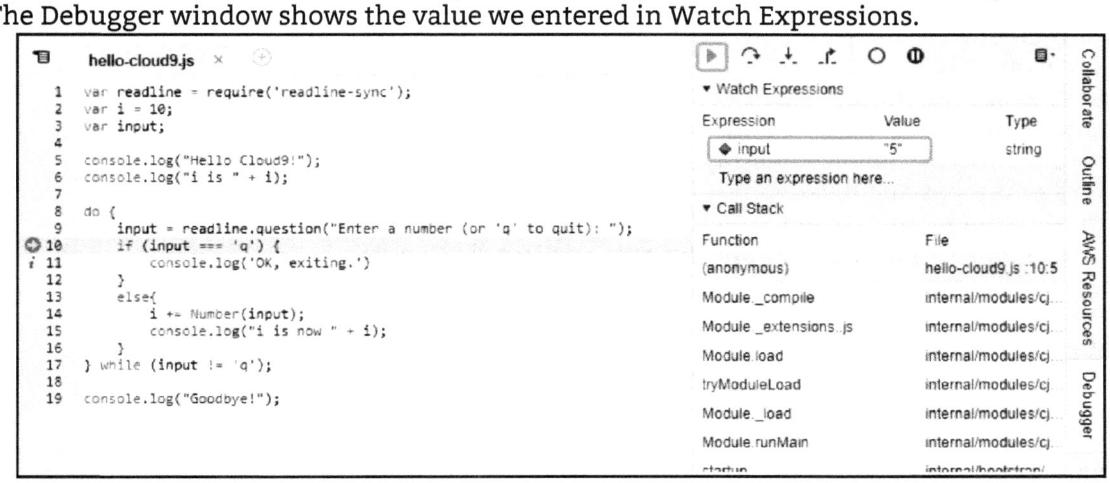

5. In the Debugger window, choose Resume, which is the blue arrow icon that is highlighted in the previous screenshot.
6. Select Stop in the Run Configuration window to stop the debugger.

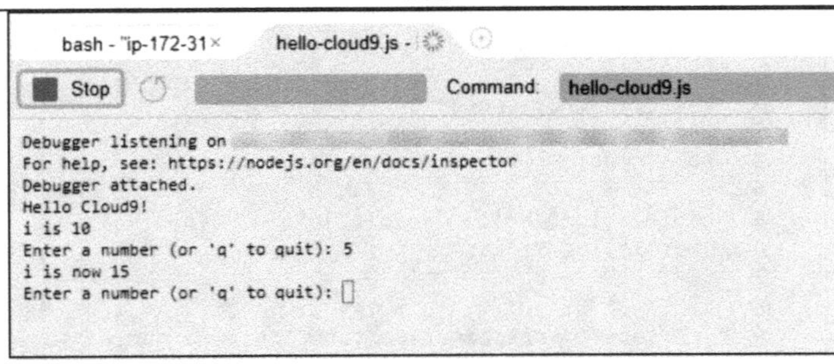

Step 3: Clean Up

- To prevent ongoing charges to our AWS account related to this tutorial, we should delete the environment.

Warning

- Deleting an environment cannot be undone.

Delete the Environment by Using the AWS Cloud9 Console

1. To open the dashboard, on the menu bar in the IDE, choose AWS Cloud9, Go To Our Dashboard.
2. Do one of the following:
   - Choose the title inside of the my-demo-environment card, and then choose Delete.

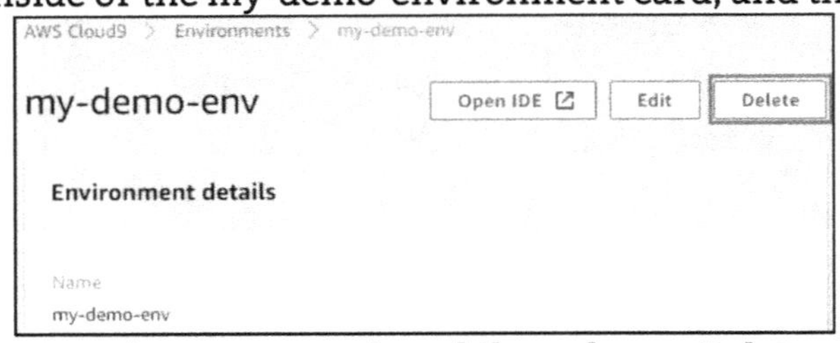

   - Select the my-demo-environment card, and then choose Delete.

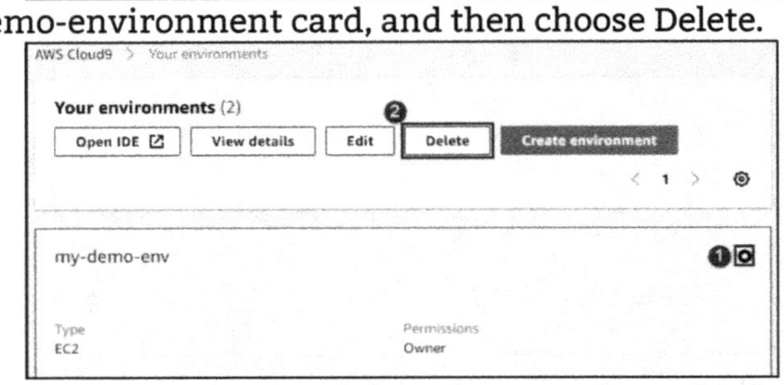

3. In the Delete dialog box, enter Delete, and then choose Delete. The delete operation will take a few minutes.

Practice Questions

1. What is cloud?
2. Define cloud computing.
3. Explain essential Characteristics of Cloud Computing.
4. Explain different Cloud Development Models.
5. Write advantages and disadvantages of Public cloud.
6. Write advantages and disadvantages of Private cloud.
7. Write advantages and disadvantages of Hybrid cloud.
8. Write Comparison between Public, Private and Hybrid Clouds.
9. Explain different Cloud Service Models: IaaS, PaaS, SaaS.
10. Write Cloud Economics benefits.
11. Write Cloud benefits.
12. Write Technical or Business risk of Cloud.
13. Explain Architecture of Cloud Computing.
14. Explain Cloud Computing Infrastructure.
15. Explain Components of Cloud infrastructure.
16. Discuss Infrastructural Constraints.
17. Enlist and explain any two Cloud Based Integrated Environment (IDE).
18. Write Differences between SaaS, PaaS, and IaaS.

2...

Virtualization

Chapter Outcomes...

- Explain the given feature of virtualization.
- Explain the characteristics of the specified virtualization type.
- Write generic steps to build a virtual machine using VMware on the given OS.
- Describe the given disadvantage of virtualization.

Learning Objectives...

- To understand Basic Concepts in Virtualization
- To learn virtualization Reference Model and Characteristics of Virtualization Environment
- To learn virtualization Examples like VMWare, Microsoft Hyper-V, etc.

2.0 INTRODUCTION

- Virtualization technology is one of the fundamental components of cloud computing, especially inregard to infrastructure-based services. Virtualization allows the creation of a secure, customizable, and isolated execution environment for running applications, even if they are untrusted, without affecting other users' applications.
- In cloud computing, the sharing and pooling resources by the applications are very important, this is called as Virtualization.
- Centralized infrastructure is used to provide applications and storage space as per demand of the end users. The users have to pay as per usage and the payments are calculated on a metered basis, the resources are scalable and the multi-tenancy is making possible.

2.1 INTRODUCTION TO VIRTUALIZATION

- Virtualization is a technique, which allows to share single physical instance of an application or resource among multiple organizations or tenants (customers). It is used by assigning a logical name to a physical resource and providing a pointer to that physical resource on demand.
- Creating a virtual machine over existing operating system and hardware is referred as Hardware Virtualization. Virtual Machines provides an environment that is logically separated from the underlying hardware.
- The machine on which the virtual machine is created is known as Host machine and Virtual machine is referred as a Guest machine. This virtual machine is managed by a software or firmware, which is known as Hypervisor.
- Virtualization is a large umbrella of technologies and concepts that are meant to provide an abstract environment whether virtual hardware or an operating system to run applications.

- The term virtualization is often synonymous with hardware virtualization, which plays a fundamental role in efficiently delivering Infrastructure-as-a-Service (IaaS) solutions for cloud computing.
- In fact, virtualization technologies have a long trail in the history of computer science and have been available in many flavors by providing virtual environments at the operating system level, the programming language level, and the application level. Moreover, virtualization technologies provide a virtual environment for not only executing applications but also for storage, memory, and networking.
- Virtualization is a kind of technology that is rapidly transforming the IT landscape and has changed the way people compute. It reduces hardware utilization, saves energy and costs and makes it possible to run multiple applications and various operating systems on the same server at the same time. It increases the utilization, efficiency and flexibility of existing computer hardware.
- Virtualization technologies have gained renewed interested recently due to the confluence of several phenomena:
  1. **Increased Performance and Computing Capacity**: Nowadays, the average end-user desktop PC is powerful enough to meet almost all the needs of everyday computing, with extra capacity that is rarely used. Almost all these PCs have resources enough to host a virtual machine manager and execute a virtual machine with by far acceptable performance. The same consideration applies to the high-end side of the PC market, where supercomputers can provide immense compute power that can accommodate the execution of hundreds or thousands of virtual machines.
  2. **Underutilized Hardware and Software Resources:** Hardware and software underutilization is occurring due to increased performance and computing capacity, and the effect of limited or sporadic use of resources. Today computers are so powerful that in most cases only a fraction of their capacity is used by an application or the system. Moreover, if we consider the IT infrastructure of an enterprise, many computers are only partially utilized whereas they could be used without interruption on a 24/7/365 basis. For example, desktop PCs mostly devoted to office automation tasks and used by administrative staff are only used during work hours, remaining completely unused overnight. Using these resources for other purposes after hours could improve the efficiency of the IT infrastructure. To transparently provide such a service, it would be necessary to deploy a completely separate environment, which can be achieved through virtualization.
  3. **Lack of Space:** The continuous need for additional capacity, whether storage or compute power, makes data centers grow quickly. Companies such as Google and Microsoft expand their infrastructures by building data centers as large as football fields that are able to host thousands of nodes. Although this is applicable for IT giants, in most cases enterprises cannot afford to build another data center to accommodate additional resource capacity. This condition, along with hardware under utilization, has led to the diffusion of a technique called server consolidation, for which virtualization technologies are fundamental.
  4. **Greening Initiatives:** Recently, companies are increasingly looking for ways to reduce the amount of energy they consume and to reduce their carbon footprint. Data centers are one of the major power consumers; they contribute consistently to the impact that a company has on the environment. Maintaining a data center operation not only involves keeping servers on, but a great deal of energy is also consumed in keeping them cool. Infrastructures for cooling have a significant impact on the carbon footprint of a data center. Hence, reducing the number of servers through server consolidation will definitely reduce the impact of cooling and power consumption of a data center. Virtualization technologies can provide an efficient way of consolidating servers.
  5. **Rise of Administrative Costs:** Power consumption and cooling costs have now become higher than the cost of IT equipment. Moreover, the increased demand for additional capacity, which translates into more servers in a data center, is also responsible for a significant increment in administrative costs. Computers in particular, servers do not operate all on their own, but they require care and feeding from system administrators. Common system administration tasks include hardware monitoring, defective hardware replacement, server setup and updates, server

resources monitoring, and backups. These are labor-intensive operations, and the higher the number of servers that have to be managed, the higher the administrative costs. Virtualization can help reduce the number of required servers for a given workload, thus reducing the cost of the administrative personnel.

2.1.1 Need of Virtualization

- Virtualization provides various benefits including saving time and energy, decreasing costs and minimizing overall risk.
  1. Provides ability to manage resources effectively.
  2. Increases productivity, as it provides secure remote access.
  3. Provides for data loss prevention.
- What makes virtualization possible? There is a software that makes virtualization possible.

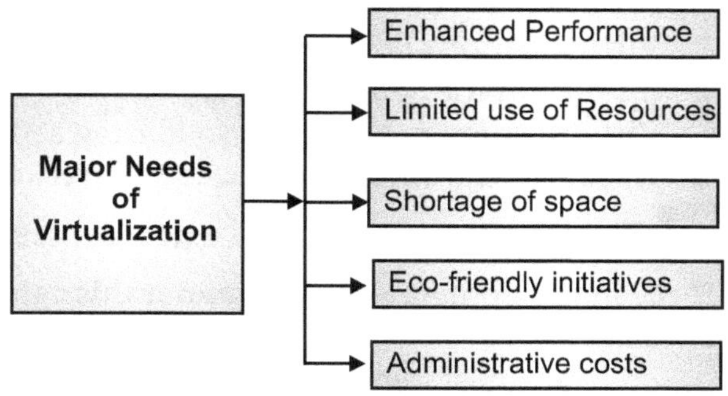

Fig. 2.1 : Need of Virtualization

This software is known as a Hypervisor, also known as a Virtualization Manager. It sits between the hardware and the operating system, and assigns the amount of access that the applications and operating systems have with the processor and other hardware resources.

- There are five major needs of virtualization which are described below:
  1. **Enhanced Performance:** Currently, the end user system i.e. PC is sufficiently powerful to fulfill all the basic computation requirements of the user, with various additional capabilities which are rarely used by the user. Most of their systems have sufficient resources which can host a virtual machine manager and can perform a virtual machine with acceptable performance so far.
  2. **Limited Use of Hardware and Software Resources:** The limited use of the resources leads to under utilization of hardware and software resources. As all the PCs of the user are sufficiently capable to fulfill their regular computational needs that are why many of their computers are used often which can be used 24/7 continuously without any interruption. The efficiency of IT infrastructure could be increase by using these resources after hours for other purposes. This environment is possible to attain with the help of Virtualization.
  3. **Shortage of Space:** The regular requirement for additional capacity, whether memory storage or compute power, leads data centers raise rapidly. Companies like Google, Microsoft and Amazon develop their infrastructure by building data centers as per their needs. Mostly, enterprises unable to pay to build any other data center to accommodate additional resource capacity. This heads to the diffusion of a technique which is known as Server Consolidation.
  4. **Eco-Friendly Initiatives:** At this time, corporations are actively seeking for various methods to minimize their expenditures on power which is consumed by their systems. Data centers are main power consumers and maintaining a data center operations needs a continuous power supply as well as a good amount of energy is needed to keep them cool for well-functioning. Therefore, server consolidation drops the power consumed and cooling impact by having a fall in number of servers. Virtualization can provide a sophisticated method of server consolidation.
  5. **Administrative Costs:** Furthermore, the rise in demand for capacity surplus, that convert into more servers in a data center, accountable for a significant increase in administrative costs. Hardware monitoring, server setup and updates, defective hardware replacement, server resources monitoring, and backups are included in common system administration tasks. These are personnel-intensive operations. The administrative costs is increased as per the number of servers. Virtualization decreases number of required servers for a given workload, hence reduces the cost of administrative employees.

Purpose of Virtualization:

1. **Abstraction:** To simplify the use of the underlying resource (e.g., by removing details of the resource's structure).

2. **Replication:** To create multiple instances of the resource (e.g., to simplify management or allocation).
3. **Isolation:** To separate the uses which clients make of the underlying resources (e.g., to improve security).

Benefits of Virtualization:

1. It helps in saving lots of cost and allows to easily maintaining it, in less cost.
2. Virtualization allows multiple operating systems on one virtualization platform.
3. It removes the dependency of heavy hardware to run the application.
4. Virtualization provides consolidating servers that are used for crashing of a server purpose.
5. It reduces the amount of space being taken by data centres and company data.

2.1.2 Virtualization Reference Model

- Three major Components falls under this category in a virtualized environment:
  1. **Guest:**
     - The guest represents the system component that interacts with the virtualization layer rather than with the host, as would normally happen.
     - Guests usually consist of one or more virtual disk files, and a VM definition file.
     - Virtual Machines are centrally managed by a host application that sees and manages each virtual machine as a different application.
  2. **Host:**
     - The host represents the original environment where the guest is supposed to be managed. Each guest runs on the host using shared resources donated to it by the host.
     - The operating system, works as the host and manages the physical resource management, and the device support.
  3. **Virtualization Layer:**
     - The virtualization layer is responsible for recreating the same or a different environment where the guest will operate. It is an additional abstraction layer between a network and storage hardware, computing, and the application running on it.
     - Usually it helps to run a single operating system per machine which can be very inflexible compared to the usage of virtualization.

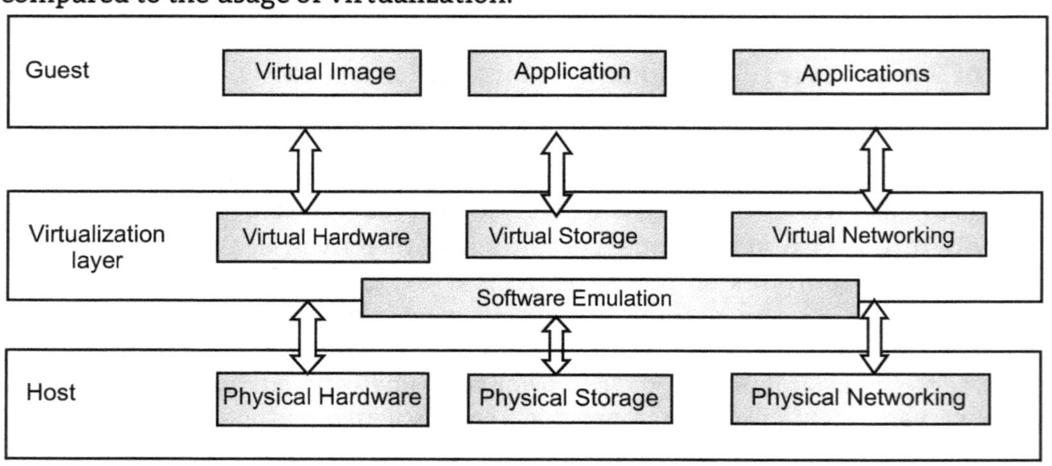

Fig. 2.2 : Virtualization Reference Model

2.1.3 Characteristics of Virtualized Environment

- Virtualization is a broad concept that refers to the creation of a virtual version of something, whether hardware, a software environment, storage, or a network. In a virtualized environment there are three major components: guest, host, and virtualization layer.
- The guest represents the system component that interacts with the virtualization layer rather than with the host, as would normally happen. The host represents the original environment where the guest is supposed to be managed.

- The virtualization layer is responsible for recreating the same or a different environment where the guest will operate shown in Fig. 2.2.
- Virtualization environment has 3 characteristics:
  1. Increased security
  2. Managed execution
  3. Portability

2.1.3.1 Increased Security

- The ability to control the execution of a guest programs in a completely transparent manner opens new possibilities for delivering a secure, controlled execution environment. All the operations of the guest programs are generally performed against the virtual machine, which then translates and applies them to the host programs.
- A virtual machine manager can control and filter the activity of the guest programs, thus preventing some harmful operations from being performed. Resources exposed by the host can then be hidden or simply protected from the guest. Increased security is a requirement when dealing with untrusted code.
- **Example 1:** Untrusted code can be analyzed in Cuckoo sandboxes environment. The term sandbox identifies an isolated execution environment where instructions can be filtered and blocked before being translated and executed in the real execution environment.
- **Example 2:** The expression sandboxed version of the Java Virtual Machine (JVM) refers to a particular configuration of the JVM where, by means of security policy, instructions that are considered potentially harmful can be blocked.

2.1.3.2 Managed Execution

- Virtualization of the execution environment not only allows increased security, but a wider range of features also can be implemented. In particular, sharing, aggregation, emulation, and isolation are the most relevant features:
  1. **Sharing:** Virtualization allows the creation of a separate computing environments within the same host. This basic feature is used to reduce the number of active servers and limit power consumption.
  2. **Aggregation:** Not only it is possible to share physical resource among several guests, but virtualization also allows aggregation, which is the opposite process. A group of separate hosts can be tied together and represented to guests as a single virtual host. This functionality is implemented with cluster management software, which harnesses the physical resources of a homogeneous group of machines and represents them as a single resource.
  3. **Emulation:** Guest programs are executed within an environment that is controlled by the virtualization layer, which is ultimately a program. Also a completely different environment with respect to the host can be emulated, thus allowing the execution of guest programs requiring specific characteristics that are not present in the physical host.
  4. **Isolation:** Virtualization allows providing guests whether they are operating systems, applications, or other entities with a completely separate environment, in which they are executed. The guest program performs its activity by interacting with an abstraction layer, which provides access to the underlying resources. The virtual machine can filter the activity of the guest and prevent harmful operations against the host.
- Besides these characteristics, another important capability enabled by virtualization is performance tuning. This feature is a reality at present, given the considerable advances in hardware and software supporting virtualization.
- It becomes easier to control the performance of the guest by finely tuning the properties of the resources exposed through the virtual environment. This capability provides a means to effectively implement a Quality of Service (QoS) infrastructure.

2.1.3.3 Portability

- The concept of portability applies in different ways according to the specific type of virtualization considered.

1. In the case of a hardware virtualization solution, the guest is packaged into a virtual image that, in most cases, can be safely moved and executed on top of different virtual machines.
2. In the case of programming level virtualization, as implemented by the JVM or the .NET runtime, the binary code representing application components (jars or assemblies) can run without any recompilation on any implementation of the corresponding virtual machine.

2.2 VIRTUALIZATION TYPES

- Virtualization covers a wide range of emulation techniques that are applied to different areas of computing.
- A virtualization types helps us better understand their characteristics and use show in Fig. 2.3.

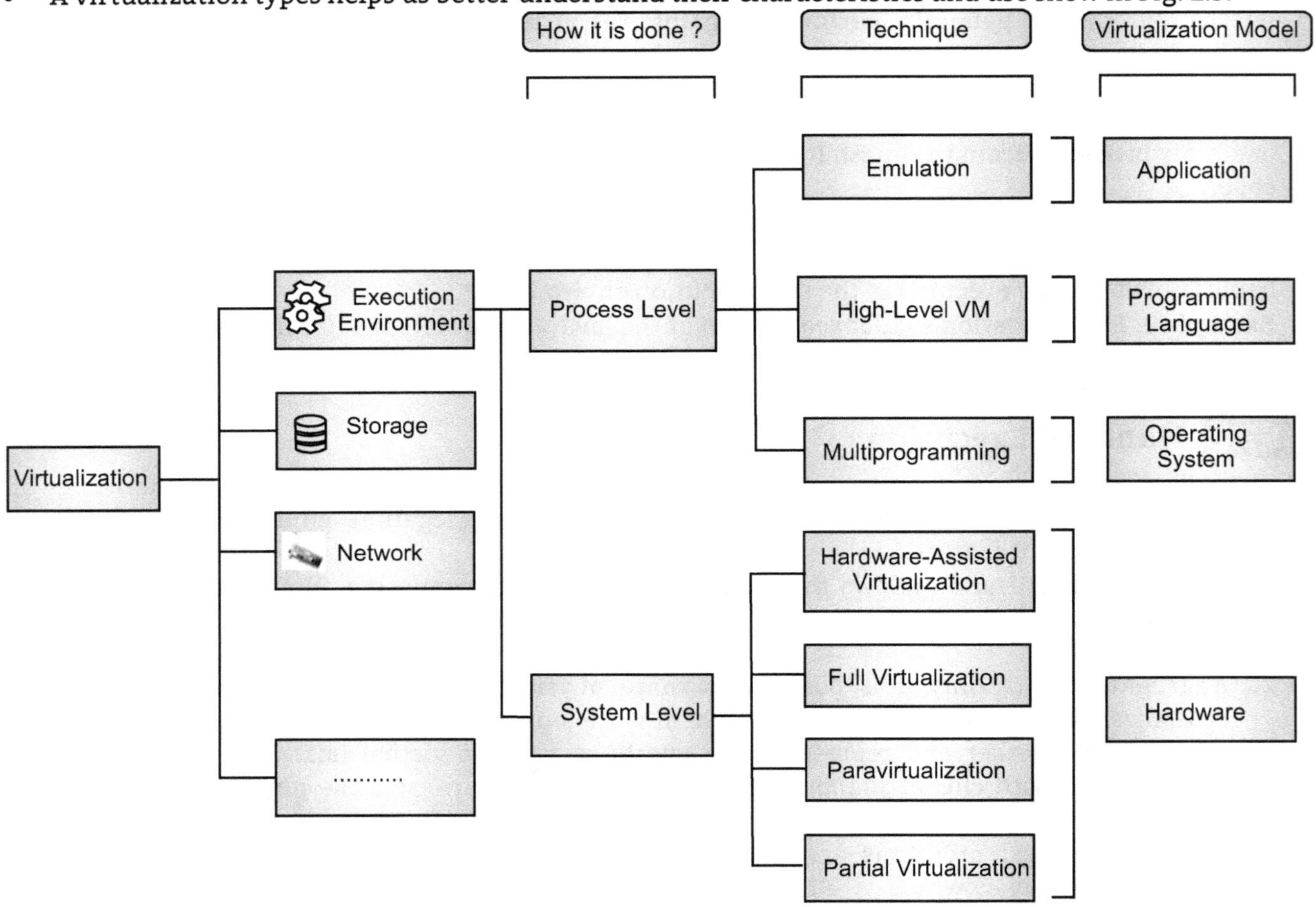

Fig. 2.3: Virtualization Types

- Virtualization have 3 main types emulations:
  - Execution Virtualization
    - Process level
    - System Level
  - Storage
  - Networks

2.2.1 Execution Virtualization

- Execution virtualization techniques further divided into two categories:
  1. **Process-level techniques** are implemented on top of an existing operating system, which has full control of the hardware.
  2. **System-level techniques** are implemented directly on hardware and do not require or require a minimum of support from an existing operating system.
- These two categories support various techniques that offers the different type of virtual computation environment: bare hardware, operating system resources, low-level programming language, and application libraries.

- All these techniques concentrate their interest on providing support for the execution of programs, whether these are the operating system, a binary specification of a program compiled against an abstract machine model, or an application.
- Therefore, execution virtualization can be implemented directly on top of the hardware by the operating system, an application, or libraries dynamically or statically linked to an application image.

2.2.1.1 Machine Reference Model

- Virtualizing an execution environment at different levels of the computing stack requires a reference model that defines the interfaces between the levels of abstractions, which hide implementation details.
- From this perspective, virtualization techniques actually replace one of the layers and intercept the calls that are directed toward it. Therefore, a clear separation between layers simplifies their implementation, which only requires the emulation of the interfaces and a proper interaction with the underlying layer.
- Machine reference model shown in Fig 2.4.
- At the bottom layer, the model for the hardware is expressed in terms of the Instruction Set Architecture (ISA), which defines the instruction set for the processor, registers, memory, and interrupt management. ISA is the interface between hardware and software, and it is important to the Operating System (OS) developer (System ISA) and developers of applications that directly manage the underlying hardware (User ISA).
- The Application Binary Interface (ABI) separates the operating system layer from the applications and libraries, which are managed by the OS. ABI covers details such as low-level data types, alignment, and call conventions and defines a format for executable programs. System calls are defined at this level.
- This interface allows portability of applications and libraries across operating systems that implement the same ABI. The highest level of abstraction is represented by the Application Programming Interface (API), which interfaces applications to libraries and/or the underlying operating system.
- For any operation to be performed in the application level API, ABI and ISA are responsible for making it happen. The high-level abstraction is converted into machine-level instructions to perform the actual operations supported by the processor.
- The machine-level resources, such as processor registers and main memory capacities, are used to perform the operation at the hardware level of the Central Processing Unit (CPU).
- This layered approach simplifies the development and implementation of computing systems and simplifies the implementation of multitasking and the co-existence of multiple executing environments.
- In fact, such a model not only requires limited knowledge of the entire computing stack, but it also provides ways to implement a minimal security model for managing and accessing shared resources.

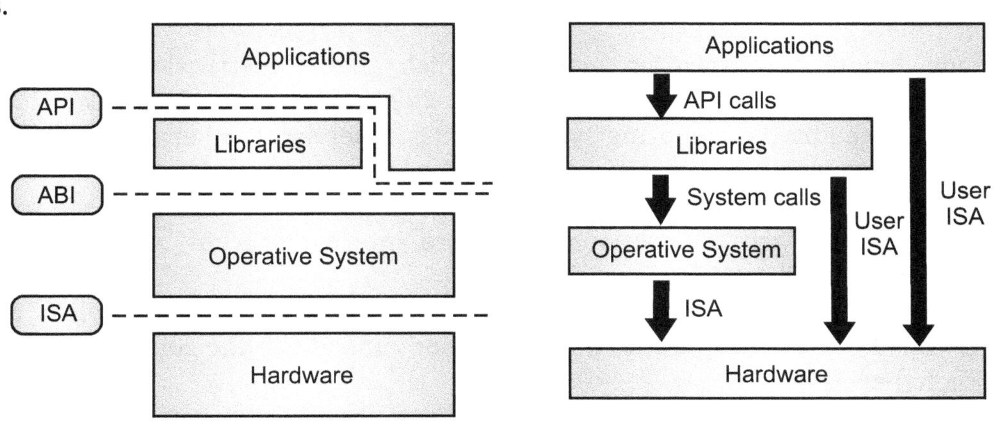

Fig. 2.4: Machine Reference Model

- This API interfaces applications to libraries and/or the core OS. For an action is to be performed in the application level API, ABI and the two which are responsible to make it done. Mainly, CPU runs on two privilege levels:
  1. **User Mode:** In this mode, memory access is restricted up to some limit whereas access to peripherals is denied.
  2. **Kernel Mode:** In this mode, CPU has instructions which manage memory and how to be accessed and it also has instructions which enable access of the peripherals like disks and network cards. From one running program to another running program, CPU switches automatically. The expansions and applications of computing system are simplified by this layered approach. Application of multitasking and co-existence of multiple executing is simplified by this layered approach.
- The instruction set has been divided into different security classes that define who can operate with them. The first distinction can be made between privileged and non privileged instructions.
- Non privileged instructions are those instructions that can be used without interfering with other tasks because they do not access shared resources. This category contains, for example, all the floating, fixed-point, and arithmetic instructions.
- Privileged instructions are those that are executed under specific restrictions and are mostly used for sensitive operations, which expose (behavior-sensitive) or modify (control-sensitive) the privileged state. For instance, behavior-sensitive instructions are those that operate on the I/O, whereas control-sensitive instructions alter the state of the CPU registers. Some types of architecture feature more than one class of privileged instructions and implement a finer control of how these instructions can be accessed.
- Fig. 2.5 shows hierarchy of privileges in the form of ring-based security: Ring 0, Ring 1, Ring 2, and Ring 3; Ring 0 is in the most privileged level and Ring 3 in the least privileged level. Ring 0 is used by the kernel of the OS, rings 1 and 2 are used by the OS-level services, and Ring 3 is used by the user.

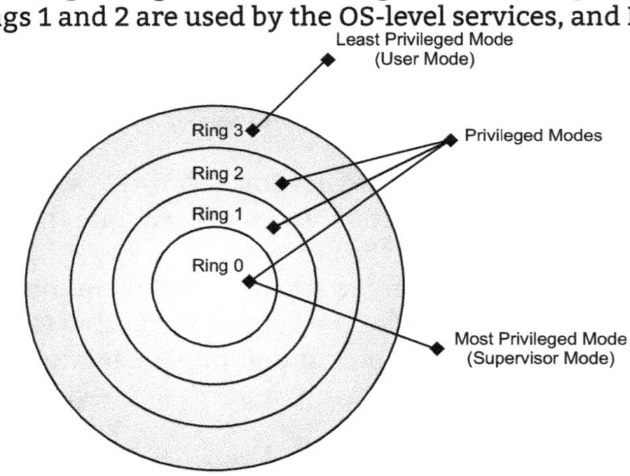

Fig. 2.5 : Security Rings and Privilege Modes

- All the current systems support at least two different execution modes: supervisor mode and user mode.
- The first mode denotes an execution mode in which all the instructions (privileged and non privileged) can be executed without any restriction. This mode, also called Master Mode or Kernel Mode, is generally used by the operating system (or the hypervisor) to perform sensitive operations on hardware level resources.
- In user mode, there are restrictions to control the machine-level resources. If code running in user mode invokes the privileged instructions, hardware interrupts occur and trap the potentially harmful execution of the instruction.
- The distinction between user and supervisor mode allows us to understand the role of the hypervisor and why it is called that. Conceptually, the hypervisor runs above the supervisor mode, and from here the prefix hyper- is used.
- In reality, hypervisors are run in supervisor mode, and the division between privileged and non privileged instructions has posed challenges in designing virtual machine managers.

- It is expected that all the sensitive instructions will be executed in privileged mode, which requires supervisor mode in order to avoid traps.
- Without this assumption it is impossible to fully emulate and manage the status of the CPU for guest operating systems. Unfortunately, this is not true for the original ISA, which allows 17 sensitive instructions to be called in user mode.
- This prevents multiple operating systems managed by a single hypervisor to be isolated from each other, since they are able to access the privileged state of the processor and change it.
- More recent implementations of ISA (Intel VT and AMD Pacifica) have solved this problem by redesigning such instructions as privileged ones.

2.2.1.2 Hardware Level Virtualization

- Hardware level virtualization is a virtualization technique that provides an abstract execution environment in terms of computer hardware on top of which a guest operating system can be run.
- In this model, the guest is represented by the operating system, the host by the physical computer hardware, the virtual machine by its emulation and the virtual machine manager by the hypervisor shown in Fig. 2.6.

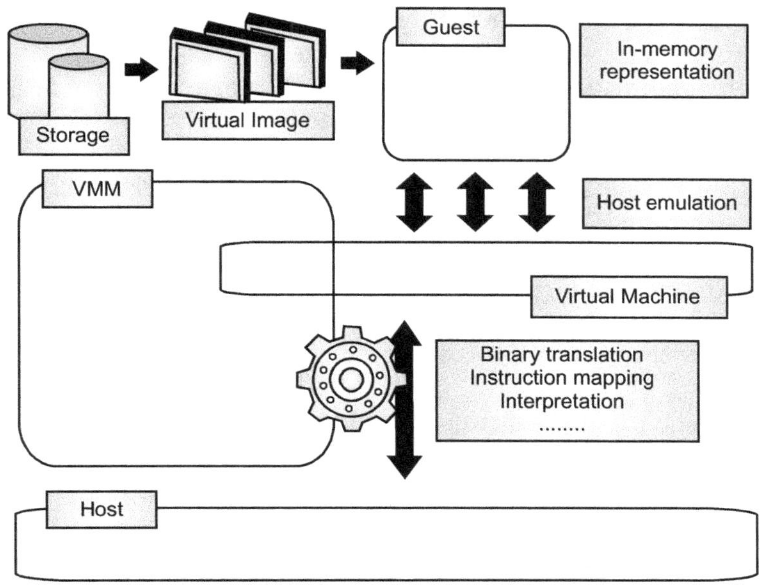

Fig. 2.6 : A Hardware Virtualization Reference Model

- The hypervisor is generally a program or a combination of software and hardware that allows the abstraction of the underlying physical hardware.
- Hardware level virtualization is also called System Virtualization, since it provides ISA to virtual machines, which is the representation of the hardware interface of a system. This is to differentiate it from process virtual machines, which expose ABI to virtual machines.

Hypervisors:

- A fundamental element of hardware virtualization is the hypervisor, or Virtual Machine Manager (VMM). It recreates a hardware environment in which guest operating systems are installed.
- There are two major types of hypervisor namely Type I and Type II shown in Fig. 2.7.
  1. **Type I:** This type of hypervisors runs directly on top of the hardware. Therefore, they take the place of the operating systems and interact directly with the ISA interface exposed by the underlying hardware, and they emulate this interface in order to allows the management of guest operating systems. This type of hypervisor is also called a native virtual machine since it runs natively on hardware.
  2. **Type II:** This type of hypervisors requires the support of an operating system to provide virtualization services. This means that they are programs managed by the operating system, which interact with it through the ABI and emulate the ISA of virtual hardware for guest operating systems. This type of hypervisor is also called a hosted virtual machine since it is hosted within an operating system.

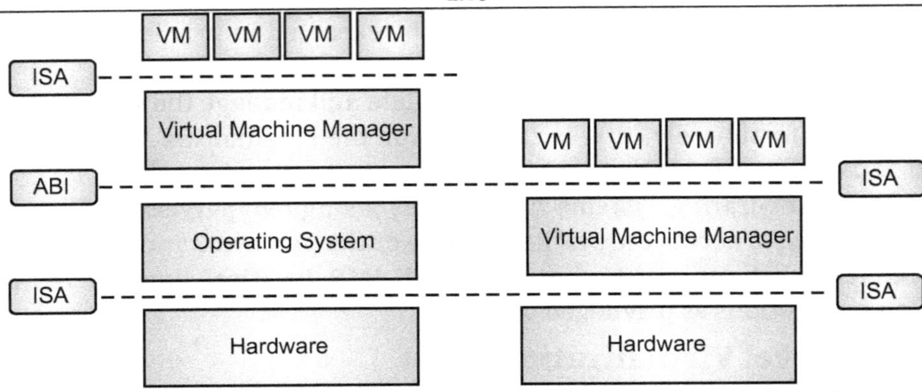

Fig. 2.7: Types of Hypervisor (Left Side is Type – I (Hosted) and Right Side is Type – II (Native) Virtual Machine)

Virtual Machine Manager (VMM):

- VMM has three main modules, dispatcher, allocator, and interpreter and it is internally organized as shown in Fig. 2.8.
- The dispatcher constitutes the entry point of the monitor and reroutes the instructions issued by the virtual machine instance to one of the two other modules.
- The allocator is responsible for deciding the system resources to be provided to the VM: whenever a virtual machine tries to execute an instruction that results in changing the machine resources associated with that VM, the allocator is invoked by the dispatcher.
- The interpreter module consists of interpreter routines. These are executed whenever a virtual machine executes a privileged instruction: a trap is triggered and the corresponding routine is executed.
- The design and architecture of a virtual machine manager, together with the underlying hardware design of the host machine, determine the full realization of hardware virtualization, where a guest operating system can be transparently executed on top of a VMM as though it were run on the underlying hardware.
- The criteria that need to be met by a virtual machine manager to efficiently support virtualization must satisfy these three properties:
  1. **Equivalence:** A guest running under the control of a virtual machine manager should exhibit the same behavior as when it is executed directly on the physical host.
  2. **Resource control:** The virtual machine manager should be in complete control of virtualized resources.
  3. **Efficiency:** A statistically dominant fraction of the machine instructions should be executed without intervention from the virtual machine manager.

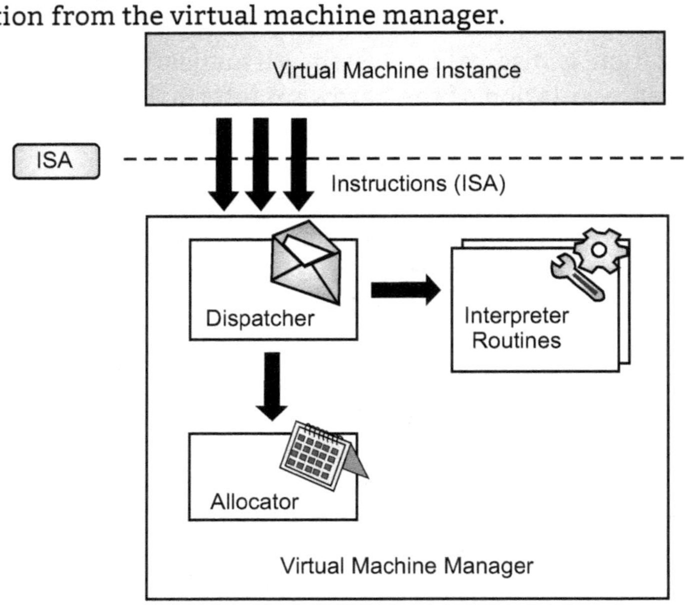

Fig. 2.8 : A Hypervisor Reference Architecture

Hardware Virtualization Techniques:

- It has four different types namely, Full Virtualization, Para-Virtualization, Partial Virtualization, and Hardware Assisted Virtualization.

1. Full Virtualization:

- Full virtualization refers to the ability to run a program, most likely an operating system, directly on top of a virtual machine and without any modification, as though it were run on the raw hardware.
- To make this possible, virtual machine managers are required to provide a complete emulation of the entire underlying hardware.
- The principal advantage of full virtualization is complete isolation, which leads to enhanced security, ease of emulation of different architectures, and co-existence of different systems on the same platform.

Advantages of full virtualization:

(i) Full virtualization technique grants the potential to combine existing systems on to the newer ones with increased efficiency and a well organized hardware.
(ii) This amazing methodology contributes effectively to trim down the operating costs engaged in repairing and enhancing older systems.
(iii) The less competent systems can be power-packed with this technique, while reducing the physical space and augmenting the overall performance of the company.
(iv) This type of virtualization provides best isolation and security for virtual machine.
(v) Truly isolated multiple guest operating system can run simultaneously on same hardware.
(vi) It's only option that requires no hardware assist or os assist to virtualize sensitive and privileged instructions.

Limitations of full virtualization:

(i) Full virtualization is usually bit slower, because of all emulation.
(ii) Hyperwiser contain the device driver and it might be difficult for new device drivers to be installer by users.

2. Para-virtualization:

- This is a not transparent virtualization solution that allows implementing thin virtual machine managers. Para-virtualization techniques expose a software interface to the virtual machine that is slightly modified from the host and, as a consequence, guests need to be modified.
- The aim of para-virtualization is to provide the capability to demand the execution of performance critical operations directly on the host, thus preventing performance losses that would otherwise be experienced in managed execution.
- This allows a simpler implementation of virtual machine managers that have to simply transfer the execution of these operations, which were hard to virtualize, directly to the host. To take advantage of such an opportunity, guest operating systems need to be modified and explicitly ported by remapping the performance critical operations through the virtual machine software interface.
- This is possible when the source code of the operating system is available, and this is the reason that para-virtualization was mostly explored in the open source and academic environment.
- This technique has been successfully used by Xen for providing virtualization solutions for Linux based operating systems specifically ported to run on Xen hypervisors.
- Operating systems that cannot be ported can still take advantage of para-virtualization by using ad hoc device drivers that remap the execution of critical instructions to the para-virtualization

Advantages of Para-virtualization:

(i) It enhances the performance notably by decreasing the number of VMM calls and prevents the needless use of privileged instructions.
(ii) It allows running many operating systems on a single server.
(iii) This method is considered as the most advantageous one as it augments the performance per server without the operating cost of a host operating system.
(iv) As a guest OS can directly communicate with hypervisor
(v) This is efficient virtualization.
(vi) Allows users to make use of new or modified device drivers.

Limitations of Para-virtualization:

(i) Para virtualization requires the guest OS to be modified in order to interact with para-virtualization interfaces.

(ii) It requires significant support and maintaibilty issues in production environment.

3. **Partial Virtualization:**

- Partial virtualization provides a partial emulation of the underlying hardware, thus not allowing the complete execution of the guest operating system in complete isolation.
- Partial virtualization allows many applications to run transparently, but not all the features of the operating system can be supported, as happens with full virtualization.
- An example of partial virtualization is address space virtualization used in time-sharing systems; this allows multiple applications and users to run concurrently in a separate memory space, but they still share the same hardware resources (disk, processor, and network).

4. **Hardware Assisted Virtualization:**

- It is a type of full virtualization where the microprocessor architecture has special instructions to aid the virtualization of hardware. These instructions might allows a virtual context to be setup so that the guest can execute privileged instructions directly on the processor without affecting the host. Such a feature set is often called a Hypervisor.
- If given instructions do not exist, Full Virtualization is still possible, however it must be done via software techniques such as Dynamic Recompilation where the host recompiles on the fly privileged instructions in the guest to be able to run in a non privileged way on the host.

Hybrid Virtualization:

- There is also a combination of Para-virtualization and Full Virtualization called Hybrid Virtualization where parts of the guest operating system use para-virtualization for certain hardware drivers, and the host uses full virtualization for other features.
- This often produces superior performance on the guest without the need for the guest to be completely para-virtualized.
- An example of this: The guest uses full virtualization for privileged instructions in the kernel but para-virtualization for I/O requests using a special driver in the guest. This way the guest operating system does not need to be fully para-virtualized, since this is sometimes not available, but can still enjoy some para-virtualized features by implementing special drivers for the guest.

2.2.1.3 Operating System Level Virtualization

- Operating system level virtualization offers the opportunity to create different and separated execution environments for applications that are managed concurrently.
- Differently from hardware virtualization, there is no virtual machine manager or hypervisor, and the virtualization is done within a single operating system, where the OS kernel allows for multiple isolated user space instances.
- The kernel is also responsible for sharing the system resources among instances and for limiting the impact of instances on each other.
- A user space instance in general contains a proper view of the file system, which is completely isolated, and separate IP addresses, software configurations, and access to devices.
- Operating systems supporting this type of virtualization are general purpose, timeshared operating systems with the capability to provide stronger namespace and resource isolation.
- This virtualization technique can be considered an evolution of the chroot mechanism in Unix systems. The chroot operation changes the file system root directory for a process and its children to a specific directory.
- As a result, the process and its children cannot have access to other portions of the file system than those accessible under the new root directory. Because Unix systems also expose devices as parts of the file system, by using this method it is possible to completely isolate a set of processes.
- Following the same principle, operating system level virtualization aims to provide separated and multiple execution containers for running applications.
- Compared to hardware virtualization, this strategy imposes little or no overhead because applications directly use OS system calls and there is no need for emulation.

- There is no need to modify applications to run them, nor to modify any specific hardware, as in the case of hardware assisted virtualization.
- On the other hand, operating system level virtualization does not expose the same flexibility of hardware virtualization, since all the user space instances must share the same operating system.
- This technique is an efficient solution for server consolidation scenarios in which multiple application servers share the same technology: operating system, application server framework, and other components.
- When different servers are aggregated into one physical server, each server is run in a different user space, completely isolated from the others.
- Examples of operating system level virtualizations are FreeBSD Jails, IBM Logical Partition (LPAR), SolarisZones and Containers, Parallels Virtuozzo Containers, OpenVZ, iCore Virtual Accounts, Free Virtual Private Server (FreeVPS), and others.

Uses of OS Virtualization:

1. Used for virtual hosting environment.
2. Used for securely allocation of finite hardware resources among a large number of distrusting users.
3. System administrator uses it to integrate server hardware by moving services on separate hosts.
4. To improvised security by separating several applications to several containers.
5. These forms of virtualization don't require hardware to work efficiently.

Advantages of OS Virtualization:

1. OS virtualization usually imposes little or no overhead.
2. OS virtualization is capable of live migration
3. It can also use dynamic load balancing of containers between nodes and a cluster.
4. The file level Copy-on-Write (CoW) mechanism is possible on OS virtualization which makes easier to back up files, more space efficient and simpler to cache than the block level copy-on-write schemes.

2.2.1.4 Programming Language Level Virtualization

- Programming language level virtualization is mostly used to achieve ease of deployment of applications, managed execution, and portability across different platforms and operating systems.
- It consists of a virtual machine executing the byte code of a program, which is the result of the compilation process. Compilers implemented and used this technology to produce a binary format representing the machine code for an abstract architecture.
- The characteristics of this architecture vary from implementation to implementation.
- Generally these virtual machines constitute a simplification of the underlying hardware instruction set and provide some high level instructions that map some of the features of the languages compiled for them.
- At runtime, the byte code can be either interpreted or compiled on the fly or jitted5 against the underlying hardware instruction set.
- Programming language level virtualization has a long trail in computer science history and originally was used in 1966 for the implementation of Basic Combined Programming Language (BCPL), a language for writing compilers and one of the ancestors of the C programming language.
- Other important examples of the use of this technology have been the UCSD Pascal and Smalltalk.
- Virtual machine programming languages become popular again with Sun's introduction of the Java platform in 1996.
- The Java virtual machine was originally designed for the execution of programs written in the Java language, but other languages such as Python, Pascal, Groovy, and Ruby were made available.
- The main advantage of programming level virtual machines, also called process virtual machines, is the ability to provide a uniform execution environment across different platforms. Programs compiled into byte code can be executed on any operating system and platform for which a virtual machine able to execute that code has been provided.

2.2.1.5 Application Level Virtualization

- Application level virtualization is a technique allowing applications to be run in runtime environments that do not natively support all the features required by such applications.

- In this scenario, applications are not installed in the expected runtime environment but are run as though they were. In general, these techniques are mostly concerned with partial file systems, libraries, and operating system component emulation.
- Such emulation is performed by a thin layer a program or an operating system component-that is in charge of executing the application. Emulation can also be used to execute program binaries compiled for different hardware architectures.
- In this case, one of the following strategies can be implemented:
  1. **Interpretation:** In this technique every source instruction is interpreted by an emulator for executing native ISA instructions, leading to poor performance. Interpretation has a minimal startup cost but a huge overhead, since each instruction is emulated.
  2. **Binary Translation:** In this technique every source instruction is converted to native instructions with equivalent functions. After a block of instructions is translated, it is cached and reused. Binary translation has a large initial overhead cost, but overtime it is subject to better performance, since previously translated instruction blocks are directly executed.
- Emulation, as described, is different from hardware level virtualization. The former simply allows the execution of a program compiled against a different hardware, whereas the latter emulates a complete hardware environment where an entire operating system can be installed.
- Application virtualization is a good solution in the case of missing libraries in the host operating system. In this case a replacement library can be linked with the application, or library calls can be remapped to existing functions available in the host system.
- Another advantage is that in this case the virtual machine manager is much lighter since it provides a partial emulation of the runtime environment compared to hardware virtualization.
- Moreover, this technique allows incompatible applications to run together. Compared to programming level virtualization, which works across all the applications developed for that virtual machine, application level virtualization works for a specific environment: It supports all the applications that run on top of a specific environment.

Benefits of Application Level Virtualization:

1. It eliminates application conflicts applications are guaranteed to use the correct version files and property file/Registry settings without any modification to the operating systems and without interfering with other applications.
2. It reduces roll-outs through instant provisioning administrators can create pre-packaged applications that can be deployed quickly locally or remotely over the network, even across slow links. Virtual software applications can even be streamed to systems on-demand without invoking a setup or installation procedure.
3. It runs multiple versions of an application Multiple versions can run on the same operating system instance without any conflicts, improving the migration to newer versions of applications and speeding the testing and integration of new features into the environment.

2.2.1.6 Storage Virtualization

- Storage virtualization is a system administration practice that allows decoupling the physical organization of the hardware from its logical representation. Using this technique, users do not have to be worried about the specific location of their data, which can be identified using a logical path.
- Storage virtualization allows us to harness a wide range of storage facilities and represent them under a single logical file system. There are different techniques for storage virtualization, one of the most popular being network based virtualization by means of Storage Area Networks (SANs). SANs use a network accessible device through a large bandwidth connection to provide storage facilities.

Characteristics of Storage Virtualization:

1. The availability of logical volumes separate from physical hard disk constraints.
2. The capability of abstracting multivendor storage devices into one group and reallocating storage space independently of size or physical location.
3. The capability of having automated storage optimization and management.

Types of Storage Virtualization:

1. **Disk Drive Virtualization** takes place when the firmware abstracts the physical cylinder, head, and sector into a single logical block address.
2. **Storage System Partitioning** occurs when the storage system creates multiple partitions from a single storage resource.
3. **Block Virtualization** happens when the software abstracts multiple disk arrays into a single storage resource.
4. **Tape Virtualization** occurs as the software abstracts both tape drives and tape media onto a single disk resource.
5. **File Virtualization** is the creation of an abstraction layer between the file servers and the clients who access those file servers.

- Currently there are three methods of storage virtualization:
  1. **Server-Based Virtualization:** This method places a management program on the host system and has the benefit of leveraging the SAN asset as it is.
  2. **Fabric-Based Virtualization:** This can be done via network switches or appliance servers. In both instances, independent appliances, such as switches, routers, and dedicated servers, are placed between servers and storage and have a storage virtualization function. The purpose behind this is to reduce the impact on the existing SAN and servers.
  3. **Storage Array-Based Virtualization:** This is a virtualization implemented at the storage system level.

2.2.1.7 Network Virtualization

- Network virtualization combines hardware appliances and specific software for the creation and management of a virtual network. Network virtualization can aggregate different physical networks into a single logical network (external network virtualization) or provide network like functionality to an operating system partition (internal network virtualization). The result of external network virtualization is generally a virtual LAN (VLAN). A VLAN is an aggregation of hosts that communicate with each other as though they were located under the same broadcasting domain. Internal network virtualization is generally applied together with hardware and operating system level virtualization, in which the guests obtain a virtual network interface to communicate with. There are several options for implementing internal network virtualization: The guest can share the same network interface of the host and use Network Address Translation (NAT) to access the network; the virtual machine manager can emulate, and install on the host, an additional network device, together with the driver; or the guest can have a private network only with the guest.
- The major advantage of network virtualization is the network productivity and capability. It facilitates the enterprises and business people who have a major number of users to keep the systems working all the time. Since network virtualization has separate channels, the speed of the network increases which allows the applications to work faster
- The most popular forms of network virtualization are explained below:
  1. **Virtual LAN (VLAN):** Ratified in the IEEE 802.1Q standard, VLANs are a method of creating independent logical networks within a shared physical network. Network administrators incorporate VLANs into their network design to logically segment broadcast domains and control the interaction between devices on different network segments. VLAN technology has evolved and is a common feature in the Application Specific Integrated Circuits (ASICs) of just about all modern day Ethernet switches. Although multiple devices can be physically connected to the same network switch, VLANs allows network administrators to create multiple virtual networks that isolate each segment from the others. Each segment utilizes a portion of the available resources (CPU, memory, bandwidth, and so on) in the host switch.
  2. **Virtual IP (VIP):** An IP address that is not connected to a specific computer or network interface in a computer. VIPs are usually assigned to a network device that is in path of the traversing network traffic. Incoming packets are sent to the VIP but are redirected to the actual interface of the receiving host(s). VIPs are mostly used for redundancy and load balancing scenarios, where multiple systems are hosting a common application and are capable of receiving the traffic as redirected by the network device.
  3. **Virtual Private Network (VPN):** A private communication network used to communicate confidentially over a public network. VPN traffic is often carried over highly insecure network mediums, such as the Internet, creating a secure channel for sensitive and confidential

information to traverse from one site to another. It is also used as a means of extending remote employees home networks to the corporate network. Although special software is usually needed to establish the connection, once established, interaction with other resources on the network is handled the same way it would be on a true physical network, without requiring any modification of the network stack or operating system.

2.2.1.8 Desktop Virtualization

- Desktop virtualization abstracts the desktop environment available on a personal computer in order to provide access to it using a client/server approach.
- Desktop virtualization provides the same outcome of hardware virtualization but serves a different purpose.
- Similarly to hardware virtualization, desktop virtualization makes accessible a different system as though it were natively installed on the host, but this system is remotely stored on a different host and accessed through a network connection.
- Moreover, desktop virtualization addresses the problem of making the same desktop environment accessible from everywhere.
- Although the term desktop virtualization strictly refers to the ability to remotely access a desktop environment, generally the desktop environment is stored in a remote server or a data center that provides a high-availability infrastructure and ensures the accessibility and persistence of the data.
- The basic services for remotely accessing a desktop environment are implemented in software components such as Windows Remote Services, VNC, and X Server.
- Infrastructures for desktop virtualization based on cloud computing solutions include Sun Virtual Desktop Infrastructure (VDI), Parallels Virtual Desktop Infrastructure, Citrix XenDesktop, and others.
- Desktop virtualization has many benefits, including a lower Total Cost of Ownership (TCO), increased security, reduced energy costs, reduced downtime and centralized management.
- Limitations of desktop virtualization include difficulty in maintenance and set up of printer drivers; increased downtime in case of network failures; complexity and costs involved in VDI deployment and security risks in the event of improper network management.

2.2.1.9 Application Server Virtualization (ASV)

- Application Server Virtualization also called as 'Advanced Load Balancing'. It enables IT departments to balance workloads of an application in an agile way. It spreads applications across servers and servers across applications.
- It also enables to manage the servers as a single instance. ASV gives a better network security compliance as only one server is visible to the public while the rest are hidden behind a reverse proxy network security appliance.
- Application server virtualization abstracts a collection of application servers that provide the same services as a single virtual application server by using load balancing strategies and providing a high availability infrastructure for the services hosted in the application server.
- This is a particular form of virtualization and serves the same purpose of storage virtualization: providing a better quality of service rather than emulating a different environment.

2.3 VIRTUALIZATION TECHNOLOGY EXAMPLES

- In this section we will study examples of virtualization technology.

2.3.1 VMware

- VMware's technology is based on the concept of full virtualization, where the underlying hardware is replicated and made available to the guest operating system, which runs unaware of such abstraction layers and does not need to be modified.
- VMware implements full virtualization either in the desktop environment or also called as Type II hypervisors, or in the server environment also called as Type I hypervisors.
- In both cases, full virtualization is made possible by means of direct execution (for non-sensitive instructions) and binary translation (for sensitive instructions), thus allowing the virtualization of architecture such as x86.

- Besides these two core solutions, VMware provides additional tools and software that simplify the use of virtualization technology either in a desktop environment, with tools enhancing the integration of virtual guests with the host, or in a server environment, with solutions for building and managing virtual computing infrastructures.
- VMware is well known for the capability to virtualize x86 architectures, which runs unmodified on top of their hypervisors. With the new generation of hardware architectures and the introduction of hardware assisted virtualization (Intel VT-x and AMD V) in 2006, full virtualization is made possible with hardware support, but before that date, the use of dynamic binary translation was the only solution that allowed running x86 guest operating systems unmodified in a virtualized environment.
- VMware achieves full virtualization by providing virtual representation of memory and I/O devices. Memory virtualization constitutes another challenge of virtualized environments and can deeply impact performance without the appropriate hardware support. The main reason is the presence of a Memory Management Unit (MMU), which needs to be emulated as part of the virtual hardware.
- Especially in the case of hosted hypervisors (Type II), where the virtual MMU and the host-OS MMU are traversed sequentially before getting to the physical memory page, the impact on performance can be significant. To avoid nested translation, the translation look-aside buffer (TLB) in the virtual MMU directly maps physical pages, and the performance slowdown only occurs in case of a TLB miss.

2.3.2 Types of VMware

- VMware is a pioneer in virtualization technology and offers a collection of virtualization solutions types, from desktop computing to enterprise computing and infrastructure virtualization.
  1. End user or Desktop virtualization.
  2. Server virtualization.
  3. Infrastructure virtualization.

2.3.2.1 End user or Desktop virtualization

- VMware supports virtualization of operating system environments and single applications on end user computers.
- It allows to install different operating systems and applications in a completely isolated environment from the hosting operating system.
- Specific VMware software-VMware Workstation, for windows operating systems, and VMware Fusion, for Mac OS X environments is installed in the host operating system to create virtual machines and manage their execution.
- Besides the creation of an isolated computing environment, the two products allows a guest operating system to leverage the resources of the host machine (USB devices, folder sharing, and integration with the Graphical User Interface (GUI) of the host operating system).
- Fig. 2.9 shows of the architecture of end user or desktop virtualization.

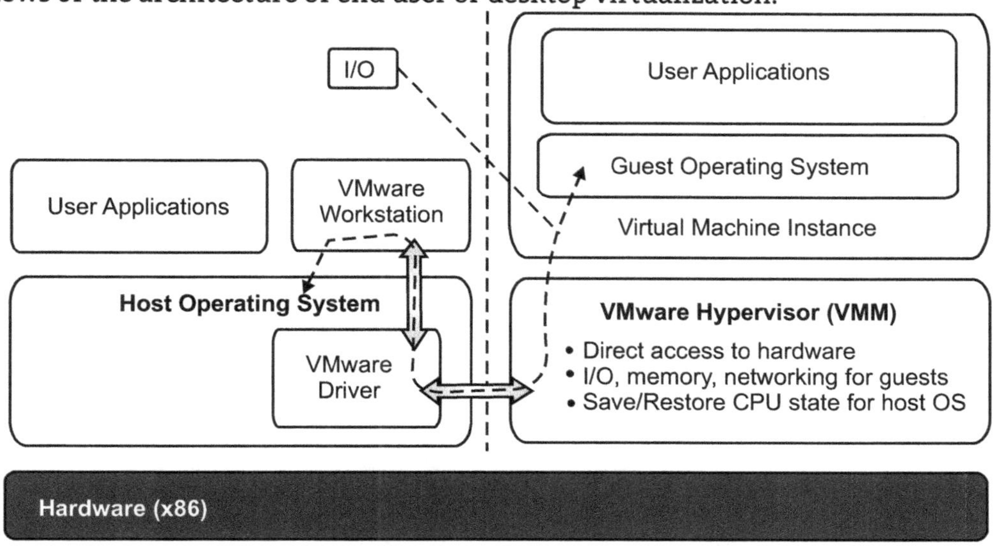

Fig. 2.9: Architecture of VMware workstation

- The virtualization environment is created by an application installed in guest operating systems, which provides those operating systems with full hardware virtualization of the underlying hardware.
- This is done by installing a specific driver in the host operating system that provides two main services:
  1. It deploys a virtual machine manager that can run in privileged mode.
  2. It provides hooks for the VMware application to process specific I/O requests eventually by relaying such requests to the host operating system via system calls.
- This architecture also called Hosted Virtual Machine Architecture. It is possible to both isolate virtual machine instances within the memory space of a single application and provide reasonable performance, since the intervention of the VMware application is required only for instructions, such as device I/O, that require binary translation.
- Instructions that can be directly executed are managed by the virtual machine manager, which takes control of the CPU and the MMU and alternates its activity with the host OS.
- Virtual machine images are saved in a collection of files on the host file system, and both VMware Workstation and VMware Fusion allows creation of new images, pause their execution, create snapshots, and undo operations by rolling back to a previous state of the virtual machine.
- Other examples of end-user computing environments virtualization are VMware Player, VMware ACE, and VMware Thin App. VMware Player is a reduced version of VMware Workstation that allows creating and playing virtual machines in a Windows or Linux operating environment. VMware ACE, a similar product to VMware Workstation, creates policy-wrapped virtual machines for deploying secure corporate virtual environments on end-user computers.
- VMware Thin App is a solution for application virtualization. It provides an isolated environment for applications in order to avoid conflicts due to versioning and incompatible applications. It detects all the changes to the operating environment made by the installation of a specific application and stores them together with the application binary into a package that can be run with VMware Thin App.

2.3.2.2 Server Virtualization

- Server virtualization is the most active segment of the virtualization industry featuring established companies such as VMware, Microsoft, and Citrix. With server virtualization one physical machine is divided many virtual servers.
- At the core of such virtualization is the concept of a hypervisor (virtual machine monitor). A hypervisor is a thin software layer that intercepts operating system calls to hardware. Hypervisors typically provide a virtualized CPU and memory for the guests running on top of them. The term was first used in conjunction with the IBM CP-370.
- VMware provided solutions for server virtualization with different approaches over time. Initial support for server virtualization was provided by VMware GSX server, which replicates the approach used for end-user computers and introduces remote management and scripting capabilities. The architecture of VMware GSX Server is depicted in Fig. 2.10.

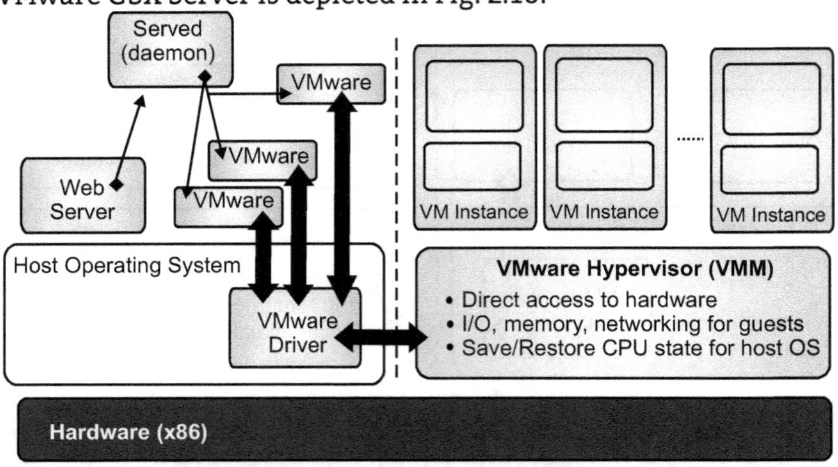

Fig. 2.10: VMware server architecture

- The architecture is mostly designed to serve the virtualization of Web servers. A daemon process, called serverd, controls and manages VMware application processes. These applications are then connected to the virtual machine instances by means of the VMware driver installed on the host operating system.
- Virtual machine instances are managed by the VMM as described previously. User requests for virtual machine management and provisioning are routed from the Webserver through the VMM by means of serverd.

2.3.2.3 Infrastructure Virtualization

- VMware infrastructure is a virtualization suite for infrastructure that provides complete overview of application availability, virtualization, resource optimization, management, and operational automation.
- VMware infrastructure integrates and virtualizes the hardware resources among two or more systems. In the virtual environment, it provides virtual resource pools to the datacenter.
- In addition to this, VMware infrastructure has a distributed architecture that provides excellent features like high availability, consolidated backup, fine-grain, policy-driven, and resource allocation of the entire virtual datacenter.
- To establish an IT enterprise, these distributed architecture services plays a major role in meeting their service level agreements and production in a cost effective manner.
- Fig. 2.11 shows infrastructure virtualization in VMware.

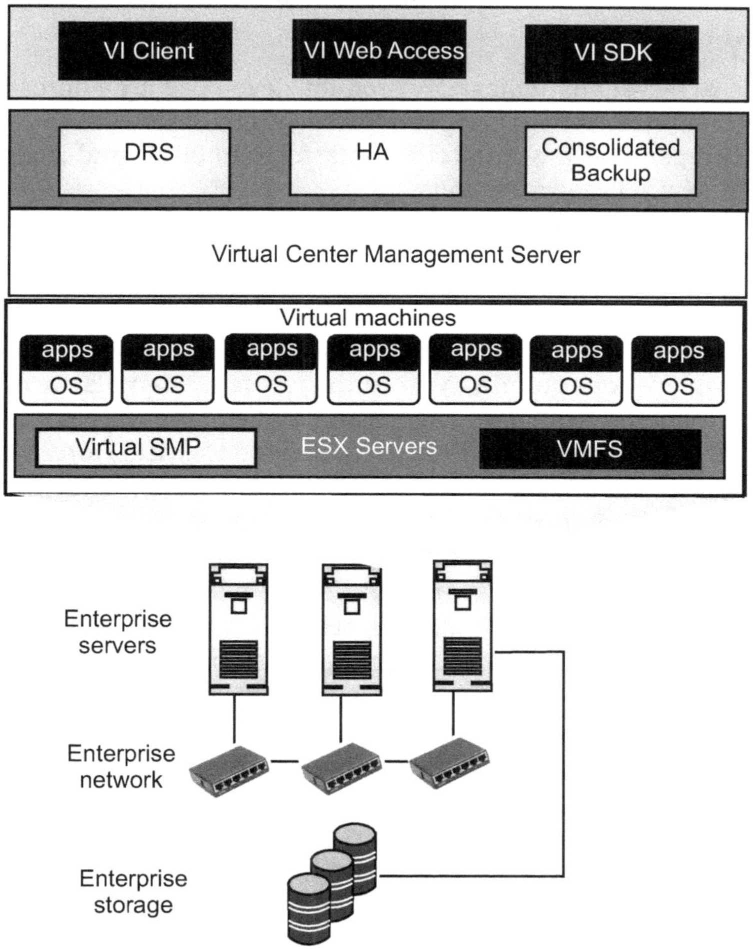

Fig. 2.11: Infrastructure Virtualization

1. **VMware ESX Server:** The virtualization layer which is production proven, and robust is run on physical servers that abstract storage, memory, processor, and networking resources across multiple Virtual Machines (VMs).
2. **Virtual Center Management Server (VirtualCenter Server):** Virtual Center Server is the central point for accolation, managing, and configuring virtual environments.

3. **VMware High Availability:** Provides features that are cost effective, easy to use, high availability to run applications on virtual machines.
4. **Virtual Infrastructure Client (VI Client):** VirtualCenter Server or individual ESX Servers connect remotely from any Windows PC, and an interface is used by client to connect.
5. **Virtual Infrastructure Web Access:** A virtual machine makes use of a web interface to manage and access remote consoles.
6. **VMware Virtual Machine File System:** ESX Server virtual machines have a high-performance file system cluster.
7. **VMware Virtual Symmetric Multi-Processing (SMP):** SMP feature is enabled for single virtual machine to convert into multiple physical processors to work parallely.
8. **VMware Virtual Motion:** To run virtual machines from one physical server to another physical server, VMotion feature is used, which allows live migration with complete transaction integrity, zero down time, and continuous service availability. If server fails, virtual machines automatically restart with production servers that have spare capacity.
9. **VMware Backup:** Consolidated Backup is easy to use. Backup can be simplified, and it reduces the overload on ESX Servers. Virtual machines have centralized agent free backup facility.
10. **VMware Infrastructure SDK:** SDK provides a third-party access to the VMware Infrastructure and provides standard interface for VMware.
11. **Distributed Resource Scheduler (DRS):** To allocates resources for virtual machines, collection of hardware, and balancing the computing capacity dynamically done using DRS.

2.3.3 Microsoft Hyper-V

- Microsoft Hyper-V is a server virtualization product developed by Microsoft Corporation, which provides virtualization services through hypervisor-based emulations.
- Microsoft introduced Hyper-V as a virtualization platform in 2008, and it continued to release new Hyper-V versions with new Windows versions.
- Hyper-V is available in three versions namely, Hyper-V for Windows Servers, Hyper-V Servers and Hyper-V on Windows 10.

2.3.3.1 Features of Hyper-V

- Features of Hyper-V are listed below:
  1. **Optimization:** The operations running within the virtualization platform can be managed from a single pane using Hyper-V Manager. The single point of management allows us to optimize the running workloads and act promptly if any issues were to arise. Moreover, each VM has a set of services and drivers (also known as integration services), which allows a considerable improvement in the performance of the guest VMs.
  2. **Portability:** Hyper-V ensures the portability of our VMs or applications between physical servers, and without affecting the system's availability. If we need to move or distribute VMs, features like live migration, storage migration, and import/export of VMs are enabled.
  3. **Remote Connectivity:** Virtual Machine Connection (VMConnect) of Hyper-V is used to connect to remote VMs. The tool allows us to remotely manage and monitor the operations that are run in the guest OS, even if the OS is not powered on yet.
  4. **Disaster Recovery and Backup:** To ensure that our virtual environment can be recovered, even after a disaster, Hyper-V allows us to create Hyper-V replicas and backups. Hyper-V replica is basically a point-in-time copy of a VM, which is then sent to another physical server for storage. If a disaster strikes, the VM can be restored from its replica. As for backups, Hyper-V applies two methods: the "Saved State" method, and the Volume Shadow Copy Service (VSS). However, the capabilities of Hyper-V replication and backup jobs are limited. Thus, it is advisable to use a third-party backup application, which maximizes VM protection and ensures high availability in a case of a disaster.
  5. **Computing Environment:** Hyper-V also allows us to build a virtual environment on the basis of a physical infrastructure in just a few clicks. With a set of integration services, we can easily create a new computing environment of our own design, which would specifically comply with our business needs and opportunities.

6. **Cost-Efficiency:** Hyper-V environments can easily be scaled up or down, requiring no extra expenses. If our business experiences grow, we can increase the number of available computing resources by creating more VMs. Installing Hyper-V is free, and requires minimal input on the part.
7. **Security:** Hyper-V ensures the protection of the host, the VMs and the data that they contain, from any malicious attacks, viruses, or an unauthorized access.
8. **Ease of Use:** An efficient virtualization platform can significantly improve the performance of our IT infrastructure. Furthermore, apart from being efficient, it is also required to be flexible and user-friendly, in order to make the user's experience comfortable and engaging. Hyper-V provides users with the ability to test out various OS or applications to see the pros and cons for themselves, with the help of high-end management tools. Hyper-V allows us to run multiple VMs on a single desktop or laptop, and can be easily integrated with other Microsoft computing services, such as Microsoft Azure.

2.3.3.2 Benefits of Microsoft Hyper-V

- Various benefits of Hyper-V are listed below:
  1. **Establish or Expand a Private Cloud Environment:** Provide more flexible, on-demand IT services by moving to or expanding the use of shared resources and adjust utilization as demand changes.
  2. **Use the Hardware More Effectively:** Consolidate servers and workloads onto fewer, more powerful physical computers to use less power and physical space.
  3. **Improve Business Continuity:** Minimize the impact of both scheduled and unscheduled downtime of the workloads.
  4. **Establish or Expand a Virtual Desktop Infrastructure (VDI):** Use a centralized desktop strategy with VDI can help us increase business agility and data security, as well as simplify regulatory compliance and manage desktop operating systems and applications. Deploy Hyper-V and Remote Desktop Virtualization Host (RD Virtualization Host) on the same server to make personal virtual desktops or virtual desktop pools available to our users.
  5. **Make Development and Test More Efficient:** Reproduce different computing environments without having to buy or maintain all the hardware we would need if we only used physical systems.

2.3.3.3 Limitations of Hyper-V

- When working with Hyper-V, there are some limitations that may be encountered, which might interfere with the virtualization process. Such limitations include:
  1. **No Native Graphical User Interface (GUI):** Thus, all configurations are implemented through Power Shell. To overcome this problem, Hyper-V Manager can be manually installed for managing Hyper-V servers.
  2. Virtualization of audio **hardware is not enabled**.
  3. Virtualized optical disk drives in the guest VM operate in a **read-only mode**.
  4. **Poor graphic performance** on CPUs without SLAT. The Windows Display Driver Model (WDDM) graphics drivers installed on the primary OS can cause the memory to overload, which leads to buffer flushing.
  5. **Live migration of guest VMs is not supported in Hyper-V** running on Windows Server 2008. Live migration implies transferring a VM from one physical server to another without interrupting the workflow. However, the feature of quick migration is available, whereby the workflow of a guest VM is suspended on one server for the period of the migration, and then resumed on another one, thus causing a brief interruption in services.
  6. **Hyper-V is not available for Windows 10 Home**. However, we can upgrade from Windows 10 Home to Windows 10 Pro by entering the system settings.
  7. Hyper-V (2012R2) provides **limited support for Windows guest OS**. Integration services are a built-in set of Hyper-V tools that can be used for better integration between the physical server and VMs.

2.3.3.4 Microsoft Hyper-V Architecture

- Hyper-V supports multiple and concurrent execution of guest operating systems by means of partitions. A partition is a completely isolated environment in which an operating system is installed and run.
- Fig. 2.12 provides an overview of the architecture of Hyper-V. Hyper-V takes control of the hardware, and the host operating system becomes a virtual machine instance with special privileges, called the parent partition.
- The parent partition (also called the root partition) is the only one that has direct access to the hardware. It runs the virtualization stack, hosts all the drivers required to configure guest operating systems, and creates child partitions through the hypervisor.
- Child partitions are used to host guest operating systems and do not have access to the underlying hardware, but their interaction with it is controlled by either the parent partition or the hypervisor itself.

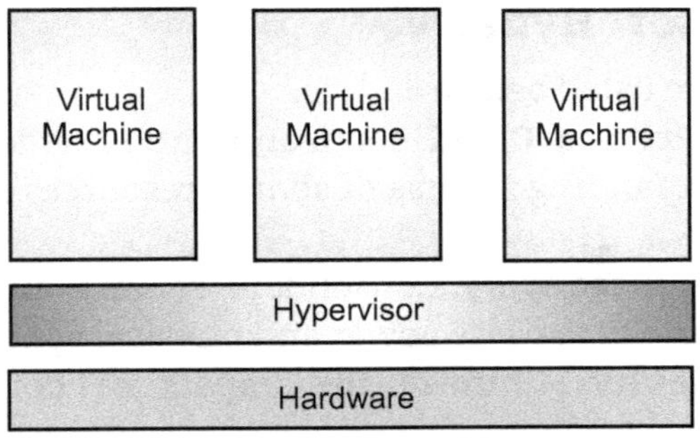

Fig. 2.12: Hyper-V Architecture

- **Hypervisor:** The hypervisor is the component that directly manages the underlying hardware (processors and memory). It is logically defined by the following components:
  1. **HyperCalls Interface** is the entry point for all the partitions for the execution of sensitive instructions. This is an implementation of the para-virtualization This interface is used by drivers in the partitioned operating system to contact the hypervisor using the standard windows calling convention. The parent partition also uses this interface to create child partitions.
  2. **Memory Service Routines (MSRs)** are the set of functionalities that control the memory and its access from partitions. By leveraging hardware-assisted virtualization, the hyper visoruses the Input/Output Memory Management Unit (I/O MMU or IOMMU) to fast track access to devices from partitions by translating virtual memory addresses.
  3. **Advanced Programmable Interrupt Controller (APIC)** component represents the interrupt controller, which manages the signals coming from the underlying hardware when some event occurs (timer expired, I/O ready, exceptions and traps). Each virtual processor is equipped with a synthetic interrupt controller (SynIC), which constitutes an extension of the local APIC. The hypervisor is responsible of dispatching, when appropriate, the physical interrupts to the synthetic interrupt controllers.
  4. **Scheduler** component schedules the virtual processors to run on available physical processors. The scheduling is controlled by policies that are set by the parent partition.
  5. **Address Manager** component is used to manage the virtual network addresses that are allocated to each guest operating system.
  6. **Partition Manager** component is in charge of performing partition creation, finalization, destruction, enumeration, and configurations.

2.3.3.5 How Hyper-V Works?

- Hyper-V is a type I hypervisor (also called native hypervisor), meaning that this software runs directly on the host's hardware and manages guest operating systems.
- Hyper-V technology is based on the isolation of VMs into separate logical units (partitions). Partitions are essentially the isolated containers in which VMs are run. The hypervisor should

include at least one parent (root) partition running Windows OS. The parent partition has the virtualization stack and can directly access hardware devices as well as memory.

- Moreover, the parent partition creates and manages the child partitions, in which guest VMs are run. Partitions present a virtual view of the operations running in the physical processor.
- If any issues occur in the physical processor, the hypervisor detects the problem and redirects it to the corresponding partition for further actions to be taken.
- The parent partition hosts Virtualization Service Providers (VSPs), while child partitions host Virtualization Service Consumers (VSCs).
- The communication between the Hyper-V components is enabled by VMBus. Thus, VMBus functions as the communications channel for redirecting requests between the parent and child partitions.

2.3.4 KVM

- Kernel based Virtual Machine (KVM) is an open source virtualization technology built into Linux®. Specifically, KVM lets we turn Linux into a hypervisor that allows a host machine to run multiple, isolated virtual environments called guests or virtual machines (VMs).
- KVM is part of Linux. If we've got Linux 2.6.20 or newer, we've got KVM. KVM was first announced in 2006 and merged into the mainline Linux kernel version a year later. Because KVM is part of existing Linux code, it immediately benefits from every new Linux feature, fix, and advancement without additional engineering.
- KVM (for Kernel-based Virtual Machine) is a full virtualization solution for Linux on x86 hardware containing virtualization extensions (Intel VT or AMD-V).
- It consists of a loadable kernel module, kvm.ko, that provides the core virtualization infrastructure and a processor specific module, kvm-intel.ko or kvm-amd.ko. KVM also requires a modified QEMU although work is underway to get the required changes upstream.
- Using KVM, one can run multiple virtual machines running unmodified Linux or Windows images. Each virtual machine has private virtualized hardware: a network card, disk, graphics adapter, etc.

2.3.4.1 KVM Features

- Various features of KVM are listed below:
  1. **Security:** KVM uses a combination of security-enhanced Linux (SELinux) and secure virtualization (sVirt) for enhanced VM security and isolation. SELinux establishes security boundaries around VMs. sVirt extends SELinux's capabilities, allowing Mandatory Access Control (MAC) security to be applied to guest VMs and preventing manual labeling errors.
  2. **Storage:** KVM is able to use any storage supported by Linux, including some local disks and network-attached storage (NAS). Multipath I/O may be used to improve storage and provide redundancy. KVM also supports shared file systems so VM images may be shared by multiple hosts. Disk images support thin provisioning, allocating storage on demand rather than all up front.
  3. **Hardware Support:** KVM can use a wide variety of certified Linux-supported hardware platforms. Because hardware vendors regularly contribute to kernel development, the latest hardware features are often rapidly adopted in the Linux kernel.
  4. **Memory Management:** KVM inherits the memory management features of Linux, including non-uniform memory access and kernel same-page merging. The memory of a VM can be swapped, backed by large volumes for better performance, and shared or backed by a disk file.
  5. **Live Migration:** KVM supports live migration, which is the ability to move a running VM between physical hosts with no service interruption. The VM remains powered on, network connections remain active, and applications continue to run while the VM is relocated. KVM also saves a VM's current state so it can be stored and resumed later.
  6. **Performance and Scalability:** KVM inherits the performance of Linux, scaling to match demand load if the number of guest machines and requests increases. KVM allows the most demanding application workloads to be virtualized and is the basis for many enterprise virtualization setups, such as datacenters and private clouds (via Open Stack).
  7. **Scheduling and Resource Control:** In the KVM model, a VM is a Linux process, scheduled and managed by the kernel. The Linux scheduler allows fine-grained control of the resources allocated to a Linux process and guarantees a quality of service for a particular process. In KVM,

this includes the completely fair scheduler, control groups, network name spaces, and real-time extensions.

8. **Lower Latency and Higher Prioritization:** The Linux kernel features real-time extensions that allows VM-based apps to run at lower latency with better prioritization (compared to bare metal). The kernel also divides processes that require long computing times into smaller components, which are then scheduled and processed accordingly.

Benefits of Kernel Based Virtualization:

1. With help of KVM module, it manages the performance critical parts of interrupts and timers by kernel based I/O emulation. It gives a capability to set limit on I/O request between virtual machine and host.
2. The KVM module allows here emulation for CPU modes not supported by physical processor and the instructions.
3. KVM module used is a part of the upstream Linux kernel as it's added to it for enhancing virtualization.
4. KVM module used here provides common interface for both Intel and AMD x86 processors which supports hardware virtualization. For Intel it is known as Intel VMX hardware assist for virtualization and for AMD it is known as AMD SVM hardware assist for virtualization.
5. It creates a bare-metal hypervisor out of the kernel. We can say it creates a native hypervisor.
6. Leverages the capability of MMU (Memory management unit) in hardware to virtualize the memory with improvement in performance.
7. A virtual machine created by it is a standard Linux process, scheduled by its native standard Linux scheduler.
8. It supports Intel's EPT (Extended Page Table) and AMD's RVI (Rapid virtualization indexing) features for memory virtualization by CPU vendors.
9. Its supports all the file system supported by main stream Linux kernel.
10. Improved utilization of resources and access to it by providing flexible storage. It's very easy to add memory, vCPU, Hard Disk to Linux KVM.
11. Supports wide range of guest operating system including windows, UNIX, Solaris and DOS.
12. All the features of the Linux like implementation of security using SELinux, wide range of hardware support and supporting Device drivers are inherited to kernel based virtual machines.
13. Secure remote management by the API provided by the virtualization modules.
14. Enhanced scalability as main stream of Linux kernel can be extended by adding modules to leverage more features.

How does KVM work?

- KVM converts Linux into a type-I (bare-metal) hypervisor.
- All hypervisors need some operating system-level components-such as a memory manager, process scheduler, Input/Output (I/O) stack, device drivers, security manager, a network stack, and more-to run VMs.
- KVM has all these components because it's part of the Linux kernel. Every VM is implemented as a regular Linux process, scheduled by the standard Linux scheduler, with dedicated virtual hardware like a network card, graphics adapter, CPU(s), memory, and disks.

2.3.4.2 Architecture of a KVM Server

- Fig. 2.13 shows the main components of a KVM Server host.

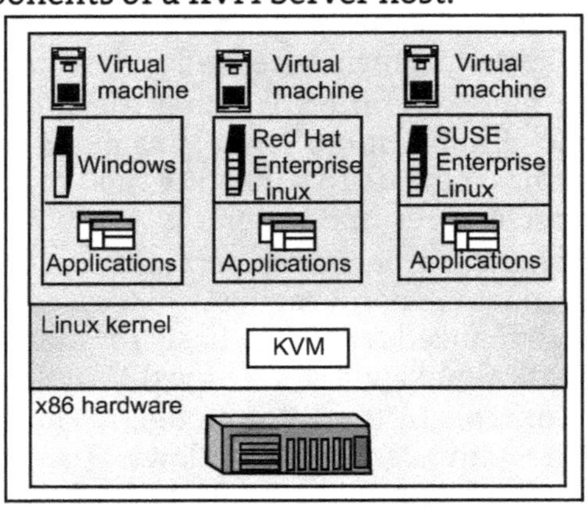

Fig. 2.13 : The Architecture of a KVM server

- We can use any type of storage that is supported by Linux to store virtual machine images, including local disks, SCSI, or network attached storage such as NFS and SAN.
- The KVM hypervisor also supports virtual machine images on shared file systems such as the Global File System (GFS2) allowing the images to be shared by multiple hosts.
- With the KVM hypervisor, we can perform live migrations and moves a running virtual machine between physical hosts with no interruption to service.
- We can save the current state of a virtual machine to disk so that we can restart running the virtual machine from its previous state at a later time.
- Because the KVM architecture hosts the virtual machine images as regular Linux processes, we can use the standard Linux security measures to isolate the images and provides resource controls.
- The Linux kernel includes SELinux along with sVIRT to isolate virtual images. In addition, we can use control groups (cgroups) to further restrict a set of tasks to a set of resources and monitor resource use.
- We can protect and secure the Kernel based Virtual Machine (KVM) environment by deploying KVM security features, such as configuring network isolation, securing storage devices, configuring secure remote management, isolating virtual machines with the sVirts.
- The KVM architecture supports the memory management features of Linux. In addition, with Kernel Same-page Merging (KSM) virtual images can share memory pages.
- If the virtual images have identical memory pages, those pages are merged into a single page that is then shared by the virtual images.
- The KVM hypervisor supports a variety of guest operating systems, including Linux distributions, Microsoft Windows, and other platforms including OpenBSD, FreeBSD, OpenSolaris, Solaris x86, and MS DOS.

2.3.5 Xen

- Xen is an open source type-I or baremetal hypervisor, which makes it possible to run many instances of an operating system or indeed different operating systems in parallel on a single machine (or host). Xen is the only type-I hypervisor that is available as open source.
- Xen is used as the basis for a number of different commercial and open source applications, such as: server virtualization, Infrastructure as a Service (IaaS), desktop virtualization, security applications, embedded and hardware appliances.
- Xen enables users to increase server utilization, consolidate server farms, reduce complexity, and decrease total cost of ownership.
- The University of Cambridge Computer Laboratory developed the first versions of Xen. The Xen Project community develops and maintains Xen Project as free and open source software, subject to the requirements of the GNU General Public License (GPL), version 2. Xen Project is currently available for the IA-3, x86-64 and ARM instruction sets.
- Xen-based technology is used for either desktop virtualization or server virtualization, and recently it has also been used to provide cloud computing solutions by means of Xen Cloud Platform (XCP). At the basis of all these solutions is the Xen Hypervisor.
- Which constitutes the core technology of Xen. Recently Xen has been advanced to support full virtualization using hardware assisted virtualization.
- Xen is the most popular implementation of para-virtualization, which, in contrast with full virtualization, allows high-performance execution of guest operating systems. This is made possible by eliminating the performance loss while executing instructions that require special management.
- This is done by modifying portions of the guest operating systems run by Xen with reference to the execution of such instructions. Therefore it is not a transparent solution for implementing virtualization. This is particularly true for x86, which is the most popular architecture on commodity machines and servers.

2.3.5.1 Components of Xen Environment

- The basic components of a Xen-based virtualization environment are the Xen hypervisor, the Dom0, any number of other VM Guests, and the tools, commands, and configuration files that let us manage virtualization.

- Collectively, the physical computer running all these components is called a VM Host Server because together these components form a platform for hosting virtual machines.
  1. **Xen Hypervisor:** The Xen hypervisor, sometimes simply called a virtual machine monitor, is an open source software program that coordinates the low-level interaction between virtual machines and physical hardware.
  2. **Dom0:** The virtual machine host environment, also called Dom0 or controlling domain, is composed of several components, such as:
     (i) The **SUSE Linux Enterprise** operating system gives the administrator a graphical and command line environment to manage the virtual machine host components and its virtual machines.
     (ii) The **xl tool** stack based on the xenlight library (libxl). Use it to manage Xen guest domains.
     (iii) **QEMU**-an open source software that emulates a full computer system, including a processor and various peripherals. It provides the ability to host operating systems in both full virtualization or para-virtualization mode.
  3. **Xen-Based Virtual Machines:** A Xen-based virtual machine, also called a VM Guest or DomU, consists of the following components:
     (i) At least one virtual disk that contains a bootable operating system. The virtual disk can be based on a file, partition, volume, or other type of block device.
     (ii) A configuration file for each guest domain.
     (iii) Several network devices, connected to the virtual network provided by the controlling domain.
  4. **Management Tools, Commands, and Configuration Files:** There is a combination of GUI tools, commands, and configuration files to help us manage and customize our virtualization environment.

2.3.5.2 Architecture of Xen

- A typical environment running Xen consists of different parts. To start with, there's Domain 0. In Xen, this is how we refer to the host operating system (OS), as it's not really a host OS in the sense that other virtual machines (VMs) domains in Xen terminology don't have to use it to get access to the host server hardware.
- Domain 0 is only responsible for access to the drivers, and if any coordination has to be done, it will be handled by Domain 0. Apart from Domain 0, there are the other VMs that are referred to as Domain U.
- Fig. 2.14 describes the architecture of Xen and its mapping onto a classic x86 privilege model.

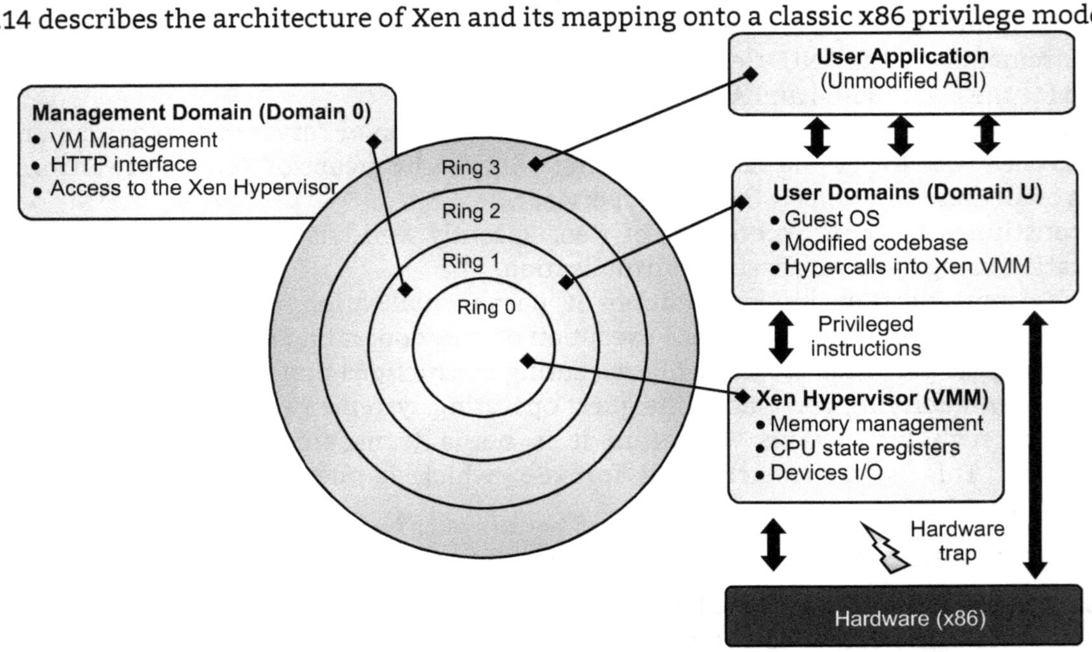

Fig. 2.14: Architecture of Xen and guest OS management

- A Xen-based system is managed by the Xen hypervisor, which runs in the highest privileged mode and controls the access of guest operating system to the underlying hardware. Guest operating systems are executed within domains, which represent virtual machine instances.
- Moreover, specific control software, which has privileged access to the host and controls all the other guest operating systems, is executed in a special domain called Domain 0.
- This is the first one that is loaded once the virtual machine manager has completely booted, and it hosts a Hyper Text Transfer Protocol (HTTP) server that serves requests for virtual machine creation, configuration, and termination. This component constitutes the embryonic version of a distributed virtual machine manager, which is an essential component of cloud computing systems providing Infrastructure-as-a-Service (IaaS) solutions.
- Many of the x86 implementations support four different security levels, called rings, where,
  - Ring 0 represent the level with the highest privileges and Ring 3 the level with the lowest ones. Almost all the most popular operating systems, except OS/2, utilize only two levels: Ring 0 for the kernel code, and Ring 3 for user application and non privileged OS code. This provides the opportunity for Xen to implement virtualization by executing the hypervisor in Ring 0, Domain 0, and all the other domains running guest operating systems-generally referred to as Domain U-in Ring 1,while the user applications are run in Ring 3.
  - This allows Xen to maintain the ABI unchanged, thus allowing an easy switch to Xen-virtualized solutions from an application point of view. Because ofthe structure of the x86 instruction set, some instructions allows code executing in Ring 3 to jump into Ring 0 (kernel mode). Such operation is performed at the hardware level and therefore with in a virtualized environment will result in a trap or silent fault, thus preventing the normal operations of the guest operating system, since this is now running in Ring 1.
  - This condition is generally triggered by a subset of the system calls. To avoid this situation, operating systems need to be changed in their implementation, and the sensitive system calls need to be reimplemented with hypercalls, which are specific calls exposed by the virtual machine interface of Xen. With the use of hypercalls, the Xen hypervisor is able to catch the execution of all the sensitive instructions, manage them, and return the control to the guest operating system by means of a supplied handler.

2.4 ADVANTAGES

2.4.1 Virtual Machine (VM)

- Virtualization enables cloud providers to serve users with their existing physical computer hardware; it enables cloud users to purchase only the computing resources they need when they need it, and to scale those resources cost effectively as their workloads grow.
- A virtual machine is a virtual representation, or emulation, of a physical computer. They are often referred to as a guest while the physical machine they run on is referred to as the host.
- In cloud computing, Virtual Machine (VM) placement is a critical operation which is conducted as part of the VM migration and aimed to find the best Physical Machine (PM) to host the VMs.

Advantages:

1. The VM (Virtual Machine) is divorced from the underlying hardware, meaning, it can be "moved" quite easily from one server to another, even whilst running. This allows for load balancing, maintenance on hardware and redundancy (High Availability).
2. Most servers are very powerful machines, and normally have more resources than the software makes use of, meaning, if it were installed directly (a bare metal install) for the most part that hardware would be sat idling, potentially. Wasting resources, cooling and electricity (i.e. Money).
3. A virtual installation, can be orders of magnitude quicker, to deploy and configure, allowing flexibility and agility in development.
4. Can use multiple operating system environments on the same computer.
5. Virtual machines can provide an instruction set architecture, or ISA, structure different than the actual computer. The ISA serves as the interface between software and hardware.

6. When we create our virtual machine, we create a virtual hard disk. So, everything on that machine can crash, but if it does, it won't affect the host machine.
7. There are security benefits to running virtual machines. For example, if we need to run an application of questionable security, we can run it in a guest operating system. So, if the application causes damage, then it will be only temporary after the guest is shut down. Virtual machines also allow for better security forensics by monitoring guest operating systems for deficiencies and allowing the user to quarantine it for analysis.

Disadvantages:

1. Virtual machines are less efficient than real machines because they access the hardware indirectly. Running software on top of the host operating system means that it will have to request access to the hardware from the host. That will slow the usability.
2. When several virtual machines are running on the same host, performance may be hindered if the computer it's running on lacks sufficient power. Our virtual machine still uses the resources of your host machine. The more powerful the host computer, the more quickly the virtual machine will run.
3. A virtual machine can be infected with the weaknesses of the host machine. As an example, process isolation is a feature usually employed by operating systems. However, there are bugs that violate it.
4. A regular computer devoid of virtual machines would then only be affected. But, a computer with a number of virtual machines would then infect each of those "machines" as well.
5. Some legacy hardware especially specialist cards, connections and the like, require a bare metal installation and are very difficult to virtualise.
6. Virtualisation is another administration layer on top of the normal network, infrastructure, server stack. Although reasonably easy to pick up, it requires knowledge of the whole stack to implement effectively.

2.4.2 VM Migration

- In particular, Virtual Machine (VM) migration is a powerful management technique that gives data center operators the ability to adapt the placement of VMs in order to better satisfy performance objectives, improve resource utilization and communication locality, mitigate performance hotspots, achieve fault tolerance, reduce energy consumption, and facilitate system maintenance activities.

Advantages:

1. **Load Balancing:** This reduces the inequality of resource usage levels across all the PMs in the cluster. This prevents some machines from getting overloaded in the presence of lightly loaded machines with sufficient spare capacity. Live migration can be used to balance the system. The overall system load can be balanced by migrating VMs from overloaded PMs to under-loaded PMs.
2. **Server Consolidation:** In order to reduce server sprawl in data centers, server consolidation algorithms are required. These algorithms are VM packing heuristics which try to pack as many VMs as possible on a PM so that resource usage is improved and unused or under-utilized machines can be turned off. Consolidation will result in reduced power consumption and thus reducing overall operational costs for data centre administrators.
3. **Hotspot and Coldspot Migration:** The detection of hotspots and coldspot are always based on thresholds which are set by the data center owner or based on the Service Level Agreements specified by the clients. Usually, a higher resource usage value close to maximum is set as the upper threshold and a very low resource usage value is set as the lower threshold. PMs having resource usage values beyond the upper threshold are said to have formed hotspots, and whose usage values below the lower threshold are said to have formed coldspot. The former implies over utilization and the latter implies underutilization, applicable across any resource dimension.
4. **Workloads Keep Changing Dynamically in Servers:** There is a sudden spike of requests (during month end, for example). Every time it happens, its not possible to provision additional servers manually. So, Virtual Machine Migration accommodates for the changing workloads automatically (It can adapt to both additional workloads or reduced workloads).

5. **A scheduled maintenance normally results:** In some downtime for the users of the server. But with Virtual Machine Migration, the VM can be migrated to some other server (for that period of scheduled maintenance) and brought back to the host server after the maintenance is completed.
6. **Virtual machine migration can also migrate Virtual Machines:** In case of unscheduled server downtime (due to some fault in server), so that users experience high availability of applications at all times.
7. **Virtual machine migration can also be used for Disaster Recovery:** This process involves setting up of similar resources in a DR site with high speed WAN links and specialized network connectivity equipment. The Virtual Machines and their memory states are frequently synchronized (replicated) between the primary servers and the servers in the DR site, so that migration can happen quickly in case of a disaster.
8. **Its easier to migrate a Virtual Machine from one server to another**, than migrating the operating system and application(s) individually.
9. Using virtual machine migration, its possible **to migrate operating systems and applications from older servers to newer servers easily and without disrupting the services.**

2.4.3 VM Consolidation

- VM consolidation techniques have been very attractive to reduce energy costs and increase resource utilization in virtualized data centers.
- Virtualization technologies allows data centers to address such resource and energy inefficiency by placing multiple Virtual Machines (VM) in a single physical server through live VM migration techniques. Reduction of energy consumption is achieved by switching idle physical servers to lower power states (e.g. suspended) while still preserving application performance requirements.
- Virtualization provides a new way to improve the power efficiency of the datacenters through consolidation. Consolidation means assigning more than one VM to a Physical server.
- Cloud computing is a modern shift in the world of IT which ensures the flexible and efficient service delivery. The main focus of cloud computing is to provide the desirable services to every user efficiently. VM consolidation in cloud computing is a very big challenge. There is still a strong need to make balanced ratio between the power consumption and performance degradation because it directly affects the services of the end-users.

Advantages:

1. Virtual Machine (VM) consolidation is an emerging solution for energy saving in cloud data centers.
2. An appropriate VM consolidation policy must change accordingly, depending on the situation
3. It is powerful technology that facilitates better use of the available data center resources.
4. It solve the data center problems such as server sprawl and underutilization of resources.
5. It reduces the performance degradation problem of data center.
6. It allows the programmers to monitoring VM status and controlling the VM placement underlying a cloud platform.

2.4.4 VM Management

- The physical resources build the physical infrastructure of a data center, which serves as a hosting environment for virtual resources. The virtual resources represent physical resources that are virtualized in order to, e.g., facilitate corresponding management tasks, such as their allocation, operation, release, monitoring and control.

Advantages:

1. It is a web console used to manage virtual machine or cluster.
2. Centralized management.
3. Full compatibility with applications.
4. Greater availability and easier recovery in case of disaster.
5. Facility for running backups.
6. Support and maintenance simplified.

7. Controlled access to sensitive data and intellectual property by keeping them safe inside the data center.
8. Hardware independence.
9. Best use of space: the fewer physical devices installed, the greater the availability of space in racks.
10. The provision of new servers is reduced to a few minutes.
11. Migrating servers to new hardware transparently.
12. Saving electrical energy

2.5 DISADVANTAGES OF VIRTUALIZATION

- Following are the disadvantages of Virtualization:

1. **Performance degradation:**
   - Performance is definitely one of the major concerns in using virtualization technology. Since virtualization interposes an abstraction layer between the guest and the host, the guest can experience increased latencies. For instance, in the case of hardware virtualization, where the intermediate emulates a bare machine on top of which an entire system can be installed, the causes of performance degradation can be traced back to the overhead introduced by the following activities:
     (i) Maintaining the status of virtual processors
     (ii) Support of privileged instructions (trap and simulate privileged instructions)
     (iii) Support of paging within VM
     (iv) Console functions
   - Furthermore, when hardware virtualization is realized through a program that is installed or executed on top of the host operating systems, a major source of performance degradation is represented by the fact that the virtual machine manager is executed and scheduled together with other applications, thus sharing with them the resources of the host.
2. **Inefficiency and Degraded User Experience:**
   - Virtualization can sometime lead to an inefficient use of the host. In particular, some of the specific features of the host cannot be exposed by the abstraction layer and then become inaccessible.
   - In the case of hardware virtualization, this could happen for device drivers: The virtual machine can sometime simply provide a default graphic card that maps only a subset of the features available in the host. In the case of programming-level virtual machines, some of the features of the underlying operating systems may become inaccessible unless specific libraries are used. For example, in the first version of Java the support for graphic programming was very limited and the look and feel of applications was very poor compared to native applications.
   - These issues have been resolved by providing a new framework called Swing for designing the user interface, and further improvements have been done by integrating support for the OpenGL libraries in the software development kit.
3. **Security Holes and New Threats:**
   - Virtualization opens the door to a new and unexpected form of phishing. The capability of emulating a host in a completely transparent manner led the way to malicious programs that are designed to extract sensitive information from the guest.
   - In the case of hardware virtualization, malicious programs can preload themselves before the operating system and act as a thin virtual machine manager toward it.
   - The operating system is then controlled and can be manipulated to extract sensitive information of interest to third parties.
4. **Expensive:**
   - One of the setbacks of virtualization is the cost. According to the CEO of an IT consulting firm, this can be quite a pricey investment upfront. A virtual server needs a one-time investment that is more than the cost of a conventional server.

- An entrepreneur who wants faster performance of tasks using technology might consider having to pay a little more to create virtual servers than upgrading new software and servers.

5. **Virtualization might not be compatible with other servers and applications:**
   - Another drawback is the possibility that not all servers and applications are virtualization friendly.
   - This can be a problem when an investment has already been made on several servers or if the applications used to run our business do not have an upgraded version that allows for virtualization.
6. **It Needs training to network administrators:**
   - Another downside of virtualization is the need to spend for training for the network administrator which is an added expense. In the case of hospital personnel, the management will have to shoulder the expenses for training doctors, nurses and administrative staff. Moreover, not all personnel are ready to learn new computer skills especially those who are not technically savvy. This can pose as a challenge.
7. **Added Expense from Easy Server Installation:**
   - Another problem seen by opponents of virtualization is the impending concern that since adding new servers can be done faster and a time might come when there are more servers than network administrators available to monitor them. This means impractical expenditure and waste of time.

Practice Questions

1. What is virtualization? What is need of virtualization?
2. Write benefits of virtualization.
3. Explain virtualization reference model.
4. Write characteristics of virtualization environment.
5. Explain need of virtualization environment.
6. Explain managed execution characteristics of virtualization environment.
7. Explain virtualization types.
8. Explain machine reference model of virtualization.
9. Explain execution environment virtualization.
10. Explain hardware level virtualization.
11. What is hypervisor? Explain it's types.
12. Explain virtual machine manager.
13. Explain different Hardware virtualization techniques.
14. Explain operating system-level virtualization.
15. Explain programming language-level virtualization.
16. Explain Application-level virtualization.
17. Explain storage virtualization, network virtualization, desktop virtualization and Application server virtualization (AVS).
18. Explain VMWare in details.
19. Explain different types of VMware.
20. Explain architecture of Architecture of VMware workstation.
21. Explain server virtualization in VMware.

22. Explain Infrastructure virtualization in VMware.
23. Explain Microsoft Hyper-V.
24. Write features of Microsoft Hyper-V.
25. Write benefits of Microsoft Hyper-V.
26. Write limitations of Hyper-V.
27. Explain Microsoft Hyper-V Architecture.
28. Explain how Hyper-V Works.
29. Enlist features of KVM.
30. Explain benefits of kernel based virtualization.
31. Explain how does KVM work?.
32. Explain architecture of a KVM Server.
33. What is XEN? Explain different components of Xen environment.
34. Explain Xen Architecture with diagram.
35. Write advantages of virtual machine, virtual machine migration, virtual machine consolidation and virtual machine management.
36. Write disadvantages of virtualization.

3...

Storage in Clouds

Chapter Outcomes...

- Explain the given component of storage system architecture.
- Write steps to design storage system for the given cloud set up.
- Compare GFS and HDFS based on the given criteria.

Learning Objectives...

- To understand Basic Concepts in Cloud Storage with its Architecture
- To learn Concepts in Virtualize Data Center (VDC)
- To study Block and File Level Storage Virtualization and Virtual Provisioning and Automated Storage Tiering
- To understand Concept of Virtual Storage Area Network (VSAN) wits its Benefits
- To learn Cloud File System such as Google File System (GFS) and Hadoop Distributed File System (HDFC)

3.0 INTRODUCTION

- Cloud storage is a service where data is remotely maintained, managed, and backed up. The service is available to users over a network, which is usually the Internet. It allows the user to store files online so that the user can access them from any location via the Internet.
- The provider company makes them available to the user online by keeping the uploaded files on an external server. This gives companies using cloud storage services ease and convenience, but can potentially be costly.
- Users should also be aware that backing up their data is still required when using cloud storage services, because recovering data from cloud storage is much slower than local backup.
- Data storage technologies are used to store and access data, applications, and virtual machines on an internal or external, local or remote (including cloud and managed service provider) basis. There are many different types of storage and points of interest to meet various usage needs and requirements.
- Storage can be found in SAN, NAS, or cloud systems, servers, workstations, laptops, and other portable devices. These various types of storage have different features and functionalities, purposes, architectures, and costs or price bands.
- Some storage solutions are purpose-built, while others leverage commercial off-the-shelf technology; others are open software based, while some are proprietary, perhaps using open source kernels. Some storage is targeted for high-performance on-line data, while others are for in active idle archive or backup/restore and data protection.
- Cloud storage is a cloud computing model in which data is stored on remote servers accessed from the internet, or "cloud." It is maintained, operated and managed by a cloud storage service provider on a storage servers that are built on virtualization techniques.

- General storage characteristics include:
  1. Internal or external to a server, or dedicated or shared with others.
  2. Performance in bandwidth, activity, or IOPS and response time or latency.
  3. Availability and reliability, including data protection and redundant components.
  4. Capacity or space for saving data on a storage medium.
  5. Energy and economic attributes for a given configuration.
  6. Functionality and additional capabilities beyond read/write or storing data.
- Different types of storage to support various application or usage scenarios include on-line or primary with a focus on providing performance and availability for active environments.
- Another type of storage is near-line or secondary, with a focus on more capacity at a lower cost, for less frequently used data. A third type of storage is off-line or tertiary, with a focus on very low cost, for inactive, idle, or dormant data.
- These three categories can be subdivided further in terms of specific usage needs or alignments in addition to meeting specific vendor product classifications.
- Storage functionalities can be implemented natively within a storage system, appliance, gateway, or virtualization device as well as via network switches, cloud point of presence gateways, and software running on servers.
- Storage functionality is also offered by cloud services that are deployed using a variety of technologies and basic building blocks discussed in this and other chapters.
- Functionalities can be embedded in a combination of hardware, firmware, and software, while other features can be found in software running on a server or appliance that is integrated or packaged as part of a solution.
- Storage services and functionalities include:
  1. Block-, file- and object-based access.
  2. Thin and dynamic provisioning or allocation.
  3. Multitenancy, partion, LUN (Logical Unit Number), or volume mapping and masking.
  4. Security, authentication, and encryption.
  5. Self-healing, high availability, RAID, snapshots, and replication.
  6. Automated data movement and storage tiering.
  7. Intelligent Power Management (IPM) or disk spin-down.
  8. Application integration and API support.
  9. Data footprint reduction (compression and de-duplication).
  10. Virtualization and cloud access.

Advantages of Cloud Storage:

1. **Usability:** All cloud storage services reviewed in this topic have desktop folders for Mac's and PC's. This allows users to drag and drop files between the cloud storage and their local storage.
2. **Bandwidth:** We can avoid emailing files to individuals and instead send a web link to recipients through the email.
3. **Accessibility:** Stored files can be accessed from anywhere via Internet connection.
4. **Disaster Recovery:** It is highly recommended that businesses have an emergency back up plan ready in the case of an emergency. Cloud storage can be used as a back up plan by businesses by providing a second copy of important files. These files are stored at a remote location and can be accessed through an Internet connection.
5. **Cost Savings:** Businesses and organizations can often reduce annual operating costs by using cloud storage; cloud storage costs about 3 cents per gigabyte to store data internally. Users can see additional cost savings because it does not require internal power to store information remotely.

Disadvantages of Cloud Storage:

1. **Data Security:** There are concerns with the safety and privacy of important data stored remotely. The possibility of private data commingling with other organizations makes some businesses uneasy.
2. **Software:** If we want to be able to manipulate the files locally through multiple devices, we will need to download the service on all devices.

3. **Usability:** Be careful when using drag/drop to move a document into the cloud storage folder. This will permanently move our document from its original folder to the cloud storage location. Do a copy and paste instead of drag/drop if we want to retain the document's original location in addition to moving a copy on to the cloud storage folder.
4. **Bandwidth:** Several cloud storage services have a specific bandwidth allowance. If an organization surpasses the given allowance, the additional charges could be significant. However, some providers allows unlimited bandwidth. This is a factor that companies should consider when looking at a cloud storage provider.
5. **Accessibility:** If we have no internet connection, we have no access to our data.

3.1 STORAGE SYSTEM ARCHITECTURE

- Storage solutions focus on the architecture or packaging of the storage system. Solutions range from small, entry-level multifunction systems to large-scale, enterprise-class systems, with many different variations between.
- System differences include high-end cache centric or monolithic frame based systems typically found in upper-price-band systems, mid-range modular, and clustered storage systems.
- These differences have become interface, protocol, and host application-independent, whereas in the past there were clear lines of delineation between different storage system architectures, similar to traditional lines of demarcation for various types of servers.
- In addition to supporting both open systems and mainframe servers natively, high end cache-centric storage systems, as their name implies, have very large amounts of cache to boost performance and support advanced feature functionality.
- Some systems support over 1000 HDDs, including ultra fast FLASH based SSD devices, fast SASHDDs (replacing Fibre Channel drives), and lower cost, high capacity SAS as well as SATA HDDs.
- While smaller mid-range storage systems can, in some cases, rival the performance of cache centric systems while consuming less power, an advantage of the larger storage systems can be to reduce the number of storage systems to manage for large scale environments.
- Mid-range and modular storage systems span from the upper end of price bands 6 and 7 for enterprise solutions to price band 1 for low-end storage solutions geared toward small and medium-sized businesses. Price bands, as their name implies, refer to how technology, including storage, can be characterized or grouped based on cost.
- The characteristics of mid-range and modular storage systems are the presence of one or two storage controllers (also known as nodes), storage processors or heads, and some amount of cache that can be mirrored to the partner controller (when two controllers exist). Dual controllers may be active/passive, with one controller doing useful work and the other in standby mode in the event of a controller failure.
- Mid-range and modular controllers attach to some amount of storage, usually with the ability to support a mix of high-performance, fast HDDs and slow, large-capacity HDDs, to implement tiered storage in a box.
- The controllers rely on less cache than cache centric solutions, but some scenarios leveraging fast processors and RAID algorithms can rival the performance of larger, more expensive cache centric systems.
- As with most storage systems, it is not the total number of HDDs, the quantity and speed of tiered-access I/O connectivity, such as iS CSI, SAS, 4GFC, 8GFC, 16GFC,or 10GbE and FCoE ports, the type and speed of the processors, or even the amount of cache memory that determines the performance.
- The performance differentiator is how a manufacturer combines the various components to create a solution that delivers a given level of performance with lower power consumption.
- To avoid performance surprises, be careful of performance claims based solely on the speed and quantity of HDDs or the speed and number of ports, processors, and memory. How the resources are deployed and how the storage management software enables those resources to avoid bottlenecks are more important.
- For some clustered NAS and storage systems, more nodes are required to compensate for overhead or performance congestion in processing diverse application workloads and performance characteristics. Other items and features to consider include support for industry standard interfaces, protocols, and technologies.

3.1.1 Cloud Storage System Architecture

- Cloud storage services software includes three modules: client, management server and storage server, the software as shown in Fig. 3.1.

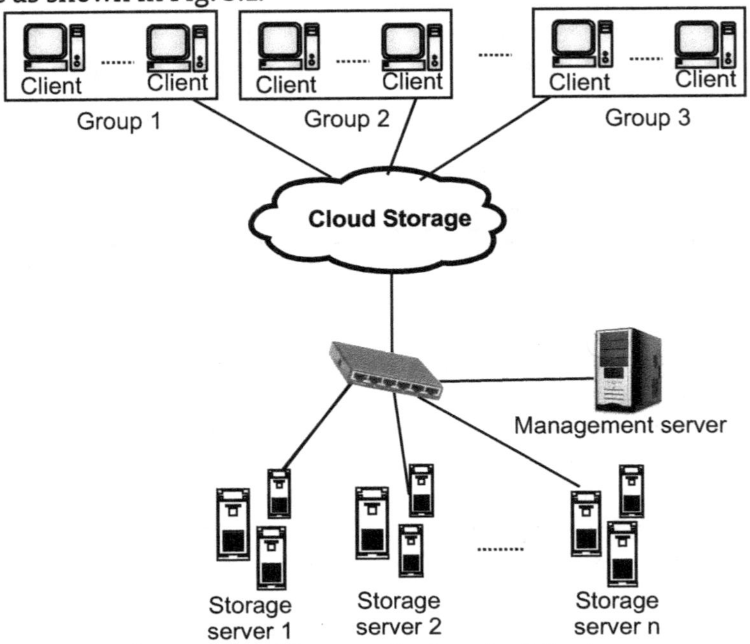

Fig. 3.1: Cloud Storage System Architecture

- Cloud storage architecture consist of following components:

1. **Client:**
   - Client software distributed in different geographic locations in need of backup host, which can be any Internet enabled device.
   - Client and management server communication between the main data backup or recovery operations preparatory work before the operation process after the completion of all requests and state feedback between the client and the storage server is simply to complete the requested backup and data recovery process.
2. **Management Server:**
   - Management Server is the service system monitoring and management center and storage server for user management task scheduling status monitoring.
   - When a client login system by the management server authentication to confirm whether the valid user.
   - Regular scanning task queue, when the arrival of the task execution time, then start a service thread, depending on the load balancing strategy, the establishment of the client and the connection between the storage server and monitor the implementation status of the task; also monitor the status of each storage server, on a regular basis spatial order, debris recovery and data migration to maintain metadata information. Management server through the logical file and physical storage mapping between data blocks to achieve the correct backup data recovery.
3. **Storage Server:**
   - The lawful management server certifies storages server node storage medium. In the management server's management, real-time response from the client's request, to receive the backup data, data storage management and is responsible for sending data to the appropriate client recovery.
   - To support the efficient running of backup and recovery operations need to store server-side design reasonable strategies for tiered storage and data migration.
   - Meanwhile, the system supports multiple storage servers, and multiple files within a single server to achieve highly scalable storage side, the way to meet the service requirements of mass data storage.

3.2 VIRTUALIZE DATA CENTER (VDC)

- A Virtual Data Center (VDC) is a pool of cloud infrastructure resources designed specifically for enterprise business needs. Those resources include compute, memory, storage and bandwidth.
- A Virtual data center can be defined as a group of cloud resources specifically designed for enterprise-specific needs.
- The basic components of a Virtual Data Center are hosts (CPU, RAM, Disk) & VNets which resides in a private environment which virtually represents a physical data center.
- The principle of the virtual data center is to give enough flexibility to the users to customize their own nodes.
- A virtual data center is a product of the Infrastructure-as-a-Service (IaaS) delivery model of cloud computing. It can provide on-demand computing, storage and networking, as well as applications, all of which can be seamlessly integrated into an organization's existing IT infrastructure.
- The premise of the virtual data center solution is to give organizations the option of adding capacity or installing a new IT infrastructure without the need to buy or install costly hardware, which takes up additional manpower, space and power. The whole data center infrastructure is provided over the cloud.
- There are two types of Data Center Architecture namely, Traditional Data Center and Virtual Data Center.

3.2.1 Traditional Data Center Architecture

- A traditional data center with four tiers is shown in Fig. 3.2. Within each tier, the datacenter core network operates through a firewall, an Ethernet based network, appropriate servers and the fiber channel storage network.
- Tier 1 aggregates the web service requests and responseelivery. Tier 2 performs the web operations, such as web and DNS services. Tier 3 conducts the application, such as a search of a database.
- Tier 4 is the vault of information and the servers that access it; for example, the backup server and storage server. The Storage Area Network (SAN) is usually used to connect disk arrays.
- For example, the Fiber Channel (FC) is a multi-gigabit-speed network technology that is used primarily for storage networking today and uses a networking hardware that is different from Ethernet.

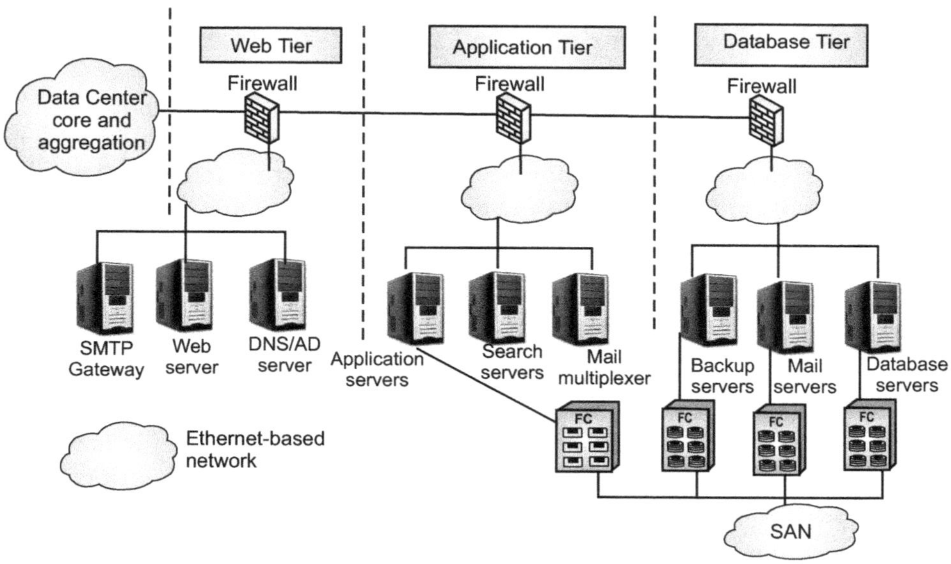

Fig. 3.2: A traditional Data Center using a 4-Tier Structure

3.2.2 A Virtualized Data Center Architecture Using Centralized Services

- In contrast to the traditional data center shown in Fig. 3.2, the physical view of a virtualized data center architecture is illustrated in Fig. 3.3. This center is virtualized and consolidated through a unified fabric interconnect, and is logically equivalent to the four tier data center.
- All the centralized services and their equipment are attached to this unified fabric interconnect shown in the fig. 3.3.

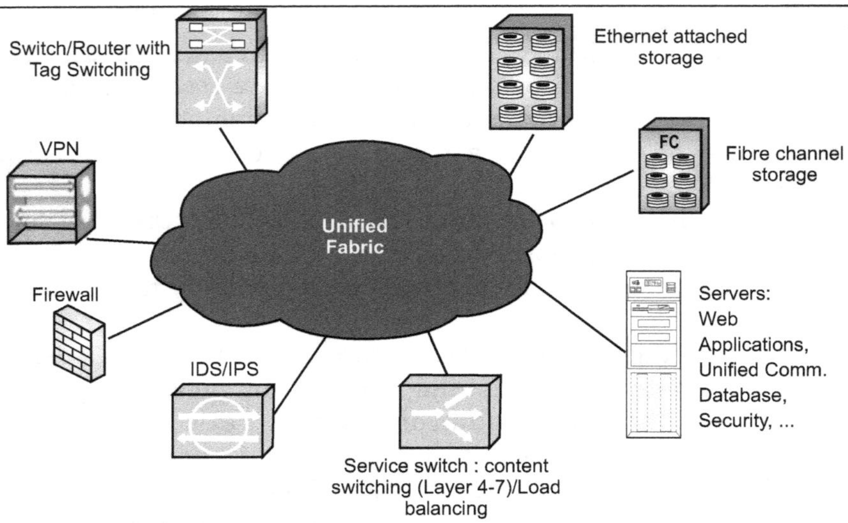

Fig. 3.3: A physical view of a virtualized data center architecture using a unified fabric interconnect and centralized services.

- The unified fabric is a lossless 10-Gbps Ethernet foundation that enables LANs, SANs, and clusters of high-performance computing networks. The IEEE standards body of the Data Center Bridging Task Group is working to create the lossless Ethernet required modifications. The Converged Enhanced Ethernet (CEE) was developed as an extended version of Ethernet for data center applications.
- Cisco refers to the technology as Data Center Ethernet (DCE). As an example, the Cisco Data Center Ethernet supports the concept of running multiple traffic types, e.g., LAN, SAN, iSCSI, etc., on a single network, while simultaneously preserving respective traffic treatments.
- The new CEE allows fewer adapters, switches, and cables and provides better utilization. In addition, this virtualized data center is service-oriented and Web 2.0 based.

3.2.3 A Consolidated Virtual Data Center Architecture

- A detail description of a consolidated data center that employs virtualization for centralized services is shown in Fig. 3.4. A unified fabric provides a single switch fabric for every type of networking in the data center.
- In this configuration, there are three areas of consolidation consisting of,
  1. **virtual routers/switches**, including a firewall and IDS/IPS in a unified fabric at the hub of the data center.
  2. **virtual servers** with load balancing.
  3. **virtual routers/switches** connected in a unified fabric at the storage end of the facility.
- This consolidation can save costs and manpower as well as provide the flexibility for dynamic central management in order to meet changing demands.

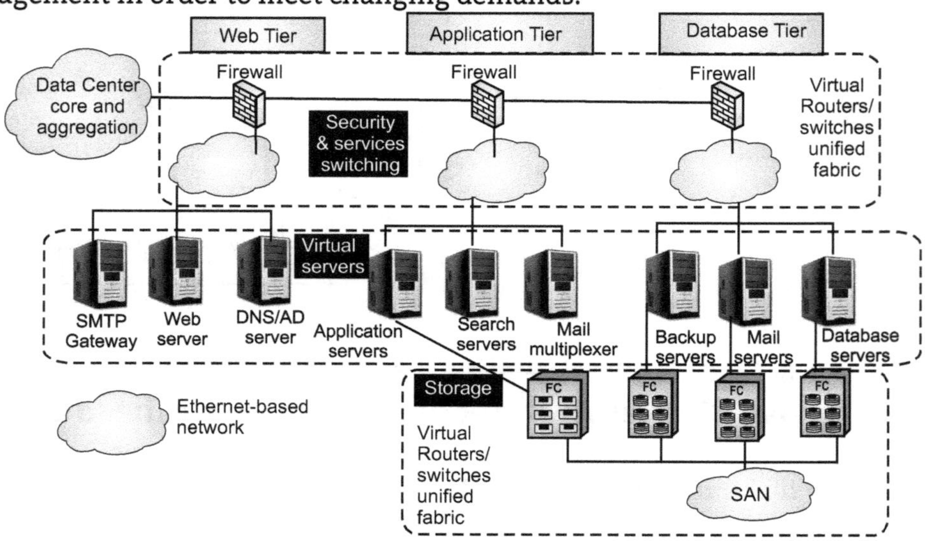

Fig. 3.4: A consolidated data center using virtualization that contains three areas of consolidation

3.2.4 Benefits of Virtual Data Center

- Various benefits of VDC are listed below:
  1. **Reduction of Costs:** Because of virtualization we can cut down management costs, economising on technical staff payments. In addition, costs about purchase, maintenance and replacement of IT hardware, known to be very expensive, are drastically reduced.
  2. **Simplified Management:** The use of virtualized servers simplifies the infrastructure management, by allowing us to administrate the machines remotely, easily and in real time.
  3. **Optimization of Resources:** Another benefits is given by the opportunity of optimizing resources, both at hardware and virtual level, and make the system more flexible and performing.
  4. **Pay-Per-Use Model:** With virtualization we can use the pay-per-use model, which enables to pay only for resources actually used. This way the customer removes waste and saves money.
  5. **Lower Consumption:** Hardware resources require a lot of energy, even if currently unused. Virtualization reduces consumption, limiting the data center's environmental impact and feed cost.
  6. **Security of Facilities and Data:** Relying on a specialized facility we can benefit of a high-level of systems security and advanced data protection, which cannot be absolutely compared with on-premise technology's safety. For instance, for anything related to the implementation of Disaster Recovery and Business Continuity systems.
  7. **High Efficiency:** Virtual machines makes the IT infrastructure more agile and increase their operational efficiency.
  8. **Integration with Managed Services:** What is one of the advantages of rely on an external provider? The chance to give the IT services management to a team of experts and focus on the core business, with total peace of mind.
  9. **The Latest Technology:** Technology changes rapidly and keep up to date can be very expensive for companies. Virtual Data Centers make at customers disposal the best technology available on the market at lower cost.
  10. **Availability and Scalability:** Virtual machines enable high scalability of resources and are characterized by a superior availability compared to physical equipment.

3.2.5 VDC Environment

- Today, data centers are essential and integral parts of any business whether small, medium, or large in size.
- The core elements of a data center are host, storage, connectivity (or network), applications, and DBMS that are managed centrally. These elements work together to process and store data.
- With the evolution of virtualization, data centers have also evolved from a classic data center to a Virtualized Data Center (VDC).
- In a VDC, physical resources from a classic data center are pooled together and provided as virtual resources. This abstraction hides the complexity and limitation of physical resources from the user.
- By consolidating IT resources using virtualization organizations can optimize their infrastructure utilization and reduce the total cost of owning an infrastructure.
- Moreover in a VDC virtual resources are created using software that enables faster deployment, compared to deploying physical resources in classic data centers.

3.2.6 Server Virtualization

- Server virtualization is a virtualization technique that involves partitioning a physical server into a number of small virtual servers with the help of virtualization software. In server virtualization, each virtual server runs multiple operating system instances at the same time.
- Server virtualization also called as a compute virtualization in cloud computing to making a virtual edition of a device or resource, such as a server, storage device, network, or an operating system where the structure splits the resources as one or more environments for execution
- Typical enterprise data centers contain a huge number of servers. Many of these servers sit idle as the workload is distributed to only some of the servers on the network. This results in a waste of expensive hardware resources, power, maintenance and cooling requirements.

- Server virtualization attempts to increase resource utilization by partitioning physical servers into several multiple virtual servers each running its own operating system and applications.
- Server virtualization makes each virtual server look and act like a physical server, multiplying the capacity of every single physical machine.
- The concept of server virtualization is widely applied in IT infrastructure as a way of minimizing costs by increasing the utilization of existing resources. Virtualizing servers is often a good solution for small to medium scale applications. This technology is widely used for providing cost effective web hosting services.

Uses of Server Virtualization:

1. To centralize the server administration.
2. Improve the availability of server.
3. Helps in disaster recovery.
4. Ease in development and testing.
5. Make efficient use of server resources.

3.2.6.1 Benefits and Limitations of Server Virtualization

Benefits of Server Virtualization:

1. Server virtualization reduces cost because less hardware is required.
2. Each server can be rebooted independently and that reboot (restart) won't affect the working of other virtual servers.
3. Live migration and Server consolidation.
4. Reduced need for physical infrastructure.
5. Reduced energy consumption and easier to backup and recover from disasters.
6. Easier to install or setup software patches and updates and Ideal in web hosting.

Limitations of Server Virtualization:

1. Possible availability issues and resource consumption.
2. Possible memory over commits.
3. Upfront costs considering the virtualization software and an organization's network
4. Software licensing.
5. IT staff with experience in virtualization may be needed because a learning curve may be involved.
6. Security may also be a concern, especially if a virtual server is on the same physical server as a separate organization.

3.2.6.2 Techniques of Server Virtualization

- There are three types of Server Virtualization techniques:
  1. **Hypervisor:**
     - A Hypervisor is a layer between the operating system and hardware. The hypervisor is the reason behind the successful running of multiple operating systems.
     - It can also perform tasks such as handling queues, dispatching and returning the hardware request. Host operating system works on the top of the hypervisor, we use it to administer and manage the virtual machines.
  2. **Para-Virtualization:**
     - In Para-virtualization model, simulation in trapping overhead in software virtualizations. It is based on the hypervisor and the guest operating system and modified entry compiled for installing it in a virtual machine.
     - After the modification, the overall performance is increased as the guest operating system communicates directly with the hypervisor.
  3. **Full Virtualization:**
     - Full virtualizations can emulate the underlying hardware. It is quite similar to Para-virtualization. Here, machine operation used by the operating system which is further used to perform Input/Output or modify the system status.
     - The unmodified operating system can run on the top of the hypervisor. This is possible because of the operations, which are emulated in the software and the status codes are returned with what the real hardware would deliver.

3.2.7 Network Virtualization

- Network virtualization is similar to server virtualization but instead of dividing up a physical server among several virtual machines, physical network resources are divided up among multiple virtual networks.
- This is useful in applications such as multi-tenant data center environments where each tenant can be allocated multiple virtual machines as well as a virtual network connecting these virtual machines.
- Oneway to do this is to provide a special label within each frame that identifies the virtual network that it belongs to. Labeling frames and forwarding data based on these labels is sometimes called network tunneling.
- Network virtualization is the method of splitting up network resources into separate bandwidth channels that are each independent from one another, and that can be assigned and reassigned to servers or other network devices.
- Its purpose is to optimize the speed, reliability, and flexibility of the network. It is particularly useful when a network experiences a large, and usually unexpected, spike in usage.

3.2.7.1 Types of Network Virtualization

- The two types of network virtualization are External Virtualization and Internal virtualization.
  1. **External Virtualization:**
     - It combines multiple networks or parts of networks into a virtual unit. External network virtualization is the combining of one or more local networks or parts of networks into a whole "virtual" network with the intended goal of improving the efficiency of a large network or data center.
     - Its two key components are the Virtual Local Area Network (VLAN) and the network switch.
     - Using these two together, system administrators can configure systems that are physically attached at the same local network into many different virtual networks.
  2. **Internal Virtualization:**
     - It uses software containers to mimic or provide the functionality of a single physical network. Internal network virtualization is a network confined to a single machine and provides network functionality to the different VMs using a single system.
     - Sometimes, it is also referred to as network in a box and it improves the overall efficiency of a single system by isolating the separate virtual environments and allowing them to communicate over a virtual network interface. This type is most commonly seen on the workstation versions of VMware and Parallels.
- Virtual networks have the following basic components:
  1. Network hardware (including network interface cards, virtual switches, and VLANs).
  2. Network storage devices.
  3. Network media (usually Ethernet or Fiber Channel).

3.2.7.2 Architecture of Network Virtualization

- In network virtualization, multiple virtual networks run with the help of a physical network as shown in Fig. 3.5.

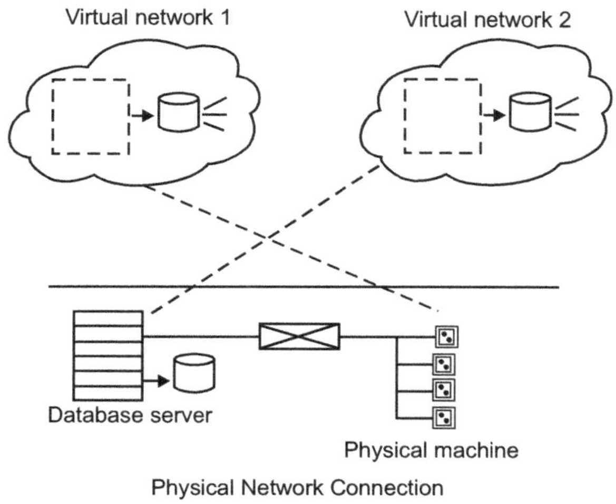

Fig. 3.5: Network Virtualization

- Network virtualization comprises rationally grouping and segmenting physical network(s) into distinct rational units known as 'virtual network(s)' and forming them to act as one or multiple separate network(s).
- It permits multiple virtual networks to share network resources. In virtual data center (VDC), network virtualization comprises virtualization of both VM and physical networks. The physical network may consist of network routers, hubs, switches, repeaters, adapters, and bridges. A VM network exists within a physical server.
- A computer on which a hypervisor runs one or more virtual machines is called a host machine, and each virtual machine is called a guest machine.
- Network virtualization permits a manager to construct multiple virtual networks in the data center (DC).
- A virtual network offers alignment of all the nodes which belong to a similar working unit in an enterprise.

3.2.7.3 Benefits and Disadvantages of Network Virtualization

- **Benefits of Network Virtualization:**
  1. Reduction of hardware expense.
  2. Energy expenses and Recoverability.
  3. More productive IT environments (i.e., efficient scaling).
  4. Improved security and recovery times.
  5. Faster in application delivery.
  6. More efficient networks, and reduced overall costs.
  7. A clear impact of network virtualization will be the reduction of physical hardware in the office space. In addition, the reduced hardware requirements will have a corresponding impact on the power consumption.
  8. Network virtualization allows our team to easily automate network and security protocols, ensuring that they are applied across an entire network infrastructure.
  9. It improves scalability business is looking to grow network virtualization provides a quick and easily scalable solution. Network virtualization allows business to respond to market demands with agility.

Disadvantages of Network virtualization:

1. Increased upfront costs (investing in virtualization software).
2. Need to license software.
3. There may be a learning curve if IT managers are not experienced.
4. Not every application and server will work in a virtualized environment.
5. Availability can be an issue if an organization can't connect to their virtualized data.

3.2.8 Desktop Virtualization

- Desktop virtualization is actually a type of illusion provided to the user using different techniques.
- It involves encapsulating and delivering either access to an entire information system environment or the environment itself to a remote client device.
- For IT organizations, desktop administration is expensive, manual, and time consuming.
- As compared to desktop virtualization, server virtualization makes datacenters more quick and effective by advanced levels of accessibility, quicker application delivery, and enhanced utilization.
- Desktop virtualization is a type of software technology used to separate the desktop and its connected application software from the physical device used by the client.
- Remote desktop virtualization works in a manner similar to client–server model in which applications can be executed on any remote desktop with different operating systems and with the help of the protocol of remote display, a user can interact with the application as shown in Fig. 3.6.
- **Components for Desktop Virtualization:** The VDI architecture consists of several components that work together to provide an end-to-end solution.
- The main components are Endpoint devices, A connection broker and VM hosting.

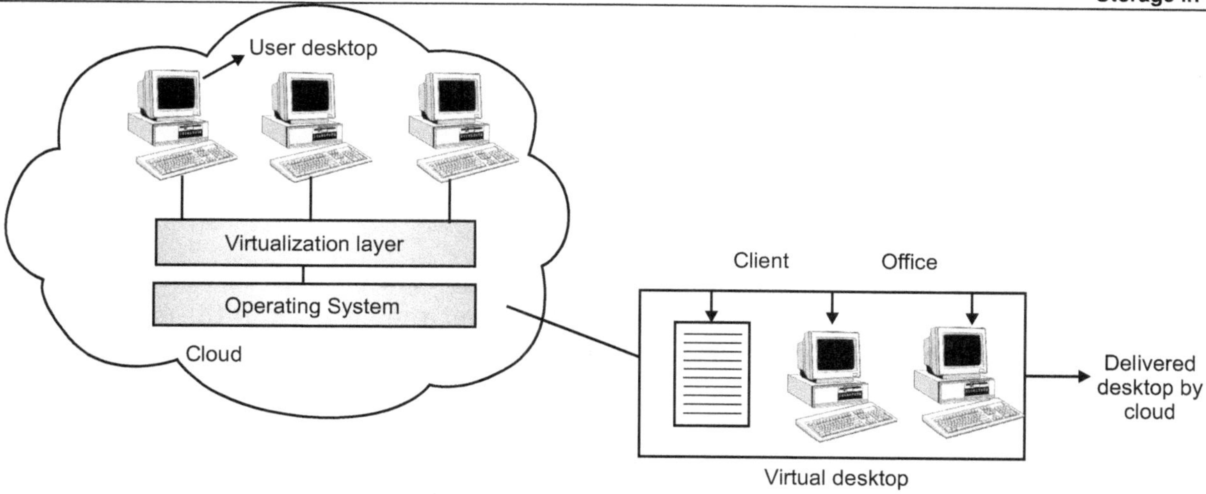

Fig. 3.6: Desktop Virtualization

- In a virtualized desktop, virtualization breaks the connection between hardware and the elements facilitate the IT staff to alter, update and organize these elements independently for greater business quickness and improved response time.

3.2.8.1 Advantages of Desktop Virtualization

1. Simpler provisioning of new desktops.
2. Installation of new applications at cheap rates so cost is low.
3. Desktop image management capabilities.
4. Increased data security (Protected reserved access to a business desktop settings).
5. Longer time given for customer desktop infrastructure.
6. Better business continuity and disaster recovery and improved deployment and management.

3.2.8.2 Techniques used for Desktop Virtualization

- There are three typical three techniques for desktop virtualization namely, Remote Desktop Services (RDS), Virtual Desktop Infrastructure (VDI) and Desktop-as-a-Service (DaaS).

1. Remote Desktop Services:

- Remote Desktop Services (RDS) is customarily called Terminal Services. It is a blanket term for characteristics of Microsoft Windows server which permits consumers to distantly access Windows applications and graphical desktops.
- In Remote Desktop Services (RDS) also known as Remote Desktop Session Host (RDSH) users remotely access desktops and Windows applications through the Microsoft Windows Server operating system. Applications and desktop images are served via Microsoft Remote Desktop Protocol (RDP). Formerly known as Microsoft Terminal Server, this product has remained largely unchanged since its initial release.
- From the end user's perspective, RDS and VDI are identical. But because one instance of Windows Server can support as many simultaneous users as the server hardware can handle, RDS can be a more cost-effective desktop virtualization option. It's also worth noting applications tested or certified to run on Windows 10 may not be tested or certified to run on the Windows Server OS.

Advantages of RDS:

(i) Data recovery in tragedy.
(ii) Operation from anyplace.
(iii) Economical.

Disadvantages of RDS:

(i) Requirement of powerful RDS.
(ii) Requirement of RDS monitoring.
(iii) Requirement of reliable network.
(iv) Requirement of right adjustment in network.
(v) Knowledgeable administrator.

2. Virtual Desktop Infrastructure:

- Virtual Desktop Infrastructure (VDI) refers to the hosting of a desktop OS running in a VM on a server in the Virtual Data Center (VDC).
- VDI allows a user to access a remote desktop environment from an endpoint device via a remote desktop delivery protocol.
- The VDI architecture consists of several components that work together to provide an end-to-end solution.
- In Virtual Desktop Infrastructure (VDI), the operating system runs on a virtual machine (VM) hosted on a server in a data center. The desktop image travels over the network to the end user's device, where the end user can interact with the desktop (and the underlying applications and operating system) as if they were local.
- VDI gives each user his or her own dedicated vertual machine running its own operating system. The operating system resources drivers, CPUs, memory, etc.-operate from a software layer called a hypervisor that mimics their output manages the resource allocation to multiple VMs and allows them to run side by side on the same server.
- A key benefit of VDI is that it can deliver the Windows 10 desktop and operating system to the end user's devices. However, because VDI supports only one user per Windows 10 instance it requires a separate VM for each Windows 10 user.

Advantages of VDI:

(i) Low price in buying desktop computers.
(ii) Centralized client operating system management.
(iii) Swift client implementation.
(iv) Reduction in the costs of desktop.
(v) Reduction in the cost of electricity.
(vi) Enhanced security of data.
(vii) Protected remote access.
(viii) Lesser applications compatibility troubles.

Disadvantages of VDI:

(i) Printing normally involves third-party appends.
(ii) Scanning is natively unsupported.
(iii) Bi-directional audio is natively unsupported.
(iv) Exhibit protocols are unsuitable for graphic design.
(v) Needs low-latency association between the virtual infrastructure and customer.
(vi) Needs enterprise class server hardware and storage areas network for VMs permanently delivered to particular users.
(vii) Needs trained IT staff

Differences between RDS and VDI:

Sr. No.	RDS	VDI
1.	Separate virtual machines are not provided to the user.	Separate virtual machines are provided to the users.
2.	Multiple operating systems instances need not be managed.	Multiple operating systems instances need to be managed.
3.	Various users share the same virtual machines and operating systems.	Same resources need not be shared.
4.	Full administration is not provided to the users because many instances of the same resources are shared by many users.	User gets full administration over resources.
5.	Less resource utilization of CPU, memory elements, etc.	More resource utilization.

3. Desktop-as-a-Service (DaaS):

- In Desktop-as-a-Service (DaaS), VMs are hosted on a cloud-based backend by a third party provider. DaaS is readily scalable, can be more flexible than on-premise solutions, and generally deploys faster than many other desktop virtualization options.
- Like other types of cloud desktop virtualization, DaaS shares many of the general benefits of cloud computing, including support for fluctuating workloads and changing storage demands, usage-based pricing, and the ability to make applications and data accessible from almost any internet-connected device.
- The drawback to DaaS is that features and configurations are not always as customizable as required.

3.2.8.3 Benefits of Desktop Virtualization

- Benefits of desktop are as follows:
  1. **Simpler Administration:** Desktop virtualization can make it easier for IT teams to manage employee computing needs. The business can maintain a single VM template for employees within similar roles or functions instead of maintaining individual computers that must be reconfigured, updated, or patched whenever software changes need to be made. This saves time and IT resources.
  2. **Cost Savings:** Many virtual desktop solutions allow us to shift more of the IT budget from capital expenditures to operating expenditures. Because compute intensive applications require less processing power when they're delivered via VMs hosted on a data center server, desktop virtualization can extend the life of older or less powerful end-user devices. On-premise virtual desktop solutions may require a significant initial investment in server hardware, hypervisor software, and other infrastructure, making cloud based DaaS wherein we simply pay a regular usage based charge.
  3. **Improved Productivity:** Desktop virtualization makes it easier for employees to access enterprise computing resources. They can work anytime, anywhere, from any supported device with an Internet connection.
  4. **Support for a Broad Variety of Device Types:** Virtual desktops can support remote desktop access from a wide variety of devices, including laptop and desktop computers, thin clients, zero clients, tablets, and even some mobile phones. We can use virtual desktops to deliver workstation like experiences and access to the full desktop anywhere, anytime, regardless of the operating system native to the end user device.
  5. **Stronger Security:** In desktop virtualization, the desktop image is abstracted and separated from the physical hardware used to access it and the VM used to deliver the desktop image can be a tightly controlled environment managed by the enterprise IT department.
  6. **Agility and Scalability:** It's quick and easy to deploy new VMs or serve new applications whenever necessary, and it is just as easy to delete them when they're no longer needed.
  7. **Better End-user Experiences:** When we implement desktop virtualization, the end-users will enjoy a feature rich experience without sacrificing functionality they have come to rely on, like printing or access to USB ports.

3.2.9 Application Virtualization

- Application virtualization also called application service virtualization is a term under the larger umbrella of virtualization.
- It refers to running an application on a thin client; a terminal or a network workstation with few resident programs and accessing most programs residing on a connected server. The thin client runs in an environment separate from sometimes referred to as being encapsulated from, the operating system where the application is located.
- Application virtualization technology offers skills to install applications without altering or making any variation to the file system, underlying OS or registry of the computing platform in which they are installed as shown in Fig. 3.7.
- In application virtualization, the virtualization concept involves a local device and an actual installed application in a remote location.

- Application virtualization is also called thin client technology. In this type of technology, the local device provides physical resources such as the CPU and random access memory that may be required to run the software but nothing is installed locally on the device itself.
- The underlying principle is to have the application and OS separated, so the application is OS independent. In these implementations, although the user interface is transparent the virtual application runs locally and the application runs remotely.

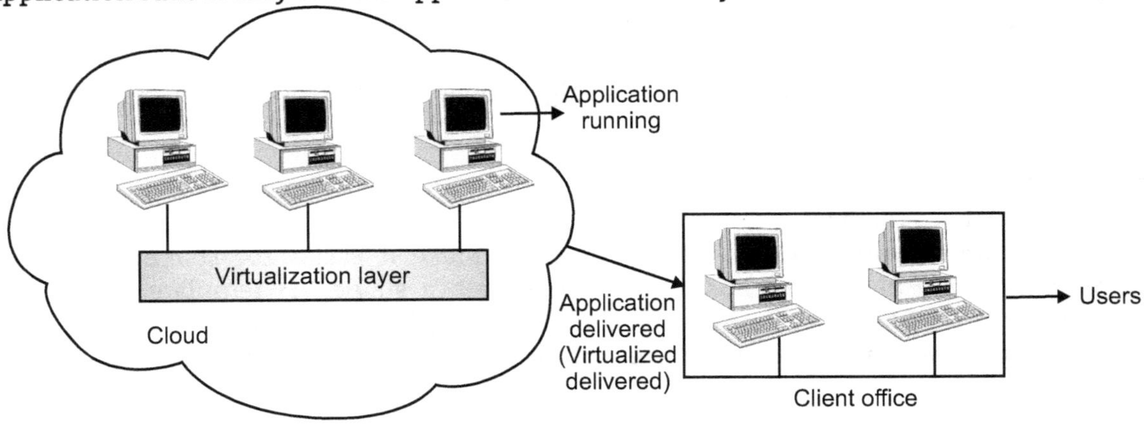

Fig. 3.7: Application Virtualization

- Technology categories that fall under application virtualization include the following:
  1. **Streaming of Application:** Before startup, rather than delivering the whole application, portions of the application's code, settings, and data are delivered according to their requirement.
  2. **VDI or Desktop Virtualization:** The application is introduced in blade PC or VM which also comprises the Operating System (OS). This makes management of infrastructure and formation of virtual desktops easy to grant access of virtual desktops. VDI may normally fill up the gaps wherever applications' streaming fails.

3.2.9.1 Advantages and Limitations of Application Virtualization

Advantages of Application Virtualization:

1. Improved workload management and reduced hardware cost.
2. Increased flexibility for working remotely
3. **Simplified Application Deployment:** Applications are never installed on to an operating System; hence the deployment of the applications is greatly simplified. Furthermore, complete removal of all application bits from a PC during retirement is assured.
4. **Simplified Operating System Image Management:** Since applications are completely different from the OS, managing OS images is simpler, especially during OS patches and upgrades. It helps to create a more dynamic desktop environment, in which the desktop is an aggregation of separately managed components.
5. **Elimination of Resource Conflicts:** Since each application has its own virtual OS resources, resource and application conflict issues are eliminated.

Limitations of Application Virtualization:

1. All software cannot be virtualized. For example, applications that require a device driver or 16-bit applications that require shared memory space cannot be virtualized.
2. Some types of software cannot be virtualized, such as anti-virus packages and applications that require heavy OS integration.

3.2.9.2 Tools used for Application Virtualization

- The tools for application virtualization include: Microsoft Application Virtualization (App-V), VMware ThinApp and Flexera Software Supporting Application Virtualization.

3.3 STORAGE VIRTUALIZATION

- Storage virtualization is the process of masking the underlying complexity of physical storage resources and presenting the logical view of these resources to compute systems in a VDC environment.

- Storage virtualization enables creating one or more logical storage on the physical storage resources. This logical or virtual storage appears as physical storage to the compute systems. The logical to physical storage mapping is performed by storage virtualization layer.
- The virtualization layer abstracts the identity of physical storage devices and creates a storage pool by aggregating storage resources from multiple heterogeneous storage arrays.
- Virtual volumes are created from these storage pools and are assigned to the compute system. Compute system remains unaware of the mapping operation and access the virtual volumes as if accessing physical storage attached to them.

3.3.1 Benefits of Storage Virtualization

- Various benefits of storage virtualization includes:
  1. **Adds or Removes Storage Without any Downtime:** Storage virtualization enables adding or removing storage without affecting application availability.
  2. **Increases Storage Utilization Thereby Reducing TCO:** It increases storage utilization by consolidating multiple heterogeneous storage resources and creating storage pools. Storage pools provide flexibility in storage resources allocation to the compute system and increase storage utilization. This considerably reduces investment in new storage resources and thereby lowers the Total Cost of Ownership (TCO).
  3. **Provides Non-Disruptive Data Migration between Storage Devices:** Data migration is required during technology refresh initiatives where newer storage systems replace the legacy storage systems. It may also be required to move data between different storage systems when performance and availability requirements change. Storage virtualization enables non-disruptive data migration (data is being accessed while migrations are in progress) between storage systems since it masks the complexity of underlying physical storage resources. It also enables support of heterogeneous, multi-vendor storage platforms.
  4. **Supports Heterogeneous, Multi-Vendor Storage Platforms**: In a virtual environment, different virtual machines running different applications can exist on a single compute system. This creates a very complex environment as there exist multiple sets of workloads and requirements. It can be extremely challenging to manage such an environment in a traditional storage environment. However, by implementing storage virtualization, the complexity in storage provisioning is removed from the environment.
  5. **Simplifies Storage Management:** Features such as storage pools, storage tiering, and virtual provisioning are key advances in storage technologies that provide this simplification.

3.3.2 Storage Virtualization at Different Layers

- Storage virtualization may be implemented at,
  1. Compute Layer (As a Storage provisioning for VMs).
  2. Network Layer (As a Block-level virtualization and File-level virtualization).
  3. Storage Layer (As a Virtual Provisioning and Automated Storage Tiering).
- At the compute layer, hypervisor allocates storage space for VMs without exposing the complexity of the physical storage.
- Block and file level virtualization are network based virtualization techniques which embed intelligence of virtualizing storage resources at network layer.
- At storage layer, both virtual provisioning and automated storage tiering simplify the storage management and help to optimize the storage infrastructure.

3.3.2.1 Compute Layer-Storage for Virtual Machines

- A 'Virtual Machine' is stored as a set of 'files' on the storage devices assigned to the hypervisor. One of the file called 'virtual disk file' represents a 'virtual disk' which is used by a VM to store its data.
- The virtual disk appears as a local physical disk drive to the VM. The size of the 'virtual disk file' represents the storage space allocated to the 'virtual disk' shown in Fig. 3.8.

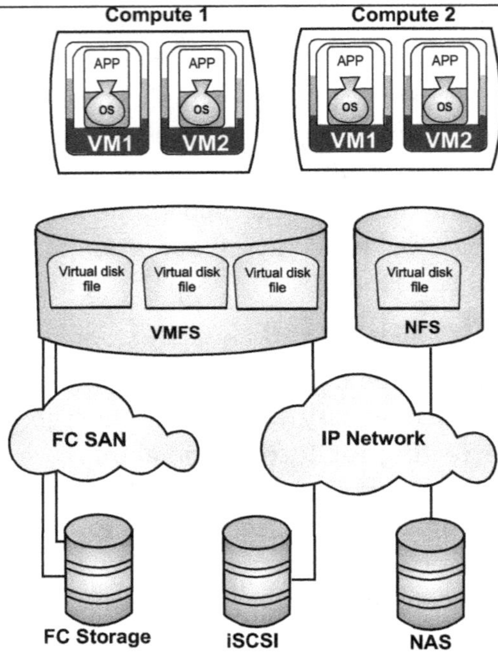

Fig. 3.8: Storage for Virtual Machines

- Hypervisor may access FC storage device, or IP storage devices such as iSCSI, and NAS devices. Virtual machines remain unaware of the total storage space available to the hypervisor and the underlying storage technologies.

3.3.2.2 Network Layer Storage Virtualization

- Network-based storage virtualization embeds the intelligence of virtualizing storage resources at network layer and provides an abstract view of physical storage resources.
- When an I/O is sent from the compute system, it is redirected through the virtualization layer at the network to the mapped physical storage.
- Virtualization applied at the network enables to pool multi-vendor storage resources and to manage these pools from a single management interface.
- It also enables non-disruptive data migration between arrays. Network based storage virtualization can be implemented in both SAN and NAS environments.
- In a SAN, virtualization is applied at the block level, whereas in NAS, it is applied at the file level.
- It has two types based on SAN and NAS namely, Block-level Virtualization and File-level Virtualization.

3.3.2.2.1 Block-Level Storage Virtualization

- Block-level storage virtualization creates an abstraction layer in the SAN, between physical storage resources and virtual volumes presented to the compute systems shown in Fig. 3.9.
- Instead of being directed to the LUNs (Logical Unit Number) on the individual storage arrays, the compute systems are directed to the virtual volumes on the virtualization appliance at the network.
- The virtualization appliance performs mapping between the virtual volumes and the LUNs on the arrays. Block-level storage virtualization enables us to combine several LUNs from one or more arrays into a single virtual volume before presenting it to the compute systems.

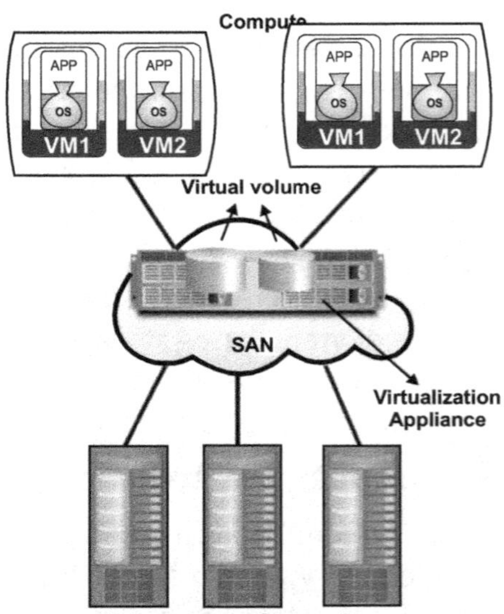

Fig. 3.9: Block-level Storage Virtualization

- It also takes a single large LUN from an array, slices it into smaller virtual volumes, and presents these volumes to the compute systems. Block-level storage virtualization supports dynamic increase of storage volumes, consolidation of heterogeneous storage arrays, and transparent volume access.
- With block-level virtualization solution in place, the virtualization appliance at the network handles the migration of data. The virtualization appliance enables storage volumes to remain online and accessible while data is being migrated.
- After data is migrated from one array to another, no physical changes are required because the compute system still points to the same port on the virtualization appliance.
- However, the mapping on the virtualization appliance should be changed to point to the new location. These changes can be performed online with no impact to end the user data access.
- Deploying block-level storage virtualization in heterogeneous arrays environment facilitates an Information Lifecycle Management (ILM) strategy, enabling significant cost and resource optimization. Low-value data can be migrated from higher performance to appropriate performance arrays or disks.

3.3.2.2.2 File-Level Storage Virtualization

- File-level storage virtualization provides an abstraction in the NAS environment and eliminates dependencies between the file and its physical location.
- Before file-level virtualization, each client knows the exact location of its file-level resources.

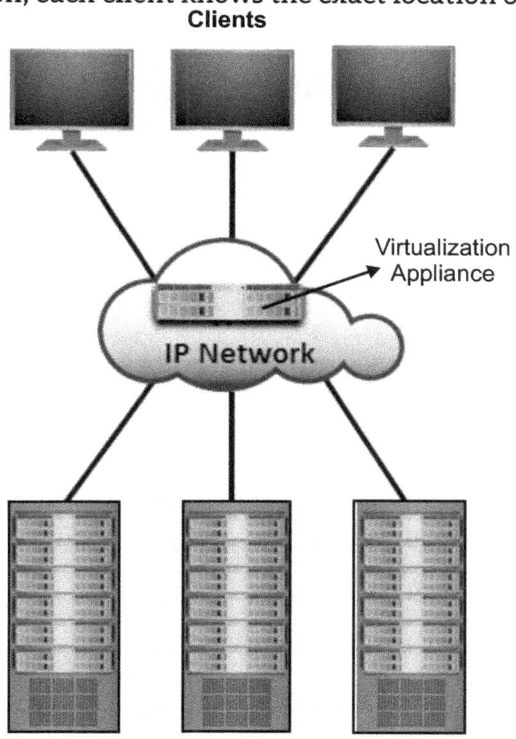

Fig. 3.10 : Multi-vendor NAS Systems

- In a data center, migrating data from a NAS to another NAS may be required for technology refresh, performance requirements, and non-availability of additional storage capacity.
- However, it is not easy to move files across this environment, and this requires downtime for NAS systems. Moreover, clients need to be reconfigured with the new path. This makes it difficult for storage administrators to improve storage efficiency, while maintaining the required service level.
- File-level virtualization simplifies file mobility. File virtualization appliance at the network creates a logical pool of storage and enables users to use a logical path, rather than a physical path to access files.

- File virtualization facilitates the movement of files between the NAS systems without any downtime i.e., clients can access their files non-disruptively while the files being migrated. Global namespace is used to map the logical path of a file to the physical path names.
- Namespace provides an abstraction layer, enabling clients to use a logical name that is independent of the actual physical location. Typically, with a standard file system such as NTFS, a namespace is associated with a single machine or file system.
- By bringing multiple file systems under a single namespace, global namespace provides a single view of the directories and files. It also provides administrators a single control point for managing files.

3.3.3 Storage Provisioning

- Storage provisioning is the process of assigning storage resources to hosts based on capacity, availability, and performance requirements.
- Storage provisioning can be performed in two ways namely, Traditional Storage Provisioning or Thick Provisioning and Virtual Storage Provisioning or Thin Provisioning.

3.3.3.1 Traditional Provisioning

- It is also known as Thick Provisioning, Thick provisioning is basically allocating the required amount of storage volumes to the hosts whereas Thin provisioning is dynamically allocating extra virtual storage volumes which can be used by the hosts on demand.
- In Traditional storage provisioning, physical storage drives are logically grouped together on which a required RAID level is applied to form a set, called RAID set. The number of drives in the RAID set and the RAID level determine the availability, capacity, and performance of the RAID set.
- Thick provisioning is basically allocating the required amount of storage volumes to the hosts whereas Thin provisioning is dynamically allocating extra virtual storage volumes which can be used by the hosts on demand.
- Individual drives in the set. Logical units are created from the RAID sets by partitioning the available capacity into smaller units. These units are then assigned to the hosts based on their storage requirements.
- Logical units are spread across all the physical drives that belong to that set. Each logical unit created from the RAID set is assigned a unique ID, called a logical unit number (LUN).
- LUNs hide the organization and composition of the RAID set from the hosts. LUNs created by traditional storage provisioning methods are also referred to as thick LUNs to distinguish them from the LUNs created by virtual provisioning methods.
- When a LUN is configured and assigned to a non-virtualized host, a bus scan is required to identify the LUN. This LUN appears as a raw storage drive to the operating system. To make this drive usable, it is formatted with a file system and then the file system is mounted.
- Whereas in a virtualized environment, the LUN is assigned to the hypervisor, which recognizes it as a raw storage drive. This drive is configured with the hypervisor file system, and then virtual storage drives are created on it.
- MetaLUN is a method to expand LUNs that require additional capacity or performance. A metaLUN can be created by combining two or more LUNs. A metaLUN consists of a base LUN and one or more component LUNs. MetaLUNs can be either concatenated or striped.
- Concatenated expansion simply adds additional capacity to the base LUN. Concatenated expansion is quick but does not provide any performance benefit. Striped expansion restripes the base LUN's data across the base LUN and component LUNs.
- In striped expansion, all LUNs must be of the same capacity and RAID level. Striped expansion provides improved performance due to the increased number of drives being striped.
- All LUNs in both concatenated and striped expansion must reside on the same storage drive type either all SSDs, Fibre Channel, or all ATA.

3.3.3.2 Virtual Provisioning

- Virtual provisioning is a strategy for efficiently managing space in a storage area network (SAN) by allocating physical storage on an "as needed" basis. This strategy is also called thin provisioning.

- Virtual provisioning enables creating and presenting a LUN with more capacity than is physically allocated to it on the storage system. The LUN created using virtual provisioning is called a thin LUN to distinguish it from the traditional LUN.
- Thin LUNs do not require physical storage to be completely allocated to them at the time they are created and presented to a hosts. Physical storage is allocated to the host "on-demand" from a shared pool of physical capacity. A shared pool consists of physical storage drives. Similar to a RAID set, a shared pool supports a single RAID protection level.
- However, unlike a RAID set, a shared pool might contain large numbers of drives. Shared pools can be homogeneous (containing a single drive type) or heterogeneous (containing mixed drive types, such as SSD, FC, SAS, and SATA drives).
- Virtual provisioning enables more efficient allocation of storage to hosts. Virtual provisioning also enables over subscription, where more capacity is presented to the hosts than is actually available on the storage system.
- Both the shared pool and the thin LUN can be expanded non-disruptively as the storage requirements of the hosts grow. Multiple shared pools can be created within a storage system, and a shared pool may be shared by multiple thin LUNs.
- When a storage pool is expanded, the sudden introduction of new empty drives combined with relative full drives cause a data imbalance. This imbalance is resolved by automating a one-time data relocation, referred to as rebalancing.
- Storage pool rebalancing is a technique that provides the ability to automatically relocate extents on physical storage drives over the entire pool when new drives are added to the pool.
- Storage pool rebalancing restripes data across all the drives both existing and new drives in the storage pool. This enables spreading out the data equally on all the physical drives within the storage pool, ensuring that the used capacity of each drive is uniform across the pool. After the storage pool capacity is increased, the capacity of the existing LUNs can be expanded.
- Despite the huge benefits of thin provisioning, over time thin volumes get less and less thin, which is called bloat. Without a way to remove the bloat, the thin volumes use all their possible space, making them like a thick volumes. This is where space reclamation comes to the rescue, by giving us a mechanism to keep thin volumes thin.
- Space reclamation is a technology that recognizes deleted data and can release the extents that host the deleted data back to the free pool on the array, where they can be used for space for other volumes.
- Virtual provisioning is designed to simplify storage administration by allowing storage administrators to meet requests for capacity on-demand.
- Virtual provisioning gives a host, application or file system the illusion that it has more storage than is physically provided. Physical storage is allocated only when the data is written, rather than when the application is initially configured.
- Virtual provisioning can reduce power and cooling costs by cutting down on the amount of idle storage devices in the array. As a result, virtual provisioning has become a part of green computing and green data center initiatives.
- The limitation for virtual provisioning is that it requires administrators to carefully monitor the usage of virtually provisioned resources to ensure that no virtual disks become full, resulting in storage errors for mission critical applications.
- One of the biggest challenges for storage administrators is balancing the storage space required by various applications in their data centers. Administrators typically allocate storage space based on anticipated storage growth.
- They do this to reduce the management overhead and application downtime required to add new storage later on. This generally results in the over-provisioning of storage capacity, which leads to higher costs, increased power, cooling, and floor space requirements, and lower capacity utilization. These challenges are addressed by Virtual Provisioning.
- Virtual Provisioning is the ability to present a logical unit (Thin LUN) to a compute system, with more capacity than what is physically allocated to the LUN on the storage array.

- Physical storage is allocated to the application "on-demand" from a shared pool of physical capacity. This provides more efficient utilization of storage by reducing the amount of allocated, but unused physical storage.

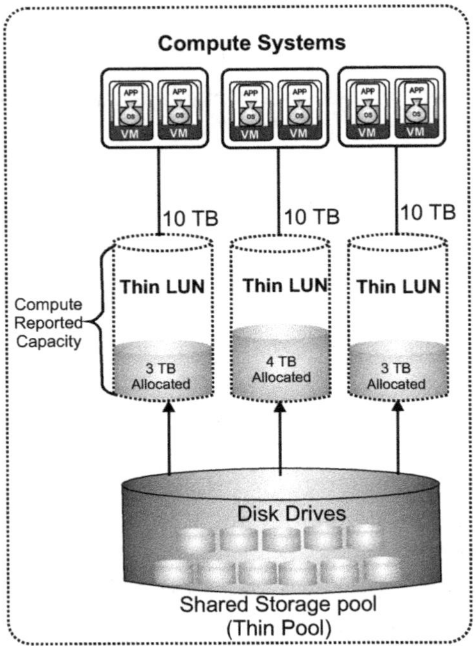

Fig. 3.11

- Fig. 3.12 shows comparison between virtual provisioning with traditional storage provisioning. The example demonstrates the benefit of better capacity utilization.

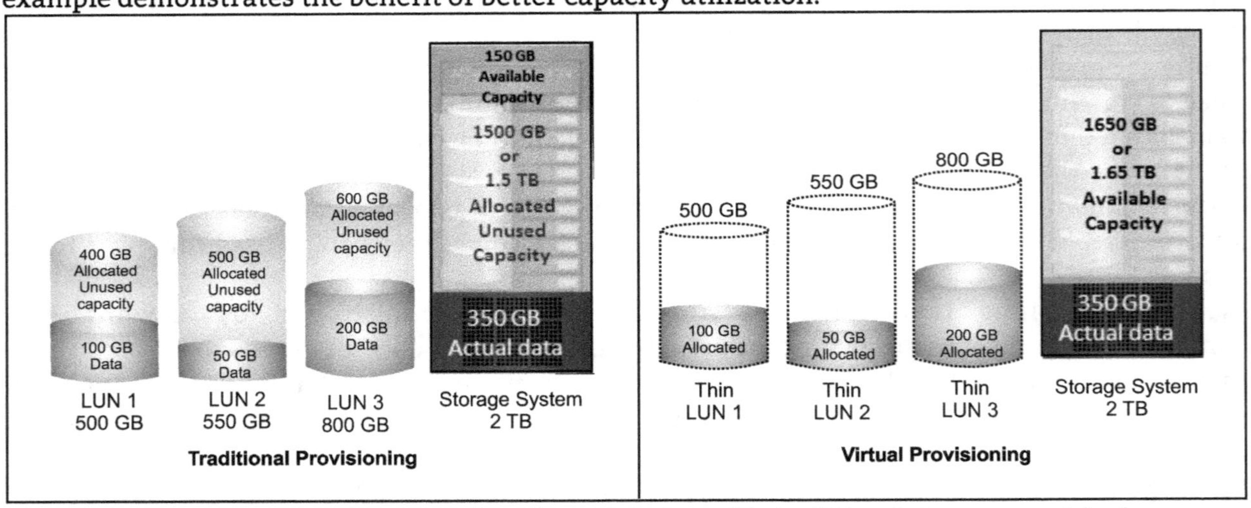

Fig. 3.12: comparison between virtual provisioning with traditional storage provisioning

- Let us assume that three LUNs are created and presented to one or more compute systems using traditional provisioning methods. The total usable capacity of the storage system is 2 TB.
- The size of LUN 1 is 500 GB, of which 100 GB contains data and 400 GB is allocated, but unused.
- The size of LUN 2 is 550 GB, of which 50 GB contains data and 500 GB is allocated, but unused.
- The size of LUN 3 is 800 GB, of which 200 GB contains data and 600 GB is allocated, but unused.
- In total, the storage system contains 350 GB of actual data, 1.5 TB of allocated but unused capacity, and only 150 GB of capacity available for other applications. Now, let us assume that a new application is installed in the data center and requires 400 GB storage capacity.
- The storage system has only 150 GB of available capacity. So, it is not possible to provide 400 GB storage to the new application even though 1.5 TB of unused capacity is available. This shows the under utilization of storage in a traditional storage provisioning environment.
- If we consider the same 2 TB storage system with Virtual Provisioning, the differences are quite dramatic. Although the system administrator creates the same size LUNs, there is no allocated unused capacity.

- In total, the storage system with Virtual Provisioning has 350 GB of actual data and 1.65 TB of capacity available for other applications, versus only 150 GB available in the traditional storage provisioning method.

3.3.3.2.1 Thin LUN

- Thin LUNs are logical devices. Physical storage need not be completely allocated to them at the time of creation. Physical storage is allocated to the Thin LUNs from the Thin pool.
- 'Thin LUN extent' is the minimum amount of physical storage that is consumed at a time by a 'Thin LUN' from a 'Thin pool'. From the operating system's perspective, Thin LUNs appear as traditional LUNs.
- Thin LUNs are best suited for situations where space efficiency is paramount. They are used for applications when the storage space consumption is difficult to predict.

3.3.3.2.2 Thin Pool

- A Thin pool comprises physical drives that provide the actual physical storage used by Thin LUNs. A Thin pool is created by specifying a set of drives and a RAID type for that pool.
- Thin LUNs are then created out of that pool (similar to traditional LUN created on a RAID group). All the Thin LUNs created from a pool share the storage resources of that pool.
- Multiple pools can be created within a storage array. Adding drives to a Thin pool increases the available shared capacity for all the Thin LUNs in the pool.
- Drives can be added to a Thin pool while the pool is used in production. The allocated capacity is reclaimed by the pool when Thin LUNs are destroyed.

3.3.3.2.3 Benefits of Virtual Provisioning

- Virtual provisioning can reduce the time required to repeatedly add storage capacity to the compute systems.
- It improves capacity utilization by reducing the amount of allocated, but unused physical storage and also avoids over-allocation of storage to the compute systems.
- Virtual provisioning reduces storage and operating costs. Storage costs are reduced through increased space efficiency in primary storage because the storage is allocated as required.
- Virtual provisioning eliminates additional investment on high-end primary storage drives due to effective storage utilization.
- Operating costs are reduced considerably because fewer disks consume less power, cooling, and floor space.
- Virtual Provisioning is less disruptive to applications, and so, administrators do not have to continually take applications off-line to increase the storage capacity.
- Capacity utilization gets improved and ease and speedy provisioning of storage.
- It has pool based view.

3.3.2.2.4 Limitations of Virtual Storage Provisioning

- Thin provisioning based storage arrays allows an administrator to over-provision the array. Over-provisioning allows an array to pretend it has more capacity than it does. This allows improved efficiency in capacity utilization.
- However, on the downside, over-provisioning introduces the risk that the array will run out of capacity and not be able to satisfy the storage demands of attached hosts. As a result, hosts will not be able to write to new areas of volumes, which may cause hosts and applications to crash. So a careful planning and foresight is required in view of the over-provisioning.
- Heavily sequential read workloads can suffer poor performance compared to thick volumes.
- There is the potential for a small write performance overhead each time new space is allocated to a thin volume.
- Over-provisioning does not simplify capacity management or storage administration. It makes it harder, and it adds pressure on the storage administrator. To gain the potential benefits, thin provisioning and over-provisioning require some good planning and foresight.

3.3.4 Storage Tiering

- Organizations are experiencing tremendous data growth, which increases their storage requirements. They are also required to meet regulatory requirements.
- The cost of storing data and meeting SLA is a serious concern. Buying more high-end storage is not a cost efficient solution for the growing data storage needs.
- Organizations require solutions that enable storing the right data at the right cost with the right access.
- Storage tiering has emerged as a means to address these challenges. It is an approach to establish a hierarchy of storage types. It helps identify active or inactive data to relocate them to an appropriate storage type.
- This enables in meeting service level requirements at an optimal cost. Each tier has different levels of protection, performance, data access frequency, and other considerations.
- For example, high performance FC drives may be configured as tier 1 storage to keep frequently accessed data to improve performance and low cost SATA drives as tier 2 storage to keep the less frequently accessed data.
- Moving the active data (frequently used data) to Solid-state drive (SSD) or FC improves the application performance. Moving the inactive data (less frequently used) to SATA can free up storage capacity in high performance drives and reduce the cost of storage. This movement of data happens based on defined tiering policies.
- The tiering policy may be based on parameters such as file type, frequency of access, performance, etc. For example, if a policy states "move the files which are not accessed for last 30 days to lower tier", then the files matching this condition are moved to the lower tier.
- Tiered storage is often referred to according to the type of disk drive or medium, by price band, by the architecture, or by its target use (on-line for files, emails, and databases; near-line for reference or backup; off-line for archives).
- The purpose of tiered storage is to configure various types of storage systems and media for different levels of Performance, Availability, Capacity, and Energy or Economics (PACE) capabilities to meet a given set of application service requirements. Other storage media, such as SSDs, magnetic tape, optical, and holographic storage devices are also used in tiered storage.
- Storage tiering means different things to different people. For some it means describing storage or storage systems tied to business, application, or information services delivery functional need.
- There are two types of storage tiering:
  1. **Manual storage tiering:** The manual storage tiering is the traditional method where the storage administrator has to monitor the storage workloads periodically and move the data between the tiers. A traditional storage tiering process is manual, repetitive, and takes few hours to few days to complete.
  2. **Automated storage tiering:** Explain in next section.

3.3.4.1 Automated Storage Tiering

- Automated storage tiering automates the storage tiering process. Data movement between tiers is performed non-disruptively, without affecting business continuity.
- Automated storage tiering eliminates manual tiering when the application workload characteristic changes over time.
- It improves application performance at the same cost or provides the same application performance at a lower cost.
- Automated Storage Tiering (AST) technologies are primarily intended to help data centers benefit from the improved performance of Flash-based media while minimizing cost and complexity. Flash-based devices such as Solid-State Disk (SSD) controller-based Flash can complete 25 to 100 times more random read operations per second than the fastest Hard Disk Drives (HDDs), but that performance comes at a premium of 15 to 20 times higher cost per gigabyte.
- The type of data migration, also referred to as storage tiering, involves moving data within a storage system for tuning or load balancing and capacity optimization(intra system).

- Depending on specific implementation, some inter and intra system data migration may require that applications be paused from updates and be in a read only mode while information is moved, while other solutions enable data to be read and written during the move.
- The granularity of the data movement varies from vendor to vendor, based on their different design philosophies and customer pain points, or challenges looking to be addressed. The data movement functionality can be done via host-based volume managers and file systems, or by vendor or third-party software running on a server or appliance, including via virtualization platforms, in addition to within storage systems.
- Storage systems that support intra system data migration do so with different objectives, including completely automated, manual, or automated with manual override and approvals.
- Some storage systems with intra system tiering promote data from slow storage to faster cache basis when active on an entire LUN, volume, file, or block basis.
- EMC has both intra and inter system movement and migration capabilities as part of their Fully Automated Storage Tiering (FAST) initiative, as domost other storage vendors to varying degrees.
- Automated tiering may help reduce storage cost per capacity, but with the potential risk of impacting quality of service or scalability.
- Data movements between tiers can happen within or between storage arrays in two ways namely, Within a storage array (Intra-array) and Between storage arrays (Inter-array).

3.3.4.2 Building Blocks of Automated Storage Tiering

- There are three major building blocks of automated storage tiering shown in Fig. 3.13.

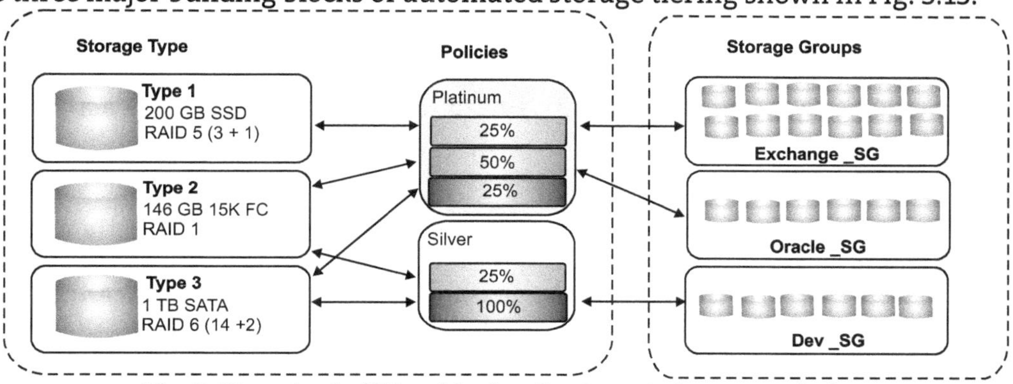

Fig. 3.13: major building blocks of automated storage tiering

1. **Storage Type** is a combination of a drive technology (SSD, FC, or SATA) and a RAID protection type. This slide displays a simple example with three storage types – one for SSD, one for FC, and one for SATA.
2. **Storage Groups** are a logical collection of LUNs that are to be managed together. In this example, three storage groups represent three different business applications. Typically, each application will have its own service level requirements.
3. **Policies** manage data movement across storage types. The data movement is done by specifying a set of tier usage rules. A policy may be applied to one or more previously defined storage groups. In our example, the Platinum policy implies that up to 25% of the Storage Group's capacity is allowed to reside on SSD, up to 50% on Fibre Channel, and up to 25% on SATA. For example, the "Silver" policy implies that all of the Storage Group's capacity (i.e. up to 100% of its capacity) may reside on SATA. Only the Fibre Channel capacity is restricted to 25% of the total capacity allocated to this Storage Group. This gives the flexibility to move the volumes included in these Storage Groups entirely to SATA, if that can produce optimal results.

3.3.4.3 Automated Storage Tiering (Intra Array)

- Automated storage tiering (Intra-array) automates the process of storage tiering within a storage array. It enables efficient use of SSDs and SATA drive technologies and provides performance and cost optimization.
- Automated storage tiering proactively monitors application workload and automatically moves the active data to higher performing SSDs tier, and inactive data to higher capacity, lower performance SATA drives tier.

- The goal is to keep the SSDs busy by storing the most frequently accessed data on them, while moving out less frequently accessed data to SATA drives.
- Data movements executed between tiers can be performed at the Sub-LUN tiering and Cache tiering.

3.3.4.4 Sub-LUN Tiering

- Traditional storage tiering moves an entire LUN from one tier of storage to another shown in Fig. 3.14.

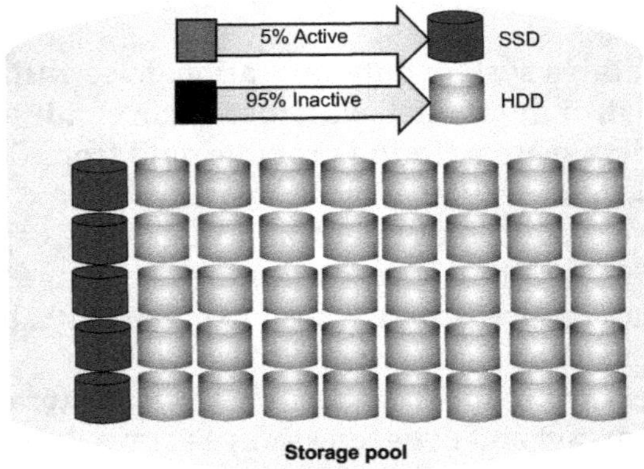

Fig. 3.14: Sub-LUN Tiering

- This movement includes both active and inactive data in that LUN. This method does not give effective cost/performance benefits. In sub-LUN tiering, a LUN is broken down into smaller segments and tiered at that level. Movement of data with much finer granularity (ex., 8MB) greatly enhances the value proposition of automated storage tiering.
- Tiering at the sub-LUN level moves more active data to faster drives and less active data to slower drives effectively

3.3.4.5 Cache Tiering

- A large cache in a storage array improves performance by retaining frequently accessed data for long period of time.
- However, configuring large cache in the storage array involves more cost. An alternate way to increase the size of the cache is by utilizing the existing SSDs on the storage array to extend the size of the cache configured in the array.
- Cache tiering uses SSDs to create a large capacity secondary cache. It enables tiering between DRAM (primary cache) and SSDs (secondary cache) shown in Fig. 3.15.
- It also enables to store large volumes of frequently accessed data on the cache tier. So, most reads are now served directly from cache tiering.
- **Benefits:** Provides excellent performance benefit during peak workload and Non-disruptive and transparent to applications

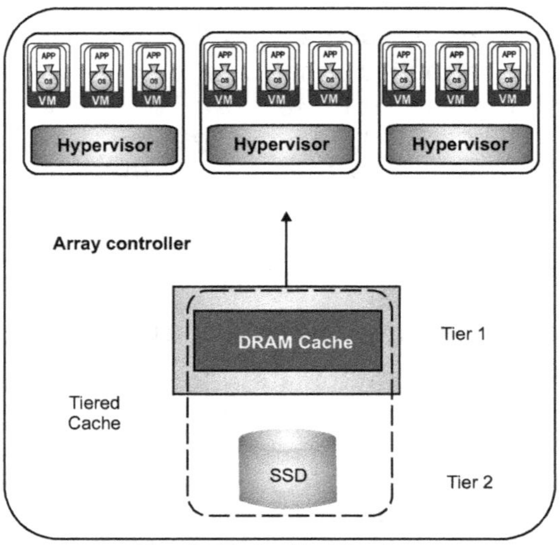

Fig. 3.15: Cache Tiering

3.3.4.6 Inter-Array Storage Tiering

- Inter-array storage tiering automates the identification of active or inactive data to relocate them to different performance/capacity tiers between the arrays.
- Fig. 3.16 shows an example of a two-tiered storage environment.

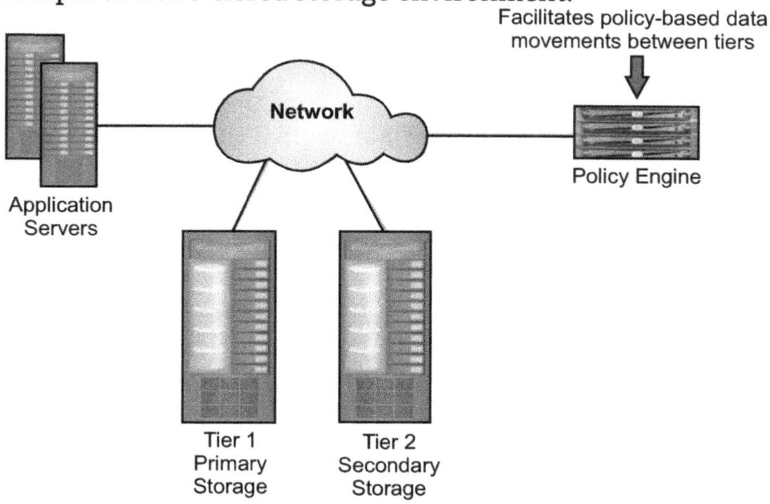

Fig. 3.16: Inter-array storage tiering

- This environment optimizes primary storage for performance and secondary storage for capacity and cost. The policy engine facilitates moving inactive or infrequently accessed data from the primary to secondary storage.
- Some of the prevalent reasons to tier data across arrays is for archival or compliance requirements. As an example, the policy engine may be configured to locate all files in the primary storage that have not been accessed in one month, and archive those files to the secondary storage.
- For each file it archives, the policy engine leaves behind a small space-saving stub file that points to the real data on the secondary storage.
- When a user tries to access the file at its original location on the primary storage, the user is transparently provided with the actual file that the stub points to, from the secondary storage.

3.3.5 Virtual Storage Area Network (VSAN) and Benefits

- When a Logical partition is created within a physical Storage Area Network (SAN), it is called Virtual Storage Area Network (VSAN). Virtualization technology enables division and allocation of entire storage area network into more logical SANs.

3.3.5.1 What is VSAN?

- A Virtual Storage Area Network (VSAN) is a logical partition in a physical storage area network (SAN). VSANs allows traffic to be isolated within specific portions of a storage area network so that if a problem occurs in one logical partition, it can be handled with a minimum of disruption to the rest of the network.
- The use of multiple, isolated VSANs can also makes a storage system easier to configure and scale out. Subscribers can be added or relocated without the need for changing the physical layout.
- A virtual SAN appliance allows unused storage capacity on virtual servers to be pooled and accessed by virtual servers as needed.
- A virtual SAN appliance is most often downloaded as a software program that runs on a Virtual Machine (VM), but some storage hardware vendors are beginning to incorporate virtual SAN appliances into their firmware.
- Depending on the vendor, a virtual SAN appliance might also be called a Software Defined Storage (SDN) appliance or simply a virtual storage appliance.
- A VSAN provides similar services and features as a typical SAN, but because it is virtualized, it allows for the addition and relocation of subscribers without having to change the network's physical layout. It also provides flexible storage capacity that can be increased or decreased over time.

- The virtual SAN or VSAN is the result of software-defined storage. It is implemented in conjunction with virtualization software such as a VMware of Microsoft Hyper-V hypervisor. For those in heavy virtualized server environments, VSANs offer simplified management and far greater scalability.
- The SAN used to be limited by the number of storage arrays that could be hooked together within one physical data center. But virtual SANs with a simple, hypervisor-converged storage design provide a way to set up storage for huge numbers of VMs. This has streamlined storage provisioning and management in virtual server environments.
- Virtual SANs can also be clustered together to provide the enterprise with greater scalability. By creating larger virtual SANs, it becomes possible to pool massive amounts of storage that can be managed centrally with relative ease.
- Further, the latest virtual SANs are moving away from proprietary hardware by using industry-standard server components to reduce storage CapEx and provide a vendor agnostic architecture.

Features of VSAN:

1. It provides converged compute and storage solution to user
2. VSAN utilizes DAS and server attached disks
3. Auto-tiering between SSD and HDD
4. It used intelligent policy driven data placement across the cluster
5. It provides support to vCenter in terms of integrated, instant storage provisioning

Enterprises are using virtual SANs because of:

1. It provides pool of internal disks for virtual server environments.
2. It stretch their storage networks across data centers lying within metropolitan distances.
3. VSAN synchronously replicate data between two geographically separate sites to provides a Recovery Point Objective (RPO) of a few minutes.
4. It set per VM policies and automate provisioning.
5. It create software defined data centers that extend on-premise storage and management services across different public clouds to give a more consistent experience.

3.3.5.2 Benefits of VSAN

1. It provides higher application performance since the local server can access data at full speed and low latency.
2. It uses centralized and consolidated storage.
3. VSAN provides data transfer and vaulting to remote sites.
4. It uses lower infrastructure cost, since there are no networked storage appliances.
5. It provides high scalability (simply put, add more servers and get more storage).
6. Not required boot storms, since OS/app stack images are stored locally.
7. It uses unified management policy (no storage silo versus server silo demarcation problems).
8. It provides high performance storage at up to 50% lower cost.
9. It uses radically simple storage (configure and manage without complex workflows).
10. It is designed for dynamic scalability and high resiliency.
11. Before the development of virtual storage technology, it was difficult for organizations to migrate to another storage platform. Since such migrations entailed application outages, lots of resources and were extremely difficult to coordinate across business units and teams, most organizations kept their storage arrays even when the technology became obsolete and vendors no longer supported them. With the advent of virtualized storage, storage managers could execute disk array swap-outs without affecting other teams and business units. With VSAN facilitating easier and nondisruptive data migration, organizations can now take advantage of the declining cost of storage to migrate to better architectures.
12. VSAN provides, simplicity, angilits and security.

3.3.5.3 Architecture of Virtual Storage Area Network (VSAN)

- A VSAN is a Virtual Storage Area Network. A SAN is a dedicated network that interconnects hosts and storage devices primarily to exchange Small Computer System Interface (SCSI) traffic.
- In SANs, we use the physical links to make these interconnections. A set of protocols runs over the SAN to handle routing, naming, and zoning. We can design multiple SANs with different topologies.

- A SAN island refers to a completely physically isolated switch or group of switches that are used to connect hosts to storage devices.
- The reasons for building SAN islands include to isolate different applications into their own fabric or to raise availability by minimizing the impact of fabric wide disruptive events.
- Fig. 3.17 portrays VSAN topology and a representation of VSANs on an MDS 9700 Director switch by per port allocation.
- Physically separate SAN islands offer a higher degree of security because each physical infrastructure contains a separate set of Cisco Fabric Services and management access. Unfortunately, in practice this situation can become costly and wasteful in terms of fabric ports and resources.

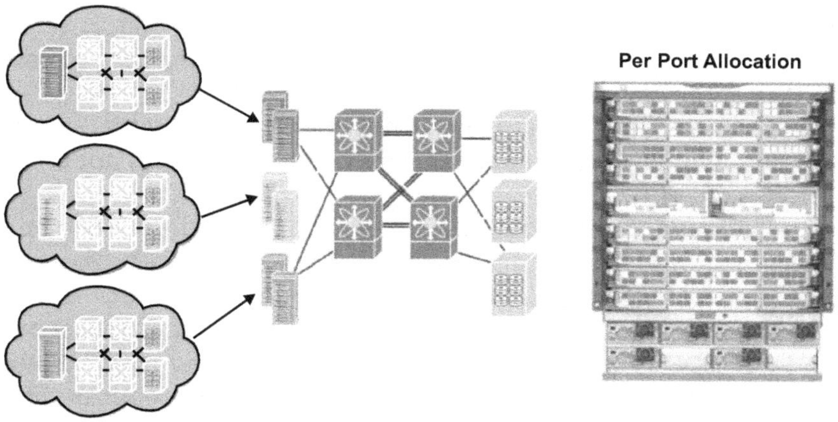

Fig. 3.17: VSAN Arcthitecture

- VSANs increase the efficiency of a SAN fabric by alleviating the need to build multiple physically isolated fabrics to meet organizational or application needs. Instead, fewer less-costly redundant fabrics can be built, each housing multiple applications and still providing island-like isolation.
- Spare ports within the fabric can be quickly and nondisruptively assigned to existing VSANs, providing a clean method of virtually growing application-specific SAN islands.
- VSANs provide not only a hardware based isolation, but also a complete replicated set of Fibre Channel services for each VSAN. Therefore, when a VSAN is created, a completely separate set of Cisco Fabric Services, configuration management capability, and policies are created within the new VSAN.

3.4 CLOUD FILE SYSTEM

- A cloud file system is a file system that creates a hub and spoke method of distributing data.
- The "hub" is the central storage area, typically located at a public cloud provider like Amazon AWS, Microsoft Azure or Google Cloud.
- The "spokes" are the organization's local locations (data centers, branch offices, remote offices). At each spoke a software or hardware appliance is installed and it acts as a cache for that location's most active data.
- A file system in the cloud is a hierarchical storage system that provides shared access to file data. Users can create, delete, modify, read, and write files and can organize them logically in directory trees for intuitive access.

Why cloud file system required?

- When we use resources in a cloud, especially a public cloud, we share the underlying physical resources with others whose intentions and resource needs are totally unknown to us.
- Typically, this sharing is between accounts rather than actual users; each tenant holding an account with a cloud provider might actually be a complex enterprise representing their own large and ever-changing set of end users.
- In a public cloud, such as those at Amazon or Rackspace, tenants are likely to be companies. In a private cloud, tenants might be departments or projects. In all of these cases, though, the important thing is that tenants don't trust each other. They might not even trust the cloud provider very much. In many situations- especially those involving medical or financial information they're not even legally allowed to extend such trust to others.

- This extreme lack of trust implies that a cloud file system must ensure that tenants are isolated from one another to a far greater degree than would be the case using a traditional distributed file system.
- In cloud both GFS and HDFS as 'cloud file systems.' The architecture of cloud file systems is illustrated in Fig. 3.18.
- Large files are broken up into 'chunks' (GFS) or 'blocks' (HDFS), which are themselves large (64MB being typical).
- These chunks are stored on commodity (Linux) servers called Chunk Servers (GFS) or Data Nodes (HDFS); further each chunk is replicated at least three times, both on a different physical rack as well as a different network segment in anticipation of possible failures of these components apart from server failures.
- When a client program ('cloud application') needs to read/write a file, it sends the full path and offset to the Master (GFS) which sends back meta-data for one (in the case of read) or all (in the case of write) of the replicas of the chunk where this data is to be found.
- The client caches such meta-data so that it need not contact the Master each time. Thereafter the client directly reads data from the designated chunk server; this data is not cached since most reads are large and caching would only complicate writes.
- In case of a write, in particular an append, the client sends only the data to be appended to all the chunk servers; when they all acknowledge receiving this data it informs a designated 'primary' chunk server, whose identity it receives (and also caches) from the Master.
- The primary chunk server appends its copy of data into the chunk at an offset of its choice; note that this may be beyond the EOF to account for multiple writers who may be appending to this file simultaneously. The primary then forwards the request to all other replicas which in turn write the data at the same offset if possible or return a failure. In case of a failure the primary rewrites the data at possibly another offset and retries the process.

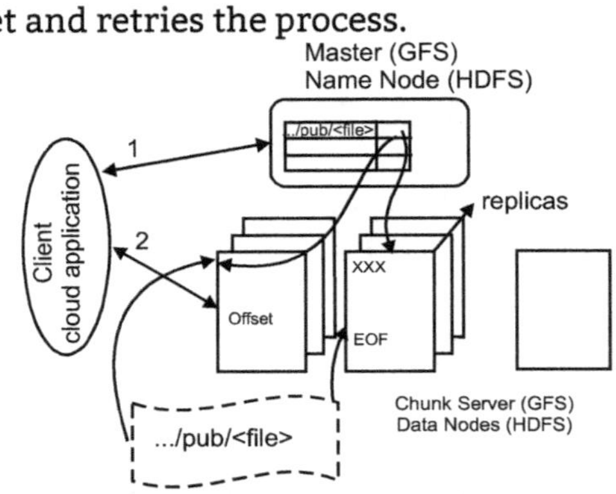

Fig. 3.18: Cloud File System

- The master maintains regular contact with each chunk server through heartbeat messages and in case it detects a failure its metadata is updated to reflect this, and if required assigns a new primary for the chunks being served by a failed chunk server.
- Since clients cache metadata, occasionally they will try to connect to failed chunk servers, in which case they update their metadata from the master and retry.
- In it is shown that this architecture efficiently supports multiple parallel readers and writers. It also supports writing (appending) and reading the same file by parallel sets of writers and readers while maintaining a consistent view, i.e. each reader always sees the same data regardless of the replica it happens to read from.
- Finally, note that computational processes (the 'client' applications above) run on the same set of servers that files are stored on.

3.4.1 Google File System (GFS)

- The Google File System, developed in late 1990s, uses thousands of storage systems built from inexpensive commodity components to provide petabytes of storage to a large user community with diverse needs.
- Thus, it should not be surprising that a main concern of the GFS designers was reliability of a system exposed to hardware failures, system software errors, application errors and, last but not least human errors.

- The system was designed after a careful analysis of the file characteristics and of the access models. Some of the most important aspects of this analysis reflected in the GFS design are:
  1. Scalability and reliability are critical features of the system; they must be considered from the beginning, rather than at later design stages.
  2. The vast majority of files range in size from a few GB to hundreds of TB.
  3. The most common operation is to append to an existing file; random write operations to a file are extremely infrequent. Sequential read operations are the norm.
  4. Users process the data in bulk and are less concerned with the response time.
  5. To simplify the system implementation the consistency model should be relaxed without placing an additional burden on the application developers.
- As a result of this analysis several design decisions were made:
  1. Segment a file in large chunks.
  2. Implement an atomic file append operation allowing multiple applications operating concurrently to append to the same file.
  3. Build the cluster around a high-bandwidth rather than low-latency interconnection network. Separate the flow of control from the data flow; schedule the high-bandwidth data flow by pipelining the data transfer over TCP connections to reduce the response time. Exploit network topology by sending data to the closest node in the network.
  4. Eliminate caching at the client site; caching increases the overhead for maintaining consistency among cashed copies at multiple client sites and it is not likely to improve performance.
  5. Ensure consistency by channeling critical file operations through a master controlling the entire system.
  6. Minimize master's involvement in file access operations to avoid hotspot contention and to ensure scalability.
  7. Support efficient check pointing and fast recovery mechanisms.
  8. Support efficient garbage collection mechanisms.
- GFS files are collections of fixed-size segments called chunks; at the time of file creation each chunk is assigned a unique chunk handle. A chunk consists of 64 KB blocks and each block has a 32bit checksum.
- Chunks are stored on Linux files systems and are replicated on multiple sites; a user may change the number of the replicas, from the standard value of three, to any desired value.
- The chunk size is 64 MB; this choice is motivated by the desire to optimize the performance for large files and to reduce the amount of metadata maintained by the system.
- A large chunk size increases the likelihood that multiple operations will be directed to the same chunk thus, it reduces the number of requests to locate the chunk and, at the same time, it allows an application to maintain a persistent network connection with the server where the chunk is located.
- Space fragmentation occurs infrequently as the chunk of a small file and the last chunk of a large file are only partially filled.

3.4.1.1 Features of Google File System

- The features of Google file system are as follows:
  1. GFS was designed for high fault tolerance.
  2. Master and chunk servers can be restarted in a few seconds and with such a fast recovery capability, the window of time in which data is unavailable can be greatly reduced.
  3. Each chunk is replicated at least three places and can tolerate at least two data crashes for a single chunk of data.
  4. The shadow master handles the failure of the GFS master.
  5. For data integrity, GFS makes checksums on every 64KB block in each chunk.
  6. GFS can achieve the goals of high availability, high performance and implementation.
  7. It demonstrates how to support large scale processing workloads on commodity hardware designed to tolerate frequent component failures optimized for huge files that are mostly appended and read.

3.4.1.2 General Architecture of Google File System

- A GFS cluster consists of a single master and multiple chunk servers and is accessed by multiple clients, as shown in Fig. 3.19.
- Each of these is typically a commodity Linux machine running a user-level server process. It is easy to run both a chunk server and a client on the same machine, as long as machine resources permit and the lower reliability caused by running possibly flaky application code is acceptable.

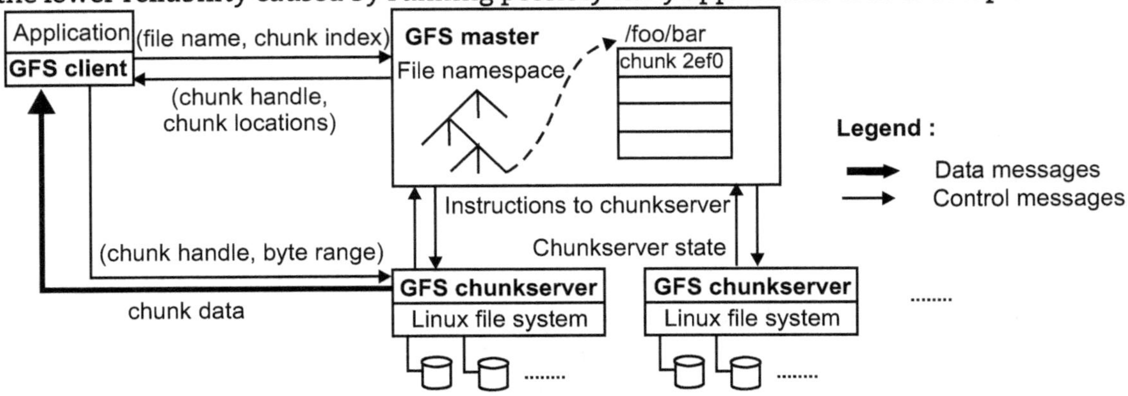

Fig. 3.19: Architecture of Google file system

- Files are divided into fixed size chunks. Each chunk is identified by an immutable and globally unique 64 bit chunk handle assigned by the master at the time of chunk creation.
- Chunk servers store chunks on local disks as Linux files and read or write chunk data specified by a chunk handle and byte range. For reliability, each chunk is replicated on multiple chunk servers. By default, we store three replicas, though users can designate different replication levels for different regions of the file namespace.
- The master maintains all file system metadata. This includes the namespace, access control information, the mapping from files to chunks, and the current locations of chunks.
- It also controls system-wide activities such as chunk lease management, garbage collection of orphaned chunks, and chunk migration between chunk servers. The master periodically communicates with each chunk server in Heart Beat messages to give it instructions and collect its state.
- GFS client code linked into each application implements the file system API and communicates with the master and chunk servers to read or write data on behalf of the application.
- Clients interact with the master for metadata operations, but all data-bearing communication goes directly to the chunk servers. We do not provide the POSIX API and therefore need not hook into the Linux vnode layer.

Advantages of GFS:

1. It reduces clients' need to interact with the master because reads and writes on the same chunk require only one initial request to the master for chunk location information.
2. Since on a large chunk, a client is more likely to perform many operations on a given chunk, it can reduce network overhead by keeping a persistent TCP connection to the chunk server over an extended period of time.
3. It reduces the size of the metadata stored on the master. This allows us to keep the metadata in memory, which in turn brings other advantages.

Disadvantages of GFS:

1. Lazy space allocation avoids wasting space due to internal fragmentation.
2. Even with lazy space allocation, a small file consists of a small number of chunks, perhaps just one. The chunk servers storing those chunks may become hot spots if many clients are accessing the same file. In practice, hot spots have not been a major issue because the applications mostly read large multi-chunk files sequentially. To mitigate it, replication and allowance to read from other clients can be done.

3.4.1.3 Architecture of Google File System Cluster

- The architecture of a GFS cluster is illustrated in Fig. 3.20.
- The master controls a large number of chunk servers; it maintains metadata such as the file names, access control information, the location of all the replicas for every chunk of each file, and the state of individual chunk servers.
- Some of the metadata is stored in persistent storage, e.g., the operation log records the file namespace, as well as the file-to-chunk-mapping. The locations of the chunks are stored only in the control structure of the master's memory and are updated at the system start up, or when a new chunk server joins the cluster. This strategy allows the master to have up-to-date information about the location of the chunks.
- System reliability is a major concern and the operation log maintains a historical record of metadata changes enabling the master to recover in case of a failure. As a result, such changes are atomic and are not made visible to the clients until they have been recorded on multiple replicas on persistent storage.
- To recover from a failure, the master replays the operation log. To minimize the recovery time, the master periodically checkpoints its state and at recovery time it replays only the log records after the last checkpoint.
- Each chunk server is a commodity Linux system. A chunk server receives instructions from the master and responds with status information. For file read or write operations an application sends to the master the file name, the chunk index, and the offset in the file.
- The master responds with the chunk. Then the application communicates directly with the chunk server to carry out the desired file operation.

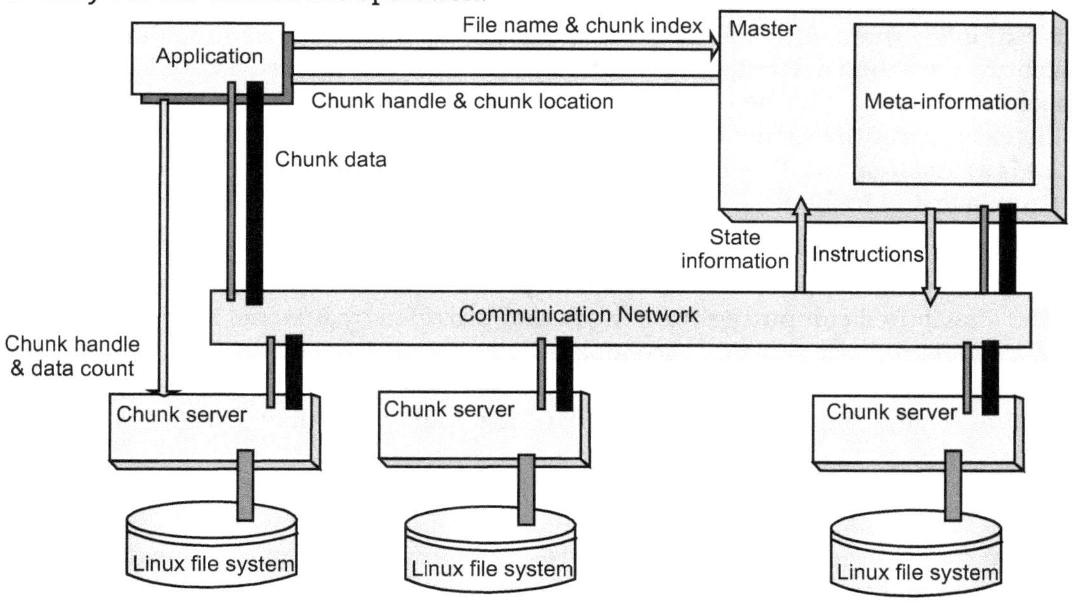

Fig. 3.20: The architecture of a GFS cluster; the master maintains state information about all system components. The master controls a number of chunk servers. A chunk server runs under Linux and uses metadata provided by the master to communicate directly with an application. The data flow is decoupled from the control flow.

- The data and the control paths are shown separately, data paths with thick lines and the control paths with thin lines. Arrows show the flow of control between an application, the master and the chunk servers.
- The consistency model is very effective and scalable. Operations, such as file creation, are atomic and are handled by the master. To ensure scalability, the master has minimal involvement in file mutations and operations such as write or append that occur frequently.
- In such cases the master grants a lease for a particular chunk to one of the chunk servers called the primary. Then, the primary creates a serial order for the updates of that chunk.

- When data for a write straddles the chunk boundary, two operations are carried out, one for each chunk. The steps for a write request illustrate a process that buffers data and decouples the control flow from the data flow for efficiency:
  1. The client contacts the master, which assigns a lease to one of the chunk servers for a particular chunk if no lease for that chunk exists; then the master replies with the ID of the primary as well as secondary chunk servers holding replicas of the chunk. The client caches this information.
  2. The client sends the data to all chunk servers holding replicas of the chunk; each one of the chunk servers stores the data in an internal LRU buffer and then sends an acknowledgment to the client.
  3. The client sends a write request to the primary once it has received the acknowledgments from all chunk servers holding replicas of the chunk. The primary identifies mutations by consecutive sequence numbers.
  4. The primary sends the write requests to all secondaries.
  5. Each secondary applies the mutations in the order of the sequence numbers and then sends an acknowledgment to the primary.
  6. Finally, after receiving the acknowledgments from all secondaries, the primary informs the client.
- The system supports an efficient check pointing procedure based on copy-on-write to construct system snapshots. A lazy garbage collection strategy is used to reclaim the space after a file deletion. In the first step the filename is changed to a hidden name and this operation is time stamped.
- The master periodically scans the namespace and removes the metadata for the files with a hidden name older than a few days; this mechanism gives a window of opportunity to a user who deleted files by mistake to recover the files with little effort.
- Periodically, chunk servers exchange with the master the list of chunks stored on each one of them; the master supplies them with the identity of orphaned chunks whose metadata has been deleted, and such chunks are then deleted, even when control messages are lost, a chunk server will carry out the housecleaning at the next heartbeat exchange with the master. Each chunk server maintains in core the checksums for the locally stored chunks to guarantee data integrity.
- CloudStore is an open-source C++ implementation of GFS that allows client access not only from C++ but also from Java and Python.

3.4.2 Hadoop Distributed File System (HDFS)

- HDFS is the file system which is used in Hadoop based distributed file system. The Hadoop is an open-source distributed computing framework and provided by Apache. Many network stations use it to create systems such as Amazon, Facebook.
- Hadoop File System was developed using distributed file system design. It is run on commodity hardware. Unlike other distributed systems, HDFS is highly faulttolerant and designed using low-cost hardware.
- HDFS holds very large amount of data and provides easier access. To store such huge data, the files are stored across multiple machines.
- These files are stored in redundant fashion to rescue the system from possible data losses in case of failure. HDFS also makes applications available to parallel processing.
- The Hadoop cores are Mapreduce and HDFS. The mapreduce can make the decomposition of tasks and integration of results. The HDFS is a distributed file system and provide the base support for the storage of file in the storage node.
- The MapReduce provides job trackers and task trackers. MapReduce is a programming model Google has used successfully in processing big data sets. A map function extracts some intelligence from raw data and a reduce function aggregates according to some guides the data output by map.
- MapReduce needs a distributed file system and an engine that can distribute, coordinate, monitor and gather the results.
- The HDFS is a master and slaver framework and which contains nodes and name node. The namenode is a center server and manage the namespace in the file system. The data node manage the data stored in it.
- The Hadoop Distributed File System (HDFS) is an open source implementation of the GFS architecture that is also available on the Amazon EC2 cloud platform.

Features of HDFS:

1. It is suitable for the distributed storage and processing.
2. Hadoop provides a command interface to interact with HDFS.
3. The built-in servers of namenode and datanode help users to easily check the status of cluster.
4. Streaming access to file system data.
5. HDFS provides file permissions and authentication.

Goals of HDFS:

1. **Fault Detection and Recovery:** Since HDFS includes a large number of commodity hardware, failure of components is frequent. Therefore HDFS should have mechanisms for quick and automatic fault detection and recovery.
2. **Huge Datasets:** HDFS should have hundreds of nodes per cluster to manage the applications having huge datasets.
3. **Hardware at Data:** A requested task can be done efficiently, when the computation takes place near the data. Especially where huge datasets are involved, it reduces the network traffic and increases the throughput.
4. **Access to Streaming Data:** HDFS is intended more for batch processing versus interactive use, so the emphasis in the design is for high data throughput rates, which accommodate streaming access to data sets.
5. **Portability:** To facilitate adoption, HDFS is designed to be portable across multiple hardware platforms and to be compatible with a variety of underlying operating systems.
6. **Accommodation of Large Data Sets:** HDFS accommodates applications that have data sets typically gigabytes to terabytes in size. HDFS provides high aggregate data bandwidth and can scale to hundreds of nodes in a single cluster.

3.4.2.1 Why should use Hadoop Distributed File System?

- It is distributed across hundreds or even thousands of servers with each node storing a part of the file system. Since the storage is done on commodity hardware, there are more chances of the node failing and, with that, the data can be lost. HDFS gets over that problem by storing the same data in multiple sets.
- HDFS works quite well for data loads that come in a streaming format. So, it is more suited for batch processing applications rather than for interactive use. It is important to note that HDFS works for high throughput rather than low latency.
- HDFS works exclusively well for large datasets, and the standard size of datasets could be anywhere between gigabytes and terabytes. It provides high-aggregate data bandwidth, and it is possible to scale hundreds of nodes in a single cluster. Hence, millions of files are supported in a single instance.
- It is extremely important to stick to data coherency. The standard files that come routinely in the HDFS fold are the read-once and write-many-times files so that the data can remain the same and it can be accessed multiple times without any issues regarding data coherency.
- HDFS works on the assumption that moving of computation is much easier, faster, and cheaper than moving of data of humongous size, which can create network congestion and lead to longer overall turnaround times. HDFS provides the facility to let applications access data at the place where they are located.
- HDFS is highly profitable in the sense that it can easily work on commodity hardware that are of different types without any issue of compatibility. Hence, it is very well suited for taking advantage of cheaply and readily available commodity hardware components.

3.4.2.2 HDFS Architecture

- The Hadoop Distributed File System (HDFS) is a distributed file system optimized to store large files and provides high throughput access to data.
- In HDFS, files are divided into blocks and distributed across the cluster. The blocks are replicated to handle hardware failure, and checksums are added for each block for corruption detection and recovery.

- Fig. 3.21 gives the high-level architecture of HDFS and a brief description of the architectural components follows. From the architectural description, it can be seen that HDFS is acentralized metadata distributed file system.

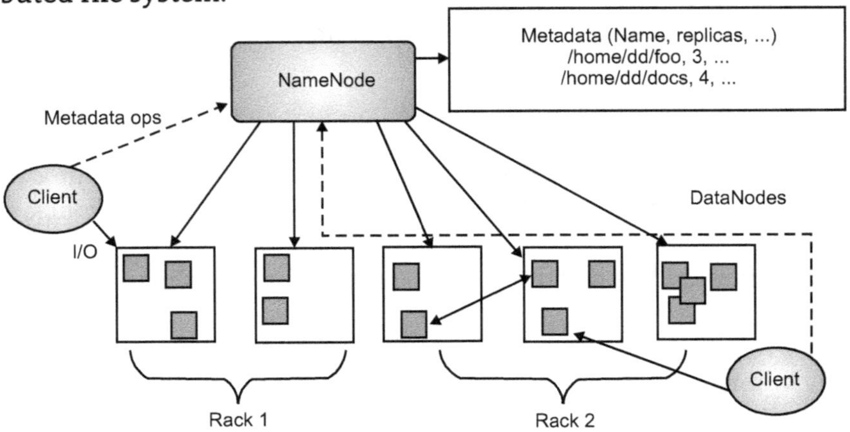

Fig. 3.21: Architecture of HDFS

- Varies components in HDFS architecture are explained below:

1. **NameNode:**
   - The NameNode is the central point of contact for the HDFS. It manages the file system's metadata. The metadata, at a high level, is a list of all the files in the file system, the mapping from each file to the list of blocks the file has. This metadata is persisted on disk.
   - As in other file systems, one of the significant attributes of the metadata that is built at runtime is the mapping from the file blocks to the physical locations of the blocks.
   - The NameNode also controls the read/write accesses to the files from clients.
   - The NameNode keeps track of the nodes in the cluster, the disk space the nodes have, and whether any node is dead. This information is used to schedule block replications for newly created files, and also to maintain a sufficient number of replicas of existing files.
2. **DataNodes:**
   - The DataNodes are the slaves in the HDFS cluster. When a client makes a request to create a file and write data to it, the NameNode assigns certain DataNodes to write the data to.
   - The blocks would be written to the first DataNode in the pipeline, and that DataNode would write the blocks to the next DataNode in the pipeline, and so on until the last DataNode. A write is considered successful when all the replicas have been successfully written. This guarantees data consistency.
   - The DataNodes also serve up blocks when clients request them to do so. They remain in touch with the NameNode, periodically send disk utilization reports, and periodically send block reports. The block reports are used by the NameNode to map theblocks of a file to its locations.
3. **The Secondary NameNode:**
   - The edits in the file system's namespace are stored in an edits log file akin to the transaction log file traditionally seen in the database world. The secondary NameNode periodically polls the NameNode and downloads the file system image file.
   - It also gets the edits log file, and merges the two. The new file system image file is then uploaded to the NameNode. This is done so that the file system image stays close to the in-memory representation of the file system in the NameNode.
   - If the NameNode ever crashes, a new NameNode can be brought up quickly with the image that was last successfully merged.
4. **The HDFS Client:**
   - The client talks to the NameNode first for any file access. For file creations, the NameNode updates its metadata for the newly created file. It also chooses DataNodes that the client should write the file blocks to.
   - For file open requests, the NameNode responds back with the set of locations that the client could read the data blocks from. If there are multiple Data Nodes from where a given block could be read, the client chooses the one that is closest to it. This reduces the amount of data sent over the network.

3.4.2.3 HDFS: (Assumptions)

1. **Hardware Failure:** Hardware malfunction is the norm other than the exception. An HDFS example may comprise of hundreds or thousands of server machines, each saving part of the file system's data. There are large number of components and each component has a non-trivial likelihood of malfunction that some components of HDFS are habitually non-functional. Therefore, detection of obvious errors and fast recovery from them is a centre architectural aim of HDFS.
2. **Streaming Data Access:** Applications running on HDFS need access to their data sets. They are not common applications that generally run on common file systems. HDFS is conceived more for batch processing other than interactive use by users. The focus is on high throughput of data access to other than reduced latency of data access.
3. **Large Data Sets:** Applications running on HDFS contain huge data sets. A usual file in HDFS is gigabytes to terabytes in size. Therefore, HDFS is adjusting to support huge files. It should supply high collective data bandwidth and range to hundreds of nodes in a single cluster that should support tens of millions of files in a single instance.
4. **Simple Coherency Model:** HDFS applications require a write-once-read-many access for files. A file one time conceived, in writing and shut, requires not be changed. This assumption simplifies data coherency matters and endows high throughput data access. A MapReduce application or a world broad web crawler application aligns flawlessly with this model. There is a design approach to support appending-writes to files in the near future.
5. **Moving Computation is Cheaper than Moving Data:** A computation demanded by an application is much more effective if it is performed beside the data it functions on. This is particularly factual when the dimensions of the data set are huge. This minimizes mesh jamming and raises the general throughput of the system.
6. **Portability over Heterogeneous Hardware and Software Platforms:** HDFS has been conceived to be effortlessly portable from one stage to another. This helps prevalent adoption of HDFS as a stage of alternative for a large set of applications.

Practice Questions

1. Write advantages and disadvantages of cloud storage.
2. Explain cloud storage system architecture.
3. Describe a virtualized data center architecture using centralized services.
4. Explain a consolidated virtual data center architecture.
5. Enlist benefits of virtual data center.
6. Explain server virtualization in details.
7. List uses of server virtualization.
8. Enlist benefits of server virtualization.
9. Enlist limitations of server virtualization.
10. Explain different server virtualization techniques.
11. What is network virtualization? Explain different types of network virtualization.
12. Write benefits of network virtualization.
13. Enlist disadvantages of network virtualization.
14. Explain desktop virtualization in details.
15. Enlist advantages of desktop virtualization.
16. Explain different techniques used for desktop virtualization.
17. Write differences between RDS and VDI.
18. Explain benefits of desktop virtualization.
19. Explain application virtualization.
20. Write advantages and limitations of application virtualization.
21. What is storage virtualization? Write down benefits of storage virtualization.

22. Explain storage virtualization at different layers.
23. Explain block-level and file level storage virtualization.
24. What is storage provisioning? Explain virtual storage provisioning.
25. Write benefits and limitations of virtual provisioning.
26. What is storage tiering? Explain automated storage tiering.
27. Discuss automated storage tiering – building blocks.
28. Explain automated storage tiering – intra array.
29. Explain inter-array of automated storage tiering.
30. What is virtual storage area network? Write its benefits.
31. Explain architecture of virtual storage-area network.
32. Explain cloud file system.
33. Write Features of Google File System.
34. Explain Google File System (GFS) architecture.
35. Explain Architecture of Google File System Cluster.
36. What are the goals of HDFS.
37. Explain why should we use Hadoop distributed file system?
38. Explain HDFS architecture.
39. Explain HDFS assumptions.

4... Cloud Monitoring and Management

Chapter Outcomes...

- Describe the given component of federated cloud computing.
- Compare different types of SLA based on the given criteria.
- Describe the given cloud interface standard.
- Explain the steps to use relevant technique for managing the given Cloud resource.

Learning Objectives...

- To understand Service Provider and User in Cloud Computng
- To learn Architecture of Federated Cloud Computing
- To study Concepts in Service Level Architecture (SLA) Management
- To understand Cloud Portal and its Functions
- To learn various Phases in Cloud Service Life Cycle
- To understand Cloud Resource Management

4.0 INTRODUCTION

- Cloud monitoring is the process of evaluating, monitoring, and managing cloud based services, applications, and infrastructure. Companies utilize various application monitoring tools to monitor cloud-based applications.
- There are multiple types of cloud services to monitor. Cloud monitoring is not just about monitoring servers hosted on AWS or Azure. For enterprises, they also put a lot of importance into monitoring cloud based services that they consume.

Benefits of Cloud Monitoring:

1. They already have infrastructure and configurations in place. Installation is quick and easy.
2. Dedicated tools are maintained by the host. That includes hardware.
3. These solutions are built for organizations of various sizes. So if cloud activity increases, the right monitoring tool can scale seamlessly.
4. Subscription based solutions can keep costs low. They do not require startup or infrastructure expenditures, and maintenance costs are spread among multiple users.
5. Because the resources are not part of the organization's servers and workstations, they don't suffer interruptions when local problems disrupt the organization.
6. Many tools can be used on multiple types of devices-desktop computers, tablets, and phones. This allows organizations to monitor apps and services from any location with Internet access.

- Cloud management is the management of cloud computing products and services.
- Public clouds are managed by public cloud service providers, which include the public cloud environment's servers, storage, networking and data center operations. Users may also option to manage their public cloud services with a third-party cloud management tool.

- Users of public cloud services can generally select from three basic cloud provisioning categories:
  1. **User Self-Provisioning:** Customers purchase cloud services directly from the provider, typically through a web form or console interface. The customer pays on a per transaction basis.
  2. **Advanced Provisioning:** Customers contract in advance a predetermined amount of resources, which are prepared in advance of service. The customer pays a flat fee or a monthly fee.
  3. **Dynamic Provisioning:** The provider allocates resources when the customer needs them, then decommissions them when they are no longer needed. The customer is charged on a pay-per-use basis.
- Managing a private cloud requires software tools to help create a virtualized pool of compute resources, provide a self-service portal for end users and handle security, resource allocation, tracking and billing.
- The cloud computing has become most popular due to its advantages. The more number of organizations are migrating to cloud to reduce the complexity of maintain resources. So cloud management becomes most challenging task.
- To reduce the complexity of management and improve the overall performance of cloud, an efficient cloud monitoring tool is required. The cloud monitoring tool helps to improve the overall performance and reduce the management complexity.

4.1 SERVICE PROVIDER AND USER

- Cloud services are also referred to as cloud types in some references. These are served by Cloud providers to their customers following a pre-agreed Service Level Agreement (SLA).
- A cloud provider is a company that delivers cloud computing based services and solutions to businesses and/or individuals. This service organization may provide rented and provider managed virtual hardware, software, infrastructure and other related services.
- Cloud services are becoming increasingly desirable for companies because they offer advantages in terms of cost, scalability and accessibility.
- A Service Level Agreement (SLA) is the bond for performance negotiated between the cloud services provider and the client.
- SLA (Service Level Agreement) is a legal contract signed between the different communicating parties in cloud based system. User stores the highly sensitive data on cloud, only if there is a proper contract signed for security and QoS maintenance assurance.
- Earlier, in cloud computing all Service Level Agreements were negotiated between a user and the service Provider.
- Nowadays, with the initiation of large utility-like cloud computing providers, most Service Level Agreements (SLA) are standardized until a client becomes a large consumer of cloud services.

Service Provider:

- Service provider is a company that offers cloud computing services - typically Infrastructure as a Service (IaaS), Software as a Service (SaaS) or Platform as a Service (PaaS) or etc., to other businesses or individuals user.
- Cloud Service Providers (CSP) are companies that offer network services, infrastructure, or business applications in the cloud.
- The cloud services are hosted in a data center that can be accessed by companies or individuals using network connectivity.
- Major cloud service providers are Cisco, Citrix, Google, IBM (SoftLayer), Oracle, Microsoft (Azure), and SAP, Rackspace, and Verizon (which acquired Terremark).
- Apple and Salesforce are also big players in cloud services, though they are mostly focused on delivering their own applications rather than hosting applications for others.

User:

- Who buy the services from service provider and pay as uses.
- Cloud service provides services to user as per user need.
- Users need is to provide less cost and more reliability and security to data.
- Provided services should be available as on demand.

4.2 AN ARCHITECTURE OF FEDERATED CLOUD COMPUTING

- Cloud Federation refers to the unionization of software, infrastructure and platform services from disparate networks that can be accessed by a client via the internet.
- The federation of cloud resources is facilitated through network gateways that connect public or external clouds, private or internal clouds (owned by a single entity) and/or community clouds (owned by several cooperating entities); creating a hybrid cloud computing environment. It is important to note that federated cloud computing services still rely on the existence of physical data centers.

Cloud Federation Benefits:

- The federation of cloud resources allows clients to optimize enterprise IT service delivery.
- The federation of cloud resources allows a client to choose the best cloud services provider, in terms of flexibility, cost and availability of services, to meet a particular business or technological need within their organization.
- Federation across different cloud resource pools allows applications to run in the most appropriate infrastructure environments.
- The federation of cloud resources also allows an enterprise to distribute workloads around the globe, move data between disparate networks and implement innovative security models for user access to cloud resources.
- Cloud computing enables companies and individuals to lease resources on demand from a virtually unlimited pool. The "pay-as-you-go" billing model applies charges for the actually used resources per unit time. This way, a business can optimize its IT investment and improve availability and scalability.
- Cloud computing promises many offering to cloud computing are as follows:
  1. **Inherently Limited Scalability of Single-Provider Clouds:** Although most infrastructure cloud providers today claim infinite scalability, in reality it is reasonable to assume that even the largest players may start facing scalability problems as cloud computing usage rate increases. In the long term, scalability problems may be expected to worsen as cloud providers serve an increasing number of on-line services, each accessed by massive amounts of global users at all times.
  2. **Lack of Interoperability Among Cloud Providers:** Contemporary cloud technologies have not been designed with interoperability in mind. This results in an inability to scale through business partnerships across clouds providers. In addition, it prevents small and medium cloud infrastructure providers from entering the cloud provisioning market. Overall, this stifles competition and locks consumers to a single vendor.
  3. **No Built-In Business Service Management Support:** Business Service Management (BSM) is a management strategy that allows businesses to align their IT management with their high-level business goals. The key aspect of BSM is Service-Level Agreement (SLA) management. Current cloud computing solutions are not designed to support the BSM practices that are well established in the daily management of the enterprise IT departments. As a result, enterprises looking at transforming their IT operations to cloud-based technologies face a non-incremental and potentially disruptive step.

Functional Requirement of Cloud Federation:

- For implementing an efficient cloud federation, there are certain functional requirements are:
  1. **Matching Cloud Service Provider with Client Requirements**: For guaranteeing the QoS according to the client requirement, SLA's between the cloud service providers must be matched with the client requirements.
  2. **Monitoring:** The usage status and the service quality of every resource need to be monitored.
  3. **Provisioning:** The resource requirements need to be properly determined and also performance degradation needs to be detected so that resources can be reconfigured and the performance of the service is maintained.
  4. **Resource Discovery:** Resources that satisfy the resource requirement of the client need to be searched and discovered by mapping them through SLA matching.

5. **Resource Management:** The configuration of the resources obtained within the same cloud or other cloud systems needs to be managed.
6. **Service Setup:** The necessary environment needs to be setup and necessary data is to be moved or copied, in order to efficiently use the delivered services.
7. **Authenticating Internetworking:** In order to provide seamless services to the customer, such that we are not aware of using a foreign cloud service provider, identity must be federated.
8. **Releasing Resources:** Services need to be monitored and performance has to be measured periodically so that unnecessary resources are released, once the client requirements are met.

Architecture of Cloud Federation:

- The client and the home cloud service provider negotiate the terms of the service level agreement. In a federated cloud, the resource requirements of the client are not limited to resources and services available with the home cloud service provider.
- In order to satisfy the client requirements, the home cloud service provider searches and identifies the appropriate foreign cloud service provider whose SLA matches with that of the client requirement.
- Fig. 4.1 shows the architecture of the Cloud Federation.
- During searching and identification, a mechanism is needed to scrutinize multiple foreign cloud service providers and identify the appropriate foreign cloud service provider(s), which satisfies the client SLA based on their capability and performance respectively.
- The reason behind considering the above two step processing is that, searching and identifying the foreign cloud based on its capability alone does not guarantee that the reliability and performance of the service mentioned in the SLA shall be achieved, even though the resources are available.
- To ensure reliability the cloud service providers are assessed for their performance metrics.

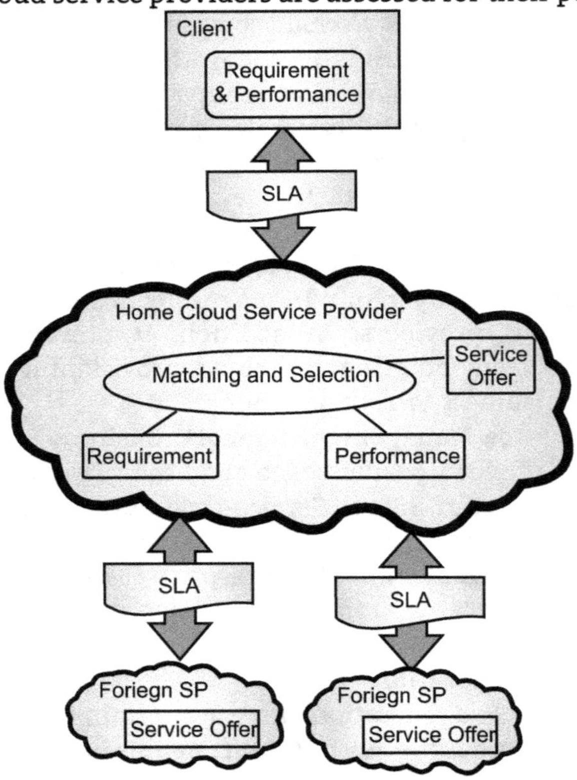

Fig. 4.1: Architecture of Cloud Federation

4.3 SERVICE LEVEL AGREEMENT (SLA) MANAGEMENT

- The purpose of Service Level Agreement (SLA) management is to manage Service Level Agreements (SALs) in a way that customer requirements are reflected and contracts are coordinated and harmonized.
- Briefly, SLA is a negotiated agreement between two parties where one is the customer and the other is the service provider.

- While SLAs have traditionally been a contract between a service provider and an enterprise customer, the expanding value chain for new generation services has made SLAs important for a myriad of partnerships.
- Basic requirement is to balance the value and quality for the customer with the costs of service.
- Service agreement management contributes to an integrated service management approach by achieving the following goals:
  1. Every service provided to a customer is covered by an SLA containing a description of the guaranteed and agreed service level.
  2. To achieve the service level targets, OLAs and UCs are established in support of the SLAs by the supply management process.
- Service Level Agreement Management is responsible for establishing, reviewing and cancellation of Service Level Agreements (SLAs) with customer.
- Service Level Agreements:
  - Are based on service design.
  - Are negotiated and agreed with the customer.
  - Need the supply management process for the supply of services (agreed in supplier contracts)on service levels (SLAs) from external partners (if needed).
  - Need the supply management process for the supply of services (agreed in UCs) on service levels (OLAs) from internal partners (if needed).

Key Components of a Service Level Agreement:

- The Key components of service level agreement are explained below:
  1. **Agreement Overview:** The agreement overview includes details such as the individuals involved, effective/expiry date as well as a general statement on what other details the particular SLA will cover.
  2. **Goals and Objectives:** The next section that should be covered is goals and objectives. Here, the purpose of the agreement, including the ability to obtain a mutual agreement, will be outlined.
  3. **Stakeholders:** This section defines the parties involved in the agreement. For example, an IT service provider and an IT customer.
  4. **Periodic Review:** There should be mention of a periodic review, which will outline the effective/expiry date, as well as the parameters regarding review timelines of a particular SLA.
  5. **Service Agreement:** Perhaps the largest section of a service level agreement comes next and is called the service agreement, which features many key components for which the service provider takes responsibility.

     Service Agreement includes:

     (i) Service scope, which looks at the specific services offered by the agreement, for example, telephone support.

     (ii) Customer requirements, which includes details on payments at agreed upon intervals.

     (iii) Service provider requirements are also a part of the service agreement and cover areas that include clarification of response times in cases of service related incidents.

     (iv) Service assumptions, here protocol on changes to services and the ways in which they are communicated to the stakeholder(s) is discussed.
  6. **Service Management:** The final portion of a service level agreement deals with service management. In this section, both service availability and service requests are covered. A concise SLA will feature information on the availability of telephone support, response time for service requests, as well as options regarding remote assistance.

Service-Level agreement Parameters:

1. **Metrics:** These are definitions of values of service properties that are measured from a service-providing system or computed from other metrics and constants. Metrics are the key instrument to describe exactly what SLA parameters mean by specifying how to measure or compute the parameter values.
2. **Function:** A function specifies how to compute a metric's value from the values of other metrics and constants. Functions are central to describing exactly how SLA parameters are computed from resource metrics.
3. **Measurement Directives:** These specify how to measure a metric.

4.3.1 Types of SLA

- There are two types of SLAs based on application hosting. These are as follows:

1. **Infrastructure SLA:**
   - The infrastructure provider manages and offers guarantees on availability of the infrastructure, namely, server machine, power, network connectivity, and so on. Enterprises manage themselves, their applications that are deployed on these server machines. The machines are leased to the customers and are isolated from machines of other customers.
   - In such dedicated hosting environments, a practical example of service-level guarantees offered by infrastructure provider Key Contractual Elements of an Infrastructural SLA are as follows
     (i) **Hardware Availability:** 99% uptime in a calendar month.
     (ii) **Power Availability:** 99.99% of the time in a calendar month.
     (iii) **Data Center Network Availability:** 99.99% of the time in a calendar month.
     (iv) **Backbone Network Availability:** 99.999% of the time in a calendar month.
     (v) **Service Credit for Unavailability:** Refund of service credit prorated on downtime period.
     (vi) **Outage Notification Guarantee:** Notification of customer within 1 hr of complete downtime.
     (vii) **Internet Latency Guarantee:** When latency is measured at 5-min intervals to an upstream provider, the average doesn't exceed 60 msec.
     (viii) **Packet Loss Guarantee:** Shall not exceed 1% in a calendar month.

- There are multiple challenges for provisioning the infrastructure on demand. These challenges are as follows:
  1. The application is a black box to the MSP (Managed Service Provider) and the MSP has virtually no knowledge about the application runtime characteristics. Therefore, the MSP needs to determine the right amount of computing resources required for different components of an application at various workloads.
  2. The MSP needs to understand the performance bottlenecks and the scalability of the application.
  3. The MSP analyzes the application before it goes on-live. However, subsequent operations/enhancements by the customer's to their applications or auto updates beside others can impact the performance of the applications, thereby making the application SLA at risk.
  4. The risk of capacity planning is with the service provider instead of the customer. If every customer decides to select the highest grade of SLA simultaneously, there may not be a sufficient number of servers for provisioning and meeting the SLA obligations of all the customers.

Application SLA:

- In the application co-location hosting model, the server capacity is available to the applications based solely on their resource demands. Hence, the service providers are flexible in allocating and de-allocating computing resources among the co-located applications.
- Therefore, the service providers are also responsible for ensuring to meet their customer's application SLOs. For example, an enterprise can have the following application SLA with a service provider for one of its application and key contractual elements of an application SLA are as follows:
  - **Service-level Parameter Metric:**
    - Web site response time (For example, max of 3.5 sec per user request).
    - Latency of web server (WS) (For example, max of 0.2 sec per request).
    - Latency of DB (For example, max of 0.5 sec per query).
  - **Function:**
    - Average latency of WS = (latency of web server 1 + latency of web server 2) /2
    - Web Site Response Time = Average Latency of Web Server + Latency of Database
  - **Measurement Directive:**
    - DB latency available via http://mgmtserver/em/latency.
    - WS latency available via http://mgmtserver/ws/instanceno/ latency.
  - **Service-Level Objective:**
    - Service assurance.
    - web site latency, 1 sec when concurrent connection, 1000.

- **Penalty:**
  - 1000 USD for every minute while the SLO was breached.
- Types of SLAs used by businesses today and based on how each one is utilized for specific situations:
  1. **Customer-Based SLA:**
     - This type of agreement is used for individual customers and comprises all relevant services that a client may need, while leveraging only one contract. It contains details regarding the type and quality of service that has been agreed upon.
     - For example, a telecommunication service includes voice calls, messaging and internet services, but that all exists under a single contract.
  2. **Service-Based SLA:**
     - This SLA is a contract that includes one identical type of service for all of its customers. Because the service is limited to one unchanging standard, it is more straightforward and convenient for vendors.
     - For example, using a service-based agreement regarding an IT helpdesk would mean that the same service is valid for all end-users that sign the service-based SLA.
  3. **Multi-Level SLA:**
     - This agreement is customized according to the needs of the end-user company. It allows the user to integrate several conditions into the same system to create a more suitable service. It addresses contracts at the following levels:

       (i) Corporate Level:
       - This SLA does not require frequent updates since its issues are typically unchanging. It includes a comprehensive discussion of all the relevant aspects of the agreement, and is applicable to all customers in the end-user organization.

       (ii) Customer Level:
       - This contract discusses all service issues that are associated with a specific group of customers. However, it does not take into consideration the type of user services.
       - An example of this is when an organization requests that the security level in one of its departments is strengthened. In this situation, the entire company is secured by one security agency but requires that one of its customers in the company is more secure for certain reasons.

       (iii) Service Level:
       - In this agreement, all aspects that are attributed to a particular service with regard to a customer group are included.

4.3.2 Life Cycle of SLA

- Each SLA goes through a sequence of steps starting from identification of terms and conditions, activation and monitoring of the stated terms and conditions, and eventual termination of contract once the hosting relationship ceases to exist.
- Such a sequence of steps is called SLA life cycle and consists of the following five phases as shown in Fig. 4.2.

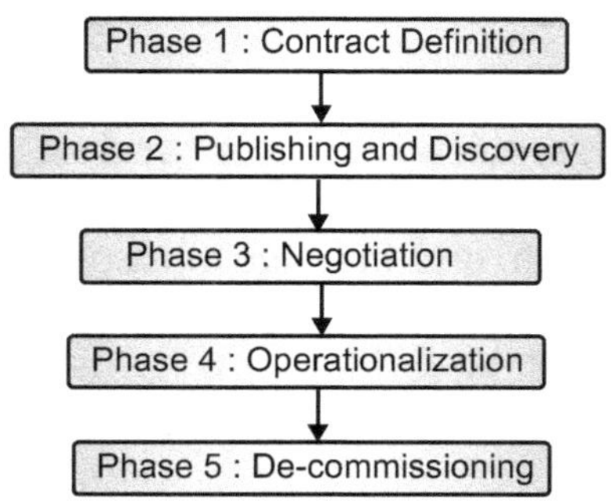

Fig. 4.2

- The phases of SLA in Fig. 4.2 are explained below:
  1. **Contract Definition:**
     - Generally, service providers define a set of service offerings and corresponding SLAs using standard templates.

- These service offerings form a catalog. Individual SLAs for enterprises can be derived by customizing these base SLA templates.

2. **Publication and Discovery:**
   - Service provider advertises these base service offerings through standard publication media, and the customers should be able to locate the service provider by searching the catalog.
   - The customers can search different competitive offerings and shortlist a few that fulfill their requirements for further negotiation.
3. **Negotiation:**
   - Once, the customer has discovered a service provider who can meet their application hosting need, the SLA terms and conditions needs to be mutually agreed upon before signing the agreement for hosting the application.
   - For a standard packaged application which is offered as service, this phase could be automated. For customized applications that are hosted on cloud platforms, this phase is manual.
   - The service provider needs to analyze the application's behavior with respect to scalability and performance before agreeing on the specification of SLA. At the end of this phase, the SLA is mutually agreed by both customer and provider and is eventually signed off.
4. **Operationalization:**
   - SLA operation consists of SLA monitoring, SLA accounting, and SLA enforcement. SLA monitoring involves measuring parameter values and calculating the metrics defined as a part of SLA and determining the deviations.
   - On identifying the deviations, the concerned parties are notified. SLA accounting involves capturing and archiving the SLA adherence for compliance.
   - As part of accounting, the application's actual performance and the performance guaranteed as a part of SLA is reported. Apart from the frequency and the duration of the SLA breach, it should also provide the penalties paid for each SLA violation.
   - SLA enforcement involves taking appropriate action when the runtime monitoring detects a SLA violation. Such actions could be notifying the concerned parties, charging the penalties besides other things.
5. **De-commissioning:**
   - SLA de-commissioning involves termination of all activities performed under a particular SLA when the hosting relationship between the service provider and the service consumer has ended.
   - SLA specifies the terms and conditions of contract termination and specifies situations under which the relationship between a service provider and a service consumer can be considered to be legally ended.

4.4 SERVICE CATALOG, MANAGEMENT AND FUNCTIONAL INFERFACES OF SERVICES

4.4.1 Service Catalog

- Service catalog is a menu based services that lists services, attributes of services, service level commitments, terms and conditions for service provisioning, and prices of services.
- Cloud service providers define, publish, and manage a list of service offerings in a service catalog. A consumer may view the service catalog to know what cloud services are available, their features and price, and consumer specific values of the services.
- Additionally, a service catalog allows a consumer to request or order a service from the catalog in a self-service way.
- The service catalog is the central source of information about the services offered by a provider to a consumer. It is fundamental to the successful transformation of an IT organization or service provider from the traditional method of delivering IT capability to delivering IT as a service.
- It does not offers consumers an unlimited number of service offerings nor does it allow them to arbitrarily choose the resources for a service.

- Rather, it offers customers a limited and standardized set of service offerings that have been pre-defined based on the provider's expertise, technology, skill of personnel, and on market demand.
- By presenting a carefully selected and standardized set of services in its service catalog, a provider can optimize its infrastructure and personnel requirements, and ensure consistent service quality, service provisioning time, and consumer satisfaction.
- Service catalog provides a central source of information on the services delivered by the service provider It is the only part of service portfolio published tocustomers It supports sale and delivery of IT services catalog is useful indeveloping solutions from one or more services
- It is a tool for service portfolio management decisions. It identifies the linkage between service asset, services and business outcomes It also identifies the demand for a service and shows how service provider will fulfill the demand
- Service Catalogue contains information of specific services for which customer are willing to pay. It is a knowledge management tool which allows employees and consultants to route their request for and about services.
- The objectives of the service catalog management process are to:
    1. Manage the information contained in the service catalog
    2. Ensure that the service catalog is accurate and reflects the current details, status, interfaces, and dependencies of all services that are being run, or being prepared to run, in the live environment, according to the defined policies
    3. Ensure that the service catalog is made available to those approved to access it in a manner that supports their effective and efficient use of service catalog information
    4. Ensure that the service catalog supports the evolving needs of all other service management processes for service catalog information, including all interface and dependency information.

Service Catalogue Composition:

- Each service in the catalogue contains the following elements:
    1. A identification label for the service.
    2. Description of services.
    3. Related service request types.
    4. Any supporting or underpinning services.
    5. Service categorization or type that allows it to be grouped with other similar services.
    6. Interfaces and dependencies between all services, and supporting components and configuration items (CIs) within the service catalogue and the CMS.
    7. Clear ownership of and accountability for the service.
    8. Associated costs.
    9. How to request the service and how its delivery is fulfilled.
    10. Escalation points and key contracts.
    11. Service level agreement (SLA) data.

Common Elements of Service Catalog:

- A service catalog includes various elements to define services. A list of common service catalog elements with explanations are provided below:
    1. **Service Category:** Services are defined using a hierarchy within the service catalog that qualifies each service under specific service category such as e-commerce, business intelligence, or database. This provides a clear view to the consumers about the type of service offered.
    2. **Service Name:** An appropriate name that enables consumers to understand what service offering is available.
    3. **Service Description:** The description tells the consumers what the service is, what business process it supports, and what value the service provides to the consumers.
    4. **Features and Options:** This is a list of features including constraints, policies, and rules to characterize a cloud service. It may provide a list of options for selection such as a list of Operating Systems (OSs) for a PaaS type of service. It may also provide technical descriptions of each option such as the software version. Further, it clarifies billing and decommissioning policies, including impact on billing if service instances are decommissioned before the subscription period is completed.

5. **Service and Support Expectations:** This catalog element describes the qualities of a cloud service such as performance and availability. It also describes the technical support parameters associated with a service such as hours of support availability.
6. **Price:** The catalog provides an indication of the price of service, including price lists for different features and options.
7. **Provisioning Timeframe:** This catalog element sets expectations for the time period required for the cloud service provider to deliver a service instance.
8. **Reference to Service-Related Documents:** The service catalog typically includes links to Service Level Agreement (SLA), service specification sheet, and any other relevant documents.

Service Catalogue Aspects:

- Service catalogue has two aspects include:
  1. **Business Service Catalogue:** It contains all the IT services delivered to the customer, together with their relationship to the business units and the business process that rely on the IT services.
  2. **Technical Service Catalogue:**
     - It contains all the IT services delivered to the customer, together with their relationship with supporting services, shared services, components, and CIs necessary to support the provision of the service to the business.
     - Service catalogue management process is responsible for providing information regarding all agreed services to all authorized persons. This process also takes care of creation and maintenance of service catalogue with correct and updated information.
     - Service catalogue manager is the process owner of this process. Any change to service portfolio or service catalogue is subject to change management process.

Service Catalogue Management Activities:

- Here are the key activities included in Service Catalogue Management:
  1. Agreeing and documenting a service definition with all relevant parties.
  2. Interfacing and Service Portfolio Management to agree the contents of the Service Portfolio Management to agree the contents of the Service Portfolio and Service catalogue.
  3. Interfacing with the business and IT Service Continuity Management on the dependencies of business units and their business processes with the supporting IT services contained within the Business Service Catalogue.
  4. Producing and maintaining a Service Catalogue and its contents, in conjunction with service portfolio.
  5. Interfacing with Business Relationship Management and Service Level Management to ensure that the information is aligned to the business and business process.

4.4.2 Cloud Interfaces

- Cloud services are consumed through cloud interfaces, which enable computing activities and administration of rented service instances.
- Based on primary purpose, these interfaces can be categorized into two types namely Management interface and Functional interface.

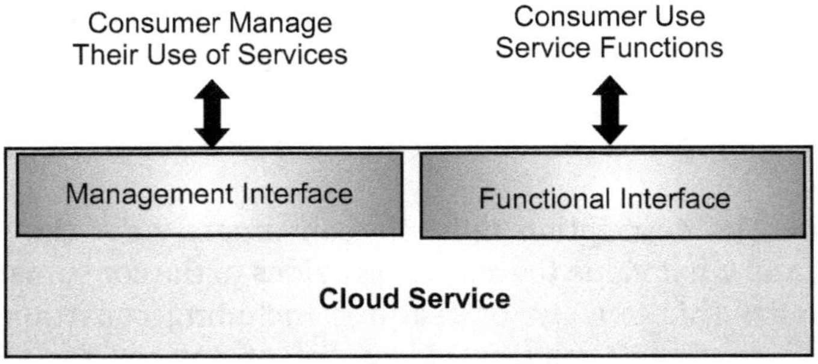

Fig. 4.3: Cloud Interfaces

- Typically, each cloud service presents an interface of each category. However, both types of interface can be combined to create a single interface for a service, or can be further divided to create more interfaces.

4.4.2.1 Management Interface

- It enables a consumer to control his use of a rented service.
- Management interface is a self-service interface that enables a consumer to monitor, modify, start, and stop rented service instances without manual interaction with the service provider. It facilitates consumers to prepare desired functional interface.
- Management functions are different for different service models.
- Based on the service model (IaaS, PaaS, or SaaS), the management interface presents different management functions.
- For IaaS, the management interface enables consumers to manage their use of infrastructure resources.
- For PaaS, the management interface enables managing the use of platform resources. The SaaS management interface enables consumers to manage their use of business applications.
- Table 4.1 shows examples of IaaS, PaaS, and SaaS management interface functions.

Table 4.1: IaaS, PaaS, and SaaS management interface functions

Sr. No.	IaaS Functions	PaaS Functions	SaaS Functions
1.	Start, stop, and configure VMs.	Configure execution/runtime environment for a business application.	Add new users.
2.	Allocate private IP addresses to VMs.	Add, configure, and delete database.	Change user roles and permissions.
3.	Add DNS server, load balancer, and public IP address.	Modify infrastructure resources that are available to applications and database.	Customize application functionality for each user.
4.	Add storage volumes of specific size.	Add authentication service to secure access to applications.	

4.4.2.2 Functional Interface

- It enables a consumer to use service functions. Functional interface presents the functional content of a service instance that enables consumers to perform computing activities.
- Similar to the management interface, the functional content is also presented differently depending on the service model.
- They are as follows:
  1. **IaaS:** The functional interface is the specifics of hardware such as processors, memory, network adapters, and storage volumes typically used by an OS.
  2. **PaaS:** The functional interface may provide an Integrated Development Environment (IDE) that consists of programming interface, libraries, and tools to develop and deploy applications. This could be offered in proprietary or commercially available coding languages. The environment enables consumers to code, compile, and run their applications on the cloud platform. The development environment may also be offered using a Software Development Kit (SDK) that a consumer can download and use for application development. After development, the consumer can upload the application onto the cloud platform.
  3. **SaaS:** The Graphical User Interface (GUI) of a business application offered as a service is an example of functional interface.

Sr. No.	IaaS Content	PaaS Content	SaaS Content
1.	Specifics of hardware, such as processors, memory, network adapters, and storage volumes.	Integrated development environment (IDE) that consists of programming interface, libraries, and tools.	Graphical user interface (GUI) of a business application.
2.		Development environment offered by software development kit (SDK).	

4.5 CLOUD PORTAL AND ITS FUNCTION

- A cloud portal is a web portal that presents service catalog and cloud interfaces, enabling consumers to order and manage cloud services in an on-demand, self-service way.

4.5.1 Cloud Portal

- A cloud portal is also accessed by the cloud administrators to manage cloud infrastructure and the lifecycle of cloud services.
- A cloud portal is an access (usually web-based) point to a cloud, which provides access to the service catalog, and facilitates self-service provisioning and ongoing access to the cloud interfaces.
- A cloud portal is also accessed by the cloud administrators to manage cloud infrastructure and the lifecycle of cloud services. Service lifecycle includes various phases of a service from its initiation to termination.
- Cloud portals are hosted on one or more (for redundancy and workload balancing) compute systems, called portal servers. Cloud portals are created using specialized development tools, called portal software.
- The portal software enables providers to design and publish cloud portals. A user (cloud administrator or consumer) may use the Uniform Resource Locator (URL) of a cloud portal to log on to the portal.

4.5.2 Cloud Portal Functions

- A cloud portal has two key functions namely, Presentation and Interaction with orchestration layer.

1. **Presentation:**
   - It is the organization and display of service information and management functions to the users.
   - A cloud portal commonly presents following elements:
     (i) **Service Catalog:** It lists and describes service offerings along with their attributes, service level, terms and conditions for provisioning, and prices. It also includes action buttons or links that allows a consumer to request or order a service from the catalog.
     (ii) **Management Interface:** It presents information about all services ordered by a consumer including order status such as on order, suspended, and available, consumption of resources by services, notification of events, and billing information. This helps monitoring and management of service instances. The management interface also includes action buttons or links, which enable a consumer to modify, stop, and start rented service instances in a self-service way.
     (iii) **Link to Functional Interface:** Once a service instance is created based on a service request, its consumer is notified in the cloud portal that the service is ready to use and is provided a link to access it. By using the link, a consumer gets access to the functional interface of a service. As described before in cloud interfaces section, the functional interface exposes the functional content of a service instance, enabling a consumer to perform computing operation.
     (iv) **Layout of Management Interface:** Management interface is commonly designed like a digital dashboard. Similar to a car's dashboard, a digital dashboard provides a summary of information pertaining to the cloud services in real-time, and also provides a central point to manage rented service instances. The management interface is presented across one or more portlets or windows. Each portlet exposes a group of management functions and service information. Service information is presented in a tabular and/or graphical view. This helps presenting information clearly and coherently, which improves content readability and simplifies management of rented service instances.
2. **Interaction with Orchestration Layer:**
   - It involves sending service request to the orchestration layer and receiving response back from the orchestration layer.
   - Once a service provisioning or management request is placed in the cloud portal, the portal routes the request to the orchestration layer where appropriate workflows are triggered to fulfill the request.

- The orchestration layer is the automation engine of the cloud infrastructure, which defines standardized workflows for process automation shown in Fig. 4.4.
- The workflows help orchestrating the execution of various system functions across the cloud infrastructure to fulfill the request.

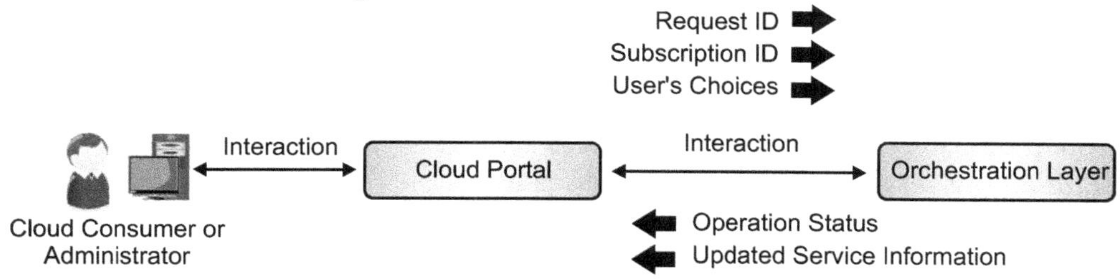

Fig. 4.4: Orchestration Layer Interaction

- A request typically carries a request identifier (ID), user's subscription ID, and user's choices. The request ID is used as a reference during interaction between the portal and the orchestration layer.
- The subscription ID is used to authenticate and authorize an operation. Users submit their choices such as service name, required resources, and location to host a service while ordering or modifying services.
- The cloud portal also receives response back from orchestration layer about service operation status such as completed, failed, and still in progress, and updated service information. Service portal presents this information to the intended users.

4.6 CLOUD SERVICE LIFE CYCLE PHASES

- A cloud service lifecycle describes the life of a cloud service from planning and optimizing the service to align with the business strategy through the design and deployment of the service to its ongoing operation and support.
- From inception to retirement, a cloud service goes through four key phases: service planning, service creation, service operation, and service termination. Each phase includes various activities as shown in Fig. 4.5.

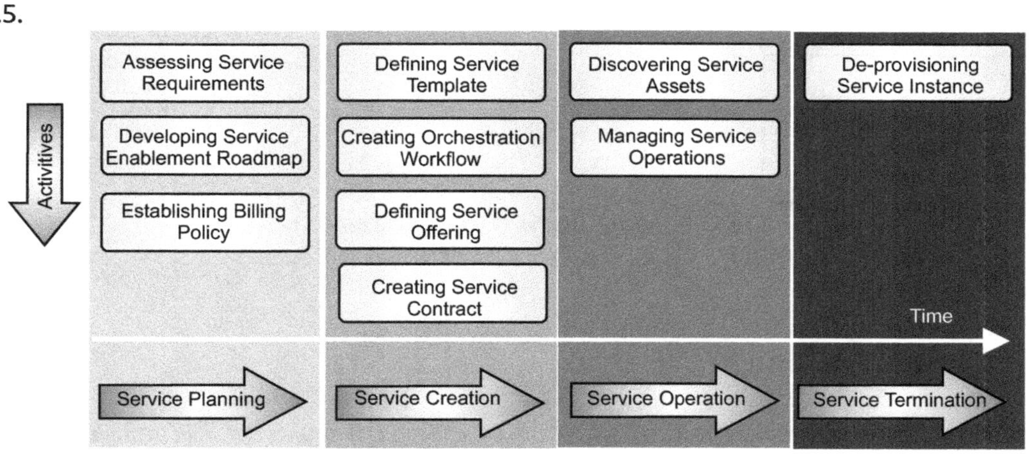

Fig. 4.5: Phases of Cloud Service Lifecycle

- The phases are as follows:

Phase 1: Service Planning

- During service planning, making business case decisions for the cloud service offering portfolio is a key factor. These decisions are made regardless of whether those services will be supported by an internal IT organization (generally referred to as IT as a Service) or provided by the existing or the new service providers who are looking to add to their portfolio of offerings.
- Service planning considers business requirements, market conditions and trends, competitive factors, required service quality and attributes, and the addition of new capabilities when required.
- Common activities during the service planning are listed as follows:
  (i) Assessing service requirements.
  (ii) Developing service enablement roadmap.
  (iii) Establishing billing policy.

Assessing Service Requirements:

- Assessment of service requirements should take into consideration both business requirements and IT capability of provider's organization as inputs shown in Fig. 4.6. These inputs are described below:

  (i) Business requirements: These include both current and future business needs. The business requirements are commonly composed of:

  - **Line Of Business (LOB) requirements** for implementing specific business functionalities. LOB refers to related products and services where a business generates revenue. Some examples of LOB requirements are listed as follows:
    - Enhancing service performance and scalability
    - Improving resource utilization
    - Eliminating unnecessary and redundant services
    - Automating and standardizing processes
    - Reducing management complexity and cost
    - Adhering to regulatory and data privacy needs

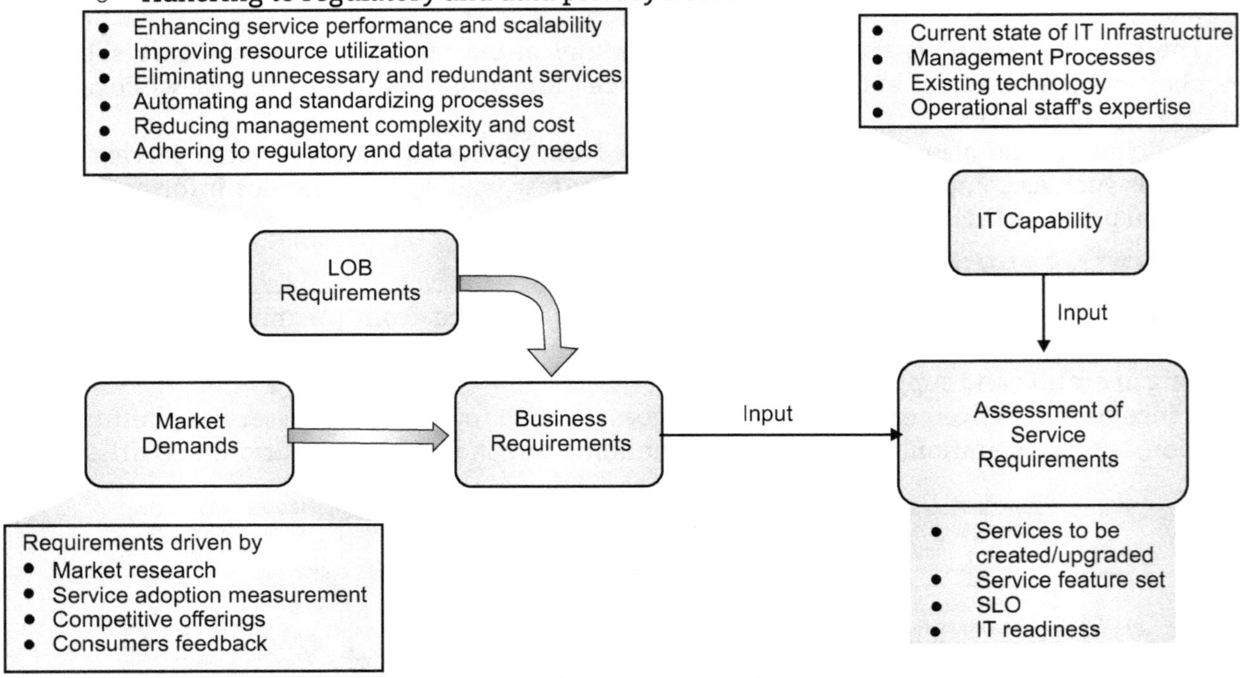

Fig. 4.6: Assessing Service Requirements

  - Market demands driven by various factors as listed as follows:
    - Market research
    - Service adoption measurement
    - Competitive offerings
    - Consumers feedback

  (ii) IT capability: This includes the current state of their IT infrastructure, management processes, technology, and expertise of the IT operational staff. Cloud administrators or architects assess and identify potential service offerings that would support the business requirements.

  (iii) Assessment of Service Requirements: Includes evaluating the services to be created and upgraded, the necessary feature set for each service, and the Service Level Objectives (SLOs) of each service aligned to consumer's needs and market conditions. SLOs are specific measurable characteristics such as availability, throughput, frequency and response time. They provide a measurement of performance of the service provider. SLOs are key elements of a Service Level Agreement (SLA) that describes what service level will be provided, how it will be supported, service location, and the responsibilities of the consumer and the provider. Cloud administrators or architects also assess the IT readiness to provide new or upgraded services. The assessment helps to evaluate the current state of IT capability relative to the capability required to deploy required services and to meet SLOs.

Developing Service Enablement Roadmap:

- A service enablement roadmap guides the strategic direction to fulfill service requirements in the provider's organization. The roadmap is the framework for needed transformation in the IT infrastructure, operations, and management.
- Also, the roadmap provides the framework for necessary cloud solutions, eliminating skill gaps of operational staff, and timeline to implement services.
- The roadmap safeguards against deviation from provider's business goals while fulfilling the service requirements.
- The service roadmap, shown in Fig. 4.7, follows a five-steps service framework. These steps are described below
  1. **Understand:** This step involves understanding the business values that the services can bring and the challenges that need to be overcome. Providers may involve internal or external cloud advisors that help accelerate understanding, promote consensus and alignment among technical and business stakeholders, and set realistic up-front expectations on services to be created or upgraded.
  2. **Plan:** This step involves analyzing the gap between existing IT capability and expected IT capability and planning for IT and business transformation. The planning includes:
     - Technical, organizational, and management process transformation planning
     - Infrastructure planning including sizing of infrastructure components, adopting new cloud solutions, licensing strategy, data protection, security, and policy compliance
     - Management and orchestration planning including deployment or upgrade of orchestrator, management tools, self-service portal, service catalog, SLA/SLO, and metering and reporting system.

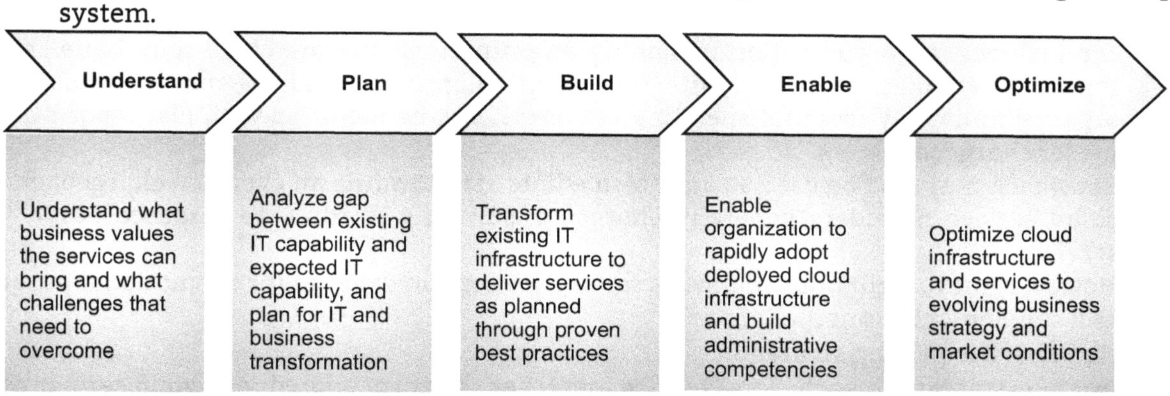

Fig. 4.7: Service Enablement Roadmap

  3. **Build:** This step involves transforming the existing IT infrastructure into a cloud infrastructure that can deliver services as planned through proven best practices. Organizations should deploy a cloud infrastructure that can take maximum advantage of their existing IT infrastructure while also implementing new processes and transitioning from legacy systems. This may require integration with existing components, policies, procedures, and management tools. Additionally, this may also require migration of applications and their workload from existing IT infrastructure to the deployed cloud infrastructure.
  4. **Enable:** This step involves adopting the deployed cloud infrastructure and building administrative competencies rapidly by an organization. This includes educating and transferring knowledge to the IT operation teams on the infrastructure design principles, on the best practices for configuration and administration, and on the ongoing service operation management and support.
  5. **Optimize:** This step involves optimizing cloud infrastructure and services to evolving business strategy and market conditions. This includes modifying orchestration and management operations, improving service performance, availability and scalability, and deploying new or value-added solutions and services.

Establishing Billing Policy:

- Cloud billing is a process of generating bills from the resource usage data for cloud services using predefined billing policies.

- Example of a billing policy could be charging consumers $3 dollar per hour for the usage of 1 CPU with a discount of 25 percent for CPU-hour greater than 30 hours. Usage data for cloud services needs to be collected by a billing system that generates bill for each consumer.
- Usage data is commonly collected from control layer that manages the provisioning of resources to the service instances.
- The billing system is responsible for accurate measurement of the number of units of service usage per consumer and reports price for the consumed units. In this way, it enables metering of cloud services, providing transparency for both the provider and the consumer of the utilized service.
- In a private cloud, chargeback and showback are commonly used for billing.
- Chargeback is the ability to measure resource consumption per business unit and charge them back accordingly.
- Showback is reporting, but not applying the charge to the business units. For showback, the business units are shown the charges usually for business accounting purposes. In either case, accurate measurement and reporting of resource usage are essential from both consumer and provider perspectives.

Factors are Considerations for Billing Policy:

- Following factors are to be taken into consideration for establishing a billing policy. They are as follows:
  1. **Provider's business goals:**
     - Service providers make billing decisions based on their business goals, such as making a profit, justifying new capital spending, influencing consumption behaviors by the business units, making IT more service aware, cost conscious and accountable, and comparing IT costs with the charges of the public service provider.
     - For instance, an organization managing an on-premise private cloud may issue showback reports to its business units, with the intent to optimize their IT spending habits. Other organizations may feel that spending habits will not be modified with just reports and may prefer chargeback.
     - Showback may also be used as an intermediate step towards an eventual chargeback. Public cloud service providers generally charge consumers according to resource usage for the service.
     - However, they might opt to deliver a service without any charge for promotional purposes or as a supplement to another service.
  2. **Service-specific pricing strategy:**
     - Pricing strategy for each cloud service identifies the costs related to a cloud service over the life of a service and plans for recovery of the cost, profit, meeting organization's Return-On-Investment (ROI) and reinvestment goals, and adjustments driven by competitive externally-provided services.
     - Once all costs are evaluated, providers should determine an appropriate chargeable unit for the service, such as duration of use, amount of bandwidth, or amount of storage capacity.
     - Ideally the chargeable unit is readily associated with the business value, the consumer perceives or receives from the service.
     - The provider determines the price per unit of usage to meet its business goals. The provider may add some margin amount over per-unit cost to define price per unit usage, or may establish price at the true cost of service, depending on the provider's business goals.

Phase 2: Service Creation:

- During service creation, providers aim at defining services in the service catalog and creating workflows for service orchestration.
- This allows a consumer to self-provision cloud services from the cloud portal and the orchestrator to automate process execution according to the workflows.
- Common activities during service creation are Defining service template, creating orchestration workflow, defining service offering and creating service contract.

Defining Service Template

- A service template is a collection of interrelated hardware and/or software components that constitute a service and work together upon deployment of a service.

- The collection of service components and their relationships are based on decisions that emanate from cloud service planning.
- On receiving a service provisioning request, hardware and/or software resources are allocated, configured, and integrated as per the service template to create an instance of the service.
- In this way, a service template provides a standard to repeatedly generate predictable instances of a specific service.
- Service templates are generally defined in the service catalog, which is presented in the cloud portal. The portal software provides standard interface to make entries about service templates along with other information described later in the 'service offering' section.
- From consumer's perspective, the service template specifics helps them to understand the hardware configuration, software, and protection mechanism for a service. From a provider's perspective, it provides guidelines to create workflows for service orchestration.
- A service template specifics may include fixed and/or customizable options. Customizable options could include a choice of OS, the approach for data protection, or a mix of storage and compute parameters. The options for service components are based on service requirements assessed during service planning.
- Service template specifics commonly covers the following entities:
  - **Service Structure:** It specifies the structure of a service that includes service components and their relationships. While planning for a service structure, an architect needs to map service requirements into component requirements of a service. For example, a SaaS type service requirement may be mapped into running a specific business application on a guest OS, deploying a database to support the application, and hosting the database and the application on VMs.
  - **Service Attribute:** It specifies configurations of service components. For example, attributes of a VM provided as a service component are: number of processors of specific processing power, memory size, and number of attached disks of specific size.
  - **Service Operation:** It specifies the management operations such as add, modify, start, and stop that can be performed on management interface of a service.

Creating Orchestration Workflow:

- Once a service template is defined, the workflows for service orchestration are created in the orchestrator based on the template specification. These workflows enable automated allocation, configuration, and integration of hardware and/or software resources for a service as per the service template.
- An orchestration workflow consists of a series of inter-related API functions to fulfill service requests invoked at the cloud portal. The cloud portal passes on the requests to the orchestrator, which interacts with appropriate cloud infrastructure components according to the workflow.
- This enables automated arrangement, coordination, and management of the service provisioning and management functions.
- Service providers want to automate these functions as much as possible. Reaching the point where a service is automated from creation to termination is one of the ultimate goals of providers.

Defining Service Offering

- Service offerings are available to consumers in the form of a service catalog presented in the cloud portal. They are defined in the service catalog using portal software that provides an administration interface to define service offerings.
- A service offering is the result of combining service template specifics with constraints, policies, rules, pricing, and SLA.
  - **Constraints** may restrict access to a service to certain individuals or groups.
  - **Policies** are principles for treating service components on a per-service or per-consumer basis. Policies could affect network and security areas, such as bandwidth quotas, firewall configuration, Quality of Service (QoS), and network traffic inspection for intrusion detection and prevention.
  - **Rules** are guidelines for deploying or scaling service instances, limiting resource allocation to the service instances, and subscription period. Rules can also be imposed for compliance requirements, disposition of consumer data upon service termination, and in a situation when a consumer requests resources beyond a specified or authorized limit.

- **Price**, if applicable, specifies the ongoing service charge, charges associated with the initial data transfer to the provider's premises, and any additional fees for support and recovery of data. These charges are determined during the service planning phase.
- **SLA** is typically a formalized contract document between a consumer and a service provider. SLA includes service level targets and responsibilities of the provider and the consumer. Service level targets are commonly the committed levels of availability, serviceability, and performance of a service. Consumer's responsibilities may include adhering to limits on resource usage and restrictions on the type of data that can be stored, or having a valid license for any software deployed on the provider's IT infrastructure. Provider's responsibilities may include ensuring privacy of the consumer's data and preventing consumer's data loss. The responsibilities of the two parties depend on the cloud service model being offered. For example, while the service provider bears most of the responsibility for a SaaS offering, the consumer of an IaaS offering is responsible for sensitive data that might reside on cloud infrastructure. If third-party providers partner with a cloud service provider, their service levels also affect the consumers. In this situation, service levels provided by the third-party providers should be factored into the SLA. Additionally, because most cloud services are available through Internet connection, service levels experienced by consumers may depend on the service levels provided by their independent Internet Service Providers (ISPs).

Creating Service Contract:

- The service contract is an agreement between the cloud service provider and the cloud service consumer stating the terms of service usage.
- The two parties enter into a contract describing agreements on pricing, SLAs, termination of service, and any specific configuration options.
- The service contract specifics is commonly presented on the cloud portal, which describes the terms and conditions for using a service.
- When a consumer wants to order or instantiate a service, the service contract must be established with the provider. By agreeing to the terms and conditions, a contract is established for the requested service.

Phase 3: Service Operation:

- The service operation phase of the cloud service lifecycle comprises ongoing management operations by cloud administrators to maintain cloud infrastructure and deployed services, meeting or exceeding SLA commitments.
- Common activities in this phase are Discovering Service Assets and Managing Service Operations.

Discovering Service Assets:

- Service assets include cloud infrastructure resources that contribute to the provisioning of a service. Examples of service assets are: compute, storage, network, security components (both physical and virtual), and business applications.
- Discovery of service assets provides cloud administrators with visibility into each asset, including physical to virtual dependencies and information about its configuration, connectivity, functions, performance, capacity, availability, and utilization.
- Discovery helps monitoring cloud infrastructure resources. In order to manage service operations, a cloud administrator needs to monitor infrastructure resources. For that, an administrator must know what resources are deployed and be able to monitor these resources. Discovery activity automatically collects information on various service assets, enabling administrators to monitor these assets centrally.
- Depending on the size of the cloud environment, discovery may involve gathering information about a large number of service assets and mapping many physical-to-virtual relationships.
- Discovery is performed using specialized tool. A discovery tool is either bundled with a management software as a feature or an independent software that passes discovered information to a management software.
- The discovery tool commonly interacts and collects necessary data from service assets through native APIs defined for these assets. An alternative discovery method is to install software agents on the service assets to expose information to the discovery tool.

- Discovery is typically scheduled by setting an interval for its periodic occurrence. Depending on provider's business requirements, a cloud administrator can change the frequency of discovery.
- Discovery may also be initiated by a cloud administrator or be triggered by an orchestrator when a change occurs in the cloud infrastructure. By default, a discovery tool discovers all service assets automatically.
- However, an administrator may manually add service assets for discovery. Manual addition is useful if administrators want to monitor only a subset of service assets.

Managing Service Operations:

- Service operation management involves all service-related operations across cloud infrastructure. It has a service-based focus, which means that all operations performed on a cloud infrastructure have a goal to meet service requirements and SLA.
- Service operation management aims at ensuring and restoring service levels while continuously optimizing management operations to increase efficiency and reduce cost.
- It ensures that management operations are efficient by using as few resources as needed without deviating from SLA commitments.
- The key management operations include the following:
  - **Monitoring and Reporting:** Monitoring is a continuous operation for tracking the status of services and service assets. The parameters that are monitored include configuration, security, performance, availability, and capacity. Reports are formulated from data gathered through monitoring. Reporting helps to organize and present current status, historical trends, operation log, and bills associated with services.
  - **Provisioning:** It configures and allocates the hardware, software, and other resources required to deliver services. Provisioning primarily involves resources management to meet capacity, availability, performance, and security requirements of cloud services.
  - **Troubleshooting:** It resolves service-related issues in the cloud infrastructure so that services can maintain their operational state.
- Increasing the degree of automation in service operation management improves IT productivity, eliminates manual errors, and optimizes resource utilization. Automating service operations as much as possible using cloud portal and orchestrator is a key goal for each service provider.
- For this, a cloud portal should provide administrative view of the cloud infrastructure and allow a cloud administrator to perform management operations through portal functions. Also, necessary management workflows need to be created at the orchestrator to automate these management operations.
- The management workflows programmatically bind and sequences several system-level management functions, which otherwise are performed by an administrator.
- Once, an administrator initiates a portal-level management operation, a predefined workflow coordinates the execution of related system functions to accomplish that management operation.
- Some management software have ability to track, correlate, and analyze system events and status. Based on their criticality, these management software may automatically take appropriate actions or trigger predefined workflows to orchestrate necessary operations.
- Examples of service operations that are commonly automated using management software are:
  - Expanding a resource pool.
  - Reclaiming overprovisioned or stranded capacity.
  - Scaling a service based on workload and utilization.
  - Validating an operation against configuration policies.
  - Identifying impending service issues and remediate them.

Phase 4: Service Termination

- The final phase of the cloud service lifecycle is service termination. Service termination denotes termination of a service by a provider or termination of service contract between a provider and a consumer. Upon termination, a service instance previously assigned to a consumer is removed.
- When a given service instance is removed, resources allocated to the service instance should be automatically returned to the resource pool for redeployment to other service instances.

- Service termination must be achieved without impacting other service instances and without compromising consumer's data, resources, and confidential information.
- A cloud service may be terminated in the two scenarios namely, Natural termination by contract agreement and Initiated termination by a provider or a consumer.

Reasons for Initiated Service Termination:

- Some common reasons for a provider to terminate service are as follows:
  - Business circumstances where the provider can no longer offer the service.
  - A disaster in provider's premises.
  - Significant consumer violation of contract terms
  - New hardware deployment or software upgrade by the provider. Typically, service providers do not want to maintain multiple versions of software and varying hardware platforms. Instead, they may offer options such as migration to new hardware and software, or a refund, or limited use of end-of-life service.
- Some common reasons for a consumer to terminate service are as follows:
  - Business circumstances where the consumer no longer needs the service.
  - The service requirement was planned to be temporary.
  - Service performance or support is not acceptable to a consumer.
- Typically, termination by the consumer is easily and quickly performed through the cloud portal. However, termination requests may be processed through a validation system and only those tenant administrators or users who have the required authority are allowed to terminate a service. Also, there could be billing implications, for example, pro-rated charges and early termination fee, depending on the terms in the service contract.

Common Activities in Service Termination

- The service termination phase usually consists the given activities:
  - **De-Provisioning Service Instance:** De-provisioning halts a service instance and releases resources from it. Automating the termination process shortens de-provisioning time. The de-provisioning activity ensures that no resources are orphaned and thus unavailable for use by other service instances.
  - **Handling Consumer's Data as Per Contract Terms:** The service contract typically includes a termination agreement that defines the terms and conditions for terminating a service. The termination agreement describes how to deal with consumer data, if a service is terminated or if the provider goes out of business. Based on the agreement, providers may return data to the consumers upon termination within a specified time duration. Some provider may also offer a data shredding service to permanently destroy all traces-including backup or secondary copies—of consumer's data from provider's premises. Such a disposal of consumer's data should be verifiable by the consumer in order to ensure that the data is not misused for malicious purpose or unintentionally.
  - **Providing Final Billing Report:** The final billing report includes service charges till the time of service termination. Depending on the terms in the service contract, a premature termination may incur early termination fees and non-refund of any subscription fee intended to cover the unused portion of the subscription period.
  - **Asking for Feedback to Improve Service:** Seeking feedback provides opportunity to understand the consumer's viewpoint about services, which can help a provider to further develop. Consumer's feedbacks are considered as a key input while planning for a new service or making decision to upgrade a service.

4.7 CLOUD RESOURCE MANAGEMENT

- A cloud is a complex system with a very large number of shared resources subject to unpredictable requests and affected by external events it cannot control.
- Cloud resource management requires complex policies and decisions for multi-objective optimization.
- Cloud computing provides a platform where resources are rented as a service to its cloud users / cloud consumers through Internet. So we can say that Cloud delivers computing as a utility as it is available to the cloud consumers on demand.

- In cloud computing, a resource can be any service which can be consumed by cloud users / cloud consumers.
- The goal of resource management in cloud computing is to provide high availability of resources, sharing of resources, fulfilling time variant servicemodel, providing efficiency and reliability on resource uses.
- From the cloud computing perspective, resource management is a process which effectively and efficiently manages all resources as well as providing QoS guarantees to cloud consumers.
- There are two ways to manage the Cloud Resource namely, Ab-initio Resource Assignment and Periodic Resource Optimization.

4.7.1 Ab-initio Resource Assignment

- It is initial resource assignment, in a manner that resources are requested by application on behalf of cloud consumers first time.
- Ab-initio resource assignment shown in Fig. 4.8 and its steps are as follows:
  1. **Request Identification:** This is the first and foremost step in Ab-initio Resource Assignment. In this step, various resources will be identified by cloud providers.
  2. **Resource Gathering / Resource Formation**: After identification of resources in step 1, gathering or formation of resources will take place. This step will identify available resources. This step may also prepare custom resources.
  3. **Resource Brokering:** This step is negotiation of resources with cloud consumers to make sure that they are available as per requirement.
  4. **Resource Discovery:** This step will logically group various resources as per the requirements of cloud consumers.
  5. **Resource Selection:** This step is to choose best resources among available resources for requirements provided by cloud consumers.
  6. **Resource Mapping:** This step will map virtual resources with physical resources (like node, link etc) provided by cloud providers.
  7. **Resource Allocation:** This step will allocate / distribute resources to the cloud consumers. It's main goal is to satisfy cloud consumers' need and revenue generation for cloud providers.

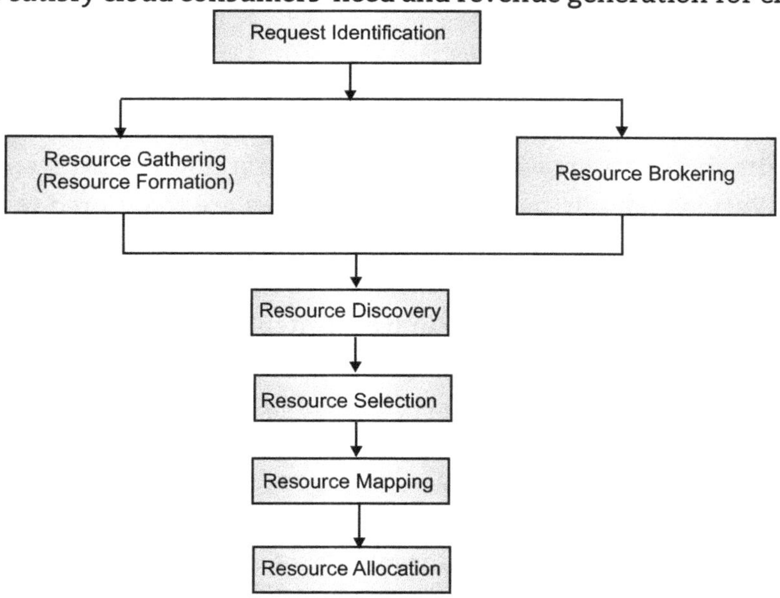

Fig. 4.8: Ab-initio Resource Assignment

4.7.2 Periodic Resource Optimization

- As name suggest this is a phase where resource management is done at regular intervals once phase 1 is completed. Here periodic resource optimization is presented as a process for two different categories of resources which are Non-virtualized resources and Virtualized resources.
- The non-virtualized resources are also called as physical resources. For both categories of resources, periodic resource optimization contains similar steps.

- The only difference is that virtualized resources can be assembled together as per the resource requirement and can be disassembled also. So periodic resource optimization for virtualized resources contains two steps more compared to non-virtualized resources which are Resource Bundling and Resource Fragmentation.

1. Non-Virtualized Resources:

- Fig. 4.9 shows non-virtualized resources.

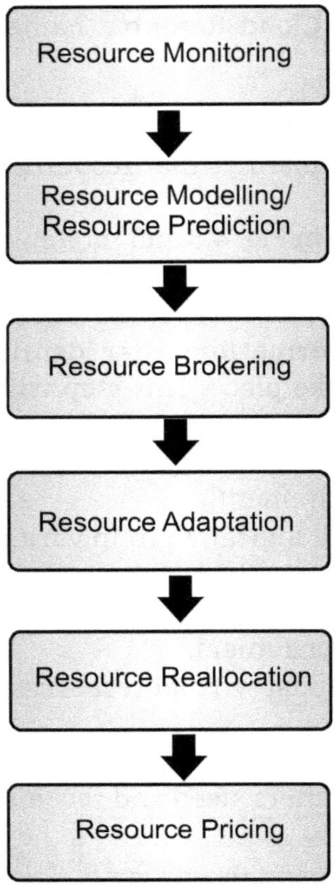

Fig. 4.9: Steps of non-virtualized resource optimization

- Non-virtualized Resources has given steps:
  - **(i) Resource Monitoring:** Resource Monitoring is the first and crucial step in Periodic Resource Optimization. Various non-virtualized cloud resources are monitored to analyze utilization of resources. This step will also monitor availability of free resources for future purpose. The major issue with cloud resource monitoring is to identify and define metrics/parameters for it.
  - **(ii) Resource Modeling / Resource Prediction**: This step will predict the various non-virtualized resources required by cloud consumers applications. This is one of the complex step as cloud resources are not uniform in nature. Due to this non uniformity, it is very difficult to predict resource requirement for peak periods and as well as for non-peak periods.
  - **(iii) Resource Brokering:** This step is negotiation of non-virtualized resources with cloud consumers to make sure that they are available as per requirement.
  - **(iv) Resource Adaptation:** As per the requirements of cloud consumers, non-virtualized cloud resources can be scaled up or scaled down. This step may increase cost from cloud providers perspective.
  - **(v) Resource Reallocation:** This step will reallocate / redistribute resources to the cloud consumers. It's main goal is to satisfy cloud consumers' need and revenue generation for cloud providers.
  - **(vi) Resource Pricing:** It is one of the most important step from cloud providers and cloud consumers perspective. Based on cloud resource usage pricing will be done.

2. Virtualized Resources Optimization:

- Fig. 4.10 shows the steps in virtualized resources optimization.

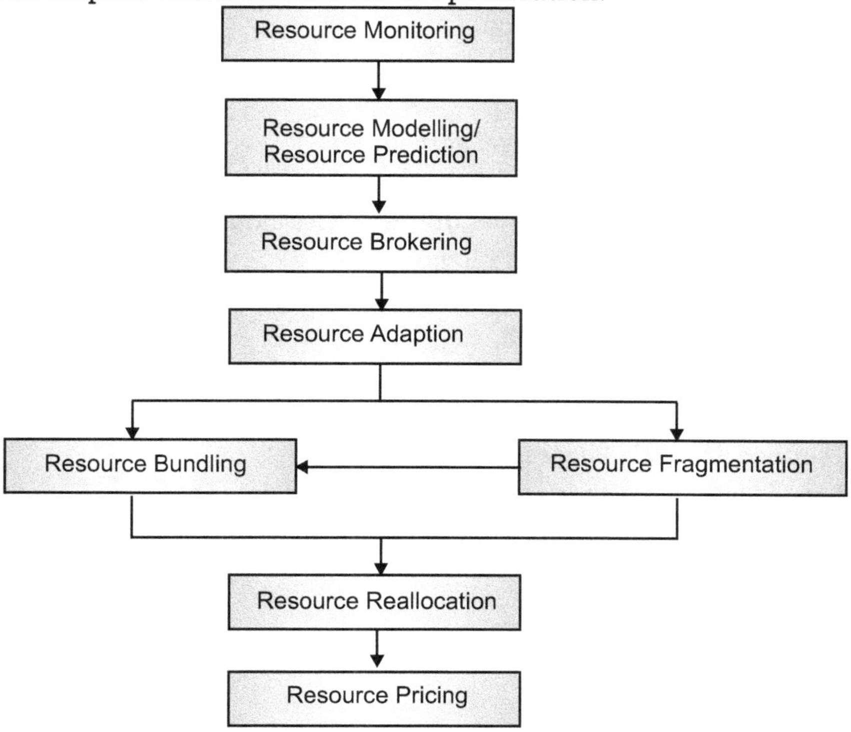

Fig 4.10: Steps of Virtualized Resource Optimization

- Virtualized resource optimization has following steps:
  1. **Resource Monitoring:** Resource Monitoring is the first and crucial step in Periodic Resource Optimization. Various virtualized cloud resources are monitored to analyze utilization of resources. This step will also monitor availability of free resources for future purpose. The major issue with cloud resource monitoring is to identify and define metrics / parameters for it.
  2. **Resource Modeling/Resource Prediction:** This step will predict the various virtualized resources required by cloud consumers applications. This is one of the complex step as resources are not uniform in nature. Due to this non uniformity, it is very difficult to predict resource requirement for peak periods and as well as for non-peak periods.
  3. **Resource Brokering:** This step is negotiation of virtualized resources with cloud consumers to make sure that they are available as per requirement.
  4. **Resource Adaptation:** As per the requirements of cloud consumers, virtualized cloud resources can be scaled up or scaled down. This step may increase cost from cloud providers perspective.
  5. **Resource Bundling:** As per the requirement various non-virtualized resources can be bundled into virtualized resources.
  6. **Resource Fragmentation:** Various virtualized resources needs to be fragmented to make non virtualized resources free. After this step various non-virtualized resources can be bundled in to virtualized resources as a part of resource bundling.
  7. **Resource Reallocation:** This step will reallocate / redistribute resources to the cloud consumers. It's main goal is to satisfy cloud consumers' need and revenue generation for cloud providers.
  8. **Resource Pricing:** It is one of the most important step from cloud providers and cloud consumers perspective. Based on cloud resource usage pricing will be done.

Practice Questions

1. Write benefits of cloud monitoring.
2. Explain service provider and user.
3. Explain architecture of federated cloud computing.

4. Describe benefits of cloud federation.
5. Explain offering to cloud computing.
6. Discuss requirements of cloud federation.
7. Explain Service Level Agreement (SLA).
8. Describe different types of SLA.
9. Explain key components of a service-level agreement.
10. Explain life cycle of SLA.
11. What is service catalog? Explain objectives of the service catalog management process.
12. Explain common elements of service catalog.
13. Explain cloud interface with its types.
14. Explain management interface of cloud.
15. Explain functional interface of cloud.
16. What is cloud portal with its functions.
17. Explain cloud service life cycle Phases.
18. Explain cloud service life cycle service planning phase in details.
19. Explain cloud service life cycle service creation phase in details.

5...

Security in Cloud Computing

Chapter Outcomes...

- Explain the given security related risk in cloud computing.
- Explain the specified feature of key security terminology for data security.
- Write steps to implement the given technology for securing the data on cloud.
- Write steps to manage the identify and access facility of given cloud set-up.
- Explain the given feature of security-as-a-cloud service.

Learning Objectives...

- To understand Fundamentals Security Concepts in Cloud chapter
- To learn Cloud Risk and its Division
- To study Technologies for Data Security and its Risks
- To understand Digital Identity and Access Management
- To study Content Level Security and Security-As- A-Cloud Service

5.0 INTRODUCTION

- Cloud computing security, consists of a set of policies, controls, procedures and technologies that work together to protect cloud based systems, data and infrastructure.
- These security measures are configured to protect data, support regulatory compliance and protect customers privacy as well as setting authentication rules for individual users and devices.
- From authenticating access to filtering traffic, cloud security can be configured to the exact needs of the business. And because these rules can be configured and managed in one place, administration overheads are reduced and IT teams empowered to focus on other areas of the business.
- Cloud security encompasses a broad range of security constraints from an end-user and cloud provider's perspective, where the end-user will primarily will be concerned with the provider's security policy, how and where their data is stored and who has access to that data.
- For a cloud provider, on the other hand, cloud computer security issues can range from the physical security of the infrastructure and the access control mechanism of cloud assets, to the execution and maintenance of security policy. Cloud security is important because it is probably the biggest reason why organizations fear the cloud.
- The Cloud Security Alliance (CSA), a nonprofit organization of industry specialists, has developed a pool of guidelines and frameworks for implementing and enforcing security within a cloud operating environment.
- Cloud computing security or, more simply, cloud security refers to a broad set of policies, technologies, applications, and controls utilized to protect virtualized IP, data, applications, services, and the associated infrastructure of cloud computing. Cloud security is the protection of data, applications, and infrastructures involved in cloud computing.

- Cloud security is a set of control-based safeguards and technology protection designed to protect resources stored online from leakage, theft, or data loss.
- Cloud service providers use a combination of methods to protect the data.
  1. **Firewalls** are a mainstay of cloud architecture. Firewalls protect the perimeter of our network security and our end-users. Firewalls also safeguard traffic between different apps stored in the cloud.
  2. **Access controls** protect data by allowing us to set access lists for different assets. For instance, we might allow specific employees application access, while restricting others. A general rule is to provide employees' access to only the tools they need to do their job. By maintaining strict access control, we can keep critical documents from malicious insiders or hackers with stolen credentials.
  3. **Data Security:** methods include virtual private networks, encryption, or masking. Virtual Private Networks (VPNs) allows remote employees to connect to corporate networks. VPNs accommodate tablets and smartphones for remote access.
  4. **Data masking** encrypts identifiable information, such as names. This maintains data integrity by keeping important information private. With data masking, a medical company can share data without violating HIPAA laws.
  5. **Threat intelligence** spots security threats and ranks them in order of importance. This feature helps us to protect mission-critical assets from threats.
  6. **Disaster recovery** is key to security since it helps you recover data that are lost or stolen.

5.1 CLOUD SECURITY FUNDAMENTALS

- Cloud security is using effective guardrails to ensure company assets such as data, application, infrastructure using cloud services can function as expected and respond to unexpected threats.
  1. **For the security folks point of view**, cloud security is defending the Confidentiality (C), Integrity (I) and Availability (A) of enterprise assets such as a data, application, infrastructure, using cloud services, from an outside or inside threat.
  2. **For the non-security background** the above mentioned CIA are the three triads of information security. There are others considerations in the mix too e.g Authentication, Authorisation etc. but, trust me, CIA is the most commonly used one to explain the risk around a threat.
- Fundamental security terms relevant to cloud computing are:
  1. **Confidentiality:**
     - Confidentiality is the characteristic of something being made accessible only to authorized parties shown in Fig. 5.1.
     - Within cloud environments, confidentiality primarily pertains to restricting access to data in transit and storage.

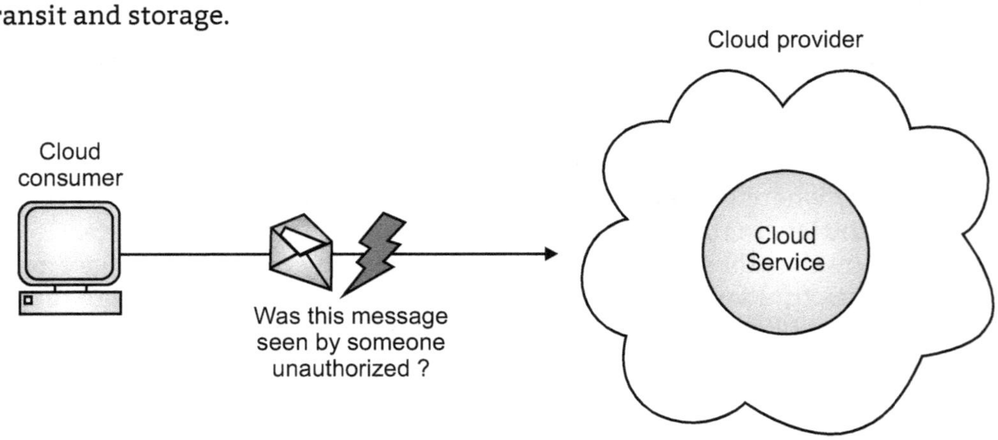

Fig. 5.1: The message issued by the cloud consumer to the cloud service is considered confidential only if it is not accessed or read by an unauthorized party.

     - Confidentiality in cloud systems is related to the areas of intellectual property rights, covert channels, traffic analysis, encryption, and inference:
       (i) Intellectual Property Rights: Intellectual Property (IP) includes inventions, designs, and artistic, musical, and literary works. Rights to intellectual property are covered by

copyright laws, which protect creations of the mind, and patents, which are granted for new inventions.

(ii) Covert Channels: A covert channel is an unauthorized and unintended communication path that enables the exchange of information. Covert channels can be accomplished through timing of messages or inappropriate use of storage mechanisms.

(iii) Traffic Analysis: Traffic analysis is a form of confidentiality breach that can be accomplished by analyzing the volume, rate, source, and destination of message traffic, even if it is encrypted. Increased message activity and high bursts of traffic can indicate a major event is occurring. Counter measures to traffic analysis include maintaining a near-constant rate of message traffic and disguising the source and destination locations of the traffic.

(iv) Encryption: Encryption involves scrambling messages so that they cannot be read by an unauthorized entity, even if they are intercepted. The amount of effort (work factor) required to decrypt the message is a function of the strength of the encryption key and the robustness and quality of the encryption algorithm.

(v) Inference: Inference is usually associated with database security. Inference is the ability of an entity to use and correlate information protected atone level of security to uncover information that is protected at a higher security level.

2. Integrity:

- Integrity is the characteristic of not having been altered by an unauthorized party shown in Fig. 5.2.
- An important issue that concerns data integrity in the cloud is whether a cloud consumer can be guaranteed that the data it transmits to a cloud service matches the data received by that cloud service.
- Integrity can extend to how data is stored, processed, and retrieved by cloud services and cloud-based IT resources.

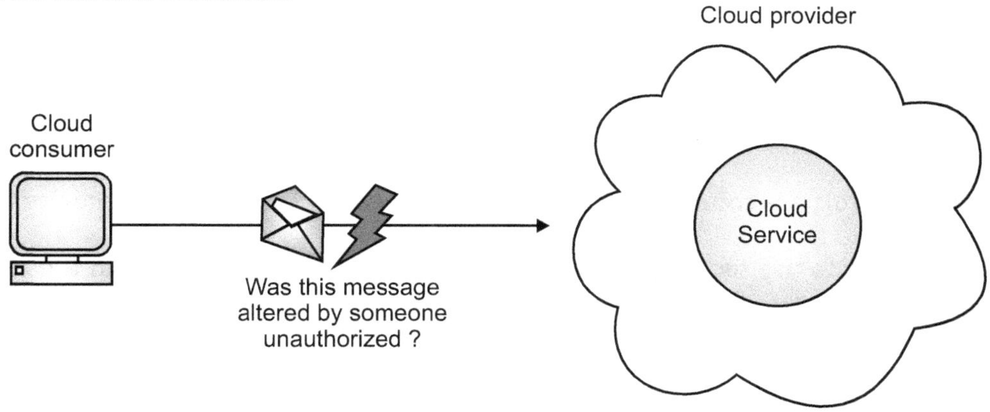

Fig. 5.2: The message issued by the cloud consumer to the cloud service is considered to have integrity if it has not been altered

- The concept of cloud information integrity requires that the following three principles are met:
  (i) Modifications are not made to data by unauthorized personnel or processes.
  (ii) Unauthorized modifications are not made to data by authorized personnel or processes.
  (iii) The data is internally and externally consistent - in other words, the internal information is consistent both among all sub-entities and with the real-world, external situation.

3. Availability:

- Availability ensures the reliable and timely access to cloud data or cloud computing resources by the appropriate personnel. Availability guarantees that the systems are functioning properly when needed.
- In addition, this concept guarantees that the security services of the cloud system are in working order. A Denial-of-Service (DoS) attack is an example of a threat against availability. The reverse of confidentiality, integrity, and availability is Disclosure, Alteration, and Destruction (DAD).

- Availability is the characteristic of being accessible and usable during a specified time period. In typical cloud environments, the availability of cloud services can be a responsibility that is shared by the cloud provider and the cloud carrier.
- The availability of a cloud-based solution that extends to cloud service consumers is further shared by the cloud consumer.

4. **Authenticity:**
   - Authenticity is the characteristic of something having been provided by an authorized source. This concept encompasses non-repudiation, which is the inability of a party to deny or challenge the authentication of an interaction.
   - Authentication in non-repudiable interactions provides proof that these interactions are uniquely linked to an authorized source. For example, a user may not be able to access a non-repudiable file after its receipt without also generating a record of this access.
5. **Threat:**
   - A threat is a potential security violation that can challenge defenses in an attempt to breach privacy and/or cause harm.
   - Both manually and automatically instigated threats are designed to exploit known weaknesses, also referred to as vulnerabilities.
   - A threat that is carried out results in an attack.
6. **Vulnerability:**
   - A vulnerability is a weakness that can be exploited either because it is protected by insufficient security controls, or because existing security controls are overcome by an attack.
   - IT resource vulnerabilities can have arrange of causes, including configuration deficiencies, security policy weaknesses, user errors, hardware or firmware flaws, software bugs, and poor security architecture.
7. **Risk:**
   - Risk is the possibility of loss or harm arising from performing an activity. Risk is typically measured according to its threat level and the number of possible or known vulnerabilities.
   - Two metrics that can be used to determine risk for an IT resource are:
     (i) The probability of a threat occurring to exploit vulnerabilities in the IT resource.
     (ii) The expectation of loss upon the IT resource being compromised.
8. **Security Controls:**
   - Security controls are counter measures used to prevent or respond to security threats and to reduce or avoid risk.
   - Details on how to use security counter measures are typically outlined in the security policy, which contains a set of rules and practices specifying how to implement a system, service, or security plan for maximum protection of sensitive and critical IT resources.
9. **Security Mechanisms:**
   - Counter measures are typically described in terms of security mechanisms, which are components comprising a defensive framework that protects IT resources, information, and services.
10. **Security Policies:**
    - A security policy establishes a set of security rules and regulations. Often, security policies will further define how these rules and regulations are implemented and enforced.
    - For example, the positioning and usage of security controls and mechanisms can be determined by security policies.

5.1.1 Cloud Security Services

- Cloud security also affects cloud software assurance include authentication, authorization, auditing, and accountability, as follows:

1. **Authentication:**
   - Authentication is the testing or reconciliation of evidence of a user's identity. It establishes the user's identity and ensures that users are who they claim to be.
   - For example, a user presents an identity (user ID) to a computer login screen and then has to provide a password.

- The computer system authenticates the user by verifying that the password corresponds to the individual presenting the ID.

2. **Authorization:**
   - Authorization refers to rights and privileges granted to an individual or process that enable access to computer resources and information assets.
   - Once, a user's identity and authentication are established, authorization levels determine the extent of system rights a user can hold.
3. **Auditing:**
   - To maintain operational assurance, organizations use two basic methods: system audits and monitoring. These methods can be employed by the cloud customer, the cloud provider or both, depending on asset architecture and deployment.
   - A system audit is a one-time or periodic event to evaluate security.
   - Monitoring refers to an ongoing activity that examines either the system or the users, such as intrusion detection.

5.1.2 Types of Auditors

- Information Technology (IT) auditors are often divided into two types: internal and external:
  - Internal auditors typically work for a given organization, whereas external auditors do not. External auditors are often Certified Public Accountants (CPAs) or other audit professionals who are hired to perform an independent audit of an organization's financial statements.
  - Internal auditors usually have a much broader mandate than external auditors, such as checking for compliance and standards of due care, auditing operational cost efficiencies, and recommending the appropriate controls.
  - IT auditors typically audit the following functions:
    1. System and transaction controls.
    2. Systems development standards.
    3. Backup controls.
    4. Data library procedures.
    5. Data center security.
    6. Contingency plans .
  - In addition, IT auditors might recommend improvements to controls, and they often participate in a system's development process to help an organization avoid costly reengineering after the system's implementation.
  - An audit trail or log is a set of records that collectively provide documentary evidence of processing, used to aid in tracing from original transactions forward to related records and reports, and/or backward from records and reports to their component source transactions. Audit trails may be limited to specific events or they may encompass all of the activities on a system.
  - Audit logs should record the following:
    - The transaction's date and time.
    - Who processed the transaction.
  - At which terminal the transaction was processed.
  - Various security events relating to the transaction In addition, an auditor should examine the audit logs for the following:
    - Amendments to production jobs.
    - Production job reruns.
    - Computer operator practices.
    - All commands directly initiated by the user.
    - All identification and authentication attempts.
    - Files and resources accessed.

Accountability:

- Accountability is the ability to determine the actions and behaviors of a single individual within a cloud system and to identify that particular individual.

- Audit trails and logs support accountability and can be used to conduct postmortem studies in order to analyze historical events and the individuals or processes associated with those events.
- Accountability is related to the concept of nonrepudiation, where in an individual cannot successfully deny the performance of an action.

5.2 CLOUD RISK

- Risk should always be understood in relation to overall business opportunity and appetite for risk sometimes risk is compensated by opportunity.
- Cloud services are not only about convenient storage, accessible by multiple devices, but include important benefits such as more convenient communication and instant multi-point collaboration.
- Therefore, a comparative analysis needs to compare not only the risks of storing data in different places but also the risks when on premises data stored on premises - e.g. a spreadsheet is emailed to other persons for their contributions, against the security issues of a spreadsheet stored in the cloud and open to collaboration between those persons.
- Therefore, the risks of using cloud computing should be compared to the risks of staying with traditional solutions, such as desktop based models.
- The level of risk will in many cases vary significantly with the type of cloud architecture being considered.
- It is possible for the cloud customer to transfer risk to the cloud provider and the risks should be considered against the cost benefit received from the services.
- However not all risks can be transferred, if a risk leads to the failure of a business, serious damage to reputation or legal implications, it is hard or impossible for any other party to compensate for this damage.
- The risk analysis in this paper applies to cloud technology. It does not apply to any specific cloud computing offering or company. This paper is not meant to replace a project specific organizational risk assessment.
- The level of risks is expressed from the perspective of the cloud customer. Where the cloud provider point of view is considered, this is explicitly stated.

5.2.1 Top Cloud Security Risks

- The most important classes of cloud specific risks are as follows:
  1. **Loss of Governance:** In using cloud infrastructures, the client necessarily cedes control to the Cloud Provider (CP) on a number of issues which may affect security. At the same time, SLAs may not offer a commitment to provide such services on the part of the cloud provider, thus leaving a gap in security defenses.
  2. **Lock-In:** There is currently little on offer in the way of tools, procedures or standard data formats or services interfaces that could guarantee data, application and service portability. This can make it difficult for the customer to migrate from one provider to another or migrate data and services back to an in-house IT environment. This introduces a dependency on a particular Cloud Provider(CP) for service provision, especially if data portability, as the most fundamental aspect, is not enabled.
  3. **Isolation Failure:** Multi-tenancy and shared resources are defining characteristics of cloud computing. This risk category covers the failure of mechanisms separating storage, memory, routing and even reputation between different tenants (e.g., so-called guest-hopping attacks). However it should be considered that attacks on resource isolation mechanisms (e.g.,. against hypervisors) are still less numerous and much more difficult for an attacker to put in practice compared to attacks on traditional OSs.
  4. **Compliance Risks:** Investment in achieving certification (e.g., industry standard or regulatory requirements) may be put at risk by migration to the cloud:
     - If the CP cannot provide evidence of their own compliance with the relevant requirements.
     - If the CP does not permit audit by the Cloud Customer (CC).

     In certain cases, it also means that using a public cloud infrastructure implies that certain kinds of compliance cannot be achieved.

5. **Management Interface Compromise:** Customer management interfaces of a public cloud provider are accessible through the Internet and mediate access to larger sets of resources (than traditional hosting providers) and therefore pose an increased risk, especially when combined with remote access and web browser vulnerabilities.
6. **Data Protection:** Cloud computing poses several data protection risks for cloud customers and providers. In some cases, it may be difficult for the cloud customer (in its role as data controller) to effectively check the data handling practices of the cloud provider and thus to be sure that the data is handled in a lawful way. This problem is exacerbated in cases of multiple transfers of data, e.g., between federated clouds. On the other hand, some cloud providers do provide information on their data handling practices. Some also offer certification summaries on their data processing and data security activities and the data controls they have in place, e.g., SAS70 certification.
7. **Insecure or Incomplete Data Deletion:** When a request to delete a cloud resource is made, as with most operating systems, this may not result in true wiping of the data. Adequate or timely data deletion may also be impossible (or undesirable from a customer perspective), either because extra copies of data are stored but are not available, or because the disk to be destroyed also stores data from other clients. In the case of multiple tenancies and the reuse of hardware resources, this represents a higher risk to the customer than with dedicated hardware.
8. **Malicious Insider:** While usually less likely, the damage which may be caused by malicious insiders is often far greater. Cloud architectures necessitate certain roles which are extremely high-risk. Examples include CP system administrators and managed security service providers.

5.2.2 Cloud Risk Division

- The risks identified in the assessment are classified into three categories namely Policy and Organizational, Technical and Legal.

5.2.2.1 Policy and Organizational Risks

- These are business related IT risks that organizations may face when considering cloud computing service providers. Such risks include lock-in, loss of governance, compliance challenges, loss of business reputation, and cloud service termination or failure.
- In addition to the risk of vendor lock-in through the use of proprietary interfaces, organizations face challenges such as complying with various regulations, even though applications and data have been migrated from a traditional data center to a cloud environment.

5.2.2.2 Technical Risks

- Organizations that deploy cloud solutions also face technical risks such as resource exhaustion, which can occur when not managing cloud resources effectively and not preparing to automatically provision additional resources when needed.
- Resource exhaustion can cause degradation of services and, in some cases, a failure to provide services at all.

5.2.2.3 Legal Risks

- Organizations must consider the legal risks of the cloud. A critical risk that must be confronted is maintaining compliance with regulations such as the Health Insurance Portability and Accountability Act (HIPAA) or the Payment Card Industry Data Security Standard (PCI DSS).
- Many organizations find it difficult or even impossible to achieve compliance while using cloud architecture. IT leaders should throughly research any applicable regulations before planning a cloud migration.

5.3 TECHNOLOGIES FOR DATA SECURITY

- Technologies for data security and privacy in cloud computing are Database Outsourcing and Query Integrity Assurance, Data Integrity in untrustworthy storage, Web Application Based Security, Multimedia Data Security.

5.3.1 Database Outsourcing and Query Integrity Assurance

- Database outsourcing has become an important component of cloud computing. Due to the rapid advancements in network technology, the cost of transmitting a terabyte of data over long distances has decreased significantly in the past decade.
- In addition, the total cost of data management is five to ten times higher than the initial acquisition costs. As a result, there is a growing interest in outsourcing database management tasks to third parties that can provide these tasks for a much lower cost due to the economy of scale.
- This new outsourcing model has the benefits of reducing the costs for running Database Management Systems (DBMS) independently and enabling enterprises to concentrate on their main businesses.
- Fig. 5.3 demonstrates the general architecture of a database outsourcing environment with clients. The database owner outsources its data management tasks, and clients send queries to the untrusted service provider.
- Let T denote the data to be outsourced. The data T are is preprocessed, encrypted, and stored at the service provider. For evaluating queries, a user rewrites a set of queries Q against T to queries against the encrypted database.

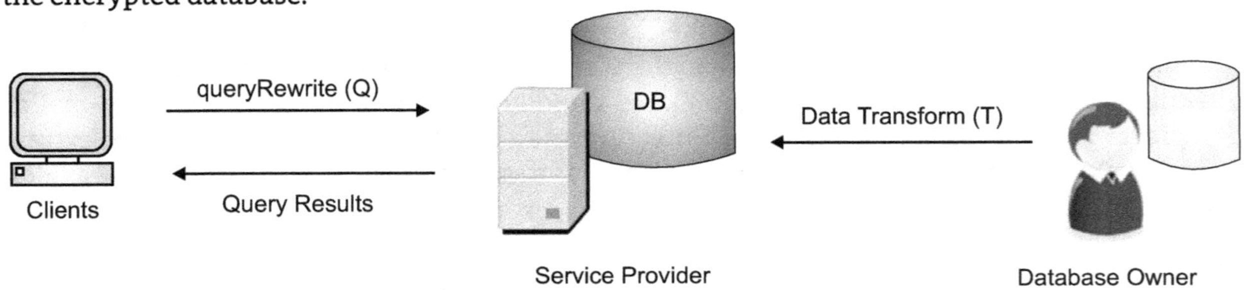

Fig. 5.3: The System Architecture of Database Outsourcing

- Generally, there are two security concerns in database outsourcing. These are data privacy and query integrity are as follows:

  1. Data Privacy Protection:
  - A Method to execute SQL queries over encrypted databases. This strategy is to process as much of a query as possible by the service providers, without having to decrypt the data. Decryption and the remainder of the query processing are performed at the clientside. Other order preserving encryption scheme for numeric values that allows any comparison operation to be directly applied on encrypted data. This technique is able to handle updates, and new values can be added without requiring changes in the encryption of other values.
  - Generally, existing methods enable direct execution of encrypted queries on encrypted datasets and allows users to ask identity queries over data of different encryptions.
  - The ultimate goal data privacy protection is to makes queries in encrypted databases as efficient as possible while preventing adversaries from learning any useful knowledge about the data.

  2. Query Integrity Assurance:
  - In addition to data privacy, an important security concern in the database outsourcing paradigm is query integrity. Query integrity examines the trustworthiness of the hosting environment.
  - When a client receives a query result from the service provider, it wants to be assured that the result is both correct and complete, where correct means that the result must originate in the owner's data and not has been tampered with, and complete means that the result includes all records satisfying the query.
  - Another method compared several signature methods that can be utilized in data authentication, and they identified the problem of completeness but did not provide a solution.

  3. Utilized an Aggregated Signature:
  - To sign each record with the information from neighboring records by assuming that all the records are sorted with a certain order. The method ensures the completeness of a selection query by checking the aggregated signature. But it has difficulties in handling multipoint selection query of which the result tuples occupy a non-continuous region of the ordered sequence.

4. **Dual Encryption:**
   - To ensure query integrity without requiring the database engine to perform any special function beyond query processing. Dual encryption enables cross-examination of the outsourced data, which consist of the original data stored under a certain encryption scheme and another small percentage of the original data stored under a different encryption scheme. Users generate queries against the additional piece of data and analyze their results to obtain integrity assurance.

5.3.2 Data Integrity in Untrustworthy Storage

- While the transparent cloud provides flexible utility of network based resources, the fear of loss of control on their data is one of the major concerns that prevent end users from migrating to cloud storage services.
- Actually it is a potential risk that the storage infrastructure providers become self interested, untrustworthy, or even malicious.
- There are different motivations whereby a storage service provider could become untrustworthy-for instance, to cover the consequence of a mistake in operation, or deny the vulnerability in the system after the data have been stolen by an adversary.
- Before cloud computing, several remote data storage checking protocols have been suggested. In practice, a remote data possession checking protocol has to satisfy the following five requirements:
  1. **Requirement #1:** It should not be a pre-requirement that the verifier has to possess a complete copy of the data to be checked. And in practice, it does not make sense for a verifier to keep a duplicated copy of the content to be verified. As long as it serves the purpose well, storing a more concise contents digest of the data at the verifier should be enough.
  2. **Requirement #2:** The protocol has to be very robust considering the untrustworthy prover. A malicious prover is motivated to hide the violation of data integrity. The protocol should be robust enough that such a prover ought to fail in convincing the verifier.
  3. **Requirement #3:** The amount of information exchanged during the verification operation should not lead to high communication overhead.
  4. **Requirement #4:** The protocol should be computationally efficient.
  5. **Requirement #5:** It is possible to run the verification an unlimited number of times.

It uses two protocols to check data integrity:

- A PDP-Based Integrity Checking Protocol.
- An Enhanced Data Possession Checking Protocol.

A PDP-Based Integrity Checking Protocol:

- Protocol based on the Provable Data Procession (PDP) technology, which allows users to obtain a probabilistic proof from the storage service providers. Such a proof will be used as evidence that their data have been stored there.
- One of the advantages of this protocol is that the proof could be generated by the storage service provider by accessing only a small portion of the whole dataset. At the same time, the amount of the metadata that end users are required to store is also small—that is, o (1).
- Additionally, such a small amount data exchanging procedure lowers the overhead in the communication channels too.
- The flowcharts of the protocol for provable data possession shown in Fig. 5.4.

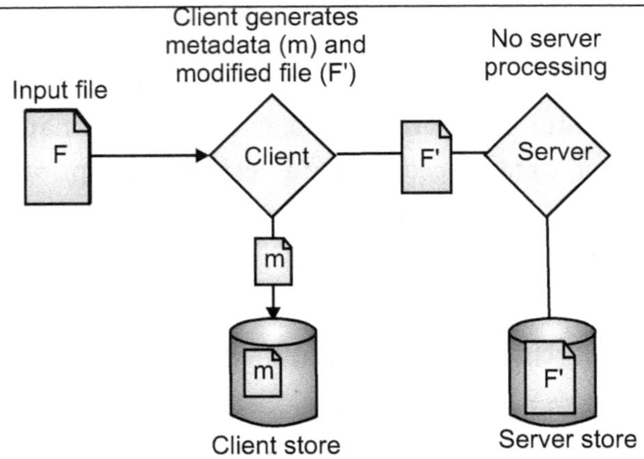

(a) Pre-process and store

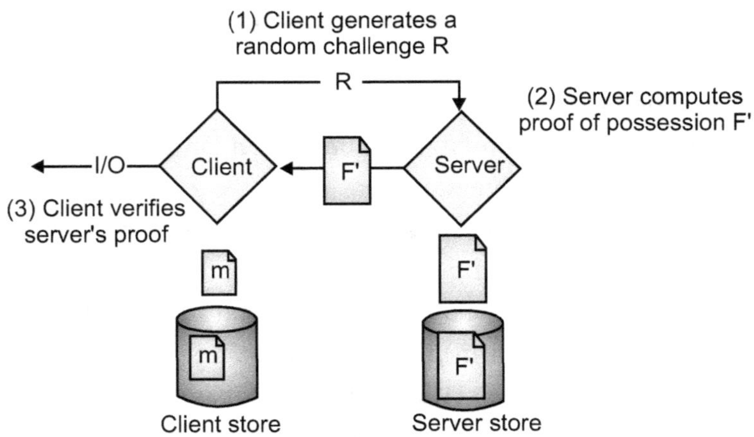

(b) Verify Server Possession

Fig. 5.4: Protocol for Provable Data Possession

- The data owner, the client in the figure, executes the protocol to verify that a dataset is stored in an outsourced storage machine as a collection of n blocks.
- Before uploading the data into the remote storage, the data owner pre-processes the dataset and a piece of metadata is generated.
- The metadata are stored at the data owner's side, and the dataset will be transmitted to the storage server.
- The cloud storage service stores the dataset and sends the data to the user in responding to queries from the data owner in the future.
- As part of pre-processing procedure, the data owner (client) may conduct operations on the data such as expanding the data or generating additional metadata to be stored at the cloud server side.
- The data owner could execute the PDP protocol before the local copy is deleted to ensure that the uploaded copy has been stored at the server machines successfully.
- Actually, the data owner may encrypt a dataset before transferring them to the storage machines.
- During the time that data are stored in the cloud, the data owner can generate a "challenge" and send it to the service provider to ensure that the storage server has stored the dataset.
- The data owner requests that the storage server generate a metadata based on the stored data and then send it back.
- Using the previously stored local metadata, the owner verifies the response. On the behalf of the cloud service provider's side, the server may receive multiple challenges from different users at the same time.
- For the sake of availability, it is highly desired to minimize not only the computational overhead of each individual calculation, but also the number of data blocks to be accessed. In addition, considering the pressure on the communication networks, minimal bandwidth consumption also implies that there are a limited amount of metadata included in the response generated by the server.

- Hence, the PDP scheme probabilistically guarantees the data integrity. It is mandatory to access the whole dataset if a deterministic guarantee is required by the user.

An Enhanced Data Possession Checking Protocol:

- The above PDP based protocol does not satisfy Requirement #2 with 100% probability. An enhanced protocol has been proposed based on the idea of the DiffieHellman scheme.
- This protocol satisfies all five requirements and is computationally more efficient than the PDP-based protocol.
- The verification time has been shortened at the setup stage of this protocol. By taking advantage of the trade-offs between the computation times required by the prover and the storage required at the verifier.

5.3.3 Web-Application-Based Security

- In cloud computing environments, resources are provided as a service over the Internet in a dynamic, virtualized, and scalable way.
- Through cloud computing services, users access business applications on line from a Web browser, while the software and data are stored on the servers.
- Therefore, in theera of cloud computing, Web security plays a more important role than ever. The Web site server is the first gate that guards the vast cloud resources.
- Since the cloud may operate continuously to process millions of dollars' worth of daily on-line transactions, the impact of any Web security vulnerability will be amplified at the level of the whole cloud.
- Web attack techniques are often referred as the class of attack. When any Web security vulnerability is identified, attacker will employ those techniques to take advantage of the security vulnerability.
- The types of attack can be categorized in Authentication, Authorization, Client-Side Attacks, Command Execution, Information Disclosure, and Logical Attacks.

1. Authentication:

- Authentication is the process of verifying a claim that a subject made to act on behalf of a given principal. Authentication attacks target a Web site's method of validating the identity of a user, service, or application, including Brute Force, Insufficient Authentication, and Weak Password Recovery Validation.
- Brute Force attack employs an automated process to guess a person's username and password by trial and error. In the Insufficient Authentication case, some sensitive content or functionality are protected by "hiding" the specific location in hide string but still remains accessible directly through a specific URL. The attacker could discover those URLs through a Brute Force probing of files and directories. Many Web sites provide password recovery service.
- This service will automatically recover the user name or password to the user if she or he can answer some questions defined as part of the user registration process. If the recovery questions are either easily guessed or can be skipped, this web site is considered to be weak password recovery validation.

2. Authorization:

- Authorization is used to verify if an authenticated subject can perform a certain operation. Authentication must precede authorization. For example, only certain users are allowed to access specific content or functionality.
- Authorization attacks use various techniques to gain access to protected areas beyond their privileges. One typical authorization attack is caused by Insufficient Authorization. When a user is authenticated to a Web site, it does not necessarily mean that she should have access to certain content that has been granted arbitrarily.
- Insufficient authorization occurs when a web site does not protect sensitive content or functionality with proper access control restrictions. Other authorization attacks are involved with session.
- Those attacks include credential/session prediction, insufficient session expiration, and session fixation.
    - In many web sites, after a user successfully authenticates with the web site for the first time, the web site creates a session and generate a unique "session ID" to identify this session. This session ID is attached to subsequent requests to the Web site as "Proof" of the authenticated session.

- Credential/Session Prediction attack deduces or guesses the unique value of a session to hijack or impersonate a user.
- Insufficient session expiration occurs when an attacker is allowed to reuse old session credentials or session IDs for authorization. For example, in a shared computer, after a user accesses a Web site and then leaves, with Insufficient Session Expiration, an attacker can use the browser's back button to access web pages previously accessed by the victim.
- Session fixation forces a user's session ID to an arbitrary value via cross site scripting or peppering the web site with previously made HTTP requests. Once the victim logs in, the attacker uses the predefined session ID value to impersonate the victim's identity.

3. Client-Side Attacks:

- The client-side attacks lure victims to click a link in a malicious web page and then leverage the trust relationship expectations of the victim for the real web site.
- In content spoofing, the malicious web page can trick a user into typing user name and password and will then use this information to impersonate the user.
- Cross-Site Scripting (XSS) launches attacker-supplied executable code in the victim's browser. The code is usually written in browser-supported scripting languages such as JavaScript, VBScript, ActiveX, Java, or Flash.
- Since the code will run within the security context of the hosting web site, the code has the ability to read, modify, and transmit any sensitive data, such as cookies, accessible by the browser.
- Cross-Site Request Forgery (CSRF) is a serve security attack to a vulnerable site that does not take the checking of CSRF for the HTTP/HTTPS request.
- Assuming that the attacker knows the URLs of the vulnerable site which are not protected by CSRF checking and the victim's browser stores credentials such as cookies of the vulnerable site, after luring the victim to click a link in a malicious web page, the attacker can forge the victim's identity and access the vulnerable web site on victim's behalf.

4. Command Execution:

- The Command Execution attacks exploit server side vulnerabilities to execute remote commands on the web site. Usually, users supply inputs to the web site to request services.
- If a web application does not properly sanitize user supplied input before using it within application code, an attacker could alter command execution on the server.
- For example, if the length of input is not checked before use, buffer overflow could happen and result in denial of service. Or if the web application uses user input to construct statements such as SQL, XPath, C/C11 Format String, OS system command, LDAP, or dynamic HTML, an attacker may inject arbitrary executable code into the server if the user input is not properly filtered.

5. Information Disclosure:

- The Information Disclosure attacks acquire sensitive information about a web site revealed by developer comments, error messages, or well-know file name conventions. For example, a web server may return a list of files within a requested directory if the default file is not present. This will supply an attacker with necessary information to launch further attacks against the system.
- Other types of Information Disclosure includes using special paths such as "." and ".." for path Traversal, or uncovering hidden URLs via predictable resource location.

6. Logical Attacks:

- Logical Attacks involve the exploitation of a web application's logic flow. Usually, a user's action is completed in a multi-step process. The procedural workflow of the process is called application logic.
- A common logical attack is Denial of Service (DoS). DoS attacks will attempt to consume all available resources in the web server such as CPU, memory, disk space, and so on, by abusing the functionality provided by the Web site.
- When any one of any system resource reaches some utilization threshold, the web site will no long be responsive to normal users. DoS attacks are often caused by Insufficient Anti-automation where an attacker is permitted to automate a process repeatedly.
- An automated script could be executed thousands of times a minute, causing potential loss of performance or service.

5.3.4 Multimedia Data Security

- With the rapid developments of multimedia technologies, more and more multimedia contents are being stored and delivered over many kinds of devices, databases and networks.
- Multimedia data security plays an important role in the data storage to protect multimedia data. Recently, how storage multimedia contents are delivered by both different providers and users has attracted much attentions and many applications.

1. Protection from Unauthorized Replication:

- Contents replication is required to generate and keep multiple copies of certain multimedia contents.
- For example, Content Distribution Networks (CDNs) have been used to manage content distribution to large numbers of users, by keeping the replicas of the same contents on a group of geographically distributed surrogates.
- Although the replication can improve the system performance, the unauthorized replication causes some problems such as contents copyright, waste of replication cost, and extra control overheads.

2. Protection from Unauthorized Replacement:

- As the storage capacity is limited, a replacement process must be carried out when the capacity exceeds its limit.
- It means the situation that a currently stored content must be removed from the storage space in order to make space for the new coming content.
- However, how to decide which content should be removed is very important. If an unauthorized replacement happens, the content which the user doesn't want to delete will be removed resulting in an accident of the data loss.
- Furthermore, if the important content such as system data is removed by unauthorized replacement, the result will be more serious.

3. Protection from Unauthorized Pre-Fetching:

- The Pre-fetching is widely deployed in multimedia storage network systems between server databases and end users storage disks.
- That is to say, If a content can be predicted to be requested by the user in future requests, this content will be fetched from the server database to the end user before this user requests it, in order to decrease user response time.
- Although the Pre-fetching shows its efficiency, the unauthorized pre-fetching should be avoided to make the system to fetch the necessary content.

5.4 DATA SECURITY RISK

- The cloud computing model opens up old and new data security risks. By its very definition, Cloud computing is a development that is meant to allow more open accessibility and easier and improved data sharing.
- Data are uploaded into a cloud and stored in a data center, for access by users from that data center or in a more fully cloud based model, the data themselves are created in the cloud and stored and accessed from the cloud (again via a data center).
- The most obvious risk in this scenario is that associated with the storage of that data. A user uploading or creating cloud based data include those data that are stored and maintained by a third-party cloud provider such as Google, Amazon, Microsoft, and so on.
- This action has several risks associated with it: Firstly, it is necessary to protect the data during upload into the data center to ensure that the data do not get hijacked on the way into the database.
- Secondly, it is necessary to the stores the data in the data center to ensure that they are encrypted at all times.
- Thirdly, and perhaps less obvious, the access to those data need to be controlled; this control should also be applied to the hosting company, including the administrators of the data center.
- In addition, an area often forgotten in the application of security to a data resource is the protection of that resource during its use-that is, during a collaboration step as part of a document workflow process.

- Other issues that complicate the area of hosted data include ensuring that the various data security acts and rules are adhered to; this becomes particularly complicated when we consider the cross border implications of cloud computing and the hosting of data in a country other than that originating the data.
- Data security risks are compounded by the open nature of cloud computing. Access control becomes a much more fundamental issue in cloud-based systems because of the accessibility of the data therein.
- If we use a system that provides improved accessibility and opens up the platform to multi-node access, then we need to take into account the risks associated with this improvement.
- One way this can be done is by adding an element of control, in the form of access control, to afford a degree of risk mitigation.
- Information-centric access control can help to balance improved accessibility with risk, by associating access rules with different data objects within an open and accessible platform, without losing the inherent usability of that platform.
- A further area of risk associated not only with cloud computing, but also with traditional network computing, is the use of content after access.
- The risk is potentially higher in a cloud network, for the simple reason that the information is outside of our corporate walls; for example, a user printing off a sensitive document within an office of a company is more likely to think twice about doing so if her colleagues can see her actions than if she prints out that document in the privacy of her own home or within the anonymity of an Internet cafe.
- Data security risks include loss of governance, isolation failure, insecure or incomplete data deletion.

5.5 DIGITAL IDENTITY AND ACCESS MANAGEMENT (DIAM/IAM)

- Digital identity holds the key to flexible data security within a cloud environment. Identity, of all the components of information technology, is perhaps the most closest to the heart of the individual.
- After all, our identity is our most personal possession and a digital identity represents who we are and how we interact with others on line.
- Digital identity can be used to form the basis of data security, not only in the cloud but also at the local network level too.
- Digital identity holds the key to securing data, if that digital identity can be programmatically linked to security policies controlling the post access usage of data.
- Identity and Access Management (IAM) in enterprise IT is about defining and managing the roles and access privileges of individual network users and the circumstances in which users are granted (or denied) those privileges.
- Those users might be customers (customer identity management) or employees (employee identity management. The core objective of IAM systems is one digital identity per individual.
- Once, that digital identity has been established, it must be maintained, modified and monitored throughout each user's "access lifecycle."

5.5.1 Why Digital Identity and Access Management (IAM)?

- Traditionally, organizations invest in IAM practices to improve operational efficiency and to follow with regulatory, privacy, and data protection requirements:

1. **Improve Operational Efficiency:**
   - Properly architected IAM technology and processes can improve efficiency by automating user on-boarding and other repetitive tasks (e.g., self-service for users requesting password resets that otherwise will require the intervention of system administrators using a help desk ticketing system).
2. **Regulatory Compliance Management:**
   - To protect systems, applications, and information from internal and external threats (e.g., disgruntled employees deleting sensitive files) and to comply with various regulatory, privacy, and data protection requirements, organizations implement an "IT general and application-level

controls" framework derived from industry standard frameworks such as ISO 27002 and Information Technology Infrastructure Library (ITIL).
  - IAM processes and practices can help organizations meet objectives in the area of access control and operational security (e.g., enforcement of compliance requirements such as "segregation of duties" and assignment of limited privileges for staff members to perform their duties). Auditors routinely map internal controls to IT controls as they support management of regulatory compliance processes including Payment Card Industry (PCI), Data Security Standards (DSSs).
- In addition to improving operational efficiencies and effective compliance management, IAM can enable new IT delivery and deployment models (i.e., cloud services). For example, federated identity, a key IAM component, enables the linking and portability of identity information across trust boundaries. As such, it enables enterprises and cloud service providers to bridge security domains through web single sign-on and federated user rovisioning.
- Some of the cloud use cases that require IAM support from the CSP include:
  - Employees and on-site contractors of an organization accessing a SaaS service using identity federation (e.g., sales and support staff members accessing Salesforce.com with corporate identities and credentials)
  - IT administrators accessing the CSP management console to provision resources and access for users using a corporate identity (e.g., IT administrators of Newco.com provisioning virtual machines or VMs in Amazon's EC2 service, configured with identities, entitlements, and credentials for operating the VMs [i.e., start, stop, suspend, and delete VMs])
  - Developers creating accounts for partner users in a PaaS platform.
  - End users accessing storage service in the cloud (e.g., Amazon S3) and sharing files and objects with users, within and outside a domain using access policy management features.
  - An application residing in a cloud service provider (e.g., Amazon EC2) accessing storage from another cloud service (e.g., Mosso).
- Since IAM features such as single sign on (SSO) allow applications to externalize authentication features, businesses can rapidly adopt as a services by reducing the time required to integrate with service providers. IAM capabilities can also help a business out source a process or service to partners with a reduced impact to the business's privacy and security; for example, employees of an order fulfillment partner of a merchant can use their federated identities to access real-time information stored in a merchant application to manage the product fulfillment process. In short, extending our IAM strategy, practice, and architecture allows your organization to extend your user access management practices and processes to the cloud. Hence, organizations with established IAM practices can rapidly adopt cloud services while maintaining the efficiency and efficacy of their security controls.

5.5.2 Benefits of Digital Identity and Access Management (IAM)

- IAM benefits are given below:
  1. Save money.
  2. Improve operational efficiency.
  3. Reduce time to deliver applications and services.
  4. Enhance security.
  5. Enhance regulatory compliance.
  6. Give more power to audit.

5.5.3 Digital Identity and Access Management (IAM) Definitions

- The basic concepts and definitions of IAM functions for any service:
  1. **Authentication:** Authentication is the process of verifying the identity of a user or system (e.g., Lightweight Directory Access Protocol [LDAP] verifying the credentials presented by the user, where the identifier is the corporate user ID that is unique and assigned to an employee or contractor). Authentication usually connotes a more robust form of identification. In some use cases, such as service-to-service interaction, authentication involves verifying the network service requesting access to information served by another service (e.g., a travel web service that is connecting to a credit card gateway to verify the credit card on behalf of the user).

2. **Authorization:** Authorization is the process of determining the privileges the user or system is entitled to once the identity is established. In the context of digital services, authorization usually follows the authentication step and is used to determine whether the user or service has the necessary privileges to perform certain operations-in other words, authorization is the process of enforcing policies.
3. **Auditing:** In the context of IAM, auditing entails the process of review and examination of authentication, authorization records, and activities to determine the adequacy of IAM system controls, to verify compliance with established security policies and procedures (e.g., separation of duties), to detect breaches in security services (e.g., privilege escalation), and to recommend any changes that are indicated for counter measures.

5.5.4 IAM Challenges

- One critical challenge of IAM concerns managing access for diverse user populations (employees, contractors, partners, etc.) accessing internal and externally hosted services.
- IT is constantly challenged to rapidly provision appropriate access to the users whose roles and responsibilities often change for business reasons. Another issue is the turnover of users within the organization.
- Turnover varies by industry and function seasonal staffing fluctuations in finance departments, for example-and can also arise from changes in the business, such as mergers and acquisitions, new product and service releases, business process outsourcing, and changing responsibilities. As a result, sustaining IAM processes can turn into a persistent challenge.
- Access policies for information are seldom centrally and consistently applied. Organizations can contain disparate directories, creating complex webs of user identities, access rights, and procedures.
- This has led to inefficiencies in user and access management processes while exposing these organizations to significant security, regulatory compliance, and reputation risks.
- To address these challenges and risks, many companies have sought technology solutions to enable centralized and automated user access management. Many of these initiatives are entered into with high expectations, which is not surprising given that the problem is often large and complex.
- Most often those initiatives to improve IAM can span several years and incur considerable cost. Hence, organizations should approach their IAM strategy and architecture with both business and IT drivers that address the core inefficiency issues while preserving the control's efficacy (related to access control).

5.5.5 IAM Architecture

- IAM is not a monolithic solution that can be easily deployed to gain capabilities immediately. It is as much an aspect of architecture shown in Fig. 5.5 as it is a collection of technology components, processes, and standard practices.
- Standard enterprise IAM architecture encompasses several layers of technology, services, and processes. At the core of the deployment architecture is a directory service (such as LDAP or Active Directory) that acts as a repository for the identity, credential, and user attributes of the organization's user pool.
- The directory interacts with IAM technology components such as authentication, user management, provisioning, and federation services that support the standard IAM practice and processes within the organization.
- It is not uncommon for organizations to use several directories that were deployed for environment-specific reasons (e.g., Windows systems using Active Directory, Unix systems using LDAP) or that were integrated into the environment by way of business mergers and acquisitions.

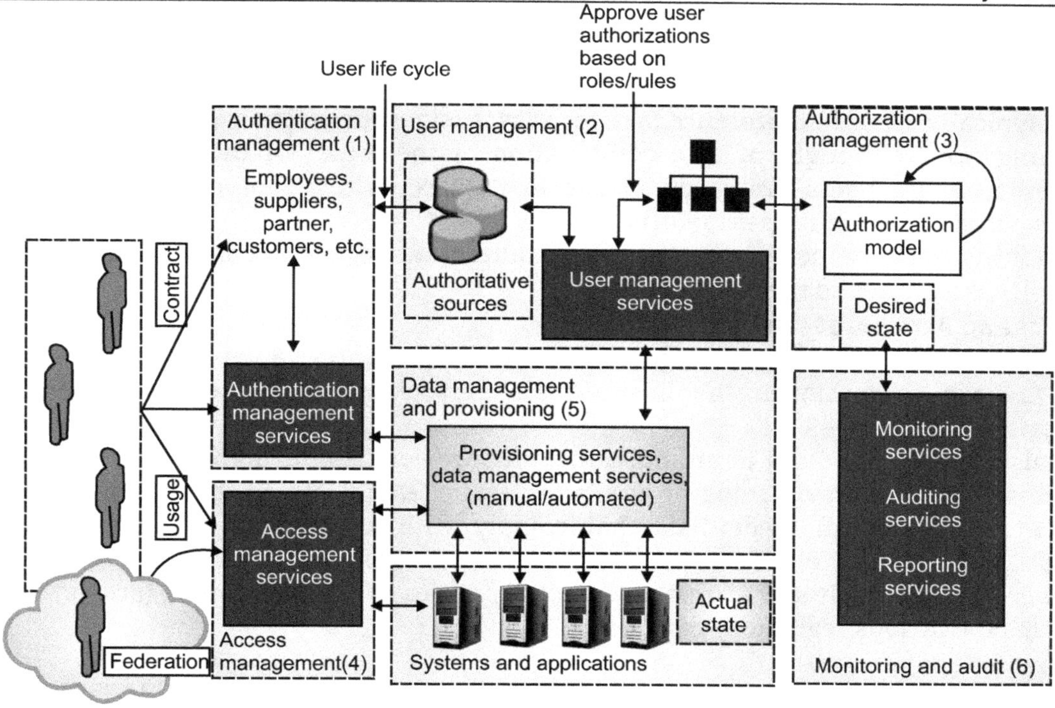

Fig. 5.5: IAM functional architecture

- The IAM processes to support the business can be broadly categorized as follows:
  1. **User Management:** Activities for the effective governance and management of identity life cycles
  2. **Authentication Management:** Activities for the effective governance and management of the process for determining that an entity is who or what it claims to be.
  3. **Authorization Management:** Activities for the effective governance and management of the process for determining entitlement rights that decide what resources an entity is permitted to access in accordance with the organization's policies.
  4. **Access Management:** Enforcement of policies for access control in response to a request from an entity (user, services) wanting to access an IT resource within the organization.
  5. **Data Management and Provisioning:** Propagation of identity and data for authorization to IT resources via automated or manual processes.
  6. **Monitoring and Auditing:** Monitoring, auditing, and reporting compliance by users regarding access to resources within the organization based on the defined policies.

5.5.6 IAM Life Cycle

- IAM processes support the following operational activities and figure 5.6 shows identity life cycle:

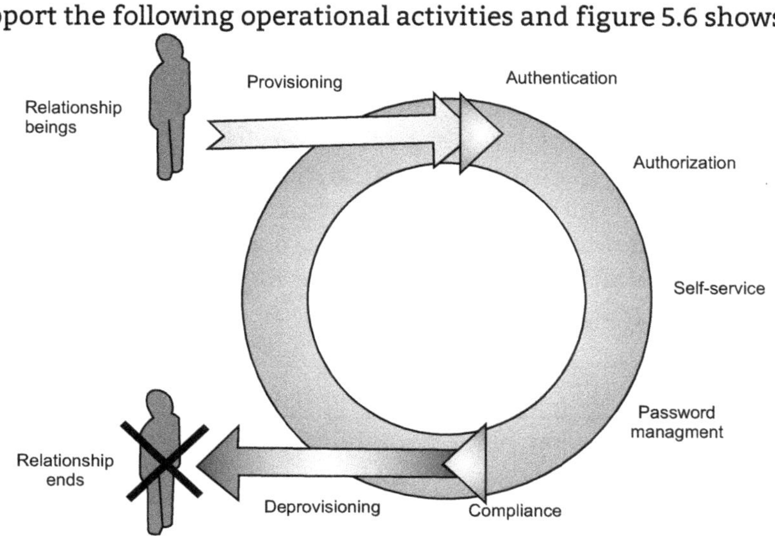

Fig. 5.6: Identity Management Life Cycle

1. **Provisioning:**
- This is the process of on-boarding users to systems and applications. These processes provide users with necessary access to data and technology resources.
- The term typically is used in reference to enterprise level resource management.
- Provisioning can be thought of as a combination of the duties of the human resources and IT departments, where users are given access to data repositories or systems, applications, and databases based on a unique user identity.
- Deprovisioning works in the opposite manner, resulting in the deletion or deactivation of an identity or of privileges assigned to the user identity.

2. **Credential and Attribute Management:**
- These processes are designed to manage the life cycle of credentials and user attributes-create, issue, manage, revoke to minimize the business risk associated with identity impersonation and inappropriate account use.
- Credentials are usually bound to an individual and are verified during the authentication process. The processes include provisioning of attributes, static (e.g., standard text password) and dynamic (e.g., one-time password) credentials that comply with a password standard (e.g., passwords resistant to dictionary attacks), handling password expiration, encryption management of credentials during transit and at rest, and access policies of user attributes (privacy and handling ofattributes for various regulatory reasons).

3. **Entitlement Management:**
- Entitlements are also referred to as authorization policies. The processes in this domain address the provisioning and deprovisioning of privileges needed for the user to access resources including systems, applications, and databases.
- Proper entitlement management ensures that users are assigned only the required privileges (least privileges) that match with their job functions.
- Entitlement management can be used to strengthen the security of web services, web applications, legacy applications, documents and files, and physical security systems.

4. **Compliance Management:**
- This process implies that access rights and privileges are monitored and tracked to ensure the security of an enterprises resources.
- The process also helps auditors verify compliance to various internal access control policies, and standards that include practices such as segregation of duties, access monitoring, periodic auditing, and reporting.
- An example is a user certification process that allows application owners to certify that only authorized users have the privileges necessary to access business sensitive information.

5. **Identity Federation Management:**
- Federation is the process of managing the trust relationships established beyond the internal network boundaries or administrative domain boundaries among distinct organizations.
- A federation is an association of organizations that come together to exchange information about their users and resources to enable collaborations and transactions (e.g., sharing user information with the organizations' benefits systems managed by a third-party provider). Federation of identities to service providers will support SSO to cloud services.

6. **Centralization of Authentication (authN) and Authorization (authZ):**
- A central authentication and authorization infrastructure alleviates the need for application developers to build custom authentication and authorization features into their applications.
- Furthermore, it promotes a loose coupling architecture where applications become agnostic to the authentication methods and policies. This approach is also called an "externalization of authN and authZ" from applications.

5.6 CONTENT LEVEL SECURITY (CLS)

- CLS was evolved to meet the market place demand and propelled by the demands of purchaser institutions.
- Content level security endows organizations to organize data and content at the organizational level, other than at the institutional level.

- CLS presents the proficiency to outlook, edit and delete data based on client functions and permissions for both application-level security and content-level security.
- The new functionality presents users with content that is applicable to them, decreasing the need for applications to run on multiple servers and permitting applications to assist different organizations inside the institution.
- The CLS solution can be rolled out over an unlimited number of distinct partitions and agencies, with each organization sustaining a concentrated outlook over all of its pertinent functions.
- Other advantages include increased usability aimed at content, new functionality that advances effectiveness and decreases mistakes and reduction in overhead cost with unlimited number of permitted users.
- CLS evolved to meet the marketplace demands and propelled by the wishes of customer institutions.
- Content Level Security (CLS) is a feature that controls who has access to edit or read content.
- The new security model has been as "content or information-centric." What this means in reality is that the content that makes up any given data object (for example, a Word document) is protected, as opposed to the file i.e., the carrier of that information being protected.
- This subtle difference in approach gives us a major advantage in terms of granularity and choice of protection level, as well as persistence of protection. We will take a word document as our example here to outline the main pros and cons of this type of security approach
- An administrator sets security levels for content according to groups that are already defined.
- The advantages that are conferred on data protected at the content level: greater control, more focused access control, increased granular protection over content, and assurance within a cloud-hosted system.
- But what, if any, disadvantages come with this type of methodology? Transfer of the data between application and database, or human-to-human transfer, can protect the data as an encrypted package, decrypted when accessis granted.
- Content centric security measures need to be compatible with both database security and secure transfer of data within a cloud environment. Protecting the content of our word document needs to be done in such a manner that it does not impact the storage of that data.

Need for Content Level Security:

- For certain businesses, there is information that should not be shared or be editable between divisions. There are two key scenarios corresponding to different levels of access:
  1. **Completely Confidential Content:** Content can be accessed only from some business units. Other units aren't aware the content exists.
  2. **Safety Reuse:** A business unit can share content to other business units but only in read-only mode.
- These scenarios are where Content Level Security (CLS), comes in, making it possible for users of to set security levels of content in relation to groups.
- CLS operates using a hierarchy of security levels, ranging from the most-permissive/open to the most-restrictive/closed. The content security levels, from most-permissive to most-restrive are:
  1. **Read and Write:** Content is viewable and editable.
  2. **Read only:** Content is viewable, but cannot be edited.
  3. **Invisible:** Content is not visible.

5.7 SECURITY-AS-A-CLOUD SERVICES

- Just like Software-as-a-Service (SaaS), the business model with Security-as-a-Service is subscription-based. In addition, Security-as-a-Service is also sometimes referred to as "SaaS" or SECaaS.
- Security as a Service can most easily be described as a cloud delivered model for outsourcing cyber security services.
- Much like Software-as-a service, SECaaS provides security services on a subscription basis hosted by cloud providers.
- Security as a service solutions have become increasingly popular for corporate infrastructures as a way to ease the in-house security team's responsibilities, scale security needs as the business grows, and avoid the costs and maintenance of on-premise alternatives.

- Security as a Service, there are two emerging provider types. The first type comprises established information security vendors who are changing their delivery methods to include services delivered through the cloud.
- The second type comprises start-up information security companies that are also emerging in this field as pure, play Cloud Service Providers (CSPs) i.e., these companies provide security only as a cloud service, and do not provide traditional client-server security products for networks, hosts, and/or applications.
- There are three impetus help to explain how security-as-a-cloud service began. As given below:
  1. The earliest first impetus is a decade old now: spam, or unsolicited email. While email is the most popular Internet resource, service providers and software developers aren't making email better, and worst of all, aggressive marketers are targeting any email user as a potential customer. Here services are designed to extend the capability of your service providers email offering. Junk mail services are only the first step. A number of other companies now provide email filtering services, both standalone security companies, as well as many Internet service providers (ISPs) which are often reselling the services of standalone security companies with their own brand.
  2. A second impetus for SECaaS is managed security services (MSSs). Managed security service providers (MSSPs) have been providing outsourced services to customers for several years, whereby the MSSPs manage an organization's network security devices, such as firewalls and intrusion detection systems (IDSs). The impetus for using MSS was, and is, the same as cloud computing: lower costs compared to in-house solutions through shared resources.
     - The difference between MSSPs and CSPs, however, is that the shared resources for MSSPs are personnel, and not infrastructure. Additionally, because many organizations are not staffed to handle round-the-clock support for such services and do not have the expertise to fully staff such positions, the shared services (i.e., personnel) model of MSSPs can be financially attractive. The MSSP model became an impetus for CSPs because it broke the strong but informal barrier to outsourcing parts of an organization's information security program. Andin this case, that outsourcing also meant off-premises management of information security devices.
     - Although outsourcing information security is often an option, initially it tended tobe outsourcing on-premises-that is, within the customer's own facilities-as opposed to off premises.
     - Of course, now outsourcing can be on-premises, off-premises, onshore, offshore, and other variations in delivery. Although this network security work is outsourced in this model, the responsibility for a customer's security remains with the customer.
     - It is the customer who is responsible for managing and monitoring the MSSP, and the customer dictates what security policies are to be enforced.
     - The MSSP monitors and manages devices (e.g., firewalls, IDSs) and data flows (e.g., Web, content, or email filtering). But these devices (including the devices that manage and monitor data flows) belong to the customer. As a result, cost savings and efficiency improvements go only so far.
     - Although this is a subscription-type service (an operational expense, or OpEx), there is still the associated Capital Expense (CapEx) of the customer's npremises hardware. With cloud computing, CapEx is further reduced because most of the devices and the monitoring and management are the responsibilities of the SaaS provider.
  3. A third impetus for SECaaS is the declining organizational efficiency of trying to provide security on the endpoints directly. Not only is there is a huge proliferation of endpoints, but they have so many configuration variables that organizational IT departments simply cannot manage them effectively. Additionally, because many of these endpoints are mobile, trying to troubleshoot configuration problems and keep security software up-to-date is a huge task. Add to those problems the fact that many mobile devices lack sufficient resources (e.g., processing power, memory, and storage capacity) to adequately handle today's endpoint protection suites and the endpoint protection situation is not looking positive. Because of these issues, and the explosive growth in malware, protecting endpoints on the endpoints is an increasing problem.

- For example, "In 2008, Symantec detected 1,656,227 malicious code threats. This represents over 60 percent of the approximately 2.6 million malicious code threats that Symantec has detected over time. This has led to a change in thinking about how to protect those endpoints. Instead of protecting endpoints on the endpoints, why not protect them through the cloud? That is, why not clean the traffic to and from the endpoints as it transits the cloud? Instead of dealing with all the complications of trying to monitor and manage the endpoints themselves, move the monitoring and management of traffic to and from the endpoint (not the monitoring and management of devices themselves) to the cloud.

Benefits of Security as a cloud Service:

1. **Cost Savings:** One of the biggest benefits of a Security as a Service model is that it saves a business money. A cloud delivered service is often available in subscription tiers with several upgrade options so a business only pays for what they need, when they need. It also eliminates the need for expertise.
2. **Latest Security Tools and Updates:** When we implement SECaaS, we get to work with the latest security tools and resources. For anti-virus and other security tools to be effective, they must be kept up to date with the latest patches and virus definitions. By deploying SECaaS throughout our organization, these updates are managed for you on every server, PC and mobile device.
3. **Faster Provisioning and Greater Agility:** One of the best things about as-a-service solutions is that the users can be given access to these tools immediately. SECaaS solutions can be scaled up or down as required and are provided on demand where and when we need them. That means no more uncertainty when it comes to deployment or updates as everything is managed for we by our SECaaS provider and visible to we through a web-enabled dashboard.
4. **Free Up Resources:** When security provisions are managed externally, the IT teams can focus on what is important to the organization. SECaaS frees up resources, gives us total visibility through management dashboards and the confidence that our IT security is being managed competently by a team of outsourced security specialists. We can also choose for our IT teams to take control of security processes if we prefer and manage all policy and system changes through a web interface.
5. **Reduced Costs:** SECaaS solutions are provided on a monthly rental basis and per license purchased.
6. **Ease of Management:** A service provider delivers total management of cloud security services, security policies, and general administration. Customizable and scalable services range from anti-virus/malware to outsourced security suite developers.
7. **Continuous Anti-Virus Updates**: SECaaS services ensure that security software is maintained with the most current virus definition and security updates.
8. Constant virus definition updates that are not reliant on user compliance. Greater security expertise than is typically available within an organization.
9. Faster user provisioning and Outsourcing of administrative tasks, such as log management, to save time and money and allow an organization to devote more time to its core competencies.
10. A web interface that allows in-house administration of some tasks as well as a view of the security environment and on-going activities.

Services Provided by SECaaS:

- It provides several services to improve information security such as Email filtering (including backup, archival, and e-discovery), Web content filtering, Vulnerability management and Identity-as-a-Service (IDaaS).

1. **Email Filtering (Including Backup, Archival, and E-Discovery):**

- SECaaS for email primarily involves cleansing spam, phishing emails, and malware included in email from an organizations incoming email stream, and then delivering that clean email securely to the organization so that it is effectively not repolluted.
- The benefits of this approach are not only more comprehensive security for clients due to the use of multiple engines, but also better performance of those client devices (because the anti-malware runs in the cloud and not on the endpoint directly), as well as far better anti-malware management.
- The anti-malware management is superior to endpoint solutions because that anti-malware isOS- and processor-agnostic, so it can be managed centrally through the cloud rather than working with multiple management systems, probably from multiple anti-malware vendors.
- This cleansing-in-the-cloud service has corollary benefits, reduced bandwidth used by email, reduced loads on organizational email servers, and improved effectiveness of a (recipient)organization's own anti-malware efforts.
- Although most attention on SECaaS involving email tends to focus on inbound email, it is also often used with outgoing email. Many organizations want to ensure that they are not inadvertently

sending malware infected emails, and cleansing outbound email through SECaaS is a good method for preventing such problems and embarrassments.

- Additionally, outside SECaaS email can be used to enforce organizational policies around the encryption of email (e.g., between specified [email] domains, such as those belonging to business partners or customers).
- This email encryption is generally performed at the (email) server-to-server level so that individual user actions and key management are not required. This is accomplished by using either Secure Sockets Layer (SSL) or Transport Layer Security (TLS) on network communications at the transport layer.
- A further benefit of SECaaS anti-malware is the collective intelligence that is gained from the visibility of all malware threats to all endpoints across an enterprise, irrespective of type (e.g., server, desktop, laptop, or mobile device), location, OS, or processor architecture. Having this greater view in a timely manner is a significant help to organizational information security teams.
- SECaaS for email also includes email backup and archiving. This service usually involves storing and indexing an organization's email messages and attachments in a centralized repository.
- That centralized repository allows an organization to index and search by a number of parameters, including date range, recipient, sender, subject, and content. These capabilities are particularly useful for e-discovery purposes, which can be extremely expensive without such capabilities.

2. Web Content filtering:

- As endpoints belonging to an organization-whether they are within an organization's facilities, at home, or on the road-try to retrieve web traffic, that traffic is diverted to a SECaaS provider that scans for malware threats and ensures that only clean traffic is delivered to end users.
- Organizations can also enforce their web content policies by allowing, blocking, or throttling traffic (use of bandwidth for that traffic reduced). Because of the number of websites accessible today, earlier URL filtering solutions deployed on organizations' premises are increasingly inefficient.
- SECaaS providers supplement that URL filtering with the examination of Hypertext Transfer Protocol (HTTP) header information, page content, and embedded links to better understand site content.
- Additionally, these services use a collective reputation scoring system to bolster the accuracy of this filtering.
- SECaaS for web content also involves scanning outbound web traffic for sensitive information(e.g., ID numbers, credit card information, intellectual property) that users could send externally without appropriate authorization (data leakage protection). Web traffic is also scanned for content analysis, file type, and pattern matching to prevent data exfiltration.
- Fig. 5.7 shows SECaaS web content filtering.

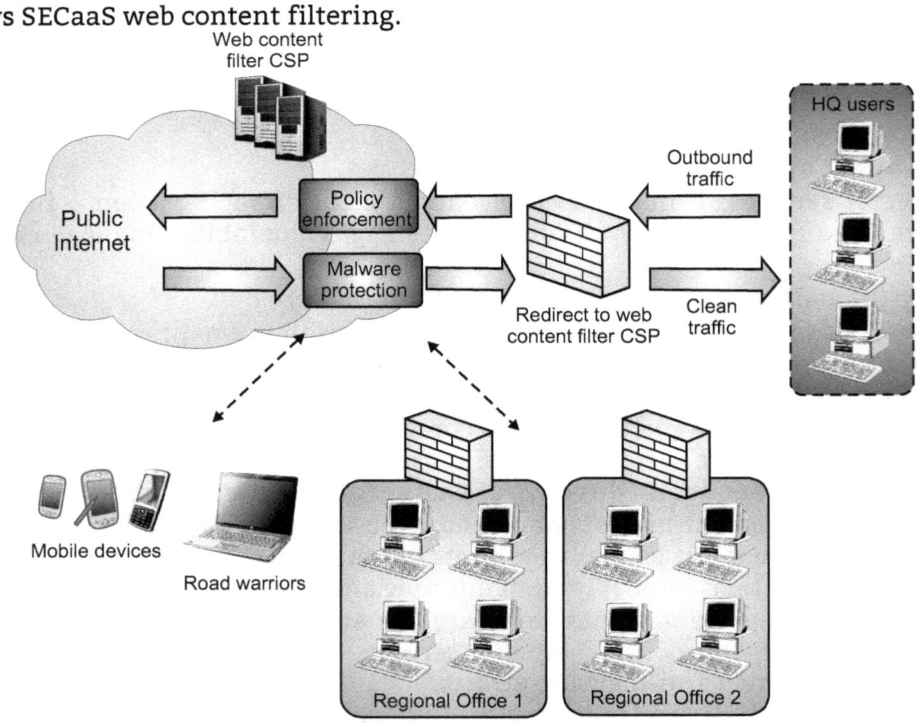

Fig. 5.7: SECaaS web content Filtering

3. Vulnerability Management:

- As the Internet facing presence of organizations has grown in size and complexity, as well as in importance to their operations, ensuring the secure configuration and operation of the systems involved has become more difficult and more important.
- There are SECaaS providers that discover, prioritize, and assess systems for vulnerabilities, and then report and remediate those vulnerabilities and verify the systems secure operation.
- Such information is also used to monitor for and report on compliance with some regulatory requirements (e.g., the Payment Card Industry's Data Security Standard).

4. Identity-as-a-service (IDaaS):

- Identity management-as-a-service (IDaaS) only recently emerged as an example of SECaaS, in comparison to email filtering, web content filtering, and vulnerability management, which are more established as SECaaS offerings.
- IDaaS attempts to provide some IAM services in the cloud. Today's relatively early IDaaS offering tends to focus on authentication, because this is the most critical problem for customers.
- Figure 5.8 shows IDaaS.
- However, the most significant problem for CSPs concerns IDaaS providers, and developing some form of collaborative meta system.
- IDaaS providers will also need to provide other IAM services for cloud customers, including authorization (groups and roles at a minimum), provisioning, and auditing.

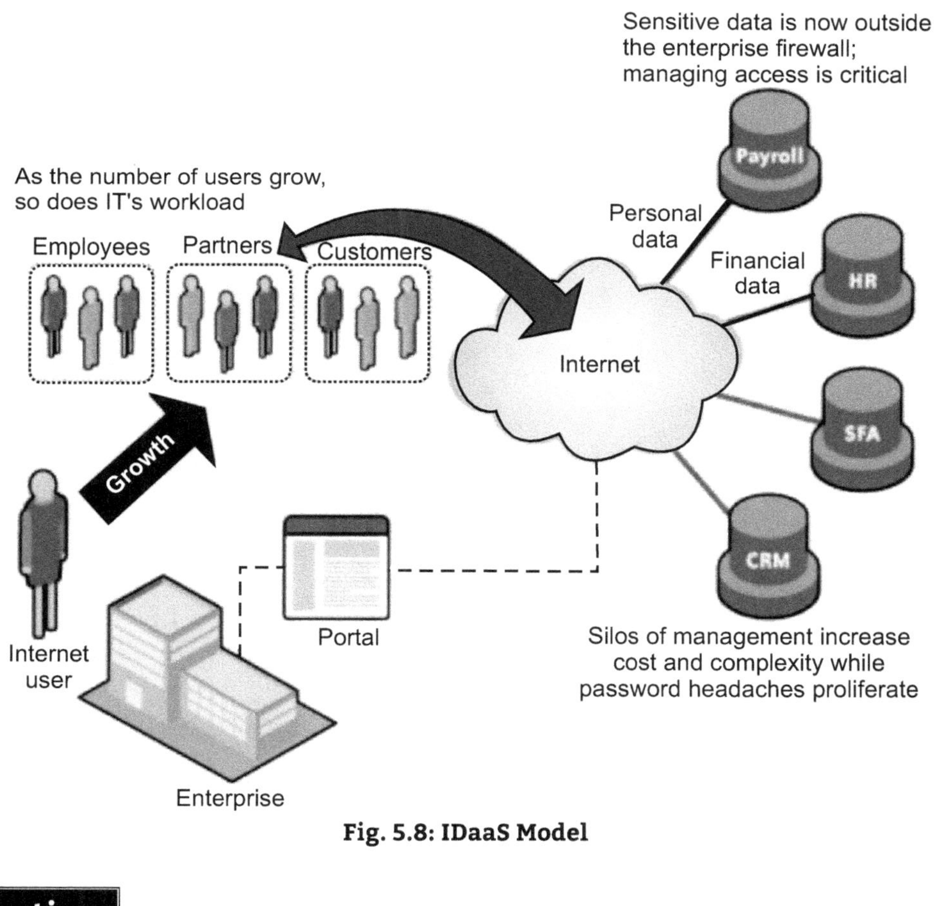

Fig. 5.8: IDaaS Model

Practice Questions

1. What is security in cloud computing?
2. Explain term Confidentiality, Integrity and Availability (CIA).
3. Describe cloud security services in details.
4. Explain different types of cloud risks.
5. Explain top cloud security risks.

6. Describe supported technologies for data security.
7. Explain database outsourcing and query integrity assurance.
8. Explain data integrity in untrustworthy storage
9. Describe protocols to checking data integrity.
10. Explain web application based security.
11. Explain multimedia data security.
12. Explain data security risk in cloud.
13. What digital identity and access management? Why it is needed?
14. Write benefits of the Benefits of IAM.
15. Explain challenges in identity and access management.
16. Explain architecture of identity and access management.
17. Describe life cycle of identity and access management.
18. Briefly explain Content Level Security (CLS).
19. Explain the need for content level security.
20. Explain why security-as-a-cloud services is needed.
21. What are the benefits of security as a cloud services.
22. Explain Services provided by security-as-a-cloud service (SECaaS).
23. What is treat? Explain in detail.

6... Trends and Future in Cloud Computing

Chapter Outcomes...

- Explain the characteristics of the given enabling technology with the IoT.
- Select relevant cloud platform for the identified application with justification.
- Describe the features of the give type of cloud based smart device.
- Compare features of the given cloud platform on the specified criteria.

Learning Objectives...

- To learn Cloud Trends in Supporting Ubiquitous Computing
- To study Enabling Technologies with the Internet of Things (RFID Sensor Networks and ZigBee Technologies, GPS)
- To understand Innovative Applications with Internet of Things
- To learn Future of Cloud Based Smart Devices, Home Based Cloud Computing etc.
- To study Cloud Platforms like Amazon AC2 and S3, Microsoft Azure, Cloudstack, InterCloud, Google App Engine, Open Source Cloud Eucalyptus, Open Stack, Open Nebulla, etc.

6.0 INTRODUCTION

- Today we can connect everything digitally to cloud computing. It provides a whole new world of jobs, applications, services, and platforms.
- We can see the future of cloud computing as a combination of cloud based software products and on-premises compute which will help to create hybrid IT solutions.
- Since the term cloud computing was first introduced more than 20 years ago, the industry has grown exponentially and is expected to continue to widen its influence on global businesses.
- Microsoft, IBM, Google, and Amazon were cloud computing trailblazers when they started promoting the concept back in the mid-2000s, and Gartner predicted the public cloud industry would grow 21.4% from 2017 to 2018, to $186.4 billion.
- Cloud computing continues to provide for the needs of adopters and it presents its own unique challenges, too. Here are five of the most pressing trends affecting the future of cloud computing.
- According to IDC, almost half of IT spending was cloud based in 2018, "reaching 60% of all IT infrastructure and 60-70% of all software, services and technology spending by 2020." So, between Gartner and IDC, no one expects cloud adoption and spending to slow down any time soon.
- There is definitely a lot of publicity around Blockchain, Quantum Computing, Machine Learning, and AI, as there should be. But at a more basic level, cloud computing is changing businesses in many ways.

- Whether it is the way they store their data, improving agility and go to market for faster release of new products and services, or how they store and protect their secure information, cloud computing is benefitting all businesses in every sector.
- Smart businesses are always looking for the most innovative ways to improve and accomplish their business objectives, i.e., make money.
- When it comes to cloud technology, more and more businesses are realizing the benefits that cloud can provide them and are beginning to seek more cloud computing options to conduct their business activities.
- And obviously, Amazon, Microsoft, Google, Alibaba, IBM, and Oracle plan to capture this spend by providing a dizzying array of IaaS and PaaS offerings to help enterprises build and run their services.
- The Internet of Things (IoT) involves the Internet connected devices we use to perform the processes and services that support our way of life. Another component set to help IoT succeed is cloud computing, which acts as a sort of front end.
- Cloud computing is an increasingly popular service that offers several advantages to IoT and is based on the concept of allowing users to perform normal computing tasks using services delivered entirely over the Internet.

6.1 CLOUD TREDNS IN SUPPORTING UBIQUITOUS COMPUTING

- The future of cloud computing systems and their innovative applications.
- The cloud trends includes use of clouds for HPC/HTC and Ubiquitous Computing, Large-Scale Private Clouds at NASA and CERN, Cloud Mashups for Agility and Scalability and Cloudlets for Mobile Cloud Computing.

6.1.1 Use of Clouds for HPC/HTC and Ubiquitous Computing

- Ubiquitous cloud computing refers to the use of Internet resources at any place and any time for any objectives.
- Today, people can access the Internet via a fixed wire or a mobile wireless connection.
- Science in the cloud has been impacted with a new research environment that leverages software and services being provided on user demand.
- New advances in research discovery are expected in high-energy physics, observatory astronomy, atmospheric modeling, biomedicine, big-data, many-cores pervasive clouds and their impact on scientific research in the information age.

6.1.2 Large-Scale Private Clouds at NASA and CERN

- In 2010, two large scale private clouds were under construction in the United States and European Union.
- The U.S. cloud, called Nebula, is developed by NASA and is designed for NASA scientists to run climate models on remote systems provided by NASA. This can save thousands of NASA users from acquiring supercomputers at their local sites.
- The EU cloud is built by CERN in Geneva. This is a large private cloud for distributing data, applications, and computing resources to thousands of scientists around the world. CERN deals with large data sets and throughput with a global workforce and a finite budget.
- Many private clouds are also under development by the IT industry, large enterprises, and other government agencies. Initially, one can see that most clouds are developed with restricted user groups.
- Once these clouds become mature and more secure to use to prove their claimed advantages, they could be converted to public clouds in the future.

6.1.3 Cloud Mashups for Agility and Scalability

- In web application development, a mashup is a web page or application that combines data, presentations, or functionality from two or more sources to create a new service.
- The main characteristics of the mashup are a combination of virtualization and aggregation. In cloud computing, the cloud has captured the computing market with dynamic resource allocation from a pool of VM resources.

6.1.4 Cloudlets for Mobile Cloud Computing

- Recently, researchers proposed a low cost infrastructure to enable cloud computing using mobile devices.
- The ides is called Cloudlet, and it offers a resource rich portal for upgrading mobile devices with cognitive abilities to access distant clouds. This portal should be designed to be trustworthy and use VMs to explore location aware cloud applications.
- The idea can be applied to opportunity discovery, fast information processing, and intelligent decision making on the road. Cloudlet makes it possible for mobile devices to access the Internet cloud easily in cost effective mobile computing services.

6.2 ENABLING TECHNOLOGIES WITH THE INTERNET OF THINGS

- In ubiquitous computing, the Internet of Things (IoT) provides a network of sensor or radio connected devices that can be uniquely identified and located in the cyber physical space.
- This IoT is mostly wirelessly connected as a self-configuring network of radio frequency tags, low-cost sensors, or e-labels. The concept is attributed to original auto-ID tracking in 1999. The term "IoT" combines RFID technology with today's IPv6-based Internet technology.
- All things (objects) have IP addresses, which can be uniquely identified. The IP identifiable objects are readable, recognizable, locatable, addressable, and/or controllable via the Internet, aided by RFID, WiFi, ZigBee, mobile networks, and GPS.
- The IoT enabling technologies are Internet of Things for Ubiquitous Computing, Radio Frequency Identification (RFID), Sensor Networks and ZigBee Technology and Global Positioning System (GPS).

6.2.1 The Internet of Things for Ubiquitous Computing

- The IoT is a natural extension of the Internet. The foundation of the IoT is Radio Frequency Identification (RFID).
- This enables the discovery of tagged objects and mobile devices by browsing an IP address or searching for a database entry.
- Whereas RFID is a kind of amoeba of the pervasive computing world, the IoT presents a vision of the future.
- In the nineteenth century, computers learned to do as instructed. In the twentieth century, computers learned to think.
- In the twenty-first century, computers want to learn how to perceive by sensing and understanding.
- Everyday objects include not only electronic devices, but also objects such as humans, animals, food, clothing, homes, vehicles, commodities, trees, hills, and landmarks.
- The IoT system could greatly reduce the chances of a company running out of stock or wasting products, as all concerned parties would know exactly what products are needed.
- Mislaid items and physical theft would be affected by the fact that the location of an item would be known to all parties. This demands that all objects on Earth be radio tagged, ranging from a milk carton to a truck container to a jumbo jet.
- Computers identify and manage all tagged objects in the same way humans do. This IoT system will improve our quality of life and make society cleaner and more secure, convenient, and enjoyable.

6.2.1.1 Ubiquitous Computing

- Ubiquitous computing is a post desktop model of human computer interaction in which information processing is integrated into everyday objects and activities.
- For daily activities, people may engage in using many pervasive devices simultaneously. They may not even be aware of the existence of the interactive devices.
- Although the idea is simple, its application is difficult. If all objects in the world were equipped with minuscule identifying devices, daily life on our planet could undergo a major transformation.
- The IoT cannot be realized without systems design and engineering, and user interfaces. Contemporary human computer interaction models, whether command line, menu driven, or GUI based, are inappropriate and inadequate to meet ubiquitous computing demands.
- The natural IoT paradigm appropriate to a ubiquitous computing world has yet to emerge. Contemporary devices that lend support to ubiquitous computing include smartphones, tablet computers, sensor networks, RFID tags, smart cards, GPS devices, and others.

6.2.1.2 Development of the Internet of Things

- In 2005, the concept of the IoT entered the limelight. The IoT should be designed to connect the world's objects in a sensory manner.
- The approach is to tag things through RFID, feel things through sensors and wireless networks, and think things by building embedded systems that interact with human activities.
- A road map for IoT development is shown in Fig. 6.1 to anticipate the desired technology advances to make the IoT a reality in 25 years.
- In 2002, the U.S. National Science Foundation (NSF) called for the convergence of cutting-edge technologies including ubiquitous computing and anotechnology.
- In April 2008, the U.S. National Intelligence Council published a report titled "Disruptive Civil Technologies," which also identified the IoT as a critical technology on U.S. interests out to 2025.
- Quantitatively speaking, the IoT should be designed to encode 50 trillion to 100 trillion objects.
- Moreover, the IoT should be designed to follows the movement of those objects. With today's population of more than 6 billion worldwide, that means every person is surrounded by 1,000 to 5,000objects on a daily basis.

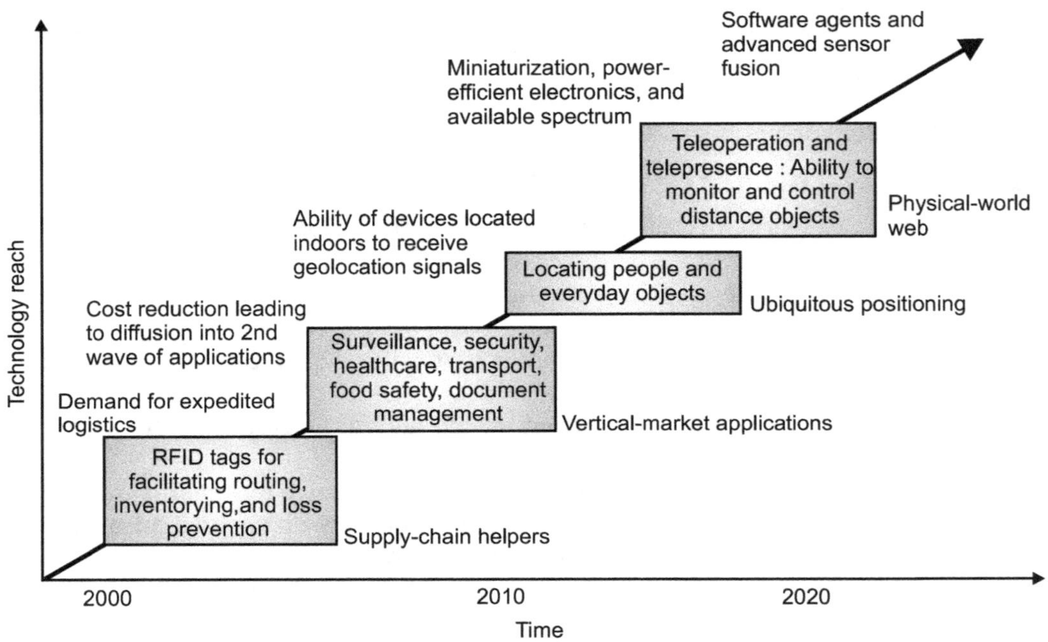

Fig. 6.1: Technology Roadmap of the IoT

6.2.1.3 Enabling and Synergistic Technologies

- Many technologies can be applied to build the IoT infrastructure and specific IoT systems for special application domains.
- Supportive technologies are divided into two categories:
  1. Enabling technologies It build up the foundations of the IoT. Among the enabling technologies, tracking (RFID), sensor networks, and GPS are critical.
  2. Synergistic technologies plays supporting roles. For example, biometrics could be widely applied to personalize the interactions among humans, machines, and objects.
- Artificial intelligence, computer vision, robotics, and telepresence can make our lives more automated in the future. The IoT development could become more mature and more sophisticated in the next 15 years.
- Fig. 6.1 shows the major technology advances and key applications that may benefit from the IoT.
- For example, supply chains are now better supported than before. Vertical market applications may represent the next wave of advances. Ubiquitous positioning is expected to become a reality as we move toward 2020.
- Beyond that, a physical IoT may be in place in a global scale. These advances will significantly upgrade human abilities, societal outcomes, national productivity, and quality of life.

6.2.1.4 Architecture of the Internet of Things

- The IoT system is likely to have an event-driven architecture. In Fig. 6.2.

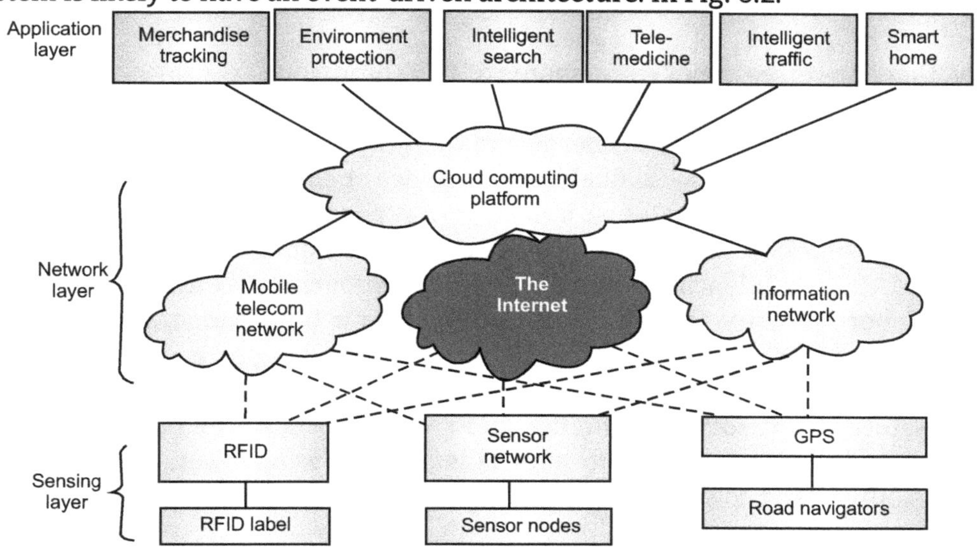

Fig. 6.2: Architecture of IoT

- IoT development is shown with a three-layer architecture.
  1. The top layer is formed by driven applications.
  2. The bottom layers represent various types of sensing devices: namely RFID tags, ZigBee or other types of sensors, and road-mapping GPS navigators.
  3. The sensing devices are locally or wide area connected in the form of RFID networks, sensor networks, and GPSes.
- Signals or information collected at these sensing devices are linked to the applications through the cloud computing platforms at the middle layer.
- The signal processing clouds are built over the mobile networks, the Internet backbone, and various information networks at the middle layer.
- In the IoT, the meaning of a sensing event does not follows a deterministic or syntactic model. In fact, the SOA model is adoptable here.
- A large number of sensors and filters are used to collect the raw data. Various compute and storage clouds and grids are used to process the data and transform it into information and knowledge formats.
- The sensed information is used to put together a decision making system for intelligence applications. The middle layer is also considered as a semantic web or grid. Some actors (services, components, avatars) are self-referenced.

6.2.2 Radio-Frequency Identification (RFID)

- RFID is applied with electronic labels or RFID tags on any objects being monitored or tracked. The tagging may be applied to any objects, such as merchandise, tools, smartphones, computers, animals, or people.
- The purpose is to identify and track the objects using radio waves or sensing signals. Some tags can be read from tens or hundreds of meters away via a wireless reader.
- Most RFID tags contain at least two major parts. One is an integrated circuit for storing and processing information, modulating and demodulating a radio-frequency (RF) signal, and other special functions.
- The other part is an antenna for receiving and transmitting the radio signals.

6.2.2.1 RFID Tags and Device Components

- There are generally three types of RFID tags:
  - Active RFID tags containing a battery and transmitting signals autonomously.
  - Passive RFID tags which have no battery and require an external source to provoke signal transmission.

- Battery-assisted passive RFID tags which require an external source to wake up the battery but have significantly higher forward link capability.
- Based on the radio frequency used, the passive RFID tags operate with from low frequency (LF) to high frequency (HF), ultra high frequency (UHF), and the microwave range. In terms of functionality, there are three major components of RFID hardware:
  - RFID tag a tiny silicon chip attached to a small antenna.
  - Reader antenna used to radiate the energy and then capture the return signal sent back from the tag. It can be integrated with a handheld reader device or connected to the reader by cable.
  - Reader the device station that talks with the tags. A reader may support one or more antennae.
- Resembling an electronic barcode, a reader device can detect signals even without a line of sight.
- Some RFID readers can identify multiple objects concurrently. And some RFID tag-reader architectures support security features such as requiring a human operator to input a challenge codebefore decoding an ID.
- RFID devices have varying sizes, power requirements, operating frequencies, amounts of rewritable and nonvolatile storage, and software intelligence.
- They operate from a few centimeters to hundreds of meters. However, larger devices having an internal power source tend to operate at longer ranges. Conversely, very smaller devices have no internal power source.

6.2.2.2 How RFID Works

- Innovations in RFID include active, semi-active, and passive RFID tags. These tags can store up to 2 KB of data and are composed of a microchip, antenna, and battery for active and semi-passive tags.
- The tag's components are enclosed within plastic, silicon, or sometimes glass. Data stored in the microchip waits to be read.
- The tag's antenna receives electromagnetic energy from an RFID reader's antenna. Using power from its internal battery or power harvested from the reader's electromagnetic field, the tag returns radio signals back to the reader.
- The reader picks up the tag's radio signals and interprets the frequencies as meaningful data.
- There are two ways to couple schemes in RFID tags namely inductively coupled and capacitively coupled.
- Fig. 6.3 shows the RFID operations between the RFID tags (e-labels), reading/writing devices, and backend computers. RFID tags are still not in widespread use by ordinary people, because they are expensive and bulky.

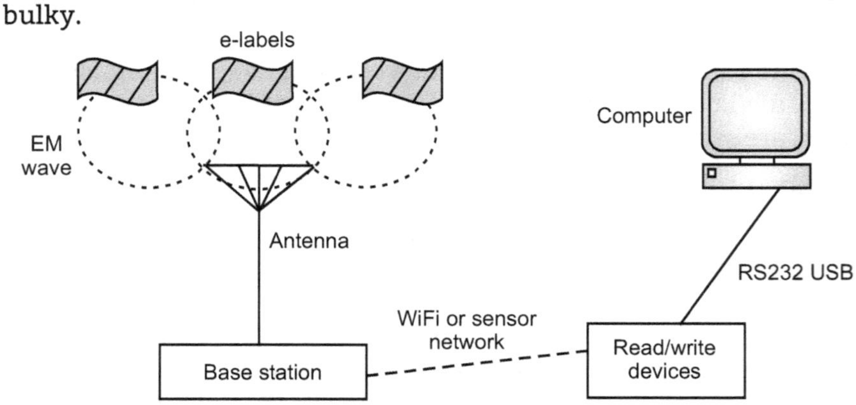

Fig. 6.3: RFID working

- They are more often used by large businesses, moving or shipping companies, and service companies. However, RFID tags can make our daily life or work much easier, more convenient, and accessible to visible or hidden objects surrounding us.
- These tags are not that expensive to produce in large quantities, and they can be made small enough to fit on almost any product or object.
- External RF antenna devices can illuminate the tag devices similar to radar illuminating a target. However, RFID is more effective at operating at shorter ranges. A variety of agencies are defining the standards and regulating the use of RFID.

- They include the International Organization for Standardization (ISO), International Electrotechnical Commission (IEC), ASTM International, DASH7 Alliance, and EPCglobal. RFID has many industrial applications including merchandise tracking and supply chain management. Its use can improve the efficiency of inventory control and accuracy of assembly line management.
- Active and semi-passive RFID tags use internal batteries to power their circuits. An active tag can also use its own battery to broadcast radio waves to a reader, whereas a semi-passive tag relies on the reader to supply its power for broadcasting.
- Active and semi-passive tags are reserved for reading over 30 to 100 meters, if repeater batteries are used to boost a tag's range.
- For example, a customer finds a pair of jeans in her size on a store shelf with a radio wand provided by the store. She can order the clothing and pay via her cell phone with the help of an RFID setting.
- Passive RFID tags rely entirely on the reader as their power source. These tags are read only up to 20 feet away. They have lower production costs, meaning they can be applied to less expensive merchandise. These tags are manufactured to be disposable. A railway car may apply active RFID tags. A bottle of shampoo may use only a passive tag.
- Another factor that influences the cost of RFID tags is data storage. There are three storage types namely read-write, read-only, and Write-Once-Read-Many (WORM).
- A read-write tag's data can be added to or overwritten. Read-only tags cannot be added to or overwritten.
- WORM tags can have additional data added once, but they cannot be overwritten. Most passive RFID tags cost 7–20 cents each. Active and semi-passive tags are more expensive, and RFID manufacturers typically do not quote prices for these tags without first determining their range, storage type, and quantity.

6.2.3 Sensor Networks and ZigBee Technology

- Today's sensor networks are mostly wireless, and are known as Wireless Sensor Networks (WSNs).
- A typical WSN consists of spatially distributed autonomous sensors to cooperatively monitor physical or environmental conditions, such as temperature, sound, vibration, pressure, motion, or pollutants.
- The development of wireless sensor networks was motivated by military applications such as battlefield surveillance.
- WSN technology is now used in many industrial and civilian application areas, including process monitoring and control, machine health monitoring, environment and habitat monitoring, health care and home automation, and intelligent traffic control.

6.2.3.1 Wireless Sensor Networks

- A WSN is a group of specialized transducers with a communications infrastructure intended to monitor and record conditions at diverse locations.
- Commonly monitored parameters are temperature, humidity, pressure, wind direction and speed, illumination intensity, vibration intensity, sound intensity, power-line voltage, chemical concentrations, pollutant levels, and vital body functions. A sensor network consists of multiple detection stations called sensor nodes, each of which is small, lightweight, and portable.
- Every sensor node is equipped with a transducer, microcomputer, transceiver, and power source. The transducer generates electrical signals based on sensed data.
- The microcomputer processes and stores the sensor output. The transceiver, which can be hardwired or wireless, receives commands from a central computer and transmits data to that computer.
- The power for each sensor node is derived from the electric utility or from a battery. A sensor node may vary in size from that of a shoebox down to a dust grain.
- The cost of sensor nodes also varies a lot, ranging from Rs 100 to a few pennies. Size and cost constraints on sensor nodes are often decided by energy, memory, computational speed, and bandwidth of the sensors used.

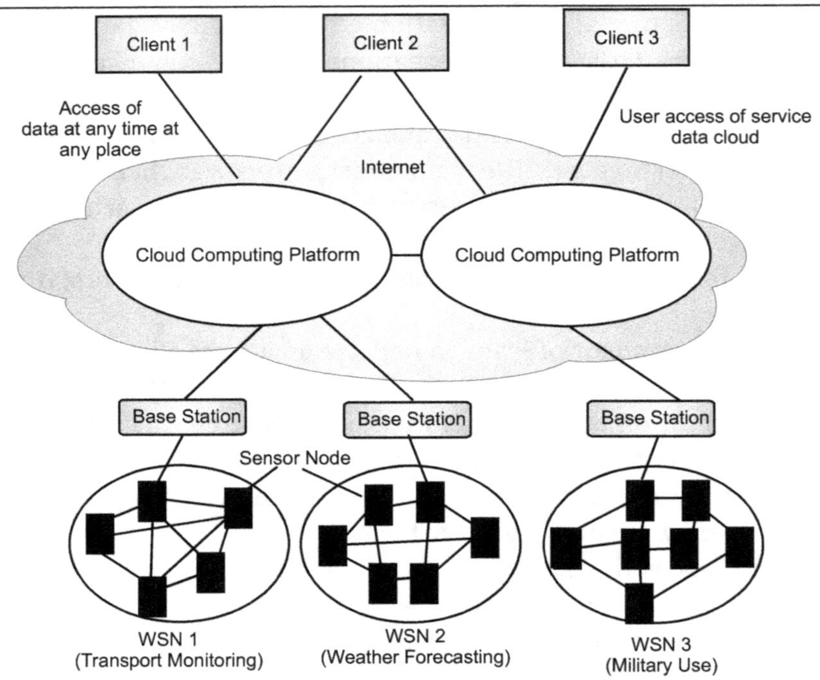

Fig. 6.4

6.2.3.2 How WSN Works

- Four classes of wireless networks supports ubiquitous computing namely Zigbee, GSM/GPRS, WiFi 802.11g and Bluetooth 802.15.1.
- The ZigBee networks are mainly used in low-cost and low-speed monitoring and control applications, such as those used in a Wireless Home Area Network (WHAN).
- The GSM/GPRS or CDMA/1 networks are cellular mobile networks that can cover a wide area for voice and data telecommunications.
- The WiFi networks specified in the IEEE 802.11b standard. WiFi is used for wirelessly accessing the Internet, reading e-mails, or conducting web page searches Bluetooth is mainly used for short distance wireless connection of computer peripherals (e.g., keyboard, mouse, printers, etc.). In terms of data rate, WiFi is the fastest (54 Mbps for 802.11g network).
- The Bluetooth with 720 Kbps and 115 Kbps for the 2.5G GPRS mobile network. ZigBee has the slowest rate of 20–250 Kbps.
- However, ZigBee has high reliability and low power/cost advantages.
- Network self-organization is expected in a sensor network. Given the large number of nodes and their potential placement in hostile locations, it is essential that the network be able to self organize; manual configuration is not feasible.
- Moreover, nodes may fail (either from lack of energy or from physical destruction), and new nodes may join the network.
- Therefore, the network must be able to periodically reconfigure itself so that it can continue to function. Individual nodes may become disconnected from the rest of the network, but a high degree of connectivity must be maintained. Collaborative signal processing is desired in a sensor network.
- To improve detection/estimation performance, it is often quite useful to fuse data from multiple sensors. This data fusion requires the transmission of data and control messages.
- A user may want to query an individual node or a group of nodes for information collected in the region. Depending on the amount of data fusion performed, it may not be feasible to transmit a large amount of the data across the network. Instead, various local sink nodes will collect the data from a given area and create summary messages. A query may be directed to the sink node nearest to the desired location.

6.2.3.3 Three Generations of Sensor Networks

- Three generations of WSN are namely First generation (1990), Second generation (2000) and Third Generation (2010).

1. **First Generation:**
   - The sensors used in the first generation were mainly vehicle-placed or air-dropped single sensors. They were quite bulky, like a shoebox, and weighed in the kilograms.
   - Networks assumed only star or point-to-point topologies and were powered by large batteries that could last hours or days.
2. **Second Generation:**
   - In the second generation, the sensors became smaller, like a pack of playing cards, and weighed in the grams, and worked with AA batteries that lasted for days or weeks. They appears in client/server or P2P configurations.
3. **Third Generation:**
   - The current generation are as large as dust particles, weigh only a negligible amount, and are used in P2P networks for embedded and remote applications.

6.2.3.4 ZigBee Network

- The term "ZigBee" is originated from the behavior of honeybees when they return to the beehive.
- This is a high-level communication protocol using small, low power, radio based sensors as specified by the IEEE 802.15.4 standard. For example, ZigBee devices are applied in WHANs in wireless light switches and consumer electronics controlled by short range radio.
- The ZigBee technology is simpler to use and less expensive than Bluetooth or WiFi. The RF applied in ZigBee results in low data rates, long battery life, and secure networking.
- The low cost allows the technology to be widely deployed in wireless control and monitoring applications.
- The low power usage allows a longer life with smaller batteries. The mesh networking provides higher availability and an extended operating range.

6.2.3.4.1 Features of Zigbee

- Features of Zigbee are given below:
  1. Support for multiple network topologies such as point-to-point, point-to-multipoint and mesh networks.
  2. Low duty cycle – provides long battery life.
  3. Low latency.
  4. Direct Sequence Spread Spectrum (DSSS).
  5. Up to 65,000 nodes per network.
  6. 128-bit AES encryption for secure data connections.
  7. Collision avoidance, retries and acknowledgements.

6.2.3.4.2 Devices supported by Zigbee

- There are three different types of ZigBee devices are as follows:
  1. **ZigBee Coordinator (ZC):** This is the most capable ZigBee device serving as the coordinator or the root of a ZigBee network. There is exactly one coordinator in each network since it is the device that started the network. It is able to store information about the network, including acting as the trust center and repository of security keys.
  2. **ZigBee Router (ZR):** This can act as an intermediate router, passing on data from end device to end device.
  3. **ZigBee End Device (ZED):** This contains just enough functionality to talk to the parent node(either the coordinator or the router). The end device cannot relay data from other devices.
- This relationship allows the node to be asleep a significant amount of the time, thereby ensuring along battery life. A ZED requires the least amount of memory, and therefore can be less expensive to manufacture than a ZR or ZC.
- ZigBee devices are required to conform to the IEEE 802.15.4 Wireless Personal Area Network (WPAN) standard. The standard specifies the lower protocol layers-the physical layer and the MAC at the data link layer. This standard operates in the unlicensed 2.4 GHz (worldwide).

6.2.3.4.3 Zigbee Protocol Architecture

- Zigbee protocol architecture consists of a stack of various layers where IEEE 802.15.4 is defined by physical and MAC layers while this protocol is completed by accumulating Zigbee's own network and application layers shown in Fig. 6.5.

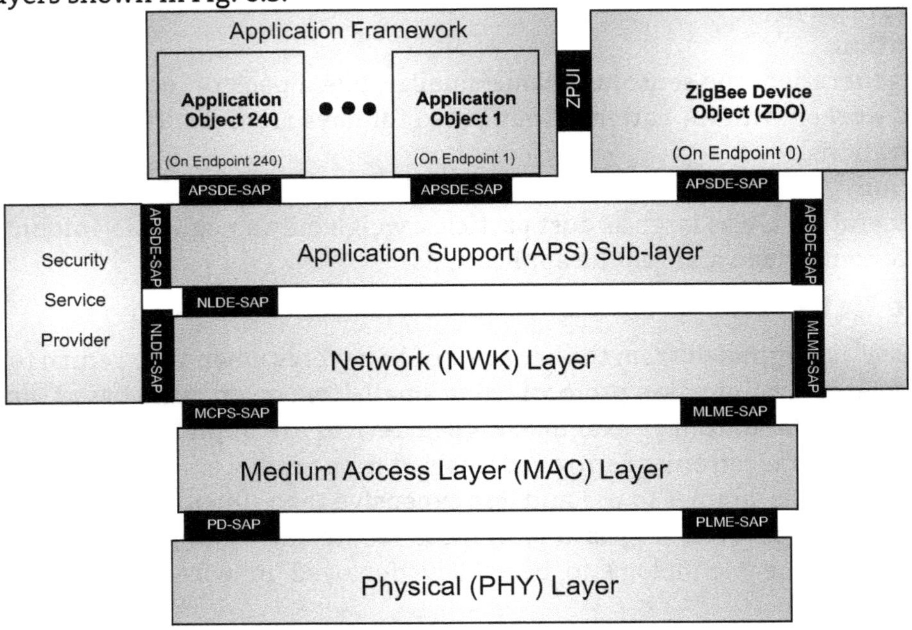

Fig. 6.5: Zigbee Protocol Architecture

- The layers in Fig. 6.5 of Zigbee are explained below:
  1. **Physical Layer:** This layer does modulation and demodulation operations up on transmitting and receiving signals respectively. This layer's supports frequency 2.4GHz, 868MHz and 915MHz.
  2. **MAC Layer:** This layer is responsible for reliable transmission of data by accessing different networks with the carrier sense multiple access collision avoidance (CSMA). This also transmits the beacon frames for synchronizing communication.
  3. **Network Layer:** This layer takes care of all network related operations such as network setup, end device connection and disconnection to network, routing, device configurations, etc.
  4. **Application Support Sub-Layer:** This layer enables the services necessary for Zigbee device object and application objects to interface with the network layers for data managing services. This layer is responsible for matching two devices according to their services and needs.
  5. **Application Framework:** It provides two types of data services as key value pair and generic message services. Generic message is a developer defined structure, whereas the key value pair is used for getting attributes within the application objects. ZDO provides an interface between application objects and APS layer in Zigbee devices. It is responsible for detecting, initiating and binding other devices to the network.

6.2.3.4.4 Applications of Zigbee

- Various applications of Zigbee are listed below:
  1. **Industrial Automation:** In manufacturing and production industries, a communication link continually monitors various parameters and critical equipments. Hence Zigbee considerably reduce this communication cost as well as optimizes the control process for greater reliability.
  2. **Home Automation:** Zigbee is perfectly suited for controlling home appliances remotely as a lighting system control, appliance control, heating and cooling system control, safety equipment operations and control, surveillance, and so on.
  3. **Smart Metering:** Zigbee remote operations in smart metering include energy consumption response, pricing support, security over power theft, etc.
  4. **Smart Grid Monitoring:** Zigbee operations in this smart grid involve remote temperature monitoring, fault locating, reactive power management, and so on.

6.2.4 Global Positioning System (GPS)

- Location-Based Service (LBS) helps people and machines find things and determine their physical where about.
- Sensors play a role in dead reckoning, but that approach does not satisfy practical needs for geo location.
- This has triggered the creation of global positioning and navigation systems. The GPS was developed in 1973 by the U.S. Air Force. The global positioning system is a satellite-based navigation system consisting of a network of 24 orbiting satellites that are eleven thousand nautical miles in space and in six different orbital paths. The satellites are constantly moving, making two complete orbits around the Earth in just under 24 hours. If you do the math, that's about 2.6 kilometers per second.
- Similar developments also occurred in the European Union, Russia, China and India.
- Generally, the GPS is augmented by other signals and cellular towers. Fixed or orbiting satellite transmitters broadcast timing signals and receiving device response signals to locate the position of moving objects.
- Radar, lidar, and sonar can all detect relative locations of things using electromagnetic, optical, and acoustic signals.
- With help from satellites, some objects can be also located by attaching active GPS devices to disclose their locations by radio, light, and/or sound.
- Since 1994, a degraded GPS has been made available for civilian applications in providing reliable positioning, navigation, and timing services.
- For anyone with a GPS receiver, the system will provide accurate location and time information for an unlimited number of users in all weather conditions, day and night, anywhere in the world.
- Each GPS satellite broadcasts a message that includes the satellite's current position, orbit, and exact time. A GPS receiver combines the broadcasts from multiple satellites to calculate its exact position using a process called triangulation. Three satellites are required in order to determine a receiver's location, though a connection to four satellites is ideal since it provides greater accuracy.
- In order for a GPS device to work correctly, it must first establish a connection to the required number of satellites. This process can take anywhere from a few seconds to a few minutes, depending on the strength of the receiver.
- For example, a car's GPS unit will typically establish a GPS connection faster than the receiver in a watch or smartphone.
- Most GPS devices also use some type of location caching to speed up GPS detection. By memorizing its previous location, a GPS device can quickly determine what satellites will be available the next time it scans for a GPS signal.

6.2.4.1 How GPS Works

- GPS consists of three parts namely Space Segment, Control Segment and User Segment.
- There are 24 satellites deployed around the Earth in fixed orbits. The satellites orbit at an altitude of approximately 20,200 KM. GPS satellites broadcast signals from space, by which each GPS receiver calculates its 3D location (latitude, longitude, and altitude) plus the current time.
- The space segment is composed of 24 satellites in medium earth orbit and also includes the boosters required to launch them into orbit. Earth twice a day in very precise orbits and transmit signals to Earth.
- GPS devices on the ground receive these signals and use a triangulation method to calculate the user's exact location. At different times, different satellites will become visible to the receiver.
- Fig. 6.6 shows, the control segment is composed of a master control station and a host of dedicated and shared ground antennas and monitor stations.
- The user segment is composed of hundreds of thousands of allied users of the secure GPS precise positioning services. Tens of millions of civil, commercial, and scientific users are only allowed to use a degraded functionality of the so-called standard positioning services that cannot be used in hostile attack purposes.
- Essentially, the GPS receiver compares the time a signal was transmitted by a satellite with the time it was received. The time difference tells the GPS receiver how far away the satellite is. With distance measured from several satellites, the receiver can determine the user's position and display it on the unit's electronic map.

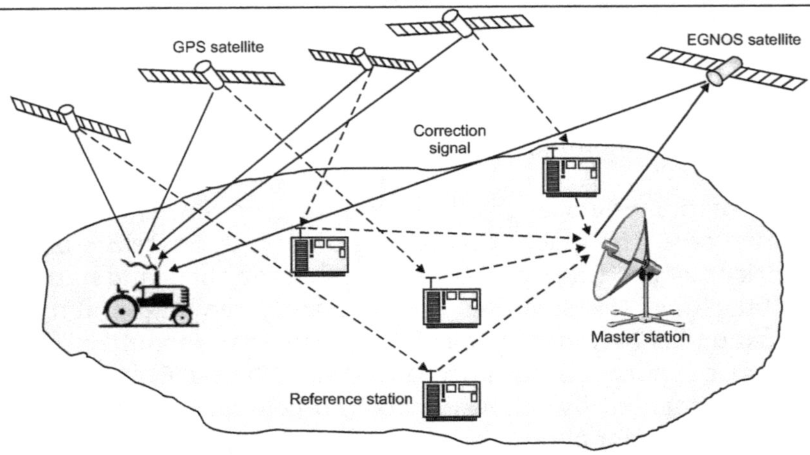

Fig. 6.6: GPS System Working Architecture

- The GPS tracking device makes it possible to track people, vehicles, and other assets, anywhere on earth.

6.2.4.2 Types of GPS

- There are two types of GPS tracking systems namely Passive GPS and Active GPS.
  1. **In passive GPS tracking,** the GPS is just a receiver, not a transmitter. Passive GPS tracking devices lack a transmission capability to send the GPS data from the vehicle. Therefore, passive GPS is also known as data loggers used primarily as recording devices.
  2. **Active GPS tracking** units incorporate a method to transmit user information from a vehicle. Although satellite uplink of data is available, cellular data communication is the most common and cost-effective. Automatic incremental updating provides a continuous source of tracking throughout a recording period. This provides current as well as historical logging positions.
- Passive GPS tracking devices store GPS location data in their internal memory which can then be downloaded to a computer or mobile for viewing at a later time, while active GPS tracking systems send the data at regular intervals to be viewed in real time.
- When real-time data is not required, passive GPS tracking devices tend to be favored more by individual consumers for their compact convenience and affordability.
- Concerned parents can install a GPS tracking unit just about anywhere in their teens' vehicles to monitor their driving habits and know where they've been going, and even law enforcement officials now rely on passive GPS tracking to trail criminal suspects and enhance civilian safety via electronic surveillance of parolees.
- Passive GPS tracking units also serve as a theft prevention and retrieval aid in consumer as well as commercial vehicles.

6.2.4.3 Operating Principles of GPS

- Knowing the distance from the receiver to a fixed-position satellite implies that the receiver is on the surface of a sphere centered at the satellite. With four satellites, the receiver location is detected at the intersection of four sphere surfaces.
- The intersection of two satellite spheres is a circle in general. This circle could be reduced to a single point, if the two spheres merely touch on their surfaces.
- Having found those two intersecting sphere surfaces, now we consider how the intersecting circle intersects with a third satellite signal sphere.
- A circle and a sphere surface intersect at zero, one, or two points. With the receiver on the surface of earth, the receiver needs to choose the point which is closest to the receiver from at most two intersecting points.
- To locate the point accurately, the receiver has to use a fourth satellite to hone in almost precisely. The fourth satellite sphere will come very close to the final two intersecting points of three satellite spheres.
- The final receiver location is thus decided by noting the closest point calculated from the two final points to the sphere surface of the fourth satellite. In the case of no error, the precise position is located.

- Otherwise, some offset-say, 10 meters from the exact location could be resulted from the error introduced. To further reduce the errors, more satellites could be involved, but this could be rather costly.
- Each satellite continually transmits messages that include the time the message was transmitted, precise orbital information (the ephemeris), and the general system health and rough orbits of all GPS satellites (the almanac).
- A GPS receiver calculates its position by precisely timing the signals sent by GPS satellites high above earth.
- A GPS receiver must be locked onto the signal of at least three satellites to calculate a 2D position (latitude and longitude) and track movement. With four or more satellites in view, the receiver can determine the user's 3D position (latitude, longitude, and altitude).
- Once the user's position has been determined, the GPS unit can calculate other information, such as speed, bearing, track, trip distance, distance to destination, sunrise and sunset times, and more. The receiver utilizes the messages it receives to determine the transit time of each message and computes the distances to each satellite.
- These distances along with the satellites' locations are used to compute the position of the receiver. This position is displayed perhaps with a moving map display or latitude, longitude, and elevation information. Many GPS units show derived information such as direction and speed calculated from positional changes.

6.3 INNOVATIVE APPLICATIONS WITH INTERNET OF THINGS

- Many innovative applications in tracking, retailing, supply chain management, smartpower grid, and smart buildings and, European IoT projects are assessed along with American Cyber-Physical System (CPS) projects for general-purpose applications.

6.3.1 Applications of the Internet of Things

- IoT has a lot of military applications along with this IoT plays important roles in environment protection, including pollution control, weather forecasting, and disaster avoidance and recovery.
- In terms of societal impacts, the IoT can make our lives more convenient and comfortable.
- Government services, law enforcement, and home and health improvements are the major beneficiaries.
- IoT applications comes under three domains, Specific Wireless Sensor Applications, Retailing and Supply-Chain Management and Smart Power Grid and Smart Buildings.

6.3.1.1 Specific Wireless Sensor Applications

- Highlighted below are several applications of sensor networks:
    - Military sensor networks to detect and gain as much information as possible about enemy movements, explosions, and other phenomena of interest.
    - Sensor networks to detect and characterize chemical, biological, radiological, nuclear, and explosive attacks and materials.
    - Sensor networks to detect and monitor environmental changes in plains, forests, oceans, and so on .
    - Wireless traffic sensor networks to monitor vehicle traffic on highways or in congested parts of a city.
    - Wireless surveillance sensor networks for providing security in shopping malls, parking garages, and other facilities.
    - Wireless parking lot sensor networks to determine whether the lot is occupied or available.

6.3.1.2 Retailing and Supply-Chain Management

- IoT applications will promote business, improve our society, and enhance economical growth.
- These include specific IoT applications in railing and logistics services and supply chain management. Many industrial, government, and community services can benefit from these applications.
- These include activities or initiatives to promote the development of better and more efficient societies, cities, and governments.

6.3.1.3 Smart Power Grid and Smart Buildings

- Environmental protection is a global issue. Green energy is desired to save energy and to reduce the effects of global warming. A critical IoT application is promotion of a smart power grid.

Smart Power Grid:

- In the past, electricity grids were simple pipes through which electricity flowed from the producer to consumers. They have however evolved gradually to become 'smart'. This has enabled them to solve the growing issue of managing the balance of the grid.
- To put it simply, the amount of electricity fed into the grid by producers must always be equal to the amount of electricity taken out by consumers. If there is too great an imbalance, incidents such as power failures or, on a larger scale, a complete blackout could occur.
- Various power companies across the United States have or are in the process of upgrading their power management and distribution systems. Various sensors at individual homes (smart thermostats) can collect information that is sent via a network to main stations (perhaps even local "hubs") that can apply complex power management and send control signals back to the grid to save energy.
- The smart grid is made possible by applying sensing, measurement, and control devices to electricity production, transmission, distribution, and consumption.
- The smart grid can be defined as a smart electrical network that combines electrical network and smart digital communication technology. A smart grid has capable of providing electrical power from multiple and widely distributed sources, like from wind turbines, solar power systems, and perhaps even plug-in hybrid electric vehicles.
- A smart grid includes an intelligent monitoring system that keeps track of all electricity flowing in the system.
- Smart meters, a digital upgrade of current utility meters, track energy usage in real time so that both the customer and the utility company know how much is being used at any given time. Energy is paid for using "time of day" pricing, meaning electricity will cost more at peak times of use.
- For example, when power is least expensive the user can allows the smart grid to turn on selected home appliances such as washing machines or factory processes that can run at arbitrary hours. At peak times it could turn off selected appliances to reduce demand.
- More involved users would be able to use the smart meter to view energy usage remotely and makes real-time decisions about energy consumption. A refrigerator or air conditioning system could be turned down remotely while residents are away.

Features of Smart Grids:

1. **Flexible:** They makes it easier to manage variations in generation and consumption better.
2. **Reliable:** Thanks to the information sent in real time and the remote management of the grid, the risk of power failures and incidents is reduced.
3. **Accessible:** All the different sources of energy can be integrated into the grid and, thanks to interconnections between grids, consumers can also take advantage of renewable energy generated in large quantities in neighbouring countries when there isn't enough in Belgium.
4. **Savings:** Better management leads to reduced costs.

What does a Smart Grid do?

- The Smart Grid represents an unprecedented opportunity to move the energy industry into a new era of reliability, availability, and efficiency that will contribute to our economic and environmental health.
- During the transition period, it will be critical to carry out testing, technology improvements, consumer education, development of standards and regulations, and information sharing between projects to ensure that the benefits we envision from the Smart Grid become a reality.

Benefits of the Smart Grid are:

1. More efficient transmission of electricity.
2. Quicker restoration of electricity after power disturbances.
3. Reduced operations and management costs for utilities, and ultimately lower power costs for consumers.
4. Reduced peak demand, which will also help lower electricity rates.

5. Increased integration of large scale renewable energy systems.
6. Better integration of customer-owner power generation systems, including renewable energy systems improved security.

Smart Buildings:

- The IoT could enhance our lives with comfort, convenience, and security, and reduce energy costs and environmental impacts.
- The IoT has been suggested in construction of smart buildings in residential, commercial, industrial, and government settings.
- This may include alarm systems, access controls, indoor climate controls, elevators, and so forth. We desire to diffuse IT into lighting, appliances, and furniture in buildings.
- A smart building can be a shopping mall or a home, a hospital or a high-rise office tower.
- Smart buildings need monitoring and regulation of heating, air conditioning, lighting, and environmental changes.
- They can oversee building security, fire suppression, and elevator operations. Smart building technologies focus on bringing more detailed monitoring and sensing "awareness" to buildings.
- A smart building is any structure that uses automated processes to automatically control the building's operations including heating, ventilation, air conditioning, lighting, security and other systems.
- A smart building uses sensors, actuators and microchips, in order to collect data and manage it according to a business' functions and services. This infrastructure helps owners, operators and facility managers improve asset reliability and performance, which reduces energy use, optimizes how space is used and minimizes the environmental impact of buildings.

Features of Smart Buildings:

1. **Systems are Connected:** The most fundamental feature of a smart building is that the core systems within it are linked. So, water meters, pumps, fire alarms, power, lighting etc are all connected. This is what makes a building "smart" – the ability of the systems within it to talk to one another.
2. **The Use of Sensors:** Sensors are an integral part of smart buildings and play an important role in collecting data to inform decisions about where to allocate resources. So, for example, footfall counters may be integrated into the building to provide information on where people are at certain times of the day and which areas are high traffic.
3. **Automation:** Information is gathered and analysed by the systems that have been put in place in a smart building – importantly, this is done constantly and in real time. This ongoing monitoring allows for automated adjustments that can control conditions across an entire building.
4. **Data:** Smart buildings generate a large volume of valuable data about their own use, which is something that regular buildings simply don't do.

Characteristics of a Smart building:

1. **People-Centric:**

- Buildings of the future are designed to function for the people who will use them. As the needs and expectations of people continuously change, the way we design and construct buildings must follow.
- **We need to ask:**
    - What will people use these buildings for?
    - How will these buildings make them comfortable, happy and productive?
    - If today's workforce values mobility, flexibility and connectivity around the work place, how should the design of these buildings address these needs?

2. **Flexible:**

- Disruption is moving at an exponential rate, continuously affecting and changing business needs, models, landscapes, and the use of buildings. To address disruption, buildings of the future should be designed with flexibility in mind. We don't want to build white elephants. Gone will be the days that buildings are designed as rigid structures that are built for one purpose and can't be changed.
- In the future, these structures and spaces will be adaptable without significant building modification: with walls that can be moved easily and essential engineering services that can be effortlessly altered and re-connected in new ways.

3. **Invisible:**

- Technologies should be embedded to a building seamlessly. It should just work, no explanations needed. The goal for smart buildings is to self-manage, learn, anticipate, and adapt on its own, without the need for the intervention or recognition of its users. Room temperatures, lighting, shading, energy and water utilisation can all be easily and automatically adjusted based on sensors and monitors.

4. **Sustainable:**

- The impact of climate change and rapid population growth to our natural resources is endangering the future of human kind, making sustainability one of the key priorities when designing buildings of the future. Thanks to advanced technologies, smart buildings can exist off the grid and develop self-sustaining ecosystems, enabling it to produce energy and collect and treat water on site.

5. **Learning:**

- Buildings of the future will not only be designed for us, they will get to know us. Every sensor, automation and monitor installed in these buildings will be integrated into a main building management system which can capture every movement within the building and enable the building to automatically modify its settings and continuously self-tune.

Benefits of Smart Buildings:

1. **Make the Occupants More Productive:** Air quality, physical comfort, security, sanitation, lighting and even room and space availability can all be delivered at an optimum level to enable occupants to perform well.
2. **Reducing Energy Consumption:** Smart buildings are greener, more energy efficient and more cost effective.
3. **End of Guesswork:** The use of sensors and cameras provides precise data on how the building is being used, which can be converted into insightful decision making. Space utilisation can be improved based on actual data, as the building generates actionable, living intelligence automatically.
4. **Significant Operational Savings:** This includes the savings that can be made in terms of everyday spend and maintenance on equipment. It also extends to the potential savings that are offered by identifying underutilised resources and the potential for growth into unused spaces.
5. **Data Protection:** Equipment, such as thermal sensors, measures data without using identifiable images of staff or the public.

- There are many benefits to implementing smart systems within a building, from cost efficiency to improving the environmentally friendly credentials of the construction. Smart buildings are relatively new today but, given the wide range of benefits that they offer, will soon become the norm.

6.4 FUTURE OF CLOUD-BASED SMART DEVICES

- In recent years there's been a lot of talk about cloud computing and cloud storage, like Microsoft Azure, Amazon Web Services, and Google Cloud.
- Almost everything in the digital world is connected to the cloud in some way or another-unless it's specifically kept in local storage for security reasons. As tech giants and startups find new ways to organize, process and present data cloud computing will become a more and more integral part of our lives.
- The future of cloud computing will most likely represent a combination of cloud based software products and on premises compute to create a hybrid IT solution that balances the scalability and flexibility associated with cloud and the security and control of a private data center.
- For years, futurists have forecast the day when a refrigerator would automatically create our grocery list and send the list to the store so your essentials could be delivered.
- The cloud's ability to provide Internet access any place and any time makes such processing a reality.
- Some devices may initially be "intelligent" with respect to their ability to control power consumption, possibly avoiding power use during peak times and costs.

6.4.1 Home Based Cloud Computing

- Today, most households have wireless network capabilities that allows family members to connect to the Web and access sites and content they desire.
- With the advent of smart devices, intelligent fabrics, and greater use of Radio Frequency Identification Devices (RFID), family members will expect on-demand personalized technology solutions.
- Using the cloud for communication, devices can coordinate activities. For example, your car may notify your home automation system that you are down the block and instruct it to light the house, turn on your favorite music, and prompt the refrigerator for a list of ready-to-cook meals.
- Home users can benefit from many aspects of cloud computing services. While many cloud vendors and providers target a great deal of their services to business clients, individual users can also find very attractive cloud packages for personal communications and other needs.
- One of the first elements of using cloud computing at home is finding the right services that benefit personal users. This may mean sifting through a series of cloud software offers.
- Some cloud computing personal services are more accessible for example, Microsoft offers aspects of cloud computing in its Office 365 and other packages. For other more specific cloud services, users may have to read through service specifications to figure out if a cloud offer is right for them.

6.4.2 Energy Aware Cloud Computing

- Data centers are not only expensive to maintain, they are also unfriendly to the environment. Carbon emissions due to data centers world wide are now more than the emissions.
- High energy costs and huge carbon footprints are incurred due to the massive amount of electricity needed to power and cool the numerous servers hosted in these data centers.
- Cloud service providers need to adopt measures to ensure that their profit margins are not dramatically reduced due to high energy costs. According to Amazon's estimate, the energy related costs of its datacenters amount to 42% of the total budget, which includes both direct power consumption and the cooling infrastructure amortized over a 15-year period.
- As a result, companies such as Google, Microsoft, and Yahoo! are building large data centers in barren desert land surrounding the Columbia River in the United States to exploit cheap hydroelectric power.
- There is also increasing pressure from governments world wide to reduce carbon footprints, which have a significant impact on climate change. To address these concerns, leading IT vendors have recently formed a global consortium, called The Green Grid, to promote energy efficiency for datacenters and minimize their impact on the environment.
- Pike research forecasts that data center energy expenditures world wide will reduce from $23.3 billion in 2010 to $16.0 billion in 2020, as well as causing a 28% reduction in greenhouse gas (GHG) emissions from 2010 levels as a result of the adoption of the cloud computing model for delivering IT services.
- Lowering the energy usage of data centers is a challenging and complex issue because computing applications and data are growing so quickly that larger servers and disks are needed to process them fast enough within the required time period.
- Green cloud computing is envisioned to achieve not only efficient processing and utilization of computing infrastructure but also minimize energy consumption.
- This is essential for ensuring that the future growth of cloud computing is sustainable. Energy efficiency is increasingly most important for information and communication technologies.
- The reasons are the increased use in advanced technologies, increased energy costs and the need to reduce GHG (GreenHouse Gas) emissions.
- These reasons called for energy-efficient technologies that tend to decrease the overall energy consumption in terms of computation, communications and storage.
- Cloud computing has been recently attracted as a promising approach for delivering these advanced technology services by utilizing the data centre resources.
- Cloud based computing can reduces the IT capital costs, labour costs, enhance productivity and also be remarkably efficient.

- One of the analyses shows that a particular organization or company that switched to the cloud has saved around 68–87% energy for its office computing and carbon emission has been reduced.
- Growth in cloud computing has some consequences because of GreenHouse Gas (GHG) emissions and sustainability. Clouds are utilized better and are less expensive to operate than the traditional data centres.
- Moreover, only the large organizations both commercial and governmental will have the capital and expertise to achieve a similar level of efficiency at a lower cost. Because of this, most of the work done in internal data centres can be outsourced to the cloud in the coming years, resulting in reductions in energy consumption, energy expenses and emissions from data centre operations.
- A research report analyzed the energy efficiency benefits of cloud computing, which includes an assessment for SaaS (Software as a Service), PaaS (Platform as a Service) and IaaS (Infrastructure as a Service) markets.
- The study examines the drivers and technical developments related to cloud computing. Market forecasts include a quantification of energy savings and reduction possibilities under a cloud computing scenario.
- By migrating to the cloud, industries can achieve significant energy savings and reduced pollution, in addition to savings from reduced server purchases and maintenance.
- The reduction in energy consumption was larger and not by a reduced number of servers. This was due to two factors namely usage of server is lower, power consumed is less and forming the servers in subset based on PUE (power usage effectiveness), reduces the energy consumption.
- **The energy aware cloud computing benefits:**
  1. **Reduces Direct Energy for Servers by 70–90%:** The operations required for far fewer servers and Google's servers are fully loaded with more efficiency. An organization that hosts its own IT services must have redundancy to prevent safety and more servers to manage the demand. From the above, it results in more servers and server utilization of 10% or less.
  2. **Reduces Energy for Server Cooling by 70–90%:** More energy consumed by server means more heat produced. This makes the AC cooling systems to work harder than their usual load. The energy 1.5 watts of cooling required for each watt of direct power consumption by the server. In addition, the large corporate data centres indirectly consume ~0.5 watts of power for each watt of direct power consumption.

6.5 CLOUD PLATFORMS

- For availing the services offered by cloud providers, cloud users need various platforms to work efficiently with different applications.
- The cloud management software is a part of the software which is responsible for the entire process of identifying the physical machine, receiving the IP address sent from the network, and producing the virtual machine.
- Cloud management software must be flexible enough to work on distinct operating systems and the hardware of sellers.

6.5.1 Amazon Web Service (ASW) EC2 and S3

- Amazon has been a leader in providing public cloud services. Amazon applies the IaaS model in providing its services.
- Amazon Web Services (AWS) is a platform that allows the development of flexible applications by providing solutions for elastic infrastructure scalability, messaging, and data storage. The platform is accessible through SOAP or RESTful Web Service interfaces and provides a Web based console where users can handle administration and monitoring of the resources required, as well as their expenses computed on a pay-as-you-go basis.
- Amazon web service solution stack are services that provide raw compute and raw storage: Amazon Elastic Compute (EC2) and Amazon Simple Storage Service (S3). These are the two most popular services, which are generally complemented with other offerings for building a complete system.
- EC2 provides the virtualized platforms to the host VMs where the cloud application can run. S3 (Simple Storage Service) provides the object-oriented storage service for users.

6.5.1.1 Amazon Elastic Compute Cloud (Amazon EC2)

- Amazon Elastic Compute Cloud (Amazon EC2) provides scalable computing capacity in the Amazon Web Services (AWS) cloud. Using Amazon EC2 eliminates the need to invest in hardware up front, so we can develop and deploy applications faster.
- We can use Amazon EC2 to launch as many or as few virtual servers as we need, configure security and networking, and manage storage.
- Amazon EC2 enables we to scale up or down to handle changes in requirements or spikes in popularity, reducing our need to forecast traffic.
- Amazon EC2's simple web service interface allows us to obtain and configure capacity with minimal friction. It provides we with complete control of our computing resources and lets you run on Amazon's proven computing environment.
- Amazon EC2 reduces the time required to obtain and boot new server instances to minutes, allowing you to quickly scale capacity, both up and down, as our computing requirements change.
- Amazon EC2 changes the economics of computing by allowing you to pay only for capacity that you actually use.
- Amazon EC2 provides developers the tools to build failure resilient applications and isolate them from common failure scenarios.

6.5.1.1.1 Features of Amazon EC2

- Amazon EC2 provides the following features:
  1. Virtual computing environments, known as instances.
  2. Preconfigured templates for the instances, known as Amazon Machine Images (AMIs), that package the bits you need for your server (including the operating system and additional software).
  3. Various configurations of CPU, memory, storage, and networking capacity for your instances, known as instance types.
  4. Secure login information for your instances using key pairs (AWS stores the public key, and you store the private key in a secure place).
  5. Storage volumes for temporary data that's deleted when you stop or terminate your instance, known as instance store volumes.
  6. Persistent storage volumes for your data using Amazon Elastic Block Store (Amazon EBS), known as Amazon EBS volumes.
  7. Multiple physical locations for your resources, such as instances and Amazon EBS volumes, known as Regions and Availability Zones.
  8. A firewall that enables us to specify the protocols, ports, and source IP ranges that can reach your instances using security groups.
  9. Static IPv4 addresses for dynamic cloud computing, known as Elastic IP addresses.
  10. Metadata, known as tags, that we can create and assign to your Amazon EC2 resources.
  11. Virtual networks we can create that are logically isolated from the rest of the AWS cloud, and that we can optionally connect to your own network, known as Virtual Private Clouds (VPCs).

Benefits of ASW EC2:

1. **ELASTIC WEB-SCALE COMPUTING:** Amazon EC2 enables we to increase or decrease capacity within minutes, not hours or days. We can commission one, hundreds, or even thousands of server instances simultaneously. We can also use Amazon EC2 Auto Scaling to maintain availability of our EC2 fleet and automatically scale our fleet up and down depending on its needs in order to maximize performance and minimize cost. To scale multiple services, we can use AWS Auto Scaling.
2. **Completely Controlled:** We have complete control of our instances including root access and the ability to interact with them as you would any machine. We can stop any instance while retaining the data on the boot partition, and then subsequently restart the same instance using web service APIs. Instances can be rebooted remotely using web service APIs, and you also have access to their console output.
3. **Flexible Cloud Hosting Services:** We have the choice of multiple instance types, operating systems, and software packages. Amazon EC2 allows you to select a configuration of memory, CPU, instance

storage, and the boot partition size that is optimal for our choice of operating system and application. For example, choice of operating systems includes numerous Linux distributions and Microsoft Windows Server.

4. **Integrated:** Amazon EC2 is integrated with most AWS services such as Amazon Simple Storage Service (Amazon S3), Amazon Relational Database Service (Amazon RDS), and Amazon Virtual Private Cloud (Amazon VPC) to provide a complete, secure solution for computing, query processing and cloud storage across a wide range of applications.
5. **Reliable:** Amazon EC2 offers a highly reliable environment where replacement instances can be rapidly and predictably commissioned. The service runs within Amazon's proven network infrastructure and data centers. The Amazon EC2 Service Level Agreement commitment is 99.99% availability for each Amazon EC2 Region.
6. **Secure:** Cloud security at AWS is the highest priority. As an AWS customer, you will benefit from a data center and network architecture built to meet the requirements of the most security-sensitive organizations. Amazon EC2 works in conjunction with Amazon VPC to provide security and robust networking functionality for your compute resources.
7. **Inexpensive:** Amazon EC2 passes on to you the financial benefits of Amazon's scale. You pay a very low rate for the compute capacity you actually consume. See Amazon EC2 Instance Purchasing Options for more details.
8. **Easy to Start:** There are several ways to get started with Amazon EC2. You can use the AWS Management Console, the AWS Command Line Tools (CLI), or AWS SDKs. AWS is free to get started. To learn more, please visit our tutorials.

6.5.1.1.2 Amazon EC2 Functionality

- Amazon EC2 presents a true virtual computing environment, allowing you to use web service interfaces to launch instances with a variety of operating systems, load them with our custom application environment, manage our network's access permissions, and run our image using as many or few systems as we desire.
- To use Amazon EC2, we simply:
  - Select a pre-configured, templated Amazon Machine Image (AMI) to get up and running immediately. Or create an AMI containing your applications, libraries, data, and associated configuration settings.
  - Configure security and network access on our Amazon EC2 instance.
  - Choose which instance type(s) we want, then start, terminate and monitor as many instances of our AMI as needed, using the web service APIs or the variety of management tools provided.
  - Determine whether we want to run in multiple locations, utilize static IP endpoints, or attach persistent block storage to our instances.
  - Pay only for the resources that we actually consume, like instance-hours or data transfer.

6.5.1.1.3 Advantages of Amazon EC2

The benefits of Amazon EC2 can be enormous in some situations. Here are a few of the immediate advantages:

- We does not have to purchase or set up a virtual server; instead, we use Amazon's hardware infrastructure. This is especially useful if we does not have an IT person on staff, or if we don't have the money to purchase a virtual server.
- As we will see later in this lesson, it's relatively painless to set up our own virtual machine on Amazon EC2.
- We can easily obtain a machine to prototype or test a new application. If our organization is in a financial crunch, all of our machines may be in use or out of date, making it difficult to try new things.
- With Amazon EC2 we can obtain a machine for a few days or weeks for a relatively low cost, in order to test or learn new software and applications. In essence, this is what you'll do in this course, as we use Amazon EC2 for just a few weeks so we can learn ArcGIS Server.
- We can easily obtain a server that is public-facing (in other words, that can be accessed by anyone on the Internet). In some organizations it takes a fair amount of paperwork, official approval, and

coordination with IT staff to get a public-facing server. This is for good reason, since any time we open up a server to the world, there are a lot more security risks that come into play.

- Setting up a public-facing server on Amazon EC2 carries somewhat less risk because the machine is not running on your organization's hardware and can be completely isolated from our network if we choose.
- We can add "auto scaling" rules that add or remove machines depending on how busy our site is at any given time. This is how Amazon EC2 gains the "Elastic" part of its name.
- This elasticity can be incredibly cost efficient for certain types of sites, such as those responding to natural disasters. Suppose that we administer a weather site, and one afternoon a string of serious tornados hits.
- Our site will see a lot more traffic that day, especially if our site gets linked to by other sites. If we were hosting your site on premises, you might run out of hardware, or it might take some time to add new machines. If we were hosting our site on Amazon EC2 with auto scaling rules, our site could temporarily expand to use whatever amount of hardware was needed.

6.5.1.1.4 EC2 Instances and AMIs

- There are two important terms that we should understand regarding Amazon EC2:
  1. **EC2 Instance:** An EC2 instance is a virtual machine running on Amazon EC2.
  2. **AMI:** An Amazon Machine Image (AMI, sometimes pronounced "ah-mee" or "Amy") determines the files, settings, and software that are applied when we create a new EC2 instance. We can think of an AMI as a blueprint for creating an EC2 instance. Also, when we work with an EC2 instance, we can save a "snapshot" of our work at any time by creating an AMI. This way, if something ever happens to our instance, we can create a new instance and continue where we left off.

1. EC2 Instances:

- EC2 instances represent virtual machines. They are created using AMI as templates, which are specialized by selecting the number of cores, their computing power, and the installed memory.
- The processing power is expressed in terms of virtual cores and EC2 Compute Units (ECUs). The ECU is a measure of the computing power of a virtual core; it is used to express a predictable quantity of real CPU power that is allocated to an instance.
- By using compute units instead of real frequency values, Amazon can change over time the mapping of such units to the underlying real amount of computing power allocated, thus keeping the performance of EC2 instances consistent with standards set by the times.
- Over time, the hardware supporting the underlying infrastructure will be replaced by more powerful hardware, and the use of ECUs helps give users a consistent view of the performance offered by EC2 instances.
- Since, users rent computing capacity rather than buying hardware, this approach is reasonable. One ECU is defined as giving the same performance as a 1.01.2 GHz 2007 Opteron or 2007 Xeon processor.
- Currently available configurations for EC2 instances are six major categories:
  - (i) **Standard Instances:** This class offers a set of configurations that are suitable for most applications. EC2 provides three different categories of increasing computing power, storage, and memory.
  - (ii) **Micro Instances:** This class is suitable for those applications that consume a limited amount of computing power and memory and occasionally need bursts in CPU cycles to process surges in the workload. Micro instances can be used for small Web applications with limited traffic.
  - (iii) **High-Memory Instance:** This class targets applications that need to process huge workloads and require large amounts of memory. Three-tier Web applications characterized by high traffic are the target profile. Three categories of increasing memory and CPU are available, with memory proportionally larger than computing power.
  - (iv) **High-CPU Instances**: This class targets compute-intensive applications. Two configurations are available where computing power proportionally increases more than memory.
  - (v) **Cluster Compute Instances:** This class is used to provide virtual cluster services. Instances in this category are characterized by high CPU compute power and large memory and an extremely high I/O and network performance, which makes it suitable for HPC applications.

(vi) Cluster GPU Instances: This class provides instances featuring graphic processing units (GPUs) and high compute power, large memory, and extremely high I/O and network performance. This class is particularly suited for cluster applications that perform heavy graphic computations, such as rendering clusters. Since GPU can be used for general-purpose computing, users of such instances can benefit from additional computing power, which makes this class suitable for HPC applications.

6.5.1.2 Amazon Simple Storage Service (S3)

- Amazon S3 (Simple Storage Service) is a scalable, high-speed, low-cost web-based service designed for online backup and archiving of data and application programs.
- It allows to upload, store, and download any type of files up to 5 TB in size. This service allows the subscribers to access the same systems that Amazon uses to run its own web sites. The subscriber has control over the accessibility of data, i.e. privately/publicly accessible.
- Amazon Simple Storage Service is storage for the Internet. It is designed to make web-scale computing easier for developers.
- Amazon S3 has a simple web services interface that you can use to store and retrieve any amount of data, at any time, from anywhere on the web.
- It gives any developer access to the same highly scalable, reliable, fast, inexpensive data storage infrastructure that Amazon uses to run its own global network of web sites. The service aims to maximize benefits of scale and to pass those benefits on to developers.
- This guide explains the core concepts of Amazon S3, such as buckets and objects, and how to work with these resources using the Amazon S3 Application Programming Interface (API).
- Amazon Simple Storage Service (Amazon S3) is an object storage service that offers industry-leading scalability, data availability, security, and performance.
- This means customers of all sizes and industries can use it to store and protect any amount of data for a range of use cases, such as websites, mobile applications, backup and restore, archive, enterprise applications, IoT devices, and big data analytics.
- Amazon S3 provides easy-to-use management features so you can organize your data and configure finely-tuned access controls to meet your specific business, organizational, and compliance requirements.
- Amazon S3 is designed for 99.999999999% (11 9's) of durability, and stores data for millions of applications for companies all around the world.

6.5.1.2.1 Amazon S3 Features

- Features of Amazon S3 are listed below:
  1. **Low Cost and Easy to Use**: Using Amazon S3, the user can store a large amount of data at very low charges.
  2. **Secure:** Amazon S3 supports data transfer over SSL and the data gets encrypted automatically once it is uploaded. The user has complete control over their data by configuring bucket policies using AWS IAM.
  3. **Scalable:** Using Amazon S3, there need not be any worry about storage concerns. We can store as much data as we have and access it anytime.
  4. **Higher Performance:** Amazon S3 is integrated with Amazon CloudFront, that distributes content to the end users with low latency and provides high data transfer speeds without any minimum usage commitments.
  5. **Integrated with AWS Services:** Amazon S3 integrated with AWS services include Amazon CloudFront, Amazon CLoudWatch, Amazon Kinesis, Amazon RDS, Amazon Route 53, Amazon VPC, AWS Lambda, Amazon EBS, Amazon Dynamo DB, etc.

6.5.1.2.2 Advantages of Using Amazon S3

- Amazon S3 is intentionally built with a minimal feature set that focuses on simplicity and robustness. Following are some of the advantages of using Amazon S3:
  1. **Creating Buckets:** Create and name a bucket that stores data. Buckets are the fundamental container in Amazon S3 for data storage.

2. **Storing Data:** Store an infinite amount of data in a bucket. Upload as many objects as you like into an Amazon S3 bucket. Each object can contain up to 5 TB of data. Each object is stored and retrieved using a unique developer-assigned key.
3. **Downloading Data:** Download your data or enable others to do so. Download our data anytime we like, or allow others to do the same.
4. **Permissions:** Grant or deny access to others who want to upload or download data into your Amazon S3 bucket. Grant upload and download permissions to three types of users. Authentication mechanisms can help keep data secure from unauthorized access.
5. **Standard Interfaces:** Use standards-based REST and SOAP interfaces designed to work with any Internet development toolkit.

6.5.1.2.3 Amazon S3 Key Concepts

- Key concepts of Amazon S3 are, Buckets, Objects, Keys, Regions and Amazon S3 Data Consistency Model.

1. **Buckets:**

- A bucket is a container for objects stored in Amazon S3. Every object is contained in a bucket.
- For example, if the object named photos/puppy.jpg is stored in the johnsmith bucket, then it is addressable using the URL http://johnsmith.s3.amazonaws.com/photos/puppy.jpg.
- Buckets serve several purposes:
  (i) They organize the Amazon S3 namespace at the highest level.
  (ii) They identify the account responsible for storage and data transfer charges.
  (iii) They play a role in access control.
  (iv) They serve as the unit of aggregation for usage reporting.

2. **Objects:**

- Objects are the fundamental entities stored in Amazon S3. Objects consist of object data and metadata. The data portion is opaque to Amazon S3.
- The metadata is a set of name-value pairs that describe the object.
- These include some default metadata, such as the date last modified, and standard HTTP metadata, such as Content-Type. We can also specify custom metadata at the time the object is stored.

3. **Keys:**

- A key is the unique identifier for an object within a bucket. Every object in a bucket has exactly one key. The combination of a bucket, key, and version ID uniquely identify each object.
- So we can think of Amazon S3 as a basic data map between "bucket + key + version" and the object itself.
- Every object in Amazon S3 can be uniquely addressed through the combination of the web service endpoint, bucket name, key, and optionally, a version.
- For example, in the URL http://doc.s3.amazonaws.com/2006-03-01/AmazonS3.wsdl, "doc" is the name of the bucket and "2006-03-01/AmazonS3.wsdl" is the key.

4. **Regions:**

- We can choose the geographical AWS Region where Amazon S3 will store the buckets that we create. We might choose a Region to optimize latency, minimize costs, or address regulatory requirements.
- Objects stored in a Region never leave the Region unless we explicitly transfer them to another Region. For example, objects stored in the EU (Ireland) Region never leave it.

6.5.1.2.4 Amazon S3 Data Consistency Model

- Amazon S3 provides read-after-write consistency for PUTS of new objects in the S3 bucket in all Regions with one caveat. The caveat is that if we make a HEAD or GET request to the key name (to find if the object exists) before creating the object, Amazon S3 provides eventual consistency for read-after-write.
- Amazon S3 offers eventual consistency for overwrite PUTS and DELETES in all Regions.
- Updates to a single key are atomic. For example, if you PUT to an existing key, a subsequent read might return the old data or the updated data, but it never returns corrupted or partial data.

- Amazon S3 achieves high availability by replicating data across multiple servers within AWS data centers. If a PUT request is successful, our data is safely stored. However, information about the changes must replicate across Amazon S3, which can take some time, and so we might observe the following behaviors:
    1. A process writes a new object to Amazon S3 and immediately lists keys within its bucket. Until the change is fully propagated, the object might not appear in the list.
    2. A process replaces an existing object and immediately tries to read it. Until the change is fully propagated, Amazon S3 might return the previous data.
    3. A process deletes an existing object and immediately tries to read it. Until the deletion is fully propagated, Amazon S3 might return the deleted data.
    4. A process deletes an existing object and immediately lists keys within its bucket. Until the deletion is fully propagated, Amazon S3 might list the deleted object.

6.5.2 Microsoft Azure

- Microsoft Windows Azure is a cloud operating system built on top of Microsoft data centers infrastructure and provides developers with a collection of services for building applications with cloud technology.
- Services range from compute, storage, and networking to application connectivity, access control, and business intelligence. Any application that is built on the Microsoft technology can be scaled using the Azure platform, which integrates the scalability features into the common Microsoft technologies such as Microsoft Windows Server 2008, SQL Server, and ASP.NET.
- Microsoft Azure is a cloud computing service formed by Microsoft to build, deploy, and manage services and applications via data centers of the Microsoft network running world wide.
- It offers SaaS, PaaS, and IaaS and supports various diverse programming devices, languages, and structures, comprising Microsoft-specific and third-party systems and software.
- The Microsoft Azure Service Bus permits applications working on Azure sites or off site tools to correspond with Azure.
- Microsoft Azure has been explained as a 'cloud layer' over numerous Windows Server systems that utilize Windows Server 2008 and a modified edition of Hyper-V, well-known as the Microsoft Azure Hypervisor for providing services' virtualization.
- The Microsoft Azure Service Bus permits applications working on Azure sites or off site tools to correspond with Azure.
- Azure offers an API built on XML, HTTP, and REST which permits a developer to interrelate with the services offered by Microsoft Azure.

How Azure can help in business?

- Azure can help in our business in the following ways:
    1. **Capitaless:** We don't have to worry about the capital as Azure cuts out the high cost of hardware. We simply pay as we go and enjoy a subscription-based model that's kind to your cash flow. Also, to set up an Azure account is very easy. We simply register in Azure Portal and select our required subscription and get going.
    2. **Less Operational Cost:** Azure has low operational cost because it runs on its own servers whose only job is to make the cloud functional and bug-free, it's usually a whole lot more reliable than your own, on-location server.
    3. **Cost Effective:** If we set up a server on our own, we need to hire a tech support team to monitor them and make sure things are working fine. Also, there might be a situation where the tech support team is taking too much time to solve the issue incurred in the server. So, in this regard is way too pocket-friendly.
    4. **Easy Back Up and Recovery Options:** Azure keep backups of all our valuable data. In disaster situations, we can recover all our data in a single click without our business getting affected. Cloud-based backup and recovery solutions save time, avoid large up-front investment and roll up third-party expertise as part of the deal.
    5. **Easy to Implement:** It is very easy to implement our business models in Azure. With a couple of on-click activities, we are good to go. Even there are several tutorials to make we learn and deploy faster.

6. **Better Security:** Azure provides more security than local servers. Be carefree about our critical data and business applications. As it stays safe in the Azure Cloud. Even, in natural disasters, where the resources can be harmed, Azure is a rescue. The cloud is always on.
7. **Work from Anywhere:** Azure gives us the freedom to work from anywhere and everywhere. It just requires a network connection and credentials. And with most serious Azure cloud services offering mobile apps, we are not restricted to which device we are got to hand.
8. **Increased Collaboration:** With Azure, teams can access, edit and share documents anytime, from anywhere. They can work and achieve future goals hand in hand. Another advantage of the Azure is that it preserves records of activity and data. Timestamps are one example of the Azure's record keeping. Timestamps improve team collaboration by establishing transparency and increasing accountability.

Microsoft Azure Services:

- Fig. 6.7 provides an overview of services provided by Azure. These services can be managed and controlled through the Windows Azure Management Portal, which acts as an administrative console for all the services offered by the Azure platform.
- Some following are the services of Microsoft Azure offers:

1. Compute Service:

- Includes Virtual Machines, Virtual Machine Scale Sets, Functions for server less computing, Batch for containerized batch workloads, Service Fabric for micro services and container orchestration, and Cloud Services for building cloud-based apps and APIs.
- Compute services are the core components of Microsoft Windows Azure, and they are delivered by means of the abstraction of roles. A role is a runtime environment that is customized for a specific compute task. Roles are managed by the Azure operating system and instantiated on demand in order to address surges in application demand.
- Currently, there are three different roles namely Web role, Worker role and Virtual Machine (VM) role.

(i) Web role:

- The web role is designed to implement scalable web applications. web roles represent the units of deployment of web applications within the Azure infrastructure. They are hosted on the IIS 7 WebServer, which is a component of the infrastructure that supports Azure.
- When Azure detects peakloads in the request made to a given application, it instantiates multiple Web roles for that application and distributes the load among them by means of a load balancer. Since version 3.5, the .NET technology natively supports Web roles; developers can directly develop their applications in Visual Studio, test them locally, and upload to Azure.
- It is possible to develop ASP.NET (ASP.NET Web Role and ASP.NET MVC 2 Web Role) and WCF (WCF Service Web Role) applications. Since IIS 7 also supports the PHP runtime environment by means of the FastCGI module, Web roles can be used to run and scale PHP Web applications on Azure (CGI Web Role).
- Other web technologies that are not integrated with IIS can still be hosted on Azure (i.e., Java Server Pages on Apache Tomcat), but there is no advantage to using a Web role over a Worker role.

(ii) Worker role:

- Worker roles are designed to host general compute services on Azure. They can be used to quickly provide compute power or to host services that do not communicate with the external world through HTTP.
- A common practice for worker roles is to use them to provide background processing for Web applications developed with web roles.
- Developing a worker role is like a developing a service. Compared to a web role whose computation is triggered by the interaction with an HTTP client (i.e., a browser), a Worker role runs continuously from the creation of its instance until it is shut down.
- The Azure SDK provides developers with convenient APIs and libraries that allows connecting the role with the service provided by the runtime and easily controlling its startup as well as being notified of changes in the hosting environment.

- As with web roles, the .NET technology provides complete support for worker roles, but any technology that runs on a windows server stack can be used to implement its core logic. For example, Worker roles can be used to host Tomcat and serve JSP-based applications.

(iii)Virtual Machine (VM) Role:

- The Virtual Machine (VM) role allows developers to fully control the computing stack of their compute service by defining a custom image of the Windows Server 2008 R2 operating system and all the service stack required by their applications.
- The Virtual Machine role is based on the Windows Hyper-V virtualization technology, which is natively integrated in the Windows server technology at the base of Azure.
- Developers can image a Windows server installation complete with all the required applications and components, save it into a Virtual Hard Disk (VHD) file, and upload it to Windows Azure to create compute instances on demand.

2. Networking:

- With Azure we can use variety of networking tools, like the Virtual Network, which can connect to on-premise data centers; Load Balancer; Application Gateway; VPN Gateway; Azure DNS for domain hosting, Content Delivery Network, Traffic Manager, Express Route dedicated private network fiber connections; and Network Watcher monitoring and diagnostics

3. Storage Service:

- Includes Blob, Queue, File and Disk Storage, as well as a Data Lake Store, Backup and Site Recovery, among others.
- Windows Azure provides different types of storage solutions that complement compute services with a more durable and redundant option compared to local storage. Compared to local storage, these services can be accessed by multiple clients at the same time and from everywhere, thus becoming a general solution for storage.

(i) Blobs:

- Azure allows storing large amount of data in the form of binary large objects (BLOBs) by meansof the blobs service. This service is optimal to store large text or binary files.
- Two types of blobsare available:

  (a) Block Blobs: Block blobs are composed of blocks and are optimized for sequential access; therefore they are appropriate for media streaming. Currently, blocks are of 4 MB, and a single block blob can reach 200 GB in dimension.

  (b) Page Blobs: Page blobs are made of pages that are identified by an offset from the beginning of the blob. A page blob can be split into multiple pages or constituted of a single page. This type of blob is optimized for random access and can be used to host data different from streaming. Currently, the maximum dimension of a page blob can be 1 TB.

- Blobs storage provides users with the ability to describe the data by adding metadata. It is also possible to take snapshots of a blob for backup purposes. Moreover, to optimize its distribution, blobs storage can leverage the Windows Azure CDN so that blobs are kept close to users requesting them and can be served efficiently.
- Azure drive: Page blobs can be used to store an entire file system in the form of a single Virtual Hard Drive(VHD) file. This can then be mounted as a part of the NTFS file system by Azure compute resources, thus providing persistent and durable storage. A page blob mounted as part of an NTFS tree is called an Azure Drive.
- Tables: Tables constitute a semi structured storage solution, allowing users to store information in the form of entities with a collection of properties. Entities are stored as rows in the table and are identified by a key, which also constitutes the unique index built for the table. Users can insert, update, delete, and select a subset of the rows stored in the table. Unlike SQL tables, there are no schema enforcing constraints on the properties of entities and there is no facility for representing relationships among entities. For this reason, tables are more similar to spreadsheets rather than SQL tables. The service is designed to handle large amounts of data and queries returning huge result sets. This capability is supported by partial result sets and table partitions. A partial result set is returned together with a continuation token, allowing the client to resume the query for large result sets. Table partitions allow tables to be divided among several servers for load-balancing purposes. Apartition is identified by a key, which is represented by three of the columns of the table. Currently, a table can contain up to 100 TB of data, and rows can have up to 255 properties, with a maximum of 1 MB for each row. The maximum dimension of a row key and partition keysis 1 KB.

- Queues, Queue storage allows applications to communicate by exchanging messages through durable queues, thus avoiding lost or unprocessed messages. Applications enter messages into a queue, another applications can read them in a first-in, first-out (FIFO) style. To ensure that messages get processed, when an application reads a message it is marked asinvisible; hence it will not be available to other clients. Once the application has completed processing the message, it needs to explicitly delete the message from the queue.
- This two-phase process ensures that messages get processed before they are removed from the queue, and the client failures do not prevent messages from being processed. At the same time, this is also a reason that the queue does not enforce a strict FIFO model: Messages that are read by applications that crash during processing are made available again after a timeout, during which other messages can be read by other clients. An alternative to reading a message is peeking, which allows retrieving the message but letting it stay visible in the queue. Messages that are peeked are not considered processed. All the services described are geo-replicated three times to ensure their availability in case of major disasters. Geo-replication involves the copying of data into a different datacenter that is hundreds or thousands of miles away from the original data center.

4. **Web + Mobile:** Creating Web + Mobile applications is very easy as it includes several services for building and deploying applications.
5. **Containers:** Azure has a property which includes container Service, which supports Kubernetes, DC/OS or Docker Swarm, and Container Registry, as well as tools for microservices.
6. **Databases:** Azure has also includes several SQL-based databases and related tools.
7. **Data + Analytics:** Azure has some big data tools like HDInsight for Hadoop Spark, R Server, HBase and Storm clusters
8. **AI + Cognitive Services:** With Azure developing applications with artificial intelligence capabilities, like the Computer Vision API, Face API, Bing Web Search, Video Indexer, Language Understanding Intelligent.
9. **Internet of Things:** Includes IoT Hub and IoT Edge services that can be combined with a variety of machine learning, analytics, and communications services.
10. **Security + Identity:** Includes Security Center, Azure Active Directory, Key Vault and Multi-Factor Authentication Services.
11. **Developer Tools:** Includes cloud development services like Visual Studio Team Services, Azure DevTest Labs, HockeyApp mobile app deployment and monitoring, Xamarin cross-platform mobile development and more.

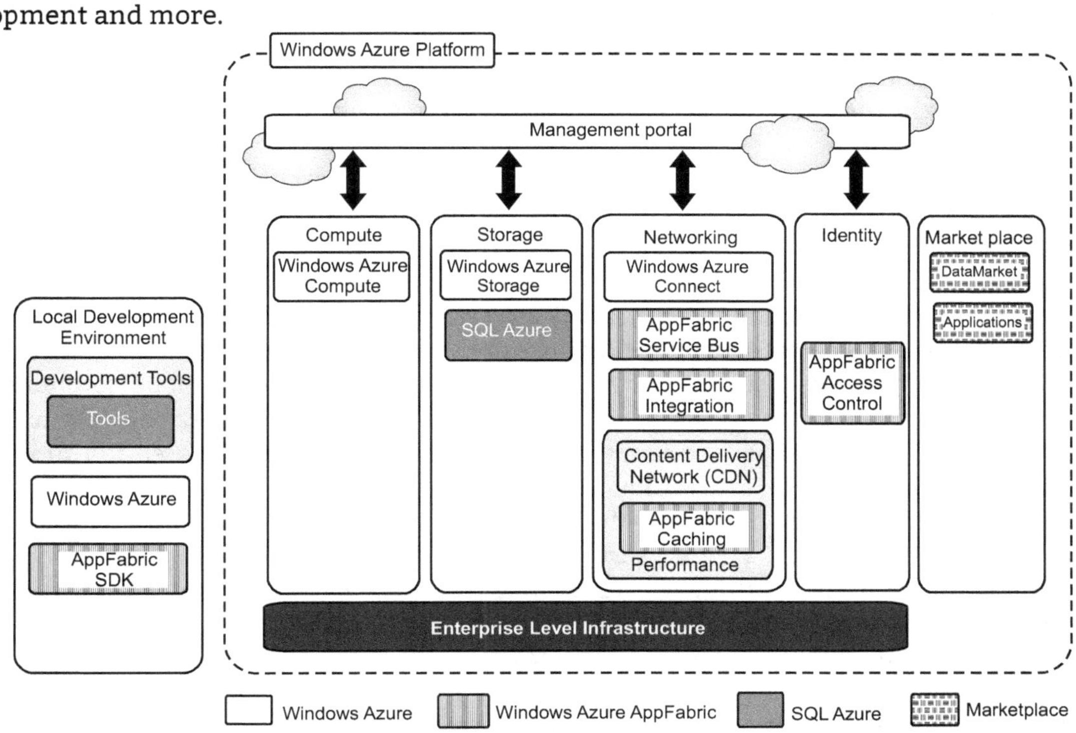

Fig. 6.7: Microsoft Windows Azure Platform Architecture with Services Provided

Benefits of Microsoft Azure:

1. Azure helps in reducing the cost of hardware by a considerable amount. Microsoft Azure pricing follows a subscription-based model that charges users for resources consumed by them. The lower operational costs become evident in MS azure with the limited requirement of infrastructure maintenance.
2. The easy implementation approaches, along with improved security in MS azure, are also prominent reasons for its popularity.
3. Most important of all, the flexible backup and disaster recovery alternatives with MS Azure improve its credibility. Azure stores backup of all your significant data that you can recover in a simple process. The interesting highlight in azure services for cloud-based backup and recovery is the time savings and avoiding massive up-front investments.
4. Another interesting aspect of MS azure is the facility for improved collaboration. Azure enables team members to access, edit, and share documents without any restrictions of time and location.
5. The use of timestamps for recording activity and data also present credible reasons for adopting MS azure. It results in better transparency and accountability.

6.5.3 Cloudstack

- Apache CloudStack is open source software designed to deploy and manage large networks of virtual machines, as a highly available, highly scalable Infrastructure as a Service (IaaS) cloud computing platform.
- CloudStack is used by a number of service providers to offer public cloud services, and by many companies to provide an on-premises (private) cloud offering, or as part of a hybrid cloud solution.
- CloudStack is a turnkey solution that includes the entire "stack" of features most organizations want with an IaaS cloud: compute orchestration, Network-as-a-Service, user and account management, a full and open native API, resource accounting, and a first-class User Interface (UI).
- CloudStack currently supports the most popular hypervisors: VMware, KVM, Citrix XenServer, Xen Cloud Platform (XCP), Oracle VM server and Microsoft Hyper-V.
- Users can manage their cloud with an easy to use Web interface, command line tools, and/or a full-featured RESTful API. In addition, CloudStack provides an API that's compatible with AWS EC2 and S3 for organizations that wish to deploy hybrid clouds.
- CloudStack is cloud software which assists users to alter the cloud according to their requirements. It controls and supports the network, storage, and compute joints in a cloud infrastructure. It is used to arrange, control, and systematize situations in cloud computing.
- CloudStack is open source software that forms the foundation for infrastructure clouds. Data center operators can quickly and easily build cloud services within their existing infrastructure to offer on-demand, elastic cloud services.
- Enterprises can use CloudStack to take on hybrid workloads, making it easier to manage legacy workloads while spinning up workloads that take advantage of the cloud model.
- CloudStack users can take full advantage of cloud computing to deliver higher efficiency, limitless scale and faster deployment of new services and systems to the end-user.
- CloudStack allows user to coordinate virtualized servers, networking and network storage to provide infrastructure-as-a-service (IaaS) just like hosting providers-but on their own hardware.
- CloudStack is an open source cloud operating system which delivers public cloud computing similar to Amazon EC2 but using our own hardware. CloudStack provides orchestration of our virtualized resources into one homogeneous environment where we can delegate the creation to users of the virtual machines using the self-service CloudStack portal.
- CloudStack provides powerful features for enabling a secure multi-tenant cloud computing environment. With one click virtual servers can be deployed from a pre-defined template. Virtualized instances can be shutdown, paused and restarted via the web interface, the command line or by calling the extensive CloudStack API.

CloudStack can be used for following Multiple Purposes:

1. Service Providers can offer virtualized hosting in an elastic cloud computing configuration.
2. Enterprises can stage development, testing and production in a consistent way easing the development and publishing processes for applications.

3. Web content providers can deploy scalable, elastic web infrastructure that can adapt to meet the demand of their readership.
4. Software-as-a-Service providers can offer true multi-tenant software hosting while securing each user's environments.

CloudStack are capable for the following:

1. Establishing an on-command, flexible cloud computing service. Service suppliers may offer self-service virtual machines, networking arrangements, and storage sizes over the Internet.
2. CloudStack may be used to construct an on-command cloud computing service along with flexibility. Service supplier provides storage and virtual machines, and much more on the Internet.
3. An organization or worker could establish an on-premise private cloud along with CloudStack.

Features and Functionality Cloudstack:

- Works with hosts running XenServer/XCP, KVM, Hyper-V, and/or VMware ESXi with vSphere.
- Provides a friendly Web-based UI for managing the cloud.
- Provides a native API.
- May provide an Amazon S3/EC2 compatible API (optional).
- Manages storage for instances running on the hypervisors (primary storage) as well as templates, snapshots, and ISO images (secondary storage).
- Orchestrates network services from the data link layer (L2) to some application layer (L7) services, such as DHCP, NAT, firewall, VPN, and so on.
- Accounting of network, compute, and storage resources.
- Multi-tenancy/account separation.
- User management.

Benefits of CloudStack

1. **Cost Effectiveness:** Cloud computing services can be costly, making it a challenge for businesses with a tight budget to avail the service that fits their needs. Apache CloudStack is a solution that allows businesses to access powerful tools to do related tasks free of charge. We do not have to pay a single penny to use and take advantage of this software's capabilities.
2. **Quality Services:** Apache CloudStack comes with tools that enable users to deliver cloud services, distribute internal workloads, or provide public workloads to clients simultaneously. This platform can assist we in offering only the best services and solutions to our clients.
3. **Powerful API:** This cloud management solution features a RESTful API that allows users to connect with an array of third-party services. Moreover, this feature lets users create and use their own applications. It also makes the process of handling API related tasks easier as it is extensively documented.
4. **An Array of Administrative Capabilities:** With Apache CloudStack, businesses can manage their users, assign management tasks, segregate cloud resources, etc. Hence, it gives them complete control over the operation. The platform allows users to comprehensively and seamlessly oversee activities within their network, particularly those that are system and cloud-related.
5. **Hypervisor Agnostic:** The software can support any hypervisor from any manufacturer. This feature makes the platform a flexible solution. Apache CloudStack can be easily integrated with visual machine monitor of any types and even be included in our own system.

6.5.4 InterCloud

- InterCloud is the concept of connected cloud networks, including public, private, and hybrid clouds. It incorporates a number of technology efforts put together to improve interoperability and portability among cloud networks.
- The InterCloud started as a research project in Cisco in 2008 and was soon taken up by the Institute of Electrical and Electronics Engineers (IEEE). The goal was to improve interoperability of cloud networks. The terms "Inter-Cloud Computing" and "InterCloud" were used to address this concept.
- The term "InterCloud" is originally attributed to the journalist and technology author Kevin Kelly, according to several sources. In addition, a series of conferences led by the IEEE about the topic. The goal is to connect different cloud computing platforms and allows the data and applications to be ported between data centers or cloud services.
- The InterCloud is a unified universal 'cloud of clouds' or it is also called as cloud of cloud and an expansion of the Internet 'network of networks' on which it is established.
- The InterCloud circumstances are based on the chief concept that every individual cloud does not contain countless physical resources or ubiquitous geographic marks.

- The InterCloud is based on scenarios where a single cloud has no infinite physical resources or ubiquitous geographic footprint. If a cloud saturates the compute and storage resources of its infrastructure, or is requested to use resources in a geography where it has no footprint, it would still be able to satisfy such requests for service allocations sent from its clients. The InterCloud scenarios would address such situations where each cloud would use the infrastructures of other clouds.
- The InterCloud is architected to enable standalone clouds to work as one; it involves not just connecting clouds but also accelerating development for cloud and unifying workload management across clouds.
- It ensures that network and security policies follow the workload, harnessing an expanded ecosystem of best-of-breed partners and service offerings. It takes advantage of global data while meeting local and regional requirements.
- The InterCloud is a new approach to business and cloud transformation. It is about the continuous delivery of reliable, available, and consistent services over the lifecycle of the application.
- It is about the business objectives being supported over the lifecycle of the transformation from legacy applications to agile development projects in cloud, to the evolution of applications to continuous integration/continuous delivery(CI/CD) and beyond.
- Several key tenets of the InterCloud exist to accomplish this:
  1. The software-defined infrastructure is fluid and ever evolving to support the ever-changing and growing demands of the business.
  2. Software-defined services support all aspects of the business application needs.
  3. Application parameters and configuration details of the application including integration, performance optimizations metrics, and service-level objectives (SLOs),
  4. Integrated application platform, any underlying dependent or loosely coupled services the application requires (message queue, Doman Name System [DNS], memcache),
  5. Network and security policies and the enforcement of those policy objectives.
  6. Data, being able to abstract data aspects of the application and provide analytics and business outcome learnings
  7. BSS (Back-Office Support Systems) being able to abstract the BSS aspects to enable complete abstraction to any existing BSS systems in the enterprise or Cisco Powered partner clouds
  8. OSS (Operational Support Systems) being able to abstract the OSS aspects to enable complete abstraction to any existing OSS systems in the enterprise or Cisco Powered partner clouds
  9. SaaS frameworks for Cisco applications and the broad range of partner independent software vendor (ISV) applications comprise broad sets of tools for multiple cloud solutions.
  10. Public cloud providers are important to support for existing use cases and use cases that make sense.
  11. Private cloud solutions will be in place for many reasons-compliance, performance, control, and so on. The key here is to support the enterprise in whatever private cloud deployment model it chooses.
  12. Enterprise is a special case of private cloud where the deployment model is the enterprise data center. Additionally, the enterprise model may want to burst to other deployment models, so managing the policies and processes of the enterprise becomes critical.
- As shown in Fig. 6.8, the broker offers three facilities to the cloud users, such as SaaS, PaaS, and IaaS. IaaS services are offered by cloud provider A, SaaS services by cloud provider B, and PaaS services are offered by cloud provider C.

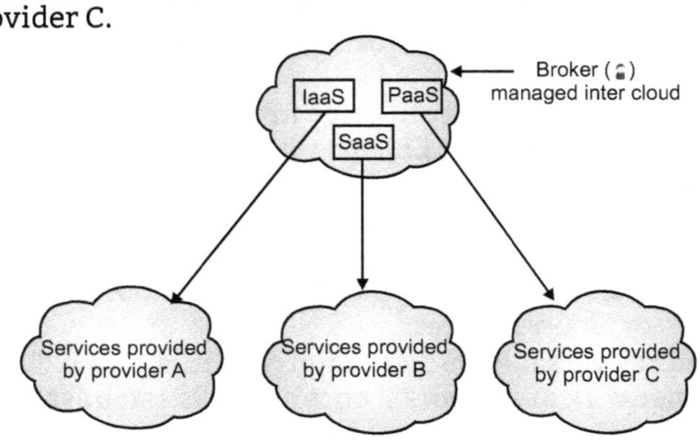

Fig. 6.8: InterCloud

- Cloud providers have been deploying data centers in multiple locations throughout the globe. For example, Amazon EC2 cloud services are available via Amazon data centers located in the United States, Europe, and Singapore.
- This disbursement is leading to the emergence of a notion, called the InterCloud, supporting scalable delivery of application services by harnessing multiple datacenters from one or more providers. In addition to enhancing performance and reliability, these InterClouds provide a powerful means of reducing energy related costs.
- One reason is that the local demand for electricity varies with time of day and weather. This causes time varying differences in the price of electricity at each location.
- Moreover, each site has a different source of energy (such as coal, hydroelectric, or wind), with different environmental costs. This gives scope to adjust the load sent to each location, and the number of servers powered on at each location, to improve efficiency.

InterCloud Architecture:

- InterCloud architecture, shown in Figure 6.9.

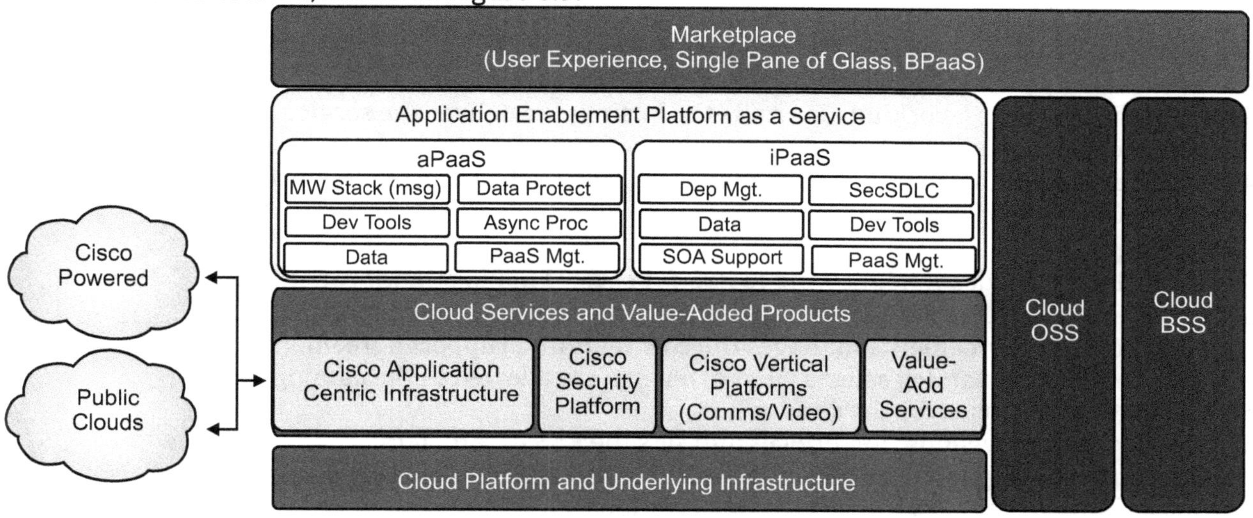

Fig. 6.9: InterCloud Architecture

- InterCloud architecture consists of the following layers:

1. **Cloud Platform and Underlying Infrastructure:**

- The OpenStack platform and underlying infrastructure consist of physical, virtual, and automation components. The beginning point for any service is the physical data center, controls, and hardware.
- Whatever services or virtualization you build on top of this infrastructure will only be as good as the underlying physical design and the security controls you integrate.

2. **Cloud Services and Value-Added Products:**

- In the layer above the OpenStack platform, services and capabilities are added by the InterCloud to enable advanced services around networking, security, NFV, data, database, load balancing, and application policy.
- As we move up the stack, it is critical to focus on the API interfaces and capabilities. This layer is also where the InterCloud Fabric (iCF) product resides to enable point-to-point secure InterCloud connectivity.
- It also includes various InterCloud products such as network products, InterCloud security, InterCloud virtualization and InterCloud services.

3. **Application Enablement Platform as a Service:**

- The InterCloud's primary use case is to enable application portability and interoperability across a world of clouds. By virtue of its broad definition, one can throw in various solutions under the PaaS umbrella.
- For our purposes we will define what PaaS encompasses by looking at what customer problems need to be solved and working backward from there. Our target audience in terms of usage of the PaaS solution on the InterCloud is the enterprise developers and enterprise IT engineering teams on the customer side; the set of decision makers for adoption of a particular PaaS offering will have a mix of technical and business roles.

4. Cloud OSS:

- The OSS consist of the following management aspects:
  - (i) Change management means managing break/fix and new features to the system following the change process and change windows.
  - (ii) Configuration management means managing the configuration.
  - (iii) Capacity management means managing the capacity needs of the physical infrastructure.
- Performance management means managing the expected performance of the systems involved in delivering the service.
- SLA management means managing the SLA thresholds set by configuration and performance management.
- Incident management means managing incidents as they occur, documenting results, and creating tickets.
- Problem management means managing incidents that happen frequently or cause major downtime.
- Service desk is the name for the support staff available to provide assistance.
- Log and event management means managing all the logs and events from the data sources.
- Reporting and analytics means analyzing the events, logs, and data generated by the services to look for incidents or problems and to enhance the performance of the system.
- Service delivery means working alongside the business to deliver the service required.
- Image/lifecycle management means managing software images and patching these images.
- Asset and license management means managing the assets and licenses of the underlying hardware and software.

5. Cloud BSS:

- The InterCloud provides the following to BSS for several management functions:
  - Accounting provides data for managing the user accounts and departments.
  - Contracts and Agreements manages the contracts and support agreements.
  - Service Offering Catalog selects what offerings are allowed in the catalog.
  - Pricing sets the price for the service.
  - Provisioning provisions the services and sets the BSS parameters.
  - Orchestration supports the dependencies and order of provisioning services.
  - Subscriptions manages the service subscriptions.
  - Metering provides usage data.
  - Entitlements sets user access levels.
  - Order manages the quote to the order fulfillment process.
  - Billing creates a single bill and shows the detailed breakdown of the service chargeable components.
  - Rating allows the cloud provider to discount the service.
  - Clearing and Settlement provides all billing remediation and settlement services.

6. Marketplace:

- The Marketplace is the curated set of products and services from Cisco and its InterCloud partners that enables enterprise customers to consume products and services in the enterprise catalog and across the global InterCloud product catalog from a simple, easy-to-use marketplace.
- The Marketplace performs the following operations:
  - Manage online user ID setup and user directory.
  - Manage identity authentication and secure site sign-in.
  - Manage an online directory of applications.
  - Manage or facilitate the purchase/consumption process.
  - Meter usage of applications.
  - Send and receive payments.
  - Manage the customer feedback system.

6.5.5 Google App Engine

- Google App Engine is a PaaS implementation that provides services for developing and hosting scalable web applications.
- App Engine is essentially a distributed and scalable runtime environment that leverages Google's distributed infrastructure to scale out applications facing a large number of requests by allocating more computing resources to them and balancing the load among them.

- The runtime is completed by a collection of services that allows developers to design and implement applications that naturally scale on App Engine.
- Developers can develop applications in Java, Python, and Go, a new programming language developed by Google to simplify the development of Web applications.
- Application usage of Google resources and services is metered by App Engine, which bills users when their applications finish their free quotas.
- The features supported by the Google app engine are Support trendy languages, Elasticity and Complete control. Google App Engine assists apps written in a variety of programming languages like Java, Python, PHP and Go.
- Google App Engine comprises the following characteristics:
  1. Mechanized scaling and load balancing.
  2. Planned jobs for activating events at particular times or normal intervals.
  3. Integration with other APIs and Google cloud services.
- With Google App Engine, users have a cloud-based platform that enables them to create, maintain, and scale apps without the need to have and/or maintain servers. Once the application is uploaded, it is ready for deployment. Scaling is also automatic and the process depends mostly on incoming traffic.
- Google App Engine offers support for a host of programming languages. The service also supports both standard and flexible environments. Users just need to pick an environment, select a language, and fire away.
- Programming languages are supported on current Google App Engine are 1. GO, 2. PHP, 3. JAVA, 4. Python, 5. NodeJS, 6. .NET, 7. Ruby, 8. Custom Runtime.

Why Google App Engine ?

- Fully managed service with zero ops (no need to work at infrastructure level at all).
- Deploy at Google Scale.
- All popular languages support.
- Lots of built-in features such as scaling up/down, logging, monitoring, diagnostics etc.
- Building quickly and time to market is short.
- Pay only for what we use.

Architecture and Core Concepts of App Engine:

- App Engine is a platform for developing scalable applications accessible through the web shown in Fig. 6.10.
- The platform is logically divided into four major components namely Infrastructure, Runtime Environment, Underlying Storage and Set of Scalable Services.

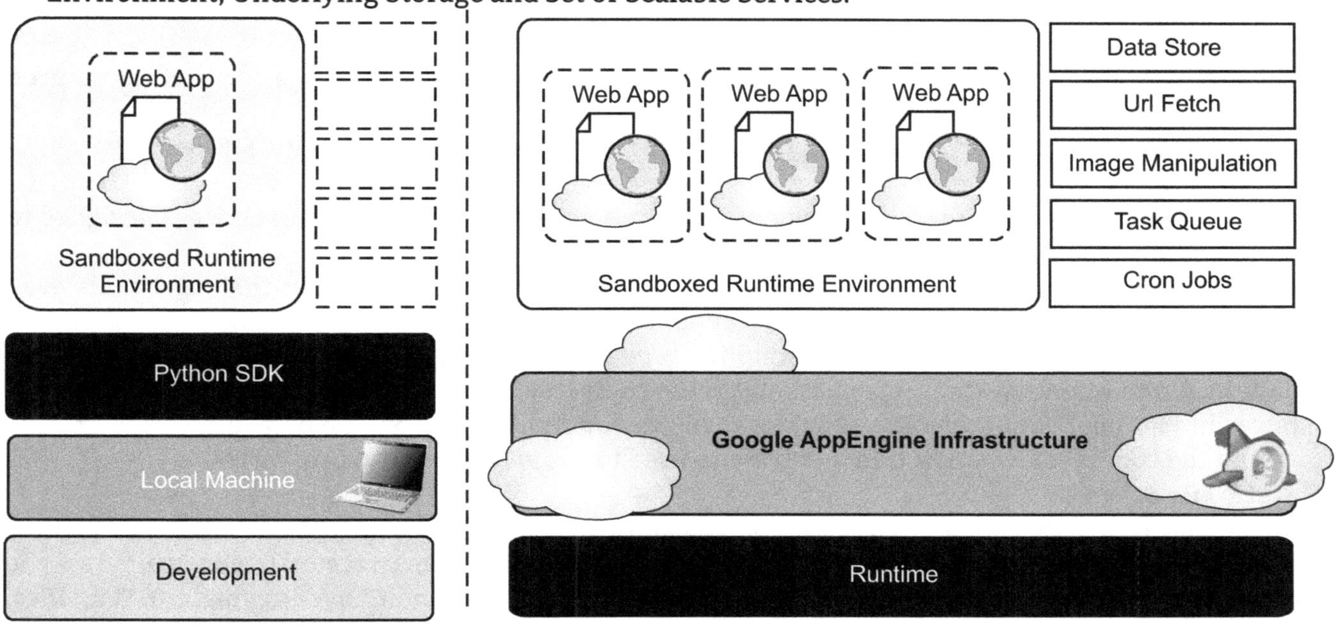

Fig. 6.10: Architecture of Google App Engine

- The components of Google App Engine in Fig. 6.10 are explained below:

Infrastructure

- App Engine hosts web applications, and its primary function is to serve users requests efficiently.To do so, App Engine's infrastructure takes advantage of many servers available within Google data centers.
- For each HTTP request, App Engine locates the servers hosting the application that processes the request, evaluates their load, and, if necessary, allocates additional resources (i.e., servers) or redirects the request to an existing server.
- The particular design of applications, which does not expect any state information to be implicitly maintained between requests to the same application, simplifies the work of the infrastructure, which can redirect each of the requests to any of the servers hosting the target application or even allocate a new one.
- The infrastructure is also responsible for monitoring application performance and collecting statistics on which the billing is calculated.

Runtime Environment:

- The runtime environment represents the execution context of applications hosted on App Engine. With reference to the App Engine infrastructure code, which is always active and running, the runtime comes into existence when the request handler starts executing and terminates once the handler has completed.
- One of the major responsibilities of the runtime environment is to provide the application environment with an isolated and protected context in which it can execute without causing a threat to the server and without being influenced by other applications. In other words, it provides applications with a sandbox.
- Currently, App Engine supports applications that are developed only with managed or interpreted languages, which by design require a runtime for translating their code into executable instructions.
- Therefore, sandboxing is achieved by means of modified runtimes for applications that disable some of the common features normally available with their default implementations. If an application tries to perform any operation that is considered potentially harmful, an exception is thrown and the execution is interrupted.
- Some of the operations that are not allowed in the sandbox include writing to the server's file system; accessing computer through network besides using Mail, UrlFetch, and XMPP; executing code outside the scope of a request, a queued task, and a cron job; and processing a request for more than 30 seconds.

Storage:

- App Engine provides various types of storage, which operate differently depending on the volatility of the data.
- There are three different levels of storage namely, In memory-cache, Storage for semi-structured data and Long term storage for static data.
- Google App Engine supports uses main two storage namely Data-Store and Static File Servers.

1. Data-Store:

- Data-Store is a service that allows developers to store semi-structured data. The service is designed to scale and optimized to quickly access data.
- Data-Store can be considered as a large object database in which to store objects that can be retrieved by a specified key. Both the type of the key and the structure of the object can vary. DataStore provides high-level abstractions that simplify interaction with Big table. Developers define their data in terms of entity and properties, and these are persisted and maintained by the service into tables in Bigtable. Data-Store also provides facilities for creating indexes on data and to update data within the context of a transaction. Indexes are used to support and speed up queries.

2. Static File Servers:

- Web applications are composed of dynamic and static data. Dynamic data are a result of the logic of the application and the interaction with the user. Static data often are mostly constituted of the components that define the graphical layout of the application (CSS files, plain HTML files, JavaScript files, images, icons, and sound files) or data files.

- These files can be hosted on static file servers, since they are not frequently modified. Such servers are optimized for serving static content, and users can specify how dynamic content should be served when uploading their applications to App Engine.

Application Services of Google App Engine:

- Applications hosted on App Engine take the most from the services made available through the runtime environment.
- These services simplify most of the common operations that are performed in Web applications includes access to data, account management, integration of external resources, messaging and communication, image manipulation, and asynchronous computation.

Pros of Google App Engine:

1. No need to buy servers or server space (no maintenance).
2. Makes solving the problem of scaling easier.
3. Free up to a certain level of consumed resources.
4. Access to google infrastructure.
5. Less likely that google(has the company) is going close shop then Heroku or Appspot.
6. Scalable.
7. Easy and cheaper (in short term).
8. Nice option for start-ups/individuals.
9. Suitable for apps that just store and retrieve data.

Cons of Google App Engine :

1. Locked into Google App Engine?
2. Developers have read-only access to the filesystem on App Engine.
3. App Engine can only execute code called from an HTTP request (except for scheduled background tasks).
4. Users may upload arbitrary Python modules, but only if they are pure-Python; C and Pyrex modules are not supported.
5. App Engine limits the maximum rows returned from an entity get to 1000 rows per Datastore call.
6. Java applications may only use a subset (The JRE Class White List) of the classes from the JRE standard edition.
7. Java applications cannot create new threads.

6.5.6 Open Source Cloud Eucalyptus

- **Eucalyptus** (Elastic Utility Computing Architecture Linking Your Programs To Useful Systems) was founded out of a research project in the computer science department at the University of California, Santa Barbara, and became a for-profit business called Eucalyptus Systems in 2009.
- Eucalyptus Systems announced a formal agreement with Amazon Web Services (AWS) in March 2012, allowing administrators to move instances between a Eucalyptus private cloud and the Amazon Elastic Compute Cloud (EC2) to create a hybrid cloud. The partnership also allows Eucalyptus to work with Amazon's product teams to develop unique AWS-compatible features.
- Eucalyptus is an open source Linux based software architecture which provides an EC2-compatible cloud computing platform and S3-compatible cloud storage platform.
- It implements scalable, efficient-enhancing and private and hybrid clouds within and organization's IT infrastructure. It gives an Infrastructure as a Service (IaaS) solution. Users can use commodity hardware.
- Eucalyptus was developed to support the High Performance Computing (HPC). Eucalyptus can be deployed without modification on all major Linux OS distributions, including Ubuntu, RHEL/CentOS, openSUSE, and Debian.
- Eucalyptus allows us to flexibly provision our own collections of resources (hardware, compute, storage, network) on an as-needed basis.
- Eucalyptus enables pooling compute, storage, network resources which can be dynamically scaled up or down as application workloads change, as well as high-availability configurations features.
- Eucalyptus offers easily API compatibility with Amazon's EC2, S3, IAM, ELB, Auto Scaling, and Cloudwatch services, as well as it provides a virtual network overlay which both isolates network traffic of different users and also allows more clusters to appear to belong to the same Local Area Network.

- Key benefits of Eucalyptus, open source software like Reduce Public Cloud Spend, Hybrid Capability, Dynamic Scalability, Infrastructure Flexibility, Security and Control, Cloud Reliability, Improved Performance, Operational Efficiency as well as Organizational Agility.

Features of Eucalyptus:

1. Linux-based controller with administration Web portal.
2. EC2-compatible (SOAP, Query) and S3-compatible (SOAP, REST) CLI and Web portal interfaces.
3. Xen, KVM, and VMWarebackends.
4. Amazon EBS-compatible virtual storage devices.
5. Interface to the Amazon EC2 public cloud.
6. Virtual networks.
7. SSH key management.
8. Image management.
9. Linux-based VM management
10. IP Address management.
11. Security Group management.
12. Volume and snapshot management.
13. Supports both Linux and Windows Virtual Machines (VMs).
14. Application Program Interface- (API) compatible with Amazon EC2 platform.
15. Compatible with Amazon Web Services (AWS) and Simple Storage Service (S3).
16. Works with multiple hypervisors including VMware, Xen and KVM.
17. Can be installed and deployed from source code or DEB and RPM packages.
18. Internal processes communications are secured through SOAP and WS-Security.
19. Multiple clusters can be virtualized as a single cloud.
20. Administrative features such as user and group management and reports.

Benefits of Eucalyptus:

1. It enables virtualization of network, servers as well as storage in a secure manner.
2. Modular design of Eucalyptus enables variety of user interfaces, bringing benefits of virtualization technology to a broad range of users as well as provides a platform for service providers to device profitable consumption based pricing models.
3. Cloud snapshot and VM features provide an exhaustive set of opportunities to improve template manipulation, cluster reliability, as well as easily automation.
4. Leverages existing virtualization technology, supports multiple hypervisors and supports Linux-based operating systems.
5. Eucalyptus provides users access to source code and an opportunity to leverage contributions from a worldwide community of developers.

Eucalyptus Architecture:

- Fig. 6.11 shows Eucalyptus Fundamental Architecture. It has following blocks:
  1. **Cluster Controller (CC):** Cluster Controller manages the one or more Node controller and responsible for deploying and managing instances on them. It communicates with Node Controller and Cloud Controller simultaneously. CC also manages the networking for the running instances under certain types of networking modes available in Eucalyptus.
  2. **Cloud Controller (CLC):** Cloud Controller is front end for the entire ecosystem. CLC provides an Amazon EC2/S3 compliant web services interface to the client tools on one side and interacts with the rest of the components of the Eucalyptus infrastructure on the other side.
  3. **Node Controller (NC):** It is the basic component for Nodes. Node controller maintains the life cycle of the instances running on each nodes. Node Controller interacts with the OS, hypervisor and the Cluster Controller simultaneously.
  4. **Walrus Storage Controller (WS3):** Walrus Storage Controller is a simple file storage system. WS3 stores the machine images and snapshots. It also stores and serves files using S3 APIs.
  5. **Storage Controller (SC):** It allows the creation of snapshots of volumes. It provides persistent block storage over AoE or iSCSI to the instances.

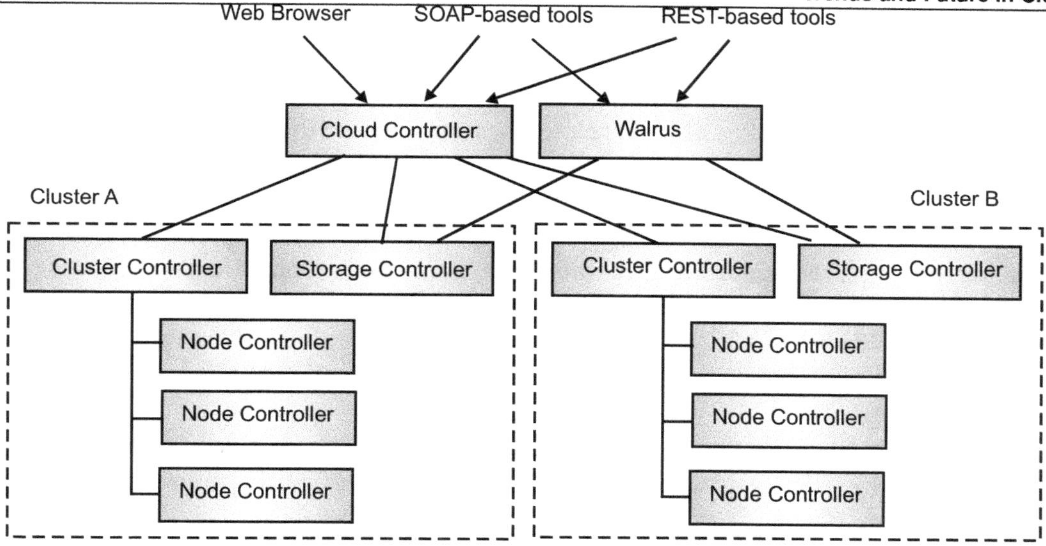

Fig. 6.11: Eucalyptus Fundamental Architecture

6.5.7 OpenStack

- OpenStack is a project originally started by NASA and Rackspace for delivering a cloud computing and storage platform.
- Today, OpenStack is a global collaboration of developers and technologists producing an open source cloud computing platform for public and private clouds.

History of OpenStack:

- In 2010, Rackspace was rewriting code for their cloud infrastructure and was considering open sourcing some of it. At the same time, NASA was also working on code for cloud infrastructure. They combined efforts and it became the base for OpenStack. The first OpenStack Summit was held in Austin, Texas in July 2010, and OpenStack has continued to meet every six months in different corners of the globe since then.
- In 2012, the OpenStack Foundation was formed, which we'll talk more about momentarily. The Foundation oversees the projects and stewards the community.
- In 2014, the OpenStack Marketplace was established, which is a portal at Openstack.org/marketplace that helps potential users navigate what was, and continues to be, a rapidly growing ecosystem of vendors who offer everything from trainings on OpenStack to "pre-packaged" distributions of OpenStack projects. The Juno release was also launched, which was widely regarded as an enterprise grade release.
- In 2015, the OpenStack Powered interoperability certification launched. The OpenStack Powered badge is for products that run fully functional instances of OpenStack and have been tested to standards agreed upon by the ecosystem of vendors and users.
- 2016 was a booming year for OpenStack, as adoption by Chinese companies skyrocketed, and a Heavy Reading survey announced that 86% of telecoms said OpenStack is important to their business. By this time, half of the Fortune 100 was also running OpenStack, and the Certified OpenStack Administrator program launched, which is a professional certification that tests fundamental OpenStack skills.
- Heading into 2017, OpenStack has continued to grow in its programmable infrastructure offering, giving users one platform for containers, vms, and bare metal.
- OpenStack is an open source platform that uses pooled virtual resources to build and manage private and public clouds. The tools that comprise the OpenStack platform, called "projects," handle the core cloud-computing services of compute, networking, storage, identity, and image services. More than a dozen optional projects can also be bundled together to create unique, deployable clouds.
- In virtualization, resources such as storage, CPU, and RAM are abstracted from a variety of vendor-specific programs and split by a hypervisor before being distributed as needed.

- OpenStack uses a consistent set of Application Programming Interfaces (APIs) to abstract those virtual resources 1 step further into discrete pools used to power standard cloud computing tools that administrators and users interact with directly.
- The technology consists of a series of interrelated projects delivering various components for a cloud infrastructure solution. OpenStack software delivers a massively scalable cloud operating system consisting of three major components:
  1. **Compute:** Open source software designed to provision and manage large networks of virtual machines, creating a redundant and scalable cloud computing platform.
  2. **Object Storage:** Open source software for creating redundant, scalable object storage using clusters of standardized servers to store petabytes of accessible data (code-named "Swift").
  3. **Image Service:** Provides discovery, registration, and delivery services for virtual disk images (code-named "Glance").
- OpenStack has attracted more than 500 member organizations, including Dell, Cisco, Citrix, HP, EMC, VMware, Red Hat, IBM and Intel, and the project is currently managed by the non-profit OpenStack Foundation.
- OpenStack is open source software for building clouds. It is programmable infrastructure that allows users to have one platform for virtual machines, containers and bare metal.
- Hundreds of companies and tens of thousands of individuals from around the world have come together to create and support OpenStack because they believe in the importance of a standardized, ubiquitous cloud platform.
- OpenStack has multiple projects under its name. The projects cover foundational elements like compute, networking and storage, but also span from telemetry to orchestration to container APIs.
- OpenStack is one of the world's largest open source projects. That means that it was created by people who contributed their time and talent to the project, and that no one "owns" OpenStack.
- OpenStack is able to constantly evolve and constantly improve because of its open source nature, and when needs arise or situations change, the community can quickly respond with innovative solutions. OpenStack is licensed under the Apache 2.0 license, which means that it is free to use, free to distribute and that others can modify OpenStack for their own needs.
- This creates a rich suite of options that all operate on the same underlying infrastructure. For users, this means we can switch between vendors or combine services without fear of being locked into a single, proprietary solution.
- OpenStack is used in everything from retail to finance to telecom to research.

Why OpenStack:

1. **Control and Flexibility:** Open source platform means you're never lockedto a proprietary vendor, and modular design can integrate with legacy orthird-party technologies to meet your business needs.
2. **Industry Standard:** More than 60 leading companies from over a dozencountries are participating in OpenStack, including Cisco, Citrix, Dell, Inteland Microsoft, and new OpenStack clouds are coming online across theglobe.
3. **Proven Software:** Run the same software that today powers some of thelargest public and private clouds in the world.
4. **Compatible and Connected:** Compatibility with public OpenStackcloudsmeans enterprises are prepared for the future-making it easy to migratedata and applications to public clouds when conditions are right—based onsecurity policies, economics, and other key business criteria.

Architecture and Components of OpenStack:

- OpenStack is made up of many different moving parts. Because of its open nature, anyone can add additional components to OpenStack to help it to meet their needs.
- But the OpenStack community has collaboratively identified nine key components that are a part of the "core" of OpenStack shown in Fig. 6.12, which are distributed as a part of any OpenStack system and officially maintained by the OpenStack community.
  1. **Nova** is the primary computing engine behind OpenStack. It is used for deploying and managing large numbers of virtual machines and other instances to handle computing tasks.

2. **Swift** is a storage system for objects and files. Rather than the traditional idea of a referring to files by their location on a disk drive, developers can instead refer to a unique identifier referring to the file or piece of information and let OpenStack decide where to store this information. This makes scaling easy, as developers don't have the worry about the capacity on a single system behind the software. It also allows the system, rather than the developer, to worry about how best to make sure that data is backed up in case of the failure of a machine or network connection.
3. **Cinder** is a block storage component, which is more analogous to the traditional notion of a computer being able to access specific locations on a disk drive. This more traditional way of accessing files might be important in scenarios in which data access speed is the most important consideration.
4. **Neutron** provides the networking capability for OpenStack. It helps to ensure that each of the components of an OpenStack deployment can communicate with one another quickly and efficiently.
5. **Horizon** is the dashboard behind OpenStack. It is the only graphical interface to OpenStack, so for users wanting to give OpenStack a try, this may be the first component they actually "see." Developers can access all of the components of OpenStack individually through an application programming interface (API), but the dashboard provides system administrators a look at what is going on in the cloud, and to manage it as needed.
6. **Keystone** provides identity services for OpenStack. It is essentially a central list of all of the users of the OpenStack cloud, mapped against all of the services provided by the cloud, which they have permission to use. It provides multiple means of access, meaning developers can easily map their existing user access methods against Keystone.
7. **Glance** provides image services to OpenStack. In this case, "images" refers to images (or virtual copies) of hard disks. Glance allows these images to be used as templates when deploying new virtual machine instances.
8. **Ceilometer** provides telemetry services, which allows the cloud to provide billing services to individual users of the cloud. It also keeps a verifiable count of each user's system usage of each of the various components of an OpenStack cloud. Think metering and usage reporting.
9. **Heat** is the orchestration component of OpenStack, which allows developers to store the requirements of a cloud application in a file that defines what resources are necessary for that application. In this way, it helps to manage the infrastructure needed for a cloud service to run.

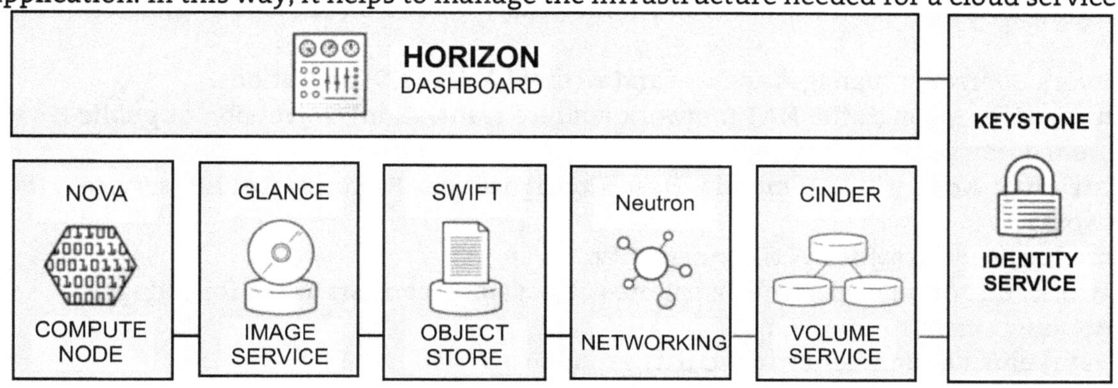

Fig. 6.12: Openstack Architecture

OpenStack Main Components:

- Currently, OpenStack focuses on the development of two aspects of cloud computing to address compute and storage aspects with the OpenStack Compute and OpenStack Storage solutions.
- "OpenStack Compute is the internal fabric of the cloud creating and managing large groups ofvirtual private servers" and "OpenStack Object Storage is software for creating redundant, scalable object storage using clusters of commodity servers to store terabytes or even petabytes of data."
- Recently, an image repository was prototyped. The image repository contains an image registration and discovery service and an image delivery service.
- Together they deliver images to the compute service while obtaining them from the storage service.

1. OpenStack Compute:

- OpenStack is developing a cloud computing fabric controller, a component of an IaaS system, known as Nova.
- The architecture for Nova is built on the concepts of shared-nothing and messaging-based information exchange. Hence, most communication in Nova is facilitated by message queues.
- To prevent blocking components while waiting for a response from others, deferred objects are introduced. Such objects include callbacks that get triggered when a response is received.
- To achieve the shared nothing paradigm, the overall system state is kept in a distributed data system. State updates are made consistent through atomic transactions.
- Nova it implemented in Python while utilizing a number of externally supported libraries and components. This in cludesboto, an Amazon API provided in Python, and Tornado, a fast HTTP server used to implement the S3 capabilities in OpenStack.
- Fig. 6.13 shows the main architecture of Open Stack Compute. In this architecture, the API Server receives HTTP requests from boto, converts the commands to and from the API format, and forwards the requests to the cloud controller.

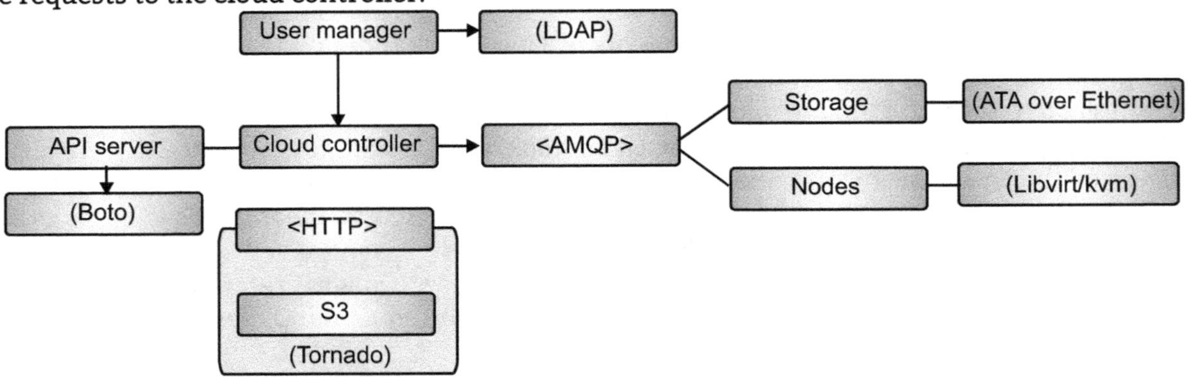

Fig. 6.13: OpenStack Nova System Architecture

- The cloud controller maintains the global state of the system, ensures authorization while interacting with the User Manager via Lightweight Directory Access Protocol (LDAP), interacts withthe S3 service, and manages nodes, as well as storage workers through a queue.
- Additionally, Novaintegrates networking components to manage private networks, public IP addressing, virtual private network (VPN) connectivity, and firewall rules. It includes the following types:
  1. Network Controller manages address and virtual LAN (VLAN) allocations.
  2. Routing Node governs the NAT (network address translation) conversion of public IPs to private IPs, and enforces firewall rules.
  3. Addressing Node runs Dynamic Host Configuration Protocol (DHCP) services for private networks.
  4. Tunneling Node provides VPN connectivity.
- The network state (managed in the distributed object store) consists of the following:
  1. VLAN assignment to a project.
  2. Private subnet assignment to a security group in a VLAN.
  3. Private IP assignments to running instances.
  4. Public IP allocations to a project.
  5. Public IP associations to a private IP/running instance.

2. OpenStack Storage

- The OpenStack storage solution is built around a number of interacting components and concepts, including a proxy server, a ring, an object server, a container server, an account server, replication, updaters, and auditors.
- The role of the proxy server is to enable lookups to the accounts, containers, or objects in OpenStack storage rings and route the requests.
- Thus, any object is streamed to or from an object server directly through the proxy server to or from the user.

- A ring represents amapping between the names of entities stored on disk and their physical locations. Separate rings for accounts, containers, and objects exist.
- A ring includes the concept of using zones, devices, partitions, and replicas. Hence, it allows the system to deal with failures, and isolation of zones representing a drive, a server, a cabinet, a switch, or even a data center.
- Weights canbe used to balance the distribution of partitions on drives across the cluster, allowing users to support heterogeneous storage resources.
- According to the documentation, "the Object Server is a very simple blob storage server that can store, retrieve and delete objects stored on local devices."
- Objects are stored as binary files with metadata stored in the file's extended attributes. This requires that the underlying file system is built around object servers, which is often not the case for standard Linux installations. To list objects, a container server can be utilized.
- Listing of containers is handled by the account server. The first release of OpenStack "Austin" Compute and Object Storage was October 22, 2010. This system has a strong developer community.

6.5.8 OpenNebula

- OpenNebula is a cloud computing tool for running various distributed data center infrastructures.
- OpenNebula is one of the most feature rich open-source Virtual Infrastructure managers. It was initially conceived to manage local virtual infrastructure, but has also included remote interfaces that make it viable to build public clouds.
- Its architecture is modular, encompassing several specialized pluggable components. The Core module orchestrates physical servers and their hypervisors, storage nodes, and network fabric.
- Management operations are performed through pluggable Drivers, which interact with APIs of hypervisors, storage and network technologies, and public clouds. The Scheduler module, which is in charge of assigning pending VM requests to physical hosts, offers dynamic resource allocation features.
- Administrators can choose between different scheduling objectives such as packing VMs in fewer hosts or keeping the load balanced. Open Nebula also supports advance reservation of capacity and queuing of best-effort leases.
- Features of OpenNebula:
  1. Linux-based controller.
  2. CLI, XML-RPC, EC2-compatible Query and OCA interfaces.
  3. Xen, KVM and VMware backend.
  4. Interface to public clouds (Amazon EC2,ElasticHosts).
  5. Virtual networks.
  6. Dynamic resource allocation.
  7. Advance reservation of capacity.
  8. Provision dynamic resources.
  9. Make advance reservations.
  10. Supportchanging environments are live migration and VM snapshots.
- OpenNebula coordinates network, storage, virtualization, security, and scrutinizing technologies to install multi-layer services as virtual machines on distributed infrastructures, merging both isolated resources and data center cloud resources as per the allotment strategies.
- OpenNebula was a guiding corporation at the Google Summer of Code 2010. OpenNebula is utilized by telecom operators, hosting suppliers, IT services suppliers, supercomputing centers, international research plans, and research labs.
- OpenNebula is a toolkit that allows building private or public deployments and also managing the virtual infrastructure. But OpenNebula goes well beyond those use cases by supporting many different cloud models, including hybrid cloud deployment.
- OpenNebula is an open source tool for virtual machines within datacenters. It supports on demand access to Amazon EC2. OpenNebula,1 an opens ource distributed VM manager that enables the dynamic placement of VMs on a pool of physical resources.
- OpenNebula extends the benefits of virtualization platforms from a single physical resource to a pool of resources, decoupling the server from the physical infrastructure and thephysical location where it resides.

- OpenNebula is focused on the efficient, dynamic, and scalable management of VMs within data centers (i.e., private clouds) that involve a large number of virtual and physical servers.
- OpenNebula can interface with a remote cloud site, being the only tool able to access on demand to Amazon EC2 in order to scale out a locally managed infrastructure.
- OpenNebula is collaborating with the most relevant cloud projects in order to promote its integration as an alternative cloud back-end product.
- OpenNebula's latest release, version 1.2, supports Xen and KVM virtualization platforms and also features support for image transfers, cloning and virtual network management.
- The OpenNebula web site provides additional information about tools for extending the functionality provided by OpenNebula, such as the Haizea3 lease management system.
- Haizea is a product that, in combination with the OpenNebula virtual infrastructure manager (VIM), can be used to manage a Xen or KVM4 cluster, allowing we to deploy different types of leases that are instantiated as virtual machines. KVM allows we to run multiple virtual machines (runningun modified Linux or Windows images), where each virtual machine has private virtualized hardware (a network card, disk, graphics adapter, etc).
- OpenNebula tries to provide a uniform cloud management layer based on service type. Its basic principle is to separate resource provisioning from the service management.
- By implementing this principle, it enables elastic cluster capacity through on-demand deployment or shutdown of virtual worker nodes which can be located in a private or public cloud, cluster partitioning through segregation and isolation of worker nodes based on service type, and heterogeneous configurations which enables a service to have multiple software configurations.

OpenNebula Architecture and its Main Components:

- OpenNebula is an open source toolkit which allows users to transform existing infrastructure into an IaaS cloud with cloud-like interfaces.
- Fig. 6.14 shows the OpenNebula architecture and its main components.

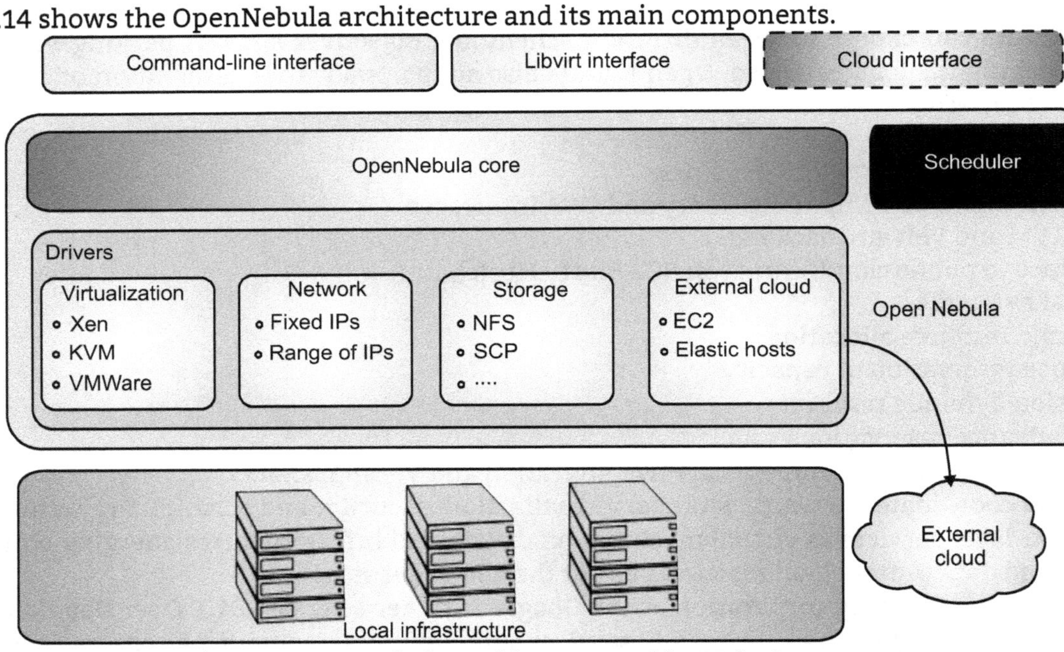

Fig. 6.14: OpenNebula Architecture and its Main Components

- The architecture of OpenNebula has been designed to be flexible and modular to allows integration with different storage and network infrastructure configurations, and hypervisor technologies.
- Here, the core is a centralized component that manages the VM fulllife cycle, including setting up networks dynamically for groups of VMs and managing their storage requirements, such as VM disk image deployment or on-the-fly software environment creation.
- Another important component is the capacity manager or scheduler. It governs the functionality provided by the core.
- The default capacity scheduler is a requirement/rank matchmaker. However, it is also possible to develop more complex scheduling policies, through a lease model and advance reservations.

- The last main components are the access drivers. They provide anabstraction of the underlying infrastructure to expose the basic functionality of the monitoring,storage, and virtualization services available in the cluster.
- Therefore, OpenNebula is not tied to any specific environment and can provide a uniform management layer regardless of the virtualization platform.
- Additionally, OpenNebula offers management interfaces to integrate the core's functionality within other data center management tools, such as accounting or monitoring frameworks. To this end, OpenNebula implements the libvirtAPI, an open interface for VM management, as well as a Command Line Interface (CLI). A subset of this functionality is exposed to external users through a cloud interface.
- OpenNebula is able to adapt to organizations with changing resource needs, including addition or failure of physical resources.
- When the local resources are insufficient, OpenNebula can support a hybrid cloud model by using cloud drivers to interface with external clouds. This lets organizations supplement their local infrastructure with computing capacity from a public cloud to meet peak demands, or implement HA strategies.
- OpenNebula currently includes an EC2 driver, which can submit requests to Amazon EC2 and Eucalyptus, as well as an ElasticHosts driver.
- Regarding storage, an Image Repository allows users to easily specify disk images from a catalog without worrying about low-level disk configuration attributes or block device mapping.
- Also, image access control is applied to the images registered in the repository, hence simplifying multiuser environments and image sharing. Never the less, users can also set up their own images.

6.5.9 Comparison of Cloud Platforms

1. Comparison of Open-Source Cloud Platforms:

Sr. No.	Feature	OpenNebula	Eucalyptus
1.	Computing Architecture	• Cluster into an IaaS cloud • Focused on the efficient, dynamic and scalable management of VMs within data centres (private cloud) involving a large amount of virtual and physical servers • Based on Haizea scheduling	• Ability to configure multiple clusters, each with private internal network addresses, into a single cloud. • Private Cloud.
2.	Virtualization Management	• Xen KVM and on-demand access to Amazon EC2	• Xen hypervisor
3.	Service	• IaaS	• IaaS
4.	Load Balancing	• Nginx Server configured as load balancer, used round-robin	• Simple load- balancing cloud controller
5.	Interoperability	• Interoperable between intra cloud services	• Multiple cloud computing interfaces using the same "back-end" infrastructure
6.	Fault Tolerance	• The daemon can be restarted and all the running VMs recovered • Persistent database backend to store host and VM information	• Separate cluster within the Eucalyptus cloud reduce the chance of correlated failure
7.	Security	• Firewall, Virtual Private	• WS-security for authentication, cloud.

2. Comparison of Some Cloud Computing Platforms

Sr. No.	Features	Different Platforms		
1.	Property	Amazon Elastic Compute Cloud (EC2).	Microsoft Azure.	Google App Engine.
2.	Focus	Infrastructure.	Platform.	Platform.
3.	Service Type	Compute, Storage (Amazon S3).	Web and non-web application.	Web Application.
4.	User Access interface	Amazon EC2 command-line tools.	Microsoft windows azure portal.	Web-based administration.
5.	Value-added service providers	Yes.	Yes.	No.
6.	Virtualization	OS level running on a Xenhypervisor.	OS level Through fabric controller.	Application container.
7.	Web APIs	Yes.	Yes.	Yes.
8.	Dynamic negotiation of QoS	None.	None.	None.
9.	Programming frame-work	Amazon Machine Images (AMI).	Microsoft.NET.	Python.

3. Comparison of cloud platforms with implementation aspects:

Sr. No.	Features	Eucalyptus	OpenNebula
1.	Cloud Character	Public.	Private.
2.	Scalability	Scalable.	Dynamical, Scalable.
3.	Cloud Form	IaaS.	IaaS.
4.	Compatibility	Suppot EC2, S3.	Open, Multi-Platform.
5.	Deployment	Dynamical Deployment.	Dynamical Deployment.
6.	Deployment Manner	Commandline.	Commandline.
7.	Transplantability	Common.	Common.
8.	VM Support	VMWare, Xen, KVM.	Xen, VMWare.
9.	Web Interface	Web Service.	Libvirt, EC2, OCCI API.
10.	Structure	Module.	Module.
11.	Reliability	-	Rollback host and VM.
12.	OS Support	Linux.	Linux.
13	Development Language	Java.	Java.

4. Comparison between ASW-EC2, Microsoft Azur and Google App Engine:

Sr. No.	Features	AWS	Microsoft Azure	Google
1.	Compute	EC2	Virtual Machines	Engine Apo Compute Engine
2.	Storage	53 CBS EFS Glacier	Blob Storage Queue Storage File Storage Disk Storage	Cloud Storage Persistent Disk
3.	Backup and Disaster Recovery		Backup Site Recovery	
4.	Database and Data warehouse	Aurora ROS DynamoDB Redshift	Data lake Store SCU. Database DocumentOB Table Storage SQL Data Warehouse	Cloud SQL Cloud Bigtable Cloud Spanner Cloud Datastore
5.	In-Memory Technology	ElastiCache	Redis Cache	
6.	Containers	Container Registry Container Service	Container Registry Container Service	Container Engine Container Registry Container Builder
7.	Servedess/FaaS	Lambda	Functions	Cloud Functions
8.	Analytics	Athena EMR Kinesis	HDlnsight Stream Analytics	ElisQuery Cloud Dataflow Cloud Dataproc Cloud Datalaba
9.	Artificial Intelligence	Lex Polly Rekognitlon Machine Learning	Machine Learning Cognitive Services Bot Service Data Lake Analytks	Cloud Machine Learning Engine Cloud Natural Language API Cloud Speech API Cloud Translation API Cloud VislonAPI
10.	Internet of Things	IoT Platform Greengrass	IoT Hub Event Hubs	

5. Comparison of open source infrastructure-as-a-service (IaaS) offerings.

Sr. No.	Criteria	Eucalyptus	OpenStack
1.	Ease of deployment and management	Amazon Web Services (AWS) – compatible API; web-based management console.	Automated deployment and management using the open source Compass system.
2.	Provisioning and orchestration	Supported by cloud controller, cluster controller, and node controller.	Uses Heat Orchestration Template, via Representational State Transfer (REST) APIs to launch multiple composite-cloud applications.
3.	Monitoring and alerts	Supports tools like Ganglia and Nagios Supported by Eucalyptus Stats and Amazon's Cloudwatch.	Supports tools like Nagios and Ganglia Supported by OpenStack Telemetry.
4.	Interoperabilit y	SupportsAWSAPI, EC2 (Elastic Compute Cloud), andS3 (Simple StorageService).	Supports RefStack and Citrix Systems' NetScaler SD-WAN.
5.	Networking modes and services	Edge, managed (virtual LAN/ non-VLAN), virtual-private-cloud networking modes.	API-driven networking service VLAN, fiat, generic routing encapsulation, and virtual extensible LAN networking modes.
6.	Storage	Allocation and deallocation of memory on demand by the storage controller.	Supported by ephemeral file system, block storage cinder, Object Storage (Swift), and shared file system.
7.	Security	Security groups (networking rules applied to all associated instances [layer 2 isolation]), identity access control.	Components for identity provisioning, password management, and authentication.
8.	Support	Supported by knowledge base, documentation, web-based issue tracking, community forum, reference architectures, and expert support from Hewlett Packard Enterprise.	Supported by Internet relay chat (IRC), documentation and community forum, and vendor support.

Practice Questions

1. Explain uses of clouds for HPC/HTC and ubiquitous computing.
2. Describe various cloud trends in supporting ubiquitous computing.
3. Explain different enabling technologies with the Internet of Things (IoT).
4. What is ubiquitous computing ? Explain the Internet of Things for ubiquitous computing.
5. Explain enabling and synergistic technologies to build the IoT infrastructure.
6. Explain architecture of the Internet of Things.

7. What is RFID? Explain RFID tags and device components.
8. Explain how RFID works.
9. What is wireless sensor networks? Explain WSN for ubiquitous computing.
10. Explain different Generations of Sensor Networks.
11. What is ZigBee Network? Write features of ZigBee.
12. Explain different devices supported by ZigBee.
13. Explain ZigBee protocol architecture.
14. Discuss applications of ZigBee.
15. What is GPS? Explain working of GPS.
16. Explain types of GPS.
17. Explain operating principles of GPS.
18. Explain innovative applications with Internet of Things.
19. Enlist wireless sensor applications.
20. What is smart power grid? Write features of smart grids.
21. List benefits of the smart grid.
22. What is smart buildings? Explain features of smart buildings.
23. Explain different characteristics of a smart building.
24. Enlist benefits of smart buildings.
25. Explain home based cloud computing with example.
26. Explain what is need of energy aware cloud computing.
27. Explain Amazon Web Service (ASW) EC2.
28. Explain Amazon Web Service (ASW) S3.
29. List the features of Amazon EC2.
30. Explain benefits of ASW EC2.
31. Describe amazon EC2 functionality.
32. Enlist advantages of Amazon EC2.
33. Explain EC2 instances and AMIs in details.
34. Enlist Amazon S3 features.
35. Write advantages of using Amazon S3.
36. Explain amazon S3 key concepts.
37. Explain amazon S3 data consistency model.
38. What is Microsoft Azure? Explain how Azure can help in business?.
39. Explain different Microsoft Azure services.
40. Enlist benefits of Microsoft Azur.
41. What is cloudstack and where it used?
42. List features and functionality CloudStack.
43. Explain benefits of CloudStack.
44. What is InterCloud? Explain InterCloud architecture.
45. What is Google App Engine? Explain, Why it is useful?

46. Explain Architecture and core concepts of Google App Engine.
47. Enlist advantages and disadvantages if Google App Engine.
48. What is Eucalyptus? Enlist Eucalyptus features.
49. Enlist Eucalyptus Benefits.
50. Explain Eucalyptus architecture.
51. What is OpenStack? Explain three major components of OpenStack.
52. Describe Architecture and Components of OpenStack.
53. Briefly explain OpenStack Compute and OpenStack Storage of Openstack.
54. Explain OpenStack Nova system architecture.
55. What is Open Nebula? Write down features of Open Nebula.
56. Explain OpenNebula architecture and its main components
57. Comparison of open-source cloud platforms OpenNebula and Eucalyptus.
58. Comparison of Cloud Computing Platforms such as Amazon EC2, Google App Engine and Microsoft Azur.

www.ingramcontent.com/pod-product-compliance
Lightning Source LLC
LaVergne TN
LVHW062200171026
850499LV00044B/1811
* 9 7 8 9 3 8 9 8 2 5 2 7 5 *